Making the World Safe for Workers

THE WORKING CLASS IN AMERICAN HISTORY

Editorial Advisors

James R. Barrett, Julie Greene, William P. Jones,

Alice Kessler-Harris, and Nelson Lichtenstein

MAKING THE WORLD SAFE FOR WORKERS

Labor, the Left,
and Wilsonian Internationalism

Elizabeth McKillen

UNIVERSITY OF
ILLINOIS PRESS
Urbana, Chicago, and Springfield

First Illinois paperback, 2018
© 2013 by the Board of Trustees
of the University of Illinois
1 2 3 4 5 C P 5 4 3 2 1
∞ This book is printed on acid-free paper.

The Library of Congress cataloged the cloth edition as follows:
McKillen, Elizabeth, 1957-
Making the world safe for workers : labor, the Left, and Wilsonian
internationalism / Elizabeth McKillen.
pages   cm. — (The working class in American history)
Includes bibliographical references and index.
ISBN 978-0-252-03787-0 (cloth : alk. paper)
ISBN 978-0-252-09513-9 (ebook)
1. Labor—United States—History—20th century. 2. Labor unions—
Political activity—United States—History—20th century. 3. Labor movement—
History—20th century. 4. International labor activities—History—20th century.
5. United States—Foreign relations—1913–1921. 6. Wilson, Woodrow, 1856–1924.
7. International Labor Organization.
I. Title.
HD8072.M3155   2013
331.880973'09041—dc23   2013009260

PAPERBACK ISBN 978-0-.252-08386-0

Dedicated to Nathan and to Isaac

Contents

Preface and Acknowledgments

IN THE SUMMER OF 2011, as I waited in stifling one-hundred-degree heat and humidity for a bus to take me from the National Archives in College Park, Maryland, to a gritty Washington, D.C., hotel, I briefly experienced a midlife crisis. What insanity, I wondered, had led me to abandon the cool streams and lakes surrounding my home in Maine for an urban swamp like Washington, D.C.? After all, nineteenth-century policymakers had been smart enough, in a day before air conditioning, to shut down government and make a reverse journey *to Maine* during the hottest summer months. More seriously, I wondered about the wisdom of devoting so much of my research life to the seemingly unglamorous subject of labor and foreign policy. Many colleagues, friends, and family, I suspected, wondered why I had not already moved on to greener research pastures.

But with the help of air conditioning and a cold beer, my doubts soon resolved themselves. The reason, I realized, that I had devoted so much time to the excavation of old labor and Left perspectives on the world of international diplomacy was simply that I believed in the subject. Books written about Woodrow Wilson's foreign policies and diplomacy at Versailles could fill a small library. By contrast, I could count on one hand the number of books devoted even partially to working-class responses to Wilson's diplomacy. Yet my own research convinced me that the World War I era witnessed one of the most important working-class debates, over the interlinking issues of national security, labor internationalism, and the best means of assuring world peace and prosperity, in U.S. history. This debate, moreover, was not contained within national borders but was part of a broader transnational dialogue among workers and labor activists about whether Wilson's schemes for transforming diplomacy would really serve the interests of ordinary people. The perspectives of working people and their organizations, I continue to believe, need to be incorporated alongside those of policymakers in any comprehensive assessment of U.S. foreign policy.

Needless to say, I have incurred many debts in pursuing this seemingly endless research journey. First, I wish to thank the wonderful research and inter-library loan staff at the University of Maine for bringing so many sources to me and making some research trips unnecessary. Second, I thank helpful librarians and archivists at the research institutions I have visited throughout the years, including National Archives II in College Park, Maryland; Schlesinger library at the Radcliffe Institute for Advanced Study at Harvard; the Houghton and Lamont libraries at Harvard University; the State Historical Society of Wisconsin Library and Archives; Memorial Library at the University of Wisconsin; the Illinois Historical Survey Collection at the University Library at University of Illinois at Urbana-Champaign; University of Washington Libraries and Archives in Seattle, Washington; the Oral History Collections at Butler Library, Columbia University (New York); New York Public Library; Tamiment Library at New York University; Northwestern University Library; Walter P. Reuther Library at Wayne State University; Chicago Historical Society/Museum; Loyola University Library and Archives (Chicago); Newberry Library (Chicago); Ohio Historical Society (Columbus); and Cambridge University Library in Cambridge, England. Earlier in my career, I was awarded a yearlong ITT International Fellowship to study women during the Irish Revolution at Trinity College, Dublin, and in the rich archives of the National Library of Ireland. Although not directly related to this project, the Irish history I absorbed during that year has strongly shaped my understanding of Irish-American labor politics and international affairs during the World War I era.

Next, I wish to thank those who helped fund this research. A timely grant from the American Council of Learned Societies in 1998–1999 helped me to initiate this research project. Subsequent grants from the Office of Research and Sponsored Programs at the University of Maine in 2005 and 2011 funded important additional research trips. A grant from the Women in the Curriculum Program at the University of Maine funded critical research on the National Women's Trade Union League and International Congress of Working Women at Schlesinger Library at the Radcliffe Institute for Advanced Studies. Two Junior Bird and Bird Fellowships from the History Department at the University of Maine also helped fund research and provide more research time.

I also wish to acknowledge the role of several conferences in shaping my thinking about labor and international affairs. Perhaps most important was a well-planned conference on the "ILO: Past and Present," at the Royal Flemish Academy of Belgium for Science and the Arts in the autumn of 2007 that helped me to better understand European and Latin American perspectives on the International Labor Organization and brought me into contact with the exciting scholarship emanating from the International Institute of Social History. In the autumn of 2008, I gave a plenary lecture at the North American

Labor History Conference at Wayne State University in Detroit at which I also received important feedback. I thank the Bernath Lecture Committee for generously sponsoring this plenary talk.

Two panels at conferences of the Society for Historians of American Foreign Relations, in 2006 and 2010, proved important, as did a 2008 conference on "Workers, the Nation State, and Beyond" at the Newberry Library in Chicago. My work on the Steering Committees of Historians Against the War and the Workers' Rights Board of Eastern Maine have also been influential in shaping my thinking about social movements and U.S. foreign policy. I thank the editors at *Diplomatic History* for including a special forum that I edited and coordinated on "Workers, Labor, and War: New Directions in the History of U.S. Foreign Relations," in their Autumn 2010 edition of that journal, which has helped to inspire a dialogue within the field on the subject.

The staff and reviewers at the University of Illinois Press deserve much praise for their help with this project. I thank Laurie Matheson for inquiring about this project at a time when my interest in it was at low ebb and for offering an early contract. This contract in turn inspired me to focus attention on completing my research and the manuscript. I also thank her for the admirable efficiency with which she guided the manuscript through the reviewing and editorial process and for her quick response to all the many questions I had during the acquisition and editorial process. Dawn Durante deserves thanks for her help with the technical aspects of the manuscript and the art that was included within it. Many thanks are due Nancy Albright for her careful and discerning copyediting of the manuscript, and to Jennifer Clark for skillfully guiding the manuscript through production. The two initial reviewers of the proposal for this project at the University of Illinois Press deserve credit for steering me away from an unworkable conceptual framework. I especially wish to thank the two subsequent reviewers of the completed manuscript, historians David Roediger and Ross Kennedy, for offering clear and insightful critiques and advice for revisions that greatly improved the manuscript.

Finally, I wish to thank colleagues, friends, students, and family who have been important to this project. Dana Frank, Thomas McCormick, James Barrett, and the late David Montgomery and Alan Dawley all read earlier versions of portions of my research and offered useful insights and support. I wish to thank Alex Grab of the University of Maine for translating Italian language articles and cartoons from the *United Mine Workers Journal*. Stefano Tijerina and Marie Carmen Sandweiss assisted with translating difficult sections and articles from Spanish language sources that were beyond my rusty Spanish language skills. Jamie Judd deserves thanks for assistance with the index. Both graduate and undergraduate students at the University of Maine have played a role in shaping my ideas about public opinion and foreign policy and will doubtless recognize some of the themes in this book.

Also important in influencing my understanding of American political opinion is my extended family, which runs the gamut from Tea Party conservatives, to Irish Catholic Democrats, to my own Socialist-labor perspectives. Such diversity of political opinion makes for some interesting family gatherings! I wish especially to acknowledge my intellectual and emotional debts to my mother, Nancy McKillen. A single parent during the second half of my childhood, her herculean efforts to keep a roof over our heads during these years inspired my own early interest in labor and women's history. She continues to be a role model in helping me to cope with the melodramas of everyday life. I also wish to acknowledge my late father Patrick McKillen's positive role in our early childhood. Elements of his legacy have also shaped my historical interests.

Finally, I thank those most directly involved in the life of this book: my spouse Nathan Godfried and our son Isaac McKillen-Godfried. Nathan, a "fellow traveler" in the history of U.S. labor and the U.S. Left, has read this manuscript almost as many times as me. I thank him not only for his constant insights about this project but for his continuous support on every front during our life together. I wish also to emphasize the way our life has been immeasurably enriched by our son Isaac, who has grown up with this book. Since Isaac has become a teenager we have not always agreed on political issues, but our far-ranging discussions have also informed my historical understanding. Let the intergenerational dialogue continue!

Making the World Safe for Workers

Introduction

MANY STUDENTS OF U.S. HISTORY AND politics are likely familiar with President Woodrow Wilson's famous pledge to make the world "safe for democracy" during World War I. Far fewer are aware that Wilson viewed the cooperation of the United States and international labor movements as critical to achieving this goal. To win domestic and international labor support for his foreign policies, Wilson solicited the help of the leaders of the American Federation of Labor (AFL). This book traces the partnership that developed between President Wilson and AFL leaders from its tentative beginnings during policy deliberations over how the United States should respond to the Mexican Revolution, through World War I, to its culmination with the creation of the International Labor Organization (ILO) as an affiliate to the League of Nations at the Versailles Peace Conference in 1919. Equally important, it details the significant opposition that developed to Wilson's and the AFL's foreign policies among a shifting array of U.S., transnational, and international labor, Socialist, and diaspora Left groups. This opposition helped to stimulate, to shape, and ultimately to undermine Wilson's efforts to create a permanent role for labor in international governance.

Recent years have witnessed a renaissance in scholarship on President Woodrow Wilson's foreign policies. Much of this literature has concerned itself with conventional state-to-state relations during the Wilson years and with the ever-popular subject of the creation of the League of Nations. But Erez Manela, in *The Wilsonian Moment*, broke the traditional mold in which much diplomatic history about Wilson is cast by moving beyond U.S. relations with the major European powers to explore the role of a transnational flow of Wilsonian ideas about self-determination in igniting anticolonial movements in the Middle East and Asia.[1] A similar transnational dialogue about Wilsonianism proved important in rekindling the spirit of labor internationalism shattered by the failure of European labor and Socialists to prevent World War I. Yet except for a core group of AFL leaders, few labor activists in the United States, Europe, or Latin America accepted the Wilsonian internationalist agenda unconditionally. Instead, Wilson's foreign policies, and his programs for incorporating labor into international governance through the proposed International Labor Organization, inspired almost continuous contention, debate, and dissent within the U.S. labor movement and at Pan-American and European labor meetings throughout Wilson's terms in office. International labor experienced no golden "Wilsonian moment" during which most labor groups aligned behind Wilson's agenda. Rather, the continuing debate over Wilson's foreign policy programs within U.S. and international labor circles exposed fundamental cleavages surrounding the question of whether the president's unique brand of liberal internationalism really served, or could be modified to serve, the interests of the world's workers.

Historians sympathetic to Wilson have typically emphasized three components of his programs: a commitment to strengthening international law, to achieving "collective security" and a more peaceful world order through a League of Nations, and to helping "oppressed nationalities" achieve self-determination and develop democratic institutions. Revisionist diplomatic historians, like many labor activists of the time period, have emphasized a fourth dimension to his programs: an underlying commitment to the pursuit of U.S. business profit and to the well-being of the international capitalist system.[2]

Even those who do not emphasize Wilson's underlying economic vision often criticize Wilson for the way he chose to implement his goals. Many, for example, argue that international law governing freedom of the seas needed to be modified in light of the evolution of new forms of submarine warfare. To insist, as Wilson did, on older rules of warfare governing freedom of the seas unfairly favored powers with large battleship fleets such as Britain. A commitment to older rules of warfare led Wilson to pursue unneutral policies that favored Britain and inexorably led the United States to war with Germany. Similarly they note that Wilson's pursuit of the League of Nations led him to neglect the need for a just peace treaty that would ensure an equitable settlement of the war. Finally they argue that Wilson's cultural and racial blinders led him to inconsistently apply principles of self-determination. Some nationality groups, Wilson believed, were not yet ready for self-determination. They needed to be guided along this path by the leading democratic powers. This rationale was used by Wilson to justify U.S. meddling in Mexico as well as U.S. military occupations of Haiti, the Dominican Republic, and Nicaragua. It was also used to justify a mandate system for the Middle East and parts of Africa that placed the populations in these areas under the suzerainty of Britain and France. These racialized beliefs additionally established the justification for ignoring the pleas of Asian anticolonialists for a hearing at Versailles.[3]

Viewing Wilson's policies through the lenses of World War I–era labor and Left dissidents, however, brings to light other concerns. U.S. labor and Socialist activists not only objected to Wilson's neutrality policies during the early stages of World War I because these policies were pro-British, but also because they were procapitalist. The U.S. business pursuit of profits, they insisted, was what led American ships into war zones and put them in harm's way. Yet it was workingmen who would be called upon disproportionately to fight and die in European trenches in the event of war. Similarly, working-class women would bear the primary burden of husbands and sons lost to war. Irish-American and German-American labor and Socialist dissenters also charged that intervening in World War I on the side of the world's largest imperial power—Great Britain—would reinforce an imperial status quo in a way that would reify an unjust international division of labor. In the wake of the Versailles Peace Conference, a heterogeneous mix of labor, Socialist, and diaspora Left activists both in the United States and abroad argued that these prophesies had come true: the Versailles Peace Treaty, League of Nations, and International Labor Organization primarily served the interests of the capitalist classes of the leading imperial powers. As the newly formed Chicago Labor Party succinctly complained, the peace treaty and accompanying covenants for the League of Nations and ILO were "dictated by the imperialists of the great world powers, in behalf of international capital, the United States assisting." European labor, as represented at the Bern International Labor and Socialist Conference in 1919, viewed the outcomes at Versailles as "more of a restoration movement rather than a basis for radical innovation" and insisted that the League of Nations seemed designed to function as an "instrument of a victorious coalition dominated by five great powers rather than an organ of international justice."[4]

Labor activists also often attached different meanings to the term *self-determination* than did the Wilson administration. For many labor and Socialist activists throughout the world, self-determination for workers could not be achieved through political democracy alone: it also required the attainment of some modicum of industrial democracy. Plans for achieving industrial democracy ranged from modest schemes for indirect kinds of worker input over managerial decisions in the workplace, to labor union participation in corporate and government economic planning, to bold Socialist and syndicalist blueprints for direct worker control or ownership of the means of production. Yet proponents of all of these types of plans converged in charging that Wilson's interventions and policies toward the social revolutions in Mexico, Ireland, and the Soviet Union seemed designed to thwart rather than promote industrial democracy.

These radical critiques helped inspire Wilson's efforts to pursue a relationship with the conservative leaders of the AFL. Recent historical scholarship has emphasized Wilson's success in capitalizing on the common intellectual turf shared by an array of progressive reformers to build a unique "left-of-center" political coalition in support of his programs.[5] But as important as the common goals apparently shared by those who participated in this coalition were Wilson's fears of those further to the left who stood outside it. Indeed, Wilson's willingness to court the AFL leadership can be understood only against the backdrop of the strong oppositional undercurrents that coursed through the U.S. and international labor movements in the early twentieth century. Wilson sought the support of the AFL leadership in aligning its significant membership behind his foreign policy goals; limiting the appeal of the alternative international agendas of the U.S. Socialist Party, IWW, and a host of immigrant and diaspora Left groups; and in winning support for his foreign policies and international programs among foreign labor movements. Over time, Wilson also accepted the logic of AFL demands for representation at the peace conference and for a role for labor in future international organizations.

Although often characterized as a pragmatic craft union movement dedicated to achieving better wages and working conditions for workers within a capitalist framework, historian David Montgomery and others have convincingly demonstrated that the AFL embodied diverse union and political traditions by the eve of World War I. A sizeable and influential minority of its members belonged to the Socialist Party. Many others supported a labor party; these numbers swelled in the aftermath of World War I to approximately one-half of the membership. The American Federation of Labor also included a few industrially organized unions, such as the United Mine Workers of America (UMWA). These industrial unions often proved more open to organizing workers of all nationality and racial groups than the more traditional craft unions. Although many AFL unions excluded women and embraced a paternalistic ethos, the International Ladies' Garment Workers' Union aggressively recruited female trade unionists, even while remaining a male-led union. Significantly, many local union chapters, municipal AFL affiliates, and constituent unions embraced a strong anti-imperialist and antiwar ethos dating back to at least the time of the Spanish-American-Cuban-Filipino War. In some cases, the oppositional foreign policy activities of local and constituent AFL unions drew inspiration from a brand of populist isolationism that enjoyed particular favor among native-born workers; in other cases it fed on the internationalist visions of immigrants.[6]

Yet AFL President Samuel Gompers rose to power, and subsequently maintained that power, by triumphing over the Socialist, radical, and immigrant Left minorities within the AFL. Gompers proved popular among more conservative elements within the AFL in part because he pursued a hands-off approach toward their membership policies. Although Gompers himself never endorsed racial or gender exclusion, he failed to intervene against those unions who did. Gompers favored national immigration restriction and condoned union practices that excluded new immigrants. Gompers also steered the organization along a conservative course by eschewing Socialist and labor party politics and by refusing to develop a systematic strategy for organizing more industrial unions. Instead Gompers favored a policy of organizing skilled workers and selectively using well-planned strikes to achieve higher wages and better working conditions. During the Progressive Era, the AFL president also embraced arbitration through third-party intermediaries such as the National Civic Federation or by government representatives as a way to resolve disputes between capital and labor.[7]

A committed anti-imperialist and pacifist as a young adult, Gompers developed a more ambiguous attitude toward U.S. imperialism in the aftermath of the Spanish-American-Cuban-Filipino War. Gompers ceased opposing U.S. imperial control over territories in the Pacific and Caribbean in return for government permission to organize unions in these areas. The AFL president reasoned that if labor standards could be raised in the new island protectorates, then the goods produced there would not undersell those made by U.S. workers and American businessmen would not be tempted to establish low-wage factories and sweatshops on the islands. Gompers developed a particularly close relationship with labor leaders in Puerto Rico and intervened on their behalf with U.S. policymakers on several occasions. Puerto Rico, in turn, became a model for Gompers in his efforts to build ties to other foreign labor movements and to influence U.S. foreign policy. As Julie Greene has recently shown, the American experiment in Panama also proved important in shaping AFL ideas about labor-organizing strategies among multiracial workforces in territories occupied by the United States.[8]

When Woodrow Wilson was elected president, Gompers welcomed the opportunity to develop an even greater rapport with officials in Washington. Gompers hailed the Clayton Anti-Trust Act championed by the Wilson administration as labor's "Magna Carta" because it exempted labor from antitrust prosecution. He also seized the opportunity to work with the newly created Labor Department and the Commission on Industrial Relations to improve mechanisms for arbitrating labor disputes.[9] Gompers anticipated that Wilson's prolabor attitude would carry over into the sphere of foreign policy and he eagerly sought labor representation at the Pan-American conferences planned by the Wilson administration in 1914–1915. Yet Wilson failed to invite labor representatives to the Pan-American conferences and at first seemed uninterested in developing a partnership with the AFL in promoting its foreign policies.

Two factors proved decisive in encouraging increased cooperation between the Wilson administration and the AFL on foreign policy issues: the growing radicalism of the Mexican Revolution and the enormous outpouring of antiwar sentiment among U.S. workers in the aftermath of the outbreak of war in Europe in 1914. When Mexican revolutionaries began violently expropriating Mexican lands owned by exploitative American capitalists like John D. Rockefeller, some American workers and Socialists cheered their audacity. But Gompers feared that these actions would inspire American businessmen to seek U.S. military intervention in Mexico to restore their properties. In an effort to avert this intervention, Gompers sought to develop a closer relationship with the president by offering him intelligence about Mexican revolutionary movements gleaned from his contacts with Mexican trade unions. On several occasions, Gompers also used his contacts with Mexican unions in efforts to defuse tensions between the United States and Mexico. Although Wilson failed to invite Gompers or other AFL leaders to serve on any formal diplomatic missions to Mexico, the relationship that developed between the two during crises over the Veracruz incident and the Pershing expedition in turn established pathways that made possible collaboration between AFL leaders and the Wilson administration during World War I.

Following the outbreak of war in Europe, Wilson officially announced U.S. neutrality and asked Americans to remain neutral in thought and action. Yet he also sought to ensure that the United States was militarily ready for possible intervention in the conflict. In 1915, he hired a team of efficiency experts to study U.S. military readiness and they soon alerted him to the dangers of possible labor unrest in undermining any future military effort. Of special concern to preparedness experts were AFL municipal labor bodies with large Irish-American, German-American, Jewish-American, or Socialist constituencies that became hotbeds of antiwar activism in 1914–1915. Also troubling was the strong antiwar sentiment within national unions in industries such as mining that might be critical to the war effort. Experts assumed that coal, in particular, would prove crucial to any future war effort, since it would fuel not only the ships that brought soldiers to Europe but also the defense plants that produced munitions. Yet the United Mine Workers, led by Irish-American John White, also became a hub of antiwar activity following the outbreak of war in Europe; the union, moreover, was heavily immigrant and multiracial in composition, boasting large numbers of Irish, Italian, Slavic and African Americans whose patriotism some preparedness activists doubted in the event of war.[10]

In response to these concerns, Wilson appointed Gompers to the Council of National Defense in 1916. Gompers subsequently used that position to assist Wilson with his industrial preparedness efforts as well as to advise the president on a host of international labor issues. This appointment in turn paved the way for the systematic incorporation of AFL leaders into policy-making circles and wartime diplomatic missions during the period of U.S. belligerency, as well as ensuring the AFL a role at Versailles.

As historian Joseph McCartin has demonstrated, Gompers and other AFL leaders viewed the war boards as a mechanism for achieving a moderate form of industrial democracy. The war boards provided significant input for labor on questions of economic and foreign policy and also afforded it a chance to promote a collective bargaining system within key industries that helped to give workers unprecedented power over the conditions and terms of their labor. Yet other scholars have preferred to emphasize the "corporat-ist" or "tripartite" dimensions of the wartime partnership that developed between business, labor, and the state during the war and have pointed to its undemocratic tendencies. The terms *corporatism* and *tripartism* are used by scholars to refer to an informal or formal process of power-sharing that often develops between organized labor, business, and the state in advanced industrial societies in an effort to resolve complex problems of domestic economic coordination as well as to promote foreign economic expansion and to deal with threats to this foreign economic expansion. In the United States, in contrast to Europe and Latin America, corporatist forms of power-sharing have often been informal. However, during World War I, World War II, and the early Cold War, this power-sharing was institutionalized within executive branch bureaucracies. Critics emphasize that although corporatist networks give some groups and individuals unprecedented access to policymakers, they exclude others. Equally important, these networks increasingly usurp some kinds of policymaking powers previously reserved for democratically elected bodies such as Congress.[11]

U.S. diplomatic historians have long recognized the importance of power-sharing partnerships among business elites, chosen labor representatives, and executive branch officials in promoting U.S. foreign policy, but their limited treatment of labor's role within these partnerships has, to date, been too narrowly construed. In particular, early scholarship on the corporatist partnership that developed between the AFL and the Wilson administration during World War I underemphasized the persistence of oppositional labor forces both in the United States and abroad in shaping this partnership and in determining the outcome of the policies it promoted.[12]

Perhaps the single most consistent opponent of the partnership that developed between the AFL and the government in promoting U.S. foreign policy during the Wilson administration was the U.S. Socialist Party. Officially established in 1901 after years of quarreling between different Socialist factions, the U.S. Socialist Party maintained a vaguely anti-imperialist orientation during its first half-dozen years but focused primarily on domestic issues. The outbreak of revolution in Mexico in 1910, however, sent a shockwave through U.S. socialism similar to that unleashed by the Bolshevik Revolution among European Socialists a few years later. Some leading U.S. Socialists, betraying their own racialized vision of the world, believed Mexican society to be too underdeveloped for socialism to triumph there. Others hailed the Mexican Revolution as the opening battle in the class war that would bring socialism to all of North America.[13]

If Socialists disagreed about many aspects of the Mexican Revolution, a consensus emerged about one point: U.S. foreign policy decision making needed to be democratized in order to prevent the business class from using its political influence to foment war with Mexico. The simultaneous drumbeats of preparedness groups who sought to dramatically increase military spending and mandate universal military service, allegedly to protect the United States from foreign invasion either by belligerent European powers or by Mexican revolutionaries, further convinced Socialists of the need for more democratic safeguards surrounding questions of war and peace. From their perspective, the greatest threat to U.S. national security was internal rather than external; the business class would not hesitate to draw the country into multiple wars to advance their own profits.

The party's innovative 1915 peace program emphasized that only the achievement of industrial democracy would ensure permanent peace. But in the interim the party demanded democratic referenda of the entire U.S. population on questions of war with either Mexico or Germany and called for removing foreign policymaking powers from the executive branch of government to Congress in order to help slow the drive toward war. To Wilson, a strong believer in executive supremacy in foreign affairs, such ideas were anathema. Likewise, the president disagreed with Socialist arguments that capitalism inevitably bred war and imperialism. Other Socialist peace proposals, however, anticipated Wilson's Fourteen Point program for international change in highlighting the need for a peace formula in Europe based on no annexations and no indemnities and in advocating an international parliament.[14]

Historian Thomas Knock has emphasized the significance of areas of overlap like these between the Socialist Party and the Wilson administration in ensuring the evolution of a left-of-center coalition in support of the president's international programs.[15] This book offers a different interpretation. Much more important than the common intellectual ground shared by the Democrats and the Socialists was the independent role played by the Socialist Party in illuminating the class underpinnings of American foreign policy and in deconstructing Wilsonian propaganda about subjects that ranged from the gendered duties of citizenship, to the war to make the world safe for democracy, to the League of Nations and ILO. In this sense, a third party committed to working-class interests at the heart of American politics proved critical, shifting the entire national debate over foreign policy to the left.

Also important in shifting the debate over American foreign policy, albeit in a more sporadic fashion, was the Industrial Workers of the World. Created in 1905, the IWW officially eschewed politics and recognized no national boundaries. IWW leaders instead focused on organizing workers into one big union that could seize control of the mines, factories, and railroads through direct action. But the IWW nonetheless promoted a strongly antimilitarist agenda after 1910, emphasizing that wars between nations were a distraction from the real war—the class war. The IWW counseled its members to avoid meaningless political demonstrations but exhorted them to "get on the job of organizing the working class to take over the industries" so as to "stop all future capitalist aggression that leads to wars and other forms of barbarism." The organizing and strike activities of the IWW posed a significant threat to the Wilson administration's effort to economically mobilize the country for war and reinforced Wilson's carrot-and-stick approach to the labor movement; the AFL leadership was rewarded for its loyalty while the IWW was brutally suppressed. Yet even with most of its leaders in jail in 1919, the IWW proved a formidable opponent of Wilson's foreign policies, offering damning indictments of the proposed International Labor Organization.[16]

A third, often neglected, tier of working-class opposition to Wilsonian foreign policy emerged among antiwar and anti-imperialist unions within the AFL. Even as Gompers moved toward alignment with the Wilson administration on critical issues in 1915–1916, the highly decentralized, federated structure of the AFL initially allowed dissent to flourish. Four case studies are used here to represent different types of oppositional foreign policy impulses within the AFL: the Seattle Central Labor Council, the Chicago Federation of Labor, the United Mine Workers and the International Ladies' Garment Workers' Union. In the case of the Seattle Council, the Socialist and nativist politics of the council's leadership proved particularly important in shaping its foreign policy agenda. By contrast, the leaders of both the Chicago Federation of Labor and the United Mine Workers were more influenced by Irish-American critiques of Wilson's foreign policy. Yet far from accepting these critiques unquestioningly, they fused them with their own ideas about economic justice, working-class citizenship duties, and the international division of labor. The male Socialist leaders of the International Ladies' Garment Workers' Union immersed themselves in the antiwar campaigns of the New York Socialist Party, but some of its midlevel female organizers were more influenced by feminist peace activities and the campaigns of the Women's Trade Union League. The integrated vision of these women emphasized the strong interconnections between industrial democracy, women's suffrage, and world peace. Denied leadership positions within the AFL, women from the ILGWU and WTUL played a prominent role in staging the International Congress of Working Women in 1919 to demand structural changes to the proposed International Labor Organization that would ensure female representation.

Also mobilizing at war's end to assert their own international agenda for the world's workers were African Americans. The voices of African Americans, even more so than those of working women, were rarely heard and almost never recorded in debates over foreign policy within the AFL. To a surprising degree, this proved true of the Socialist Party as well, inspiring some African American Socialists to leave the party during the war. Although more committed to organizing African American workers than the AFL, the IWW press also seemed to largely ignore African American foreign policy concerns during the war or to subsume them under the mantle of class unity. But during the final stages of the war, African Americans joined women in mobilizing on their own behalf to influence the postwar order. Some African American leaders and groups, such as W. E. B. Du Bois and the NAACP, sought to work with the Wilson administration and the international institutions it created in advancing the well-being of workers of color throughout the world. By contrast, African American Socialists such as A. Phillip Randolph and Hubert Harrison, and Black Nationalists under the leadership of Marcus Garvey, proved to be highly perceptive critics of the League and ILO and launched movements and campaigns that helped to swell the tide of working-class disenchantment with the Wilson administration.[17]

In sum, a formidable, although shifting, array of U.S. labor, Socialist, and diaspora Left groups challenged the Wilsonian internationalist agenda between 1912–1920, stimulating a vital debate within working-class America about whether terms like national security, national interest, and citizenship duties were really so class neutral as policymakers and preparedness activists claimed. Similarly, workers deconstructed Wilsonian rhetoric about making the world safe for democracy and wondered whether such a mission really meant making the world safe for capitalism. If so, many doubted that workers in either the United States or abroad would really benefit. Finally, workers wondered about the logic of collective security; would the League of Nations and ILO establish mechanisms for achieving international peace and justice or would they instead reinforce an imperial status quo in ways that helped foment revolution and provoked future wars?

Externally, Wilson and Gompers encountered resistance not only from the revolutionary movements of Mexico, Ireland, and the Soviet Union, but also from moderate European Socialist and labor leaders as well as social policy experts who vied with Gompers to have their agendas for international labor and economic reform heard by those at the Versailles Peace Conference. Particularly important was British Labour Party politician Arthur Henderson, who emerged as an informal leader of the Inter-Allied labor movement during the war, much to Gompers's chagrin. Although many British and European labor leaders found Wilson's rhetoric about a new diplomacy inspiring, they boycotted the Versailles Conference when the leaders of the Allied powers refused to allow German labor representatives to attend. Yet Henderson and the Allied Socialists nonetheless exercised indirect influence through European social policy experts, Belgian Socialists, and former British Labour Party representative George Barnes who sat on the Commission on International Labor Legislation at Versailles. French trade union leader Léon Jouhaux also returned early from the Bern labor conference to ensure that European labor had a voice in the commission's deliberations.[18]

The initial blueprints for the ILO came from the British, while the Americans crafted the first Labor Bill of Rights to be incorporated into the Versailles Treaty. Yet both the constitution for the ILO and the final Labor Bill of Rights were ultimately shaped by multiple compromises made during the deliberations of the Commission on International Labor Legislation. The framework for the ILO, moreover, was further modified to address European criticism before and during the first ILO convention in Washington, D.C., in October 1919. Yet while these compromises mollified European Socialists and trade unionists, they only further inflamed passions against the ILO in the United States, giving rise to a strange political alliance between U.S. labor reformers and conservative Republicans who mobilized to exclude the Labor Bill of Rights and the covenant of the ILO from the Versailles Peace Treaty upon which the Senate would vote. Although Gompers and the Wilson administration had assumed that the labor clauses of the treaty would increase its popularity in the United States, they instead proved a political liability.

The multiple labor debates that developed over Wilson's and the AFL's foreign policies and international programs deserve historical attention for several reasons. First, they demonstrate an obvious but often overlooked point: a broad range of labor, Socialist, and Left activists were vitally concerned with foreign policy and international politics during the World War I era. Although the new "transnational" labor history has recently shed welcome light on a range of significant issues involving labor and international affairs, its leading practitioners have suggested the need to deemphasize the importance of the nation-state as a "discrete" unit of analysis. As a result, this newly developing field has largely neglected questions of national foreign policies as well as the "wars of position" within nation-states that determined which labor groups exercised influence over national foreign policies and under what conditions. Instead, transnational historians have tended to focus on global economic developments, ties between labor movements across national boundaries, labor problems at sites of empire, international labor migrations, and the history of international labor institutions.[19]

Yet national foreign policies clearly played a critical role in shaping all of the above, as was well recognized by labor activists of the early twentieth century. Not only U.S. but also labor, Socialist, and diaspora Left activists throughout the world closely followed U.S. foreign policy during the World War I era because they realized that seismic shifts were occurring in the tectonic plates in which the old international political system had been embedded. The United States, they recognized, might prove one of the most significant diplomatic actors in the emerging new world order. Yet although Wilson spoke a new diplomatic language, from the beginning of his term in office labor activists judged his words against his actions and often found them wanting. Against this backdrop of suspicion, labor and Socialist organizations mobilized to ensure that their voices were heard on a host of foreign policy and international issues that they assumed might have a critical impact on the well-being of workers, ranging from questions of war and peace, to the disposition of empires, to the international division of labor, and to the question of how to create international organizations that would advance rather than undermine the quest for industrial democracy. The outcome of the debate over these questions would help to shape international labor relations as well as U.S. foreign policy for the remainder of the century.

Second, an examination of labor debates over foreign policy during this era suggests that historians have underestimated the strength of antiwar impulses within American labor, and of Wilson's fears of this antiwar sentiment, in convincing the president to forge a partnership with the AFL and to appoint Gompers to the Council of National Defense in 1916. Wilson's fears increased rather than diminished in 1917 following his declaration of war against Germany. U.S. labor, far from rallying behind the flag as Wilson anticipated, demonstrated high levels of both political and industrial unrest, helping to explain—if not to justify—Wilson's attempts to suppress dissent. Yet Wilson and AFL leaders soon discovered that opposition to their foreign policy programs among workers was a multiheaded hydra that proved impossible to destroy entirely; even as they successfully crushed one form of dissent, other forms emerged. The war for position and influence among labor groups was thus fought on multiple battlefields and its outcome proved far more inconclusive than has often assumed.[20]

Third, the AFL's incorporation into government policymaking circles during the war, and the debates that it engendered within the AFL as well as among other labor groups, sheds light on the evolution of a little considered component of Wilson's internationalist agenda: his blueprints for how to deal with international social and class unrest. Although historians have written extensively on Wilson's relationship with both imperial and revolutionary governments during this period, they have largely neglected his policies toward the international labor and Socialist movements. Yet these movements strongly concerned Wilson because he correctly understood that class unrest abroad could undermine his efforts to create a new world order as surely as could the opposition of imperial governments. Primarily focused on German "autocracy" in 1917, Wilson's focus expanded following the Bolshevik Revolution in November 1917 to include a concern with the growing social unrest in Europe and Britain. As the preeminent European historian Arno Mayer emphasized several decades ago, Wilson faced potential challenges to his diplomacy in Europe in 1918 not just from the "parties of order," but also from the "parties of movement," or those committed to change in Europe. Yet Wilson enjoyed a receptive audience among the European Left precisely because he spoke the language of reform. If Wilson had been willing to cultivate an alliance with these forces of change in Europe, he might have helped to advance his bargaining position at Versailles.[21]

Wilson, however, proved a victim of the form of class collaboration he chose to embrace at home. In particular, Wilson relied for advice in dealing with the European Left on those few AFL leaders and prowar Socialists he incorporated into government circles, while ignoring the voices of the American Left whom he tried to repress. Yet AFL leaders and prowar Socialists, who traveled to Europe on several diplomatic missions during the war, viewed events there through uniquely myopic lenses and tended to oversimplify the enormous differences emerging between moderate Socialists and Labor Party activists on the one hand, and those promoting Bolshevism and social revolution on the other. They thus offered Wilson poor intelligence that kept him from fully capitalizing on the strong support for some of his programs among the Inter-Allied labor and Socialist group led by Arthur Henderson. By simultaneously alienating the American Left, Wilson also helped to pave the way for the defeat of the treaty in the United States.

Finally, the debate within labor and Socialist circles over Wilson's and the AFL's international programs offers a unique lens through which to view questions of public opinion and U.S. foreign policy. U.S. diplomatic historians have often been accused of promoting a Washington-centric view of U.S. foreign policy that primarily emphasizes the perspectives of U.S. policymakers and opinion makers who live within the Washington beltway. But in recent years, they have tried to remedy this problem in two ways. First, they have developed a more critical perspective by increasingly using foreign archives and sources in their studies. Second, the field has embraced a "new cultural turn" that has emphasized the importance of better understanding the cultural lenses through which policymakers have viewed issues. In particular, they have explored the importance of cultural ideas about gender and race in shaping the world views of policymakers and in influencing their decision making. Some studies have also suggested the importance of cultural values as a tool used by policymakers to build public consent for their policies. Common gender and racial icons, they suggest, have been particularly important components of government propaganda efforts. Students of World War I era propaganda suggest that it was highly successful in mobilizing U.S. support for Wilson's foreign policy.[22]

But the vigorous U.S. labor debates over virtually every component of Wilson's foreign policy agenda suggest that historians may have overestimated the hegemonic power of U.S. national appeals during the World War I era. Building on older bodies of labor and social history that have been neglected by diplomatic historians, this manuscript illuminates the diverse working-class subcultures and labor organizations that impeded the efforts of Wilson and the AFL to align the U.S. working class behind their foreign policy programs. Equally important, it details competing transnational flows of information within working-class circles that tended to undercut support for Wilsonianism. On the one hand, workers enjoyed access through the Socialist Party and their unions to the alternative international agendas of European Socialists, British Labour Party activists, syndicalists and communists. On the other hand, the swirling transnational dialogues surrounding the revolutionary upheavals in Ireland, Mexico, and the Soviet Union profoundly influenced immigrants. An almost continuous stream of international labor visitors and revolutionaries enlivened local labor meetings between 1914 and 1920 and inspired heady aspirations for a new world order. Against this backdrop, both Wilson's and Gompers's handiwork at Versailles proved a bitter disappointment.

Also inspiring opposition to Wilson's and Gompers's handiwork at Versailles were competing ideas about the racial and gendered division of labor within the world economy. In this sense, hegemonic appeals using racial and gender icons tended to backfire or proved ineffectual. Conservatives often assumed that the League of Nations and ILO would subvert the racial division of labor both at home and abroad. For example, they feared that the ILO might try to undermine the authority of white southerners by regulating the conditions of African American labor in the South. Similarly, they worried that the League of Nations and ILO would give nations like Haiti with predominantly nonwhite populations a voice in international affairs equal to that of the United States. By contrast, many labor and diaspora Left activists argued that because the ILO and League of Nations were inherently undemocratic in structure they would tend to reinforce imperial infrastructures in ways that perpetuated the existing racial division of labor. African Americans pointed in particular to the mandate system created under the auspices of the League of Nations as an example of the new kinds of structures that imperial powers would use to continue to exploit workers of color.[23]

Significantly, even many white immigrant workers considered themselves members of oppressed races during this period. For example, Irish-Americans held regular "Irish race conventions" not only to advance the cause of independence for Ireland but also to uplift the Irish race. The class vision of Irish-American labor leaders in turn became inextricably connected to this racial vision. They opposed the League and ILO not only because Wilson had failed to deliver on his promise of self-determination for Ireland, but also because they believed these institutions would reinforce the existing dominance of the British Empire in ways that particularly exploited workers of Irish and Indian heritage. The progressive wing of the Irish community even reached out to African Americans in an effort to forge solidarity between oppressed races in opposing imperialism. Jewish-American Socialists made similar overtures.[24] Yet others within immigrant communities, as David Roediger, Jim Barrett, and other scholars have demonstrated, responded to their "racial inbetweenness" by pursuing whiteness and by promoting exclusionary practices toward nonwhites. In this way, racial identity among white immigrants could turn on a pivot, alternately fostering incisive critiques of imperialism and brutal race riots in 1919 that ultimately shattered class solidarity and the dream of industrial unions, a labor party, and international labor solidarity in the postwar era.[25]

Women trade unionists, meanwhile, objected to the ILO because it failed to establish a policy mandating representation for women. The early protective legislation passed by the first ILO convention in 1919, moreover, demonstrated that men were more concerned with excluding women from some kinds of professions than with helping to advance gender equality. Although the International Congress of Working Women did not assume an irreconcilable position on the ILO, the group did seek to change its structure in fundamental ways, and in so doing to alter the structural impediments to women's economic advancement throughout the world. When Wilson proved hostile to the International Congress of Working Women, he alienated a powerful new group of voters in 1920: working women.[26]

Labor and working-class debates over Wilsonian foreign policy thus illuminate a critical underside to U.S. public opinion on foreign policy and international questions during this period. The labor, Socialist, and diaspora Left proved far more significant in swelling the tide of opposition to the Versailles Peace Treaty and to U.S. participation in the League of Nations and ILO than has commonly been assumed. Equally important, their criticisms of Wilson's foreign policies afford an important new analytical lens through which to view the Wilsonian internationalist principles that would dominate American diplomacy for much of the twentieth century.

The chapters in this manuscript are divided into four thematic sections, each dealing with a particular debate that developed within labor circles over Wilson's and the AFL's foreign policies. Each section is preceded by a short prologue that introduces the relevant foreign policies as well as the labor actors—both domestic and foreign—who would prove most important in debating these policies. Part I considers the catalytic role of Wilson's policies toward the Mexican Revolution in reviving debate within American labor and Socialist circles, as well as within the Mexican-American immigrant Left, about U.S. foreign policy and its significance for American workers. It also explores the efforts of the AFL to forge a tentative relationship with the Wilson administration that would give labor more input on foreign policy questions. Part II examines the debate within the Socialist Party and AFL over Wilson's neutrality and preparedness policies and considers AFL President Samuel Gompers's appointment to the Council of National Defense and his successful efforts to secure a pledge from leading AFL unions of their loyalty to the government in the event of war. It also briefly considers the failed efforts of left-wing Socialists and IWW activists to develop a viable strategy for staging general strikes to stop the war and prevent U.S. involvement in it. A broader discussion of the IWW, however, is postponed to the chapters on U.S. belligerency. Since the IWW leadership repudiated political lobbying as an effective form of antiwar action, it proved relatively less important to the purely political debates over preparedness than either the Socialist Party or the AFL. By contrast, its economic campaigns during the period of U.S. belligerency were viewed as a direct threat to the war effort and provoked brutal repression from government authorities.

In Part III, I consider the theme of collaboration and resistance during the period of U.S. belligerency. Among the topics explored here are the continued resistance of the Socialist Party to the war, the antiwar culture of the IWW and its decision to continue strike and organizing activities despite government pleas for patriotic unity, and the AFL's collaboration with the government in promoting its war policies both at home and abroad. Part IV considers the AFL leadership's role in creating the ILO at Versailles and examines the strong opposition to U.S. membership in this organization that coalesced by the time the ILO held its first foundational meeting in Washington, D.C., in the autumn of 1919. Separate sections in chapter seven consider the importance of the International Congress of Working Women and African American Leftist groups in shaping the debate over the ILO in the United States. A conclusion considers the significance of the labor/Left debate over Wilsonian foreign policy both for U.S. diplomacy and for the U.S. labor movement in the twentieth century.

One final note on methodology is important here. Although this manuscript is based on over ten years of archival and primary research, it is also unapologetically an effort at synthesis. A common complaint lodged against the field of labor history is that it has produced a rich body of community and case studies but too few broad narratives that explore the significance of working-class agitation for understanding larger historical patterns and questions.[27]

Because this study attempts just such a broad narrative, I have necessarily relied on synthesizing existing literature as well as my own primary research. Among the diverse bodies of secondary literature on which this manuscript draws are those relating to the Mexican borderlands, European labor history, U.S. diplomatic history, U.S. immigration history, African American history, gender history, and several schools within U.S. labor history, including the older institutional labor history, the "new" labor history that came to the fore in the 1970s and 1980s, and the even newer transnational labor history. Although all of these different historical subspecialties have yielded some incremental information on questions of U.S. labor and foreign policy, their practitioners have all too often failed to engage in meaningful dialogue with one another. A final goal of this manuscript is to bring these divergent fields into conversation with one another, as well as with my own primary research discoveries. For summaries of the diplomatic history literature on Wilson's foreign policies, see especially the prologue sections. For an examination of some of the methodological debates in other fields that seem critical to questions about U.S. labor and foreign policy, see the relevant endnotes. For a summary of the major primary sources used in this study, as well as a key to how they are abbreviated in the endnotes, see the guide supplied at the end of this manuscript.

Figure P.1. *United Mine Workers Journal*, April 30, 1914, 1. This cartoon portrays Uncle Sam as willing to flex his muscles to protect oil interests in Mexico but not to defend striking miners and their families from wanton murder in Ludlow, Colorado. The Ludlow massacre and U.S. occupation of Veracruz happened within a few days of each other and catalyzed a debate over the Wilson administration's domestic and foreign priorities.

PROLOGUE: WILSON, THE WESTERN
HEMISPHERE, AND MEXICO

President Wilson is perhaps best remembered for his policies toward World War I and his role in creating the League of Nations at Versailles. Yet he first cut his diplomatic teeth on foreign policies toward the Western hemisphere and developed many of his ideas about collective security and self-determination while trying to forge closer relations with Latin America. Renouncing both the "Big Stick" and "Dollar Diplomacy" policies of his predecessors, Wilson initially sought to encourage a new spirit of Pan-Americanism based on the ideals of national equality and mutual cooperation. One of the problems with the Monroe Doctrine, Wilson proclaimed, was that the United States had issued it unilaterally, without seeking the advice or consent of Latin Americans. Wilson therefore proposed a new "Pan American Pact," to the nations of Argentina, Brazil, and Chile that would be based on a "[m]utual guarantee of political independence under republican forms of government and mutual guarantees of territorial integrity." Wilson later used similar wording in Article 10 of the League of Nations Covenant. Simultaneously with his effort to promote the Pan American Pact, Wilson sponsored a Pan American Financial Conference to encourage economic cooperation and interdependence in the Western hemisphere; for the president, economic and political reform clearly went hand in hand.[1]

Yet Pan-Americanism soon foundered on the shoals of Wilson's almost continuous interventions in the affairs of Latin American states. Perhaps most strikingly, Wilson ordered the military occupations of Haiti and the Dominican Republic during 1915 and 1916, and strengthened the U.S. financial controls over these countries established by the Taft administration. The U.S. Navy governed the Dominican Republic until 1924 despite continuous peasant resistance. In Haiti, U.S. marines engaged in a brutal guerrilla war that left at least 2,250 dead; the marines finally departed only in 1934. Wilson, like his predecessors, also intervened repeatedly in Nicaragua and continued President Taft's policies of financial supervision over this country.[2]

To his critics, Wilson's policies clearly seemed hypocritical. Yet, as Trygve Throntveit has recently argued, Wilson never really embraced the ideal of full and immediate self-determination for all would-be nation-states who sought it. Rather, Wilson emphasized that democracy was a "stage of development"; some colonial peoples, as well as weaker nations seeking their independence from the hegemony of more powerful states, required a "period of political tutelage" before they would be ready to exercise "entire control over their affairs." The United States, Wilson believed, was ideally suited to tutor underdeveloped countries in the ways of democracy because of the superiority of its political and economic institutions. The son of a Presbyterian minister, Wilson also insisted that Americans were the "custodians of the spirit of righteousness" and had been given a special covenantal responsibility by God to guide the world along the path toward democracy and uplift. For Wilson, U.S. trade and capitalist investment abroad could serve not only to promote U.S. prosperity but also to guide underdeveloped nations along the path toward democracy and progress, so long as these economic transactions were conducted in a moral manner. To assure that a moral compass guided U.S. economic expansion, Wilson sought to extend Progressive Era regulatory legislation to the export, international finance, and foreign investment realms.[3]

These beliefs in turn set the stage for Wilson's interventions in the Mexican Revolution. By the time Wilson assumed office, revolution had already raged in Mexico for more than two years. Like many progressives, Wilson sympathized with the moderate revolutionary Francisco Madero, who overthrew the government of Porfirio Díaz in 1911. Under Díaz, foreign investments in Mexico had increased exponentially, but critics charged that these investments came at the expense of the Mexican people. Díaz's dictatorial and corrupt politics, as well as his expropriation of communally held peasant lands, also inspired criticism on both sides of the border. Madero promised to end the corruption and to guide Mexico along a path of moderate reformism. But when General Victoriano Huerta overthrew Madero, Wilson learned how difficult it could be to guide revolutionary countries along the path toward American-style democracy. Although most European powers recognized Huerta's government, Wilson refused, insisting that it was a "government of butchers."[4]

When Huerta's troops arrested several American sailors and then quickly released them during an incident in Tampico, Mexico, during 1914, Wilson used it as a justification to militarily occupy the nearby port of Veracruz and to stop a German arms shipment intended for Huerta. The U.S. occupation, rather than undermining support for Huerta, temporarily increased his popularity. Yet other revolutionary forces in Mexico soon came to the fore, among them the Constitutionalists led by Venustiano Carranza and General Pancho Villa, agrarian radicals directed by Emiliano Zapata, and anarcho-syndicalists whose allegiances were divided between two groups: the Casa Del Obrero Mundial and the Partido Liberal Mexicano (PLM). Significantly, the home base of the PLM was Los Angeles, ensuring that it would play a particularly important role in shaping the U.S. working-class debate about the revolution, despite the outlaw status of its exiled leaders, Ricardo and Enrique Flores Magón.[5]

As revolution continued to convulse Mexico, American business groups with property interests there mounted concerted campaigns on behalf of a more thorough-going military occupation of Mexico. Following a border raid by Pancho Villa into Columbus, New Mexico, in the spring of 1916 that left seventeen Americans dead, Wilson launched a military expedition led by General John Pershing that penetrated deeply into Mexico. Many assumed that the much anticipated U.S. military occupation of Mexico was imminent. Pershing's expedition particularly alarmed American labor, Socialist, and Mexican émigré groups like the Partido Liberal Mexicano who paid only sporadic attention to Wilson's machinations in the Caribbean; nearly all assumed that an American protectorate in Mexico would be an economic disaster both for U.S. and Mexican workers. They disagreed strongly, however, about how to prevent U.S. war with, or military occupation of, Mexico; how to permanently end imperialism; and whether Wilson was a friend or foe of working people. Long before the "Wilsonian Moment" blossomed in Asia, important factions within U.S. and Mexican labor would come to view Wilson as a fraud, setting the stage for the future war of position between the AFL leadership and its opponents over U.S. foreign policy toward World War I and the League of Nations.[6]

1   The Mexican Revolution as Catalyst

IN THE SPRING OF 1914, two dramatic events dominated the U.S. labor and Socialist press and illustrated compellingly the ways in which the class struggle in the United States was related to the social and political upheaval that had been occurring in Mexico since 1910. On April 20, in the small town of Ludlow, Colorado, a dispute between the United Mine Workers of America (UMWA) and the Colorado Fuel and Iron Company triggered a violent attack by national guardsmen on a tent colony constructed to house miners' families after they were evicted from their company-owned homes. Guardsmen fired indiscriminately into the tent colony and then set it ablaze. At least sixty people died in the fire, most of them women and children. The attack provoked outrage across the country but soon competed for headlines with President Wilson's decision to send U.S. troops to occupy the Mexican port of Veracruz on April 21. Nineteen U.S. soldiers and several hundred Mexicans died in this assault.[1]

Wilson claimed that the occupation of Veracruz was a response to the Mexican military's decision to arrest American sailors who had gone ashore for provisions. But the Socialist and labor press questioned why the American navy was docked off the coast of Mexico. They charged that the real motives behind the occupation were to protect the American-owned oil fields in nearby Tampico from revolutionary violence and, possibly, to launch a war of conquest against Mexico that would turn it into an economic subsidiary of U.S. corporations. Muckraking Socialist journalists eagerly revealed that John D. Rockefeller was the principal stockholder in the Colorado Fuel and Iron Corporation as well as a major investor in the Tampico oil fields. UMWA, IWW, and Socialist publications compared the killing of miners' families in Ludlow with that of innocent civilians in Veracruz and indignantly asserted that American soldiers, many of working-class origin, had "no business doing the dirty work of capitalism" in either the United States or Mexico. Particularly striking was a UMWA cartoon that juxtaposed an image of a muscular Uncle Sam using military might to protect oil fields in Mexico with an image of Uncle Sam sleeping while women and children were murdered at Ludlow (Figure P.1).[2]

Figure 1.1. *Regeneración* (paper of the Los Angeles based Partido Liberal Mexicano—PLM), June 13, 1914, 2. Leaders of the PLM, as this cartoon indicates, believed that Mexican revolutionaries were too influenced by President Wilson's promises to aid the cause of reform in Mexico. They instead insisted on the need for Mexico to free itself from U.S. imperial domination through a social and economic revolution led by the peasantry and labor.

Such exposés and attempts to connect the exploitation of U.S. and Mexican workers were common following the outbreak of revolution in Mexico in 1911. Left-leaning journalists who traveled to Mexico to report on the revolution unfailingly noted the dominant presence of U.S. corporations in the country and drew parallels between their labor practices in the United States and Mexico. Mexican-American émigré groups seeking to prevent

U.S. intervention in the Mexican Revolution and to encourage American labor groups to financially support various revolutionary groups in Mexico also highlighted the connections. As Ricardo Flores Magón, the passionate Mexican-American labor activist, anarchist, and founder of the influential Los Angeles–based Partido Liberal Mexicano (PLM) explained, "The Mexican Revolution is labor's revolution for the Mexicans have been stripped to the bone by the very powers which labor is organized to fight. . . . The profits wrung from American labor have been taken across the Mexican border and used to grind out even vaster fortunes by slavery of the grossest type." Flores Magón argued that if the American business class succeeded in crushing the Mexican Revolution, then Mexican immigration to the United States would continue to increase, thereby depressing wages in the United States. Equally important, "[t]he wealth of the magnates of American industry" would continue "to flow into Mexico, to then, a land of permission for all the adventurers and all the exploiters" and "the manufactures of [the] United States would be transplanted to Mexico."[3]

By extensively publicizing such economic interconnections, the U.S. Left and Mexican émigré community helped to stimulate an interest among U.S. trade unionists and labor activists of all political persuasions in the Mexican Revolution, in U.S. foreign policy, and in developing new forms of international labor power. Most labor and Socialist groups converged in seeking to prevent a U.S. war with Mexico and in believing that a permanent military occupation of Mexico would be economically harmful to workers on both sides of the border. But they often disagreed radically in their assessments of Wilson's foreign policies, their views of different revolutionary groups in Mexico, and the kinds of international influence they sought for workers. Underlying these conflicts were differences about whether industrial democracy and an end to imperialism could be achieved within a capitalist context.

The complex and sometimes shifting international perspectives of U.S. labor, Socialist, and Mexican-American immigrant Left groups are best envisioned along a continuum with the anarcho-syndicalist leadership of the Partido Liberal Mexicano at one end of the spectrum and the AFL leadership at the opposite end. Other Socialist, labor, and immigrant Left groups tended to position themselves somewhere in between these polarities, depending upon their ideological orientation, assessments of the changing balance of power among different labor groups in the American Southwest and Mexico, and the particular event. Even affiliates of the PLM and AFL sometimes gravitated away from the policies of their national organizations and toward other positions on the spectrum when it seemed to better suit local or specific industrial needs.

Although the PLM has received much attention from Mexican, Mexican Borderlands, and labor historians, it has understandably fallen under the radar of most U.S. diplomatic historians. At the time of the outbreak of the Mexican Revolution, PLM leaders Ricardo and Enrique Flores Magón lived a marginal hand-to-mouth existence on a commune outside of Los Angeles and exercised no significant influence in Washington, D.C., usually an important criteria for whether actors are included in diplomatic history books. Yet as a number of studies have recently demonstrated, communities of immigrants and political exiles can sometimes play critical roles as conduits in transnational chains of anti-imperialist politics. The importance of the PLM was twofold. First, they connected many Mexican migrants and Mexican-Americans to the revolutionary struggle in Mexico. Second, they devoted a significant component of their enormous energies upon arriving in the United States in 1904 to trying to educate Americans about foreign policy issues, especially those related to Latin America and Mexico. At first posing as liberals seeking to rid Mexico of a corrupt ruler and to improve working conditions for Mexican workers, they won significant support among both American labor leaders and Mexican Americans. Yet following the outbreak of revolution in Mexico in 1911, the PLM embraced a much more controversial anarcho-syndicalist agenda and urged revolutionaries to expropriate both foreign and Mexican capitalists and turn over the land, mines, and factories directly to Mexican workers.[4]

Initially sympathetic toward Wilson, the PLM soon became one of the administration's most bitter critics. Wilson, claimed PLM leaders, was particularly dangerous because he posed as a reformer even while seeking greater imperial controls over Mexico and other parts of Latin America than other U.S. leaders. PLM activists tailored their foreign policy agenda accordingly, arguing that the prime task of U.S. workers should be to prevent the U.S. government from intervening in the Mexican Revolution and artificially propping up newly emerging figures of government authority, such as Francisco Madero and Venustiano Carranza who sought to quell the violence and preserve capitalist authority over workers. U.S. workers should instead economically and militarily support the PLM, whose goal was genuine social as well as political revolution in Mexico. By thwarting U.S. imperialism, American workers would be helping themselves, since they were also hurt by capital mobility.

Not surprisingly, the PLM's strongest support within the U.S labor movement after 1911 came from the IWW, which shared its syndicalist beliefs as well as its generally negative view of the Wilson administration. Some IWW activists participated in PLM forays into Mexico, while others organized "direct action" campaigns to support the PLM. Although a few disputes emerged between a Los Angeles–based IWW local and the PLM, the IWW leadership remained generally supportive of PLM goals and even considered launching a general strike to prevent U.S. intervention in Mexico when an invasion seemed imminent.

By contrast, AFL leaders distanced themselves from the PLM once it embraced anarcho-syndicalism. Far from seeking the radical forms of workers' control envisioned by the PLM, AFL President Samuel Gompers favored a moderate agenda for Mexico that included gaining government recognition of the democratic rights of workers and government support for curbing the worst capitalist abuses. To that end, the AFL initially supported recognition of the reformist government of Francisco Madero. Like the PLM, Gompers and his closest colleagues in the AFL executive council opposed U.S. military intervention in the Mexican Revolution at the behest of U.S. corporations. However, they sought to prevent intervention by cooperating with the Wilson administration rather than by using obstructionist tactics such as strikes. Yet other groups within the AFL, such as the United Mine Workers, that had extensive interests in the Borderlands, proved far more critical of the Wilson administration's policies toward Mexico. Although not opposed to Gompers's efforts to influence Wilson's policies, they anticipated the need for more militant campaigns to offset the influence of business groups over foreign policy in Washington, D.C. These disagreements in turn foreshadowed some of the divisions that would occur within the AFL over World War I.

The PLM's embrace of anarcho-syndicalism also encouraged divisions among Socialists, with some expressing sympathy for its campaigns to expropriate foreign and domestic landholders and business owners and others emphasizing that the group should promote incremental nonviolent change in Mexico. Socialists also tended to disagree about Wilson's foreign policies, with a few emphasizing that the administration had done a good job of preventing full-scale war with Mexico given the pressures exerted on it by interventionist groups, and others highlighting the ways in which Wilson's military forays into Mexico had violated Mexican sovereignty. Yet, inspired by both the Mexican Revolution and the evolving preparedness movement, Socialists overwhelmingly agreed on one point: the need to make foreign policy more subject to democratic checks and balances. The Socialist Party's campaign on behalf of a democratic diplomacy placed it at odds with President Wilson, who was a firm believer in executive supremacy in foreign affairs. In contrast to Wilson, Socialists also sought a full repudiation of the Monroe Doctrine and demonstrated skepticism toward the concept of a Pan-American concert of powers to bring harmony to the Western hemisphere. Like their anarchist and syndicalist comrades, Socialists doubted that imperialism could be permanently banished until workers achieved democratic control of industry. But in the interim they sought to limit the power of the government to involve the country in unnecessary wars and foreign entanglements that might further buoy the power of the owning classes at the expense of workers.

The Mexican question thus helped to catalyze a debate within U.S. labor, Socialist, and immigrant Left circles over Wilsonian internationalist principles that would grow significantly in coming years.

IMPERIAL BACKDROP

If for President Wilson the Mexican question was but a small part of his vision for a new Pan American order in the Western Hemisphere, for labor and Socialist groups the pattern was reversed; they tended to view hemispheric foreign policy issues through the prism of their experiences with the complex labor systems that developed in the American Southwest and Mexican Borderlands in the aftermath of the Mexican-American War (1846–1848). In this sense, the debate over the Mexican Revolution forced labor groups to confront the legacies of past U.S. imperial adventures in a way that Wilson did not. Under the terms of the Treaty of Guadalupe Hidalgo that ended the Mexican-American War in 1848, Mexico confirmed the annexation of Texas by the United States and ceded to its northern neighbor an enormously large area that now constitutes the states of California, Nevada, Utah, New Mexico, and part of Colorado for the meager sum of fifteen million dollars. In 1853, the Gadsden Purchase added a small but strategic territory lying between Arizona and the Mexican border to the bargain.[5]

A windfall for the United States, these forced land cessions deprived Mexico of one-half of its territory and three-quarters of its natural resources. Approximately one hundred and twenty thousand Mexican people were brought under the control of the U.S. government as a result of the land transfers.[6] The situation of Mexicans in the annexed territories was quite different than that of European immigrants to the United States, for as a Chicano slogan put it, Mexicans didn't voluntarily cross a border in search of work, rather the "border crossed" them. The relationship between Anglos and Mexicans in the Southwest became that of "conquerors and conquered," leading some historians to compare the plight of Mexican Americans to that of occupied peoples like the Palestinians or Algerians. As in Palestine and Algeria, a caste system developed in the Southwest whereby indigenous Mexican and

Indian peoples were expropriated and relegated to the lowest-paying, most subordinate forms of work.[7]

Yet historians also emphasize that there was a "mosaic character" to the pattern of economic development imposed by annexation. In some areas and industries, the effects of U.S. annexation were felt immediately, as in California, where the Anglo and European population increased tenfold between 1848 and 1850, placing enormous pressure upon Mexicans to sell long-held lands. In Arizona, Anglos quickly displaced Mexican mine owners and skilled workers through both legal and illegal means and relegated them to the most menial, dangerous, and low-paying positions in the mines. Similar developments occurred in the railroad industry. By contrast, in the Southwestern countryside, where Anglo and Mexican ranchers had long coexisted relatively peacefully and had frequently intermarried, life continued "virtually unchanged for several decades" after annexation.[8]

But between 1910 and 1920, improvements in irrigation and other farming techniques made land in the Southwest more arable and led to an agricultural revolution. Anglo commercial farmers soon displaced Mexican ranchers in the agricultural Borderlands of Texas and New Mexico by using lucrative cash inducements, mortgage and tax indebtedness, manipulations of the cattle and sheep markets, and fraud and coercion to claim Mexican lands.[9] The growth of commercial agriculture and other new types of business in the Southwest combined with the dislocation created by the Mexican Revolution to spur dramatically increased emigration from Mexico between 1910 and 1920. The net result was a constantly growing and ever more proletarianized Mexican population in the United States, many of whom understandably blamed the United States for their economic woes.[10]

Anglo workers often reinforced the caste system that developed in the Southwest by excluding Mexicans from their trade unions. This was especially true of local AFL unions, although the United Mine Workers proved an important exception. The IWW, because it emphasized organizing industrial unions, also often made an effort to include both Anglos and Mexicans on equal terms. But because IWW organizing efforts were still in their infancy in the Southwest, IWW unions were not widely available to Mexican workers. Where AFL unions controlled hiring, they often prevented Mexicans from obtaining skilled jobs. In other cases, they barred Mexican workers who fit the occupational criteria for union membership from their ranks. AFL trade unionists justified these practices on the grounds that Mexicans depressed wages and crossed picket lines, although the Department of Labor failed to find any evidence to substantiate these claims. The animosity of AFL unions

toward Mexicans increased proportionately as emigration from Mexico ac-
celerated. Complaints about Mexican labor multiplied in the annual Texas
State Federation of Labor conventions after 1910, and the El Paso and Houston
Central Labor Councils took the lead in pressuring city and state governments to avoid hiring Mexican-born workers. Reacting to these pressures,
both the Texas State Federation of Labor and American Federation of Labor
began to aggressively promote Mexican immigration restrictions, but they
were initially unsuccessful in stimulating action on the issue from either the
United States or the Mexican government.[11]

That Mexico proved uninterested in hindering emigration was hardly
surprising for it experienced a series of economic aftershocks in the wake of
the U.S. land grab that followed the Mexican-American War and underwent
what many would consider to be "dependent" economic development.[12]
Deprived of some of its richest land and most profitable natural resources,
Mexican rulers struggled in the nineteenth century to modernize the country
by reforming agriculture and encouraging foreign investment. Prior to the
1850s, at least 25 percent of the land in Mexico had been held communally
under the terms of charters granted to pueblos, or Mexico's villages. But in
1856, the Mexican government outlawed communal landholding and declared that land held by pueblos would be subdivided among peasants. When
peasants refused to accept individual holdings, the communally held lands
were often seized as "unclaimed" and sold or given to wealthy Mexicans or
foreigners. The practice of seizing communally held land reached its peak
under the government of Porfirio Díaz and inspired much disenchantment
with the regime.[13]

Also provoking opposition to the Díaz regime was its open door policy
toward foreign investments. Convinced that foreign capital could help modernize the Mexican economy, Díaz encouraged American companies to invest
heavily in building Mexico's railroads and in developing its lucrative petroleum fields and silver, copper, and gold mines. Large companies like Texaco
and Standard Oil soon dominated Mexico's oil industry and established seg-
regated work colonies of Mexican and U.S. workers. In the mineral mining
industries, Anglo owners and supervisors lived as "aristocrats" by comparison
with Mexican workers. The salary ratio of managers to workers in the United
States was about 2.5 to 1; in Mexico it was 20 to 1. Mexican workers became a
subjugated workforce in their own country as well as in the United States.[14]

Díaz's policies also encouraged U.S. investments in sugar, coffee, and hen-
nequin plantations and in cattle ranches, sawmills, and rubber companies.
In addition, U.S. businessmen of modest means but substantial ambition

established bars, casinos, dance halls, and whorehouses in Mexico. Many wealthy Americans bought up estates to use as vacation homes. Between 1910 and 1920, three thousand Americans moved to Mexico each year. These U.S. immigrants, whether of wealthy or modest means, and whether engaged in agriculture, mining, or industry, "stepped," in John Mason Hart's words, "into the middle of [the] deepening dispute over land" in Mexico.[15]

THE PARTIDO LIBERAL MEXICANO AND THE BIRTH OF A TRANSNATIONAL ANTI-IMPERIALIST MOVEMENT

Among those who broke with the Díaz regime over its land and investment policies were Ricardo and Enrique Flores Magón. Born and raised in a remote rural area of the southern Mexican state of Oaxaca, Ricardo and Enrique led a "marginal middle-class" existence for most of their youth. Their father was a lieutenant colonel in the Mexican army who had fought with Porfirio Díaz in the revolt of 1876. Yet Ricardo and Enrique's parents, suggest John Mason Hart, became disillusioned with Díaz because they thought he had betrayed the "political ideals of nineteenth-century liberalism" through his dictatorial and corrupt policies. Both parents also clung to local communal traditions in the face of capitalist modernization schemes imposed on the countryside by Díaz. Ricardo and Enrique inherited the family anger toward the Díaz regime and became active in oppositional liberal politics during their days as law students in the 1890s. After abandoning law school partly because of the family's dire financial circumstances, the brothers emerged as leaders of a faction that sought to radicalize and expand the liberal movement by appealing to discontented industrial workers and peasants.[16]

Because Ricardo Flores Magón, like many other Mexican intellectuals and oppositional politicians, believed that the Mexican federal government and foreign capitalists had played an almost entirely destructive role in Mexican life, he was attracted to anarchist philosophies even as a young man and immersed himself in the literature of leading European anarchist thinkers. Ricardo was also apparently much influenced as a youth by the Haymarket affair. But during his early political career in Mexico, Flores Magón posed not as an anarchist but as a reform liberal who attacked Díaz for violating the central tenets of liberalism and selling Mexico's patrimony to foreigners.[17] The Flores Magón brothers were repeatedly imprisoned for their political activities in Mexico and fled to the United States, settling first in San Antonio, then in St. Louis, and finally in Los Angeles. The early Los Angeles–based PLM, like Ricardo Flores Magón himself, focused on inspiring opposition to the

Díaz regime, building a sense of both Mexican pride and class consciousness among its members, improving the conditions of Mexican workers on
both sides of the border, encouraging Mexicans to create or join unions, and
building coalitions with all major U.S. labor organizations.[18]

Perhaps most critical in spreading the PLM's message during its early years
was its newspaper *Regeneración* which boasted between fifteen and twenty
thousand subscribers by 1906. PLM editorial musings, moreover, often re-
verberated far beyond these subscribers because the paper was read aloud at
PLM meetings and social functions to those who were illiterate or could not
afford to subscribe. *Regeneración* even played an important role in several
strikes, including a brutal conflict between workers and managers at the
Cananea Copper Company in Sonora, Mexico, in 1906. Partly owned and
managed by Americans, the company paid U.S. workers two to four times as
much as their Mexican counterparts. PLM activists from the United States
solicited the support of Mexican workers there and they in turn helped to
build local PLM organizations. Copies of *Regeneración* circulated throughout
Cananea and helped stimulate discussion about the unjust conditions at the
mine. A strike erupted, provoking violent confrontations between employers
and employees that were suppressed only through the combined military
might of U.S. and Mexican armed forces. These kinds of bold strike activities
against U.S. corporate power, though typically unsuccessful, brought favorable
publicity to the PLM among workers on both sides of the border. Spreading with lightning speed, approximately 350 PLM "grupos" and liberal clubs
formed throughout the American Southwest and Northern Mexico during
the first decade of the twentieth century, and the PLM soon became the most
important voice of the Mexican émigré Left.[19]

The influence of the PLM, suggest historians, can be fully appreciated only
by recognizing the way in which local PLM clubs became a part of the cultural
infrastructure on both sides of the Mexican border. Such clubs often served
simultaneously as "Mutualistas" that offered Mexican workers support during
labor struggles, social centers, and forums for political debate. Often, women
took part in the activities of PLM clubs, sponsoring dances and other types of
social events to raise funds for PLM activities and sometimes forming their
own affiliated organizations such as Luz y Vida (Light and Life). Many local
clubs also sponsored their own newspapers. Not surprisingly, PLM chapters
sometimes developed in ways not anticipated by the PLM leadership, since
local activists tended to cooperate with those forces in the community most
sympathetic to them, whatever their official politics or affiliation. The independence of some of these local chapters helps explain why many failed to

follow the PLM leadership down an anarcho-syndicalist path after 1911, even while still continuing to organize under a PLM banner. But before the Mexican Revolution, these groups proved to be important conduits for transmitting the PLM leadership's liberal agenda for labor reform back and forth across the border. Indeed, the cultural and political influence that the PLM exerted through these local chapters may help explain why so much of its liberal agenda for labor reform made it into the Mexican Constitution in 1917 despite the Flores Magón's drift to anarchism and subsequent imprisonment.[20]

The PLM's labor activism and its coalition-building efforts also attracted the support of a broad range of U.S. Socialist and trade union activists prior to the Mexican Revolution. The PLM helped publicize the plight of Mexico under Díaz in U.S. Left and labor circles, and virtually all major U.S. labor groups supported the reformist agenda for Mexico issued by the PLM in 1906. When PLM leaders were imprisoned in 1908 for their political and labor organizing activities, the Socialist Party, AFL, and IWW all defended the Flores Magón brothers and worked for their release. Both AFL and IWW unions, moreover, began to work closely with the PLM in organizing Mexican workers in the mining districts of Arizona. IWW unions also spread, with the blessing of PLM activists, into Northern Mexico. The growing popularity of the IWW among Mexican workers in turn worried Gompers and Mother Jones of the United Mine Workers and led them to seek even closer ties between the AFL and the PLM.[21]

But the cozy relationship between the PLM and leading U.S. Socialist and labor groups changed dramatically following the outbreak of revolution in Mexico. When PLM leaders received word of the armed uprising in Mexico against the Díaz regime, they urged Mexican peasants and workers to reclaim the lands they had once held as well as to occupy Mexico's factories, mines, and mills and begin running them for themselves. In an influential anarchist "manifesto" issued in 1911, the PLM declared war on the oppressive triumvirate of capital, clergy, and authority and outlined the steps that PLM-backed revolutionary cells should take in seizing land and businesses in Mexico and in bringing agricultural and industrial production under the control of Mexican peasants and workers.[22] Although women were not encouraged to engage in revolutionary violence, PLM leaders urged that Mexican workers manage productive enterprises "without distinction of sex," since male dominion over women was as much anathema as capitalist authority over workers. U.S-based PLM leaders, along with some of their supporters in the IWW, also staged a failed invasion of Baja, California, in the hopes of establishing model anarchist colonies there.[23]

Although these activities initially won accolades from the IWW, they shocked many of the PLM's other American allies, who had assumed that the PLM would embrace the reformist agenda of Mexican revolutionary leader Francisco Madero. But PLM leaders denounced Madero as just another bourgeois politician who sought to establish a new and more efficient government for the "protection of the interests of the rich." They insisted that for the Mexican Revolution to be meaningful it must be a social rather than political revolution that emanated from, and empowered, the Mexican working classes.[24]

By contrast, some leading Socialist and AFL leaders insisted that Mexican workers were unprepared to assume control of either agricultural or industrial production. In a series of influential articles written for the Socialist press, Eugene Debs argued that it was impossible to move Mexico from feudalism to socialism overnight. The masses of Mexican workers and producers, he insisted, were "ignorant, superstitious, unorganized and all but helpless in their slavish subjection." Mexican workers needed to be trained and educated before they would be ready to take control of the means of production. The Mexican nation must also pass through a stage of bourgeois democracy before it would be ready for socialism. He denounced the PLM for causing needless bloodshed and argued that PLM activists needed to lay down their arms so that Madero could restore stability to Mexico and initiate a process of democratic reform that would set in motion a peaceful transition to socialism.[25] AFL leaders, for their part, also denounced the tactics of the PLM as unnecessarily violent and called on them to lay down arms and accept the new Madero government. Even Mother Jones, of the United Mine Workers, who had previously lobbied vigorously for the release of the Flores Magóns from prison, now denounced them.[26]

But PLM leaders argued that it was American labor and Socialist activists who were out of touch with reality. Perhaps in response to Debs's condescending portrait of Mexico and Mexicans, William Owen, editor of the English-language section of the PLM newspaper *Regeneración*, suggested that it had become "fashionable to pity the [Mexican] peon as a victim of a feudalism from which we superior beings freed ourselves long ago [but] nothing could be more erroneous." The Mexican peon was instead the "victim of the most up-to-date capitalism being milked scientifically by Wall Street syndicates." The Mexican worker, moreover, was in the forefront of resistance to "expanding international capitalism" and should be emulated rather than pitied by the world's workers.[27]

Because of their recent experiences with corrupt national regimes like that of Porfirio Díaz, suggested PLM leaders, Mexicans understood that government was part of the problem rather than part of the solution. Although Mexican workers looked to the past for answers, it was not a feudalistic past. Rather, they sought to recreate the communal traditions of landholding and local self-government that had dominated in Mexico before the rise of powerful national governments and to extend these practices to industrial enterprise. Mexican history, suggested Ricardo Flores Magón, demonstrated that when "Pedro and I are equal economically" and have equal opportunity to use "natural wealth such as the land, waters, forests, mines" or the "wealth created by the hand of man, such as machinery, houses, railroads," then there was no need for a "chief" or, in other words, for a government to resolve disputes. Despite imprisonment for their Baja activities, PLM leaders continued throughout the 1912–1914 period to fund guerrilla units in Mexico and to encourage U.S. workers to support those forces promoting social revolution in Mexico. They also sought to educate U.S. workers to fight against American intervention in the Mexican conflict. Indeed PLM leaders argued that they stayed in the United States precisely so that they could continue to use it as a base to enlighten both American and Mexican workers about the real nature of the revolutionary struggle in Mexico and to prevent shortsighted U.S. policies toward the conflict.[28]

At first optimistic that Woodrow Wilson, as a scholar, would pursue more enlightened foreign policies than his predecessors, PLM leaders soon became outspoken critics of the president. The Flores Magón brothers' first impressions of Woodrow Wilson were forged while they were still in jail at MacNeil Island in Puget Sound, serving time for violating neutrality laws during the Baja Campaign. The PLM junta appealed to Wilson to review the case against Ricardo and Enrique Flores Magón, suggesting that they believed the president to be a man who could "see beyond the narrow limits of a ledger due to his background as a scholar." They were also encouraged by the president's "unprecedentedly bold stand" against "plutocracy." Wilson subsequently studied the case but refused to grant clemency to any of the PLM activists. The incident inspired an early distrust of Wilson and reaffirmed PLM notions that principles of justice and liberty were trampled upon as surely in so-called model republics like the United States as they were in the worst dictatorships. They also criticized the Wilson administration's early foreign policy, characterizing the United States as "an empire of crime" controlled by trusts that suppressed the rights of workers from West Virginia to Nicaragua.[29]

When Wilson proclaimed an interest in land reform issues and honest government in Mexico, the PLM junta warned workers not to listen to the "mermaid songs" of either the U.S. president or his lackeys in Mexico, among whom they initially included both Pancho Villa and Veunustiano Carranza. If Wilson were really interested in land reform, they suggested, he would begin in the United States where there were millions who didn't have a "lump of dirt" upon which they could rest their heads. What Wilson and his Mexican lackeys actually sought was U.S. control of the lands, the mines, the factories, the warships, and the railroads of Mexico. Only Emiliano Zapata, the agrarian revolutionary whose programs asserted the right of peasants to reclaim their communal lands, escaped the PLM's wrath. In a representative cartoon, the PLM portrayed the U.S. president carrying a music box that played the tune of agrarian promises while the monkeys Pancho Villa and Venustiano Carranza marched in front (figure 1.1). Workers, argued PLM leaders, needed to understand that government had only one function: to protect the interests of the rich. U.S. and Mexican workers must work to prevent both a U.S. military invasion of Mexico and the triumph of another bourgeois government there.[30]

The PLM's attacks on Carranza earned it the enmity of a fellow anarcho-syndicalist group: the Casa del Obrero Mundial (Casa), centered in Mexico City. Because Carranza pledged to support labor reform, Casa entered into a military alliance with him and formed "red brigades" to fight against the forces of Pancho Villa and Emiliano Zapata. Despite its anarchist orientation, Casa was attracted by Carranza's insistence that he sought a social revolution in Mexico and lured by the idea of developing a close working relationship with the new revolutionary government. The PLM, however, bitterly castigated Casa, arguing that it had been duped by the Carranza regime. Meanwhile, Casa leaders denounced the Magonistas as "renegades thousands of miles away who are exaggerating events in Mexico." When Carranza crushed Casa after general strikes broke out throughout the country, Enrique Flores Magón argued that "as soon as Carranza felt himself master of the situation, he kicked overboard his old friends the workingman." The division between the Casa and PLM highlighted the binational orientation of the latter: having experienced dire persecution and labor conditions in two countries, the PLM proved far more distrustful of both U.S. and Mexican governmental authorities than the Mexico City–based anarchists.[31]

By contrast, despite some disagreements over the Baja campaign and the land questions, the IWW and U.S. anarchist community remained generally sympathetic and supportive of the PLM during this period. The IWW leadership's major complaint about the PLM was that it placed too much emphasis on the redistribution of land to small villages and individual farmers. The IWW press instead insisted that large farming collectives would prove more viable. Small landholders in Mexico, they argued, would be as vulnerable to capitalist exploitation as American farmers and would soon find themselves at the mercy of loan sharks, mortgage holders, the railroad trust, grain speculators, and the beef trust. They believed that the PLM's emphasis on attacking land monopoly had led them to mismanage the Baja revolt. Meanwhile a dispute also simmered between the PLM and a Spanish-language IWW local in Los Angeles over claims that the PLM propagandized against the use of the IWW technique of sabotage. The chapter also claimed that the PLM undermined local labor struggles by acting as though Mexican American workers could be "free" only if they returned to Mexico to fight.[32]

But despite these disagreements, the PLM and IWW shared much in common, including a belief in the virtues of direct economic action by workers to achieve their goals, a distrust of government—especially the Wilson administration—and a belief in the desirability of workers' direct control and ownership of the means of production. When a U.S war with Mexico seemed to loom after the occupation of Veracruz, the IWW embraced a direct action technique long promoted by the PLM to stop U.S. war plans. Big Bill Haywood of the IWW called for a general strike by American labor to tie up industry and prevent mobilization for war. Since war tensions eased relatively quickly, the strike never came to fruition but it demonstrated the IWW's emphasis on direct economic action rather than political lobbying as the best means to fight imperialism.[33] The anarchist press, meanwhile, continued to publish the PLM's treatises to American workers, and leading anarchists Emma Goldman and Alexander Berkman played a key role in amnesty campaigns designed to secure the Flores Magóns' release from jail for the Baja campaigns.[34]

THE AFL'S ALTERNATIVE AGENDA

In contrast to either the PLM or IWW, which portrayed Wilson in their publications as a smooth-talking enemy of the people, the AFL leadership viewed Wilson as a friend of labor. Since Wilson had encouraged labor to participate in policymaking circles through the recently created Commission on Industrial Relations and the Department of Labor, AFL leaders also hoped the administration would invite AFL participation in its Mexican and Pan-American initiatives. To achieve that end, Gompers tried to align AFL policy toward Mexico behind that of the Wilson administration. At first cautious about taking a stand on the Mexican Revolution, the AFL Executive Council in 1912 announced its support for the reformist government of Francisco Madero and the AFL convention passed a resolution opposing U.S. intervention in Mexico. But when Huerta overthrew Madero, Gompers wavered. Anti-interventionist forces in the AFL sought to pass another resolution in 1913 opposing all armed U.S. intervention in Mexico. At the request of Gompers and the Committee on International Relations, however, this resolution was changed to a denunciation of American economic interests who were trying to foment war. Following the U.S. occupation of Veracruz, Gompers refused to join the chorus of those denouncing the Wilson administration. AFL Vice President James Duncan, meanwhile, declared the AFL's opposition to IWW proposals for a general strike to prevent U.S. war with Mexico.[35]

But following Huerta's resignation, the AFL convention announced its support for the leaders of the Constitutionalist forces of Venustiano Carranza. AFL leaders supported Carranza despite his anti-American animus because he was favored by major Mexican labor groups such as Casa and seemed committed to creating a democratic and capitalist Mexico. In its Executive Council Report, the AFL also praised Carranza for his land redistribution programs. At the Executive Council's behest, Gompers wrote President Wilson and asked him to grant diplomatic recognition to Carranza. Gompers urged Wilson to recognize Carranza's government in part because the Mexican leader was a friend of the labor movement and of reform in Mexico. But in a pointed reference, Gompers also emphasized that the Mexicans "must learn to be free. They have the right to this freedom without unwarranted outside interference even from those who seek their welfare." Wilson seemed favorably influenced by Gompers's letter and when the president granted de facto recognition to the Carranza government three weeks later, Gompers implied that he had played a role in shaping the administration's policies.[36]

Gompers also asked the Wilson administration for labor representation on the American commission that was to participate in the Pan American Financial Conference held from May 24–29, 1915. The Wilson administration planned the conference to encourage closer industrial, commercial, and political relations between the United States and other Latin American countries. Like the Pan American Pact, the Pan American Conference was in some ways an antecedent to the League of Nations in that it was designed to promote institutionalized cooperation between nations in the Western hemisphere that would help facilitate free trade and thereby discourage war. Gompers argued that labor should be included in the conference because someone needed to represent "people and not just profits" at the conference. He complained to administration officials that without labor input the conference would be used by "the great corporate interests of the various countries" to "manipulate conditions and events." Gompers's attitude toward the conference foreshadowed his corporatist orientation toward foreign policy during World War

I. He sought to make foreign policy decision making more democratic by ensuring that labor was represented alongside business interests on government diplomatic missions and in government councils.[37]

Yet Wilson denied Gompers's request and the AFL Executive Council instead made plans to initiate exchanges between North and South American labor movements and to hold a Pan American labor convention. The AFL Executive Council rationalized that if North and South American employers were to be united, then "wage earners of these countries must also be united for their common protection and betterment." AFL leaders hoped to demonstrate both to business and government leaders who had recently denied them access to the Pan American Conference that labor had the capacity to organize on an international basis. Particularly important in shaping Gompers's thinking on the issue was Puerto Rican organizer and Socialist Santiago Iglesias. A trusted advisor of Gompers on Puerto Rican affairs, Iglesias attended the Pan American Conference and came back convinced that government and business efforts to more effectively coordinate investment strategies posed a threat to workers throughout the Western hemisphere. Businessmen would use the knowledge they obtained at the conferences to invest in or create factories and mills wherever labor was cheapest. Exchanges between the AFL and Latin American labor movements would culminate at the end of World War I in the creation of the Pan American Federation of Labor. But in the interim, these exchanges were more important in encouraging closer ties between U.S. and Mexican labor groups.[38]

Of particular importance, Gompers worked through Socialist allies like Iglesias and John Murray to establish a friendly relationship with Casa. Although the PLM had condemned Casa for its alliance with Carranza, many AFL leaders viewed their pact with the Constitutionalists favorably, taking it as a sign that Mexican labor was developing a more pragmatic orientation. Murray's contacts with Casa helped convince Gompers to support diplomatic recognition of the Carranza regime.[39] When a new crisis soon loomed over the Pershing expedition, Gompers encouraged Casa to send Mexican labor representatives to the United States to consult with him about ending the crisis. Even as they were meeting in Washington, word reached Gompers and the Mexican delegation of a clash between U.S. and Mexican troops at Carrizal, Mexico, in which U.S. soldiers were taken prisoner. Gompers telegrammed Carranza asking him in the "name of justice and humanity" and "in the interest of a better understanding between the peoples and governments of the United States and Mexico" to release the American soldiers. When Carranza released the prisoners several hours later, Gompers again believed that he and the AFL had played a role in shaping diplomacy between the two countries. Adding credence to Gompers's beliefs was a subsequent telegram from Carranza indicating that he had received the AFL's message and done as requested. But other historians have stressed that Carranza intended to release the prisoners even before Gompers's message and simply wished to use Gompers and the AFL for further leverage in Washington.[40]

If so, Carranza's strategies were successful because the AFL Executive Council, as well as the Mexican labor delegates then meeting with them, proposed the appointment of a joint commission to resolve the conflict. When such a commission was subsequently formed, Gompers asked for labor representation on it, but his requests were denied. The Wilson administration, however, did seek Gompers's advice on a proposal that was never implemented involving a neutral zone along the U.S. border that would be controlled by representatives from the United States, Mexico, and other Latin American countries. Mexican labor delegates also suggested including labor representatives to supervise the neutral zone. The plan demonstrated that the U.S. government, like its Mexican counterpart, sought to use the AFL as an intermediary when it was expedient, setting the stage for the AFL's future incorporation into government circles.[41]

Although the AFL leadership largely supported Wilson's foreign policy toward Mexico and Latin America and sought a cooperative relationship with the administration, constituent and local AFL unions were often far more critical. Perhaps the single-most important critic of the Wilson administration's Mexican policies within the AFL was the United Mine Workers of America (UMWA), which continued to draw linkages between the brutal murders of workers and their families in Ludlow, Colorado, and the American attack on the residents of Veracruz, Mexico. Writing in the wake of the Veracruz occupation, UMWA President John White insisted that the United States did not "need to go to Mexico to find war. We have a war in Colorado that transcends in barbarity any contest south of the Rio Grande." The UMWA circulated a petition to its locals as well as municipal labor bodies such as the Seattle Central Labor Council that it then sent to the president and to Congress urging "For God's Sake. . . . Leave Mexico Alone and Come into Colorado To Relieve These Miner's Wives and Children Who Are Being Slaughtered by the Dozen by the Murderous Mine Guards." Such public confrontations with Wilson, and efforts to humiliate him, were clearly of a different nature than Gompers's private conciliatory correspondence with the president.[42]

When President Wilson declared himself a "friend of the Mexican peon" during the late spring of 1914 who sought to "return ownership of the land to the workers on the land," the UMWA continued its public campaign against the president and joined the PLM in asking why he didn't intervene at home to redistribute land in the United States. During 1915, when war between the United States and Mexico again seemed imminent, the UMWA paper urged the president to recognize an "unmistakable lesson" to be learned from the war that had engulfed all the major powers in Europe: "the way to continuous peace does not lie through domination over alien races."[43] Although the UMWA supported Gompers's efforts to use labor contacts in Mexico to promote peace, as well his initiatives in trying to sway Wilson himself, its own tactics suggested that these kinds of cooperative strategies might not be enough. UMWA leaders stopped short of supporting IWW proposals for strike actions to stop a Mexican intervention, but when preparedness groups mobilized in 1915–1916, it would hold a conference in an effort to encourage better strategizing about how labor could influence national foreign policy, especially with respect to questions of war and peace. Many local and constituent AFL unions proved interested in the UMWA conference; Gompers and the AFL Executive Council did not.[44]

Unsurprisingly, the PLM proved even more critical of its one-time ally, denouncing the AFL as a "medieval guild system," whose members scoffed "at the rights of weaker peoples" and who were "on the look-out for any pickings the invasion of Mexico may bring."[45] PLM leaders and their IWW allies clearly perceived that the AFL was actually helping to reinforce the capitalist and industrial status quo rather than promoting the true interests of workers. By contrast, the AFL leadership emphasized that it was advancing the cause of industrial democracy in both the United States and the Western hemisphere more generally by gaining a voice for labor in government circles, by serving as a model of how interested labor groups might carve a role for themselves in diplomatic negotiations, and by lobbying on behalf of the idea of labor representation in hemispheric forums like the Pan American Conference. These contrasting visions of the linkages between workers' struggles, industrial democracy, and international affairs in turn competed with a third imaginary: that of the Socialist party.

THE SOCIALIST PARTY ALTERNATIVE

Although some Socialists worked with the AFL in promoting better labor relations with Mexico and applauded the AFL's efforts at preserving peace, the party's agenda nonetheless diverged significantly from that of the AFL. Like Gompers, several prominent Socialists such as Lincoln Steffens, Upton

Sinclair, and John Spargo enjoyed close relations with President Wilson and corresponded or conferred with him regarding his Mexican policies. Others, like Jack Reed, publicly supported Wilson's Mexican policies, believing that he had helped to prevent business interests from driving the country into war. Socialists, moreover, assumed that they had, along with the AFL and other peace groups, helped to guide Wilson's policies away from war. Particularly important, for example, was Lincoln Steffen's personal relationship with the president. Following the occupation of Veracruz, Steffens criticized the president's policies, telling him "You can't commit rape a little." But Steffens nonetheless continued to work with the president and, along with Gompers and the American Union Against Militarism, claimed credit for helping to prevent war following the incident at Carrizal in 1916. Thomas Knock argues that Wilson's cautious policies toward Mexico and World War I helped to forge a liberal-Left alliance that accounted for a shift in the Socialist vote away from the Socialist presidential candidate Allen Benson and in favor of Wilson in 1916.[46]

Yet if some Socialists were attracted by Wilson's antiwar rhetoric in 1916, the majority wing of the Socialist Party remained committed to Benson and focused their energies on discrediting Wilson's foreign policies by demonstrating his hypocrisy and duplicity. Leading the charge in the attack on the Wilson administration's Mexican policy was John Kenneth Turner. Turner, a native of California, first became active in Socialist politics while in Los Angeles, also home to the PLM. When leaders of the PLM were jailed for allegedly violating the neutrality laws in 1906, the Los Angeles Socialist Party took an interest. Turner soon befriended PLM prisoners and, influenced by their accounts of Díaz's abuses, traveled to Mexico with PLM member Lazaro Gutiérrez de Lara to write an expose on his policies. Turner's articles about conditions in Mexico first appeared in *American Magazine* and the Socialist press and were later published as a best-selling book entitled *Barbarous Mexico*. The book bitterly condemned Díaz's policies and also indicted foreign capitalists for their role in robbing Mexico of its wealth.[47]

Unlike some other leading Socialists, Turner subsequently became a bitter critic of the Wilson administration's Mexican policies. Following the occupation of Veracruz, Turner returned to Mexico to report on conditions there. Turner charged that Wilson's Mexican policies were deceptive and argued that Wilson acted as though he were merely defending "sweet humanity" in intervening at Veracruz when his purpose was instead "to feed the insatiable rapacity of Oily John Rockefeller, Sisal Hemp McCormick . . . and all of the rest of the silk-hatted American vultures which hover and scream above the body of prostrate Mexico."[48] He also condemned Wilson's secret negotiations with Victoriano Huerta, Pancho Villa, and Venustiano Carranza and argued that the president was practicing the same kind of secret diplomacy he condemned among the European powers. During both the Veracruz and Carrizal incidents, Turner called for the United States to withdraw its troops from Mexico, arguing that the presence of U.S. soldiers on foreign soil was bound to result in war. He also emphasized that the U.S. constitution did not grant the president the power to militarily intervene in the affairs of other countries. Only Congress, he suggested, had the right to declare war.[49]

Turner next set his sights on U.S. actions in Haiti, the Dominican Republic, and Nicaragua, and was among the first American journalists to report on U.S. military interventions and financial machinations there. In several muckraking articles, Turner detailed the ways in which the governments of Santo Domingo and Haiti had been secretly overthrown by U.S. forces working on behalf of the "sugar trust, Morgan money trust and militarist-imperialist-jingo interests in general." In other articles, Turner detailed the complexities of the financial directorates that the United States had established in Haiti and the Dominican Republic and highlighted the ways in which they limited these countries' national sovereignty. Turner also extensively reported on U.S. military atrocities in Nicaragua and on the way in which Wilson tried to silence information about these atrocities. Wilson, argued Turner, had subverted the constitution by engaging in acts of war in Mexico, Haiti, the Dominican Republic, and Nicaragua without the authorization of Congress. Turner suggested that if it were true, as some claimed, that war was legalized murder, then in the case of Wilsonian diplomacy the murder was not even "legalized."[50]

In opinion pieces prior to the election in 1916, Turner insisted that Wilson "has SAID more fine things, probably, than any President before him, not excepting even Washington and Lincoln." He argued, however, that "ALL the fine things he has said have been FLATLY CONTRADICTED by other things he has said—or by things he has DONE."[51] In an effort to prevent the antiwar vote from going to Wilson, he emphasized that if war with Mexico was avoided in 1916, credit should go not to Wilson but to the following: first, to the Socialist party for publicizing Wilson's war-mongering policies there; second, to organized labor for mediating between the president and Carranza, third, to peace groups who lobbied on behalf of arbitration rather than war; fourth, to the patience of Carranza; and fifth, to the strength of Carranza's armaments.[52]

Not surprisingly, it was the viewpoints of Turner rather than Wilson sympathizers like Reed or Steffens that dominated the Socialist Party's 1916 foreign policy platforms; emphasizing points of convergence with the Democrats hardly made for good politics. The party asked for a radical democratization of foreign policy powers in order to prevent the president from engaging in secret war-mongering diplomacy in the future. Chief among its demands were planks calling for national referendum votes of all men and women on questions of war and peace and for the removal of diplomatic functions from the State Department and president to Congress. The party also opposed the Monroe Doctrine on the grounds it promoted interference in Latin American affairs and called for slashing the military budget and encouraging arbitration of international disputes. John Kenneth Turner personally called on Americans to elect one dozen Socialists to Congress in order to fight against "Latin American murder, Secret Diplomacy, Dollar Aggression, the Morganized Monroe Doctrine and another World War with America at its center."[53] Following Wilson's reelection, the leading Socialist newspaper, the *Appeal to Reason*, argued that Wilson and Republican presidential candidate Charles Evans Hughes represented essentially the same capitalist interests and that "the only thing that is settled by this campaign is that the interests back of Mr. Wilson and Mr. Hughes still have the power to cause an overwhelming majority of the American people to vote against their own interests."[54]

Political exigencies as well as direct ties to the Flores Magón brothers thus drove the majority wing of the Socialist Party in a different direction from the AFL in 1916. Although individual Socialists, like AFL leaders, often used whatever contacts they had with the Wilson administration to promote peace with Mexico, the Socialist Party and Socialist press had a vested interest in demonstrating the folly of Wilson's foreign policies. Their analyses of Wilson's international programs were therefore routinely more critical of the president than the AFL's. The Socialist Party went far in 1916 toward developing an anti-imperialist critique of U.S. foreign policies that emphasized the ways in which the Wilson administration was beholden to capitalist interests and pursued international policies injurious to workers in both developed countries like the United States and developing countries like Mexico. It was this anti-imperialist impulse that led the Socialist Party to promote a radical democratization of foreign policy decision making that would place the power over war and peace directly in the hands of the American public and remove diplomatic powers from the president and give them to Congress. By contrast, AFL leaders accepted the corporatist and progressive assumption that the executive branch of government could serve as a neutral arbiter between business and labor interests in shaping both domestic and international policies if labor was guaranteed equal access to government channels and included on diplomatic missions and commissions in numbers comparable to corporate interests. Although both the Socialist Party and AFL sought to avoid a U.S. war in Mexico the methods they used in trying to guarantee workers a voice in shaping the government's Mexican policies were therefore quite different. The long-term repercussions of their differing paths to power would become painfully apparent to Socialists following U.S. intervention in World War I.

LOCAL MUTATIONS

In the meantime, events in the Borderlands demonstrated how the programs of immigrant Left, Socialist, and labor groups could mutate in response to local needs and produce quite unintended results. As tensions along the Mexican border increased in 1915, a group of jailed Huertistas—or followers of assassinated revolutionary leader General Huerta—drew up blueprints for an irredentist uprising called the Plan of San Diego that was designed to liberate the states of New Mexico, Arizona, California, Nevada, and Texas from U.S. control. The Plan of San Diego decreed that Mexicans, Negroes, Orientals, and Indians in these territories needed to be emancipated and, shockingly, called for the death of all Anglo males over the age of sixteen. Such racist proposals clearly did not draw on PLM teachings for inspiration, since PLM leaders consistently advocated international labor solidarity and an ethos of mutual support between workers of different racial backgrounds during strikes. But on the day the uprising was to begin, new proletarian language was introduced into the plan that drew deeply, if selectively, on the intellectual legacies of the PLM. According to Douglas Monroy, this draft "marked a substantial revision of the document in which anarchist notions of 'universal love,' the 'proletariat,' communal property and 'social revolution' replaced race revenge." The new language increased the appeal of the plan to PLM supporters in Borderland areas as did the harsh treatment of innocent Mexican Americans in the aftermath of the first few attacks. In Texas, the Plan drew the support of PLM-affiliated ranchers of Mexican ancestry who were being dispossessed or displaced by Anglo commercial farmers. To such PLM members, the plan to liberate Texas from Anglo control seemed quite consistent with the PLM goal of liberating workers and peasants from capitalist oppression through direct action.[55]

Among the most important of the PLM sympathizers recruited to the Plan of San Diego was Aniceto Pizaña, whose small Texas ranch was attacked by U.S. authorities. Investigators found ten years' worth of copies of *Regeneración* as well as correspondence with PLM leaders and presumed that both Pizaña and the PLM must be behind the Plan of San Diego. Yet Pizaña later wrote Ricardo Flores Magón that he joined the revolt only after the unprovoked attack on his ranch resulted in the loss of his son's leg. Pizaña fled to Mexico after the attack and subsequently played a leading role in launching border raids. Although the Plan called for the death of all Anglo males, historian Benjamin Heber Johnson suggests that the raids and killings in Texas were in fact directed against local segregationists and that the perpetrators had some knowledge of local politics. Between three thousand and five thousand Mexicans and Mexican Americans took part in the revolt, many of them local PLM supporters, and launched over twenty-seven border raids. Also participating in some of the raids were Japanese, Germans, and African Americans. Thirty-three Americans lost their lives, twenty-four were wounded, and several thousand dollars' worth of property was destroyed. The Carranza government chose to cooperate with the U.S. government in an effort to stop the raids and ultimately captured Aniceto Pizaña. Wilson praised Carranza for helping to stop the border raids and used it as an important rationale in defending his decision to recognize the Carranza government. In an unintended way, PLM activists in Texas thus helped to secure U.S. government recognition of a regime they opposed.[56]

Although no evidence was ever found linking the PLM junta directly to the Plan of San Diego, the PLM backgrounds of some of the Plan's leaders and the defense of Aniceto Pizaña in *Regeneración* suggested conspiracy to government prosecutors. On February 18, 1916, they entered *Regeneración*'s offices and arrested Ricardo and Enrique Flores Magón, with William Owen charged in absentia. During their trial in May and June, the brothers highlighted the extent to which they had become Americans as well as Mexicans and cited the traditions of Thomas Jefferson and other American founding fathers in defending their right to free speech. They also tried to differentiate themselves from the racist aspects of the Plan of San Diego, emphasizing that they had always fought on behalf of the rights of all workers. As Enrique explained, they recognized that the "lumber camps of Colorado and West Virginia are practically the same as the hell-holes of the Yucatan and the Valle Nacional. . . . Our massacres of Rio Blanco and Cananea have their parallel in Ludlow, Cour D'Alene and West Virginia." They were not aliens as the prosecutors tried to portray them. Rather, "The world is our country, and all men are our countrymen."[57]

The government failed to meet legal standards for proving conspiracy but convicted them on lesser charges that amounted to using the pages of *Regeneración* to incite insurrection. While out on appeal, Ricardo continued to publish *Regeneración* intermittently, and in a way destined to provoke repression, began criticizing the U.S. government's military preparedness efforts and Wilson's decision to declare war against Germany. That the Flores Magóns now took an interest in the U.S. war effort as well as Mexican issues suggested the degree to which they had come to view themselves as part of an international working class and therefore as responsible for the well-being of Anglo and Mexican-American workers in the United States as well as the Mexican people.[58]

Ricardo Flores Magón ridiculed Wilson's claim that the United States entered the European conflict to defend its freedom, suggesting that "the European conflict did not endanger the liberty of the American people but the liberty of plundering that the bourgeoisie abrogates to itself." Demonstrating their familiarity with Socialist efforts to democratize diplomacy, they also suggested that the war demonstrated that democracy was a sham, for no democratic referendum was held on the issue of whether the United States should enter the war. Ricardo cautioned U.S. workers against getting caught up in the patriotic fervor of the time, arguing that patriotism had been "invented by the rich and the politicians so that the people may be disposed to tear each other to pieces when it be to the convinience [sic] of their masters."[59] The junta joined other groups in protesting conscription and the suppression of free speech during the war. Enrique also hinted that Mexican-American labor activists were unfairly targeted for military service: he reported with irony that the first pick in the national lottery for conscription was a striking Mexican miner. The Flores Magóns's critiques of conscription doubtless endeared them to many Mexican-Americans who were forced to register at the point of a gun for conscription so that Anglos could claim a fifty-dollar reward for reporting those who failed to comply with conscription laws. As Benjamin Heber Johnson has argued, "the process of draft registration in South Texas made the war appear much more like forced labor recruitment than it did the glorious defense of democracy."[60]

Not surprisingly, the Flores Magóns were soon rearrested for violating the newly enacted Espionage Act that made it illegal to obstruct conscription. Under the loose legal standards established by this legislation, Ricardo was sentenced to twenty years on charges of conspiracy, publishing false statements that interfered with U.S. military efforts, mailing "indecent" materials, and "printing in a foreign language matters dealing with politics without filing a translation with the Post Master." Ricardo would die while serving his sentence at Leavenworth.[61]

But even as the Los Angeles–based PLM leadership languished in prison, the revolutionary seeds that the PLM sowed in other parts of the United

States and Mexico were yielding new hybrid forms of radical discontent. In the Texas cotton belt, former PLM activists worked with the Texas Socialist Party under the leadership of Irish-born Tom Hickey to organize Mexican-American tenant formers. In 1914, Hickey formed a Texas "Land League" that seemed inspired both by his knowledge of the Irish Land League created by Michael Davitt and by his admiration for Mexican revolutionaries. In the *Rebel*, a colorful Texas Socialist newspaper that he founded and edited, Hickey wrote glowingly of Irish and Mexican tenants who had solved the land problem during their respective revolutions by simply seizing land that was rightfully theirs. Hickey also published the PLM's land distribution program in the *Rebel* and became quite active in the defense campaigns for the Flores Magóns. Relying on Mexican organizers, the Texas Socialist Party recruited over one thousand Mexican-American renters to the Land League. Although the Land League was primarily concerned with issues of tenant rights, it also became deeply involved in political campaigns launched by the Socialist Party to oppose Wilson's interventions in the Mexican Revolution.[62]

Other PLM activists played an important role in a series of copper strikes in Clifton-Morenci, Arizona, between 1915–1918 that threatened to undercut U.S. military preparedness and, later, the U.S. war effort. Such strike activities drew the attention of the Wilson administration for, as Colin MacLachlan has written, Wilson's "fear that a truculent working class might undermine industrial production and hinder military expansion approached paranoia." Wilson's short-term answer to the strikes was to order federal troops to occupy the copper camps. But Wilson also sought to redress the problems in the mines by sending federal mediators to arbitrate differences between workers and managers. Not surprisingly, these mediators chose to negotiate with AFL representatives rather than those from the IWW, thereby effectively shutting the IWW out of the mines.[63]

Also left out of Wilson's equation for pacifying the Southwest was the PLM, because Wilson chose to ignore pleas to grant amnesty to the Flores Magóns. Yet neither the PLM's nor the IWW's influence waned easily, compelling the Wilson administration to develop a closer relationship with the AFL leadership to tame labor unrest in the Southwest during World War I. After neglecting to include the AFL in the Pan American Conferences, the U.S. government would help to bankroll the early Pan American Federation of Labor at war's end. Such funding demonstrated that the Wilson administration, like the AFL leadership, remained worried about the popularity of anarcho-syndicalism among Mexican, Mexican-American, and Anglo workers, despite the imprisonment of the Flores Magón brothers.[64]

CONCLUSIONS

In recent years, transnational historians have suggested the value of tracing the flow of ideas and movements across national boundaries. Clearly the labor debate over the Mexican revolution demonstrates the value of this approach; radical ideas and revolutionaries traveled back and forth across the U.S-Mexican border with great regularity during the early twentieth century. Yet the horizontal dialogue that developed among labor groups and that linked workers' struggles in Mexico with those in the United States intersected a vertical debate within U.S. society over American foreign policy toward Mexico. Strikingly, even the PLM, whose anarcho-syndicalist platform called for the destruction of all forms of government power over workers, displayed a strong interest in U.S. foreign policy because they recognized that U.S. intervention in Mexico could destroy the social revolution they sought to foment there.

If labor and Socialist participants in the debate over U.S. foreign policy toward Mexico disagreed about many essentials, most converged in trying to prevent a U.S. military occupation of Mexico. Although Wilson claimed that his military interventions in Mexico were designed to help the Mexican people rather than to protect American corporate interests, only the AFL leadership took Wilson's rhetoric at face value. Leaders of the United Mine Workers expressed nearly as much outrage at the president for his efforts to portray his interventions as humanitarian in intent as did the PLM, IWW, and Socialists. Even Gompers, although convinced that Wilson was committed to genuine humanitarian reform in Mexico, argued that a full-scale military occupation of the country would be a mistake because Mexicans needed to determine their own form of government.

Significantly most groups purporting to speak for U.S. workers also doubted that protecting American economic investments abroad from revolutionary attacks was a vital national security interest. Indeed, U.S. Socialist and labor groups feared U.S. capital flight and sought to keep U.S. investments in the United States. PLM leaders encouraged this belief, arguing that Díaz's open door economic policies had impoverished workers in both the United States and Mexico while reaping enormous profits for U.S. corporations. U.S. imperial interventions in Mexico, they also emphasized, undermined the efforts of both Mexicans and Americans to achieve democratic control of industry.

Yet if labor and Socialist groups tended to agree on these two basic points, they diverged on many others. In the long term they disagreed over whether industrial democracy or an end to imperialism could be achieved within a capitalist context. In the short term, they disagreed about what types of international influence to seek for workers. Convinced that Wilson was a misguided friend of labor too easily wooed by business interests, the AFL leadership pursued a corporatist partnership with the Wilson administration in promoting U.S. foreign policy. This partnership would come to fruition during World War I. By contrast, others clearly judged Wilson a traitor of the working class and sought to develop alternative forms of foreign policy influence that ranged from improving labor's lobbying power and use of the media, to promoting third-party politics, to utilizing strike activity to paralyze economic mobilization for war and military interventions.

The next battle in the war of position that emerged among labor and Socialist groups over U.S. foreign policy would be a largely ideological one; a polyglot of groups purporting to speak for labor would battle each other as well as preparedness organizations and the Wilson administration for the right to define the nation's security interests and the duties of working-class citizenship following the outbreak of World War I.

PART II

World War I and the U.S. Labor Debate over Neutrality and Preparedness

Figure P.2. *United Mine Workers Journal*, July 29, 1915, 1. One of the largest and most diverse AFL unions, the United Mine Workers of America emerged as a leading opponent of U.S. intervention in World War I in 1915–1916. This cartoon was clearly aimed at discouraging U.S. workers from supporting increased levels of military preparedness or aid to any of the belligerents.

PROLOGUE: PRESIDENT WILSON, WORLD WAR I, AND THE U.S. DEBATE OVER NEUTRALITY AND PREPAREDNESS

Only a few short months separated the Wilson administration's occupation of the Mexican port of Veracruz from the outbreak of war in Europe during the late summer of 1914. A seemingly minor incident precipitated the so-called "Great War." On June 28, 1914, an assassin apparently linked to a Slavic nationalist group gunned down Archduke Franz Ferdinand, heir to the Hapsburg throne of Austria-Hungary. The assassination set in motion two alliance systems that had been created by the European powers to defend their international interests and empires: the Triple Alliance, that included Germany, Austria-Hungary, and Italy, and the Triple Entente comprised of France, Russia, and Great Britain. When Austria-Hungary declared war on Serbia on July 28 in the wake of the assassination of the Archduke, it provoked a "chain reaction." Germany, anticipating a possible response by the Triple Entente powers, declared "preventive" war on Russia and France and on August 4 invaded Belgium. Great Britain then declared war on Germany. Japan soon joined the war on the side of the Allies; Turkey aligned with the Central Powers. Italy entered the war in 1915 on the side of the Allies. Colonial armies from Africa and Asia played an important role in the fighting on both sides of the conflict.[1]

President Wilson, on the other hand, issued a "Proclamation of Neutrality" only shortly after the outbreak of the conflict and urged Americans to remain neutral in thought and action. Yet although the Atlantic Ocean seemed a natural barrier to invasion, American ships and passengers soon found themselves in harm's way. Britain began seizing neutral ships headed to continental Europe and searching them for "contraband" that it defined broadly to include foodstuffs and cotton. Germany responded by declaring a war zone around Britain and threatening to sink all enemy ships in this area—including commercial ones—with its new fleet of submarines. Germany also warned all neutral passengers to avoid traveling on enemy ships and urged neutral ships to avoid the war zone due to the danger of misidentification.[2]

The violations against U.S. shipping and death of U.S. passengers that followed unleashed a stormy debate within American society about how to define the nation's vital security interests as well as about citizenship duties. To a degree that might seem surprising to twenty-first-century Americans accustomed to unlimited U.S. military commitments around the globe, many U.S. workers at the onset of World War I believed that American national security interests stopped at American borders or at the ocean's edge. They opposed the use of U.S. military forces to defend U.S. business interests abroad or to protect Americans engaged in foreign travel and applied this reasoning both to the revolution in Mexico and to the European crisis. As a Seattle trade unionist explained in the wake of the sinking of the *Lusitania*, if there were an invasion of the United States, he would encourage his three sons to "shoulder a gun to protect Seattle, but to hunt up men to kill—I didn't raise my boys to that end."[3]

Both President Wilson and preparedness activists, by contrast, sought to encourage Americans to embrace a broader definition of American security interests and citizenship duties. For many of the preparedness groups that sprouted across the American political landscape in 1914–1915, either a threat to U.S. economic interests or an imminent German victory that would destabilize the international balance of power were sufficient justifications to involve the United States in the European war. But even if the United States failed to intervene in the European conflict, they suggested, greater military readiness and universal military training would be of value in their own right. Stronger military defenses would make other nations think twice before invading the United States or attacking its ships and foreign properties. Universal (male) military training would prove a positive social good, reminding Americans of the duties of citizenship in a democracy, bolstering the flagging masculinity of American men, and helping to hold in check those feminist forces seeking to undermine male authority in the home, society, and politics.

Although Wilson struggled to prevent U.S. intervention in the war for almost three years, his evolving definition of U.S. national security was in some ways even more all-encompassing than those of many preparedness activists and war hawks: he assumed

that the defense of international law governing the rights of neutrals was vital to the protection of American national interests.
His assumptions, Wilson scholars have convincingly argued, were
based both on his calculations about the vital role of investments
and foreign trade in sustaining American economic health and
his moral belief that international law was vital to the advance of
mankind. These same beliefs led him to begin promoting the idea
of a League of Nations by early 1915. Wilson's sense of American
exceptionalism also informed his policies; only the United States,
he assumed, could deliver the world from the chaos in which it
was now engulfed and protect democratic values. Although Wilson failed to spell out what his vision meant in terms of citizen
obligations until his declaration of war, the responsibilities were
potentially formidable—at least until the League of Nations could
ensure collective security among nation-states.[4]

Until recently, diplomatic historians have tended to portray the
debate over U.S. neutrality as a two-way dialogue between an antiwar Wilson and his more hawkish opponents—mostly, but not
exclusively Republicans—who favored greater levels of military
preparedness and earlier U.S. intervention in the war. Wilson,
they have insisted, won the overwhelming support of the majority of Americans for his neutrality policies and largely subsumed
his potential critics on the Left with his cautious policies toward
the war. But a new study by Ross Kennedy has emphasized the
importance of a consistent third voice in the debate over neutrality: a pacifist contingent that disagreed strongly with both the
preparedness groups and the Wilson administration about the
European conflict. Pacifists, in contrast to Wilson, doubted that
German submarine warfare constituted a genuine threat to the
security of most Americans. They instead argued that the greatest threat to American security lay within American borders; the
formidable block of military and business interests promoting
preparedness exercised significant influence in Washington, D.C.,
and sought to involve the country in perpetual wars—ranging
from Europe, to Mexico, and to other parts of Latin America.
At first convinced that Wilson was less likely to intervene in the
European conflict than many of his Republican rivals, they grew
increasingly concerned that his policies were tilting toward Britain in an un-neutral way in 1915–1916.[5]

Kennedy emphasizes that the pacifists' vision of national security was quite narrow; they believed in the use of military force only to prevent an invasion of the United States. But in another way, as Alan Dawley has argued, pacifist ideas about how to assure permanent peace were far-ranging. Many pacifists were social reformers deeply involved in international reform movements who assumed that war would end only when societies throughout the world were fundamentally transformed, whether through the enfranchisement of women, the realization of racial equality, the destruction of imperialism, or the achievement of industrial democracy. In this sense, they defied the conventional image of opponents of war as provincial isolationists. Pacifist influence was widespread within the Socialist and labor movements and at first hindered Gompers's efforts to win support for Wilson's foreign policy agenda.[6]

The first chapter in this section explores the critical role of the Socialist Party in shaping the political debate over Wilson's foreign policies as well as the pacifist agenda, while the second considers the internal political debate that raged within the American Federation of Labor over its policies toward the war.

2 The Outbreak of World War I and the Socialist "War on War"

Woodrow Wilson did keep us out of war, but it was not because the men back of him did not want war. It was because the American working class told Johnny Rockefeller and Willie Hearst if they wanted their American millions protected to shoulder their little muskets, put on their little uniforms and do their own fighting.

—Kate Richards O'Hare, quoted in Omaha Daily News, October 23, 1916, p 5.

ON AUGUST 8, 1914, only a few days after European powers declared war against one another, a remarkable mass protest meeting staged by the New York and New Jersey Socialist Parties attracted over ten thousand Socialists and trade unionists to Union Square in New York City despite "broiling" hot weather. Troubled by the apparent breakdown of international labor solidarity in Europe, the organizers took pains to include speakers from "every nation now in arms in Europe," including "Russians, Germans, Frenchmen, Englishmen, Italians, Austrians, Poles, and Scandinavians," who addressed the audience in multiple languages. Most speakers blamed the capitalist quest for markets for causing the war. As Frank Sieverman, an "ex-international officer" of the Boot and Shoeworkers Union explained, "the war in Europe was not a war between kings, for kings are but the trumpets through which the real rulers of the world, the capitalist class, sound their commands." The capitalist class above all sought markets for their surplus goods, leading to the quest for colonies and the resulting nationalist rivalries over empire that had provoked the war.[1]

Frank Cassidy, Socialist Party representative and chairman of the meeting, emphasized slightly different themes. He asserted that the war was staged by the ruling classes of Europe because "their thrones and kingdoms were in danger from the growth of the working class movement in all countries." War provided an easy way to turn workers against each other and keep them in subjection. Because the ruling classes had quickly "commandeered all the lines of transportation and communication," they had taken European Socialists and labor leaders "by surprise" and prevented them from staging the mass strikes that might have prevented war. Since European Socialists and workers were currently unable to stop the carnage, it was the responsibility of U.S. labor and Socialist activists to revive the spirit of international labor solidarity and bring an end to the war. The meeting passed a resolution on behalf of the "workers of all nationalities" demanding that the U.S. government use "every possible agency at its command . . . to stop this abominable and monstrous conflict now in progress" and to "prohibit the industrial and money masters of this country from furnishing to the belligerent powers any money, food supplies, munitions of war and any other commodity that will in anyway assist to prolong this butchery." As Anne Maley, the sole woman speaker at the meeting exclaimed, "No arms for European slaughter! No bread for European butchers!" Maley and others argued that by enforcing an embargo on Europe, the United States might be able to "starve" the war and bring an early peace.[2]

Although the embargo effort ultimately failed, meetings like the one in New York signaled the beginning of a prolonged effort on the part of U.S. Socialist and labor activists to learn from the mistakes of their European counterparts, prevent U.S. involvement in the European conflict, and perhaps bring peace to Europe. Leading the charge in the effort to create a viable working-class antiwar movement was the Socialist Party, whose political credibility had been sullied by the breakdown of international Socialist solidarity in Europe. Yet as the New York meeting demonstrated, the Socialist Party often worked hand in hand with immigrant Left organizations, as well as with local and constituent AFL and IWW unions—especially those with large Socialist, German-American, Jewish-American or Irish-American constituencies—in its antiwar campaigns. Collectively declaring "war on war," these groups not only sought to revive international labor solidarity in ways that facilitated an early peace but also strongly contested the Wilson administration's definitions of U.S. national security, preparedness, and citizenship responsibilities. Their activism proved an important part of the broader pacifist movement and, as Kate Richards O'Hare argued, may have helped to delay U.S. involvement in the war in ways not commonly realized. Equally significant, the Socialists who led the "war against war" delineated a blueprint for reforming international diplomacy and protecting the international interests of workers that differed in significant ways from that of the Wilson administration.

Antiwar protests like the one in New York often paradoxically fostered a sense of both international labor solidarity and *messianic Americanism* among participants. Alan Dawley has defined "messianic Americanism" as the "belief that America has a God-given mission of redemption."[3] For President

Wilson and his closest advisors, the United States was exceptional because of its superior Anglo-Saxon Protestant culture, its highly developed democratic institutions, and its stable capitalist economy. Wilson believed that in the context of World War I the United States could help make "the world safe for democracy" by spreading its democratic ideals and culture, by encouraging the rule of law in international relations, and by creating strong international organizations that would enforce international law and promote peace and democracy through collective security.

By contrast, the U.S. Socialist sense of American exceptionalism was cut of a different cloth. For American Socialists, the United States was exceptional not because of the Anglo-Saxon Protestant cultural backgrounds of many of its elites, but because of the diverse cultures of its working classes, an idea prominently on display at the New York meeting. Many believed that the diverse international roots of American workers, along with their continuing transnational ties to former homelands, might make the Socialist-led antiwar movement in the United States the ideal vehicle for promoting world peace.[4] Socialists also quite clearly differed from Wilson in their assumptions about capitalism. For Wilson and his advisors, U.S. capitalism was unique because it was so successful. By contrast, for many U.S. Socialists and trade unionists, capitalism found its most brutal expression in the United States; battle-toughened U.S. laborites and Socialists might therefore be better trained to resist the patriotic deceptions of the capitalist ruling classes than their counterparts in Europe. Finally, while U.S. Socialists had as much admiration for U.S. democratic institutions as American elites, they believed that the democratic revolution begun by the founding fathers was far from complete. In the long run they sought democratic control of industry through collective ownership of the means of production; in the short run they favored more democratic input for workers over both domestic and foreign policy. Although supportive of some of Wilson's ideas about international law and collective security through international organizations, they believed that democratic majoritarian rule must be the bedrock upon which these institutions were built. The U.S. Socialist and labor movements, they anticipated, would be well situated to serve as a voice for international democracy at war's end.

Recent historical research on U.S. socialism has emphasized its decentralized nature and has focused on the rich regional political subcultures it helped to cultivate. Historian Paul Buhle estimates that states like Arkansas, Missouri, and Texas each had more than a dozen Socialist newspapers in the World War I era. In urban areas, the Socialist press often catered to immigrants and the foreign language federations within the U.S. Socialist Party, as well as to Socialist splinter groups. The Chicago area alone boasted at least a dozen or more Socialist papers on the eve of the war, including ones published in Slovakian, Slovenian, Bohemian, Polish, and German, as well as a Christian Socialist paper. New York was famous for its Yiddish Socialist newspapers and its Jewish Socialist culture and also boasted a significant and highly vocal African American Socialist community in Harlem.[5]

This chapter, however, refocuses attention on the National Executive Committee of the Socialist Party as well as the Socialist Party newspapers with the largest circulations, for they played the most critical roles as "first responders" in national political debates over the war and citizenship duties, and offered a powerful counterpoint to preparedness propaganda as well as to the neutrality policies of the Wilson administration. The party leadership also initiated early efforts to inspire a Socialist-negotiated peace in Europe and mediated, although not always successfully, conflicts between different factions within the U.S. Socialist Party. Prominent left-wing Socialist leaders, for their part, worked with cooperating IWW leaders in an unsuccessful effort to devise a plan for implementing a general strike to oppose war. Although this chapter focuses primarily on the Socialist leadership and the party's major press outlets, the role of Socialists in shaping local and industrial antiwar labor subcultures within the AFL is taken up in chapter 3, and local cooperation between Socialists and the IWW is considered in chapter 4. The strained relationship between African Americans and the Socialist Party leadership, and the significant role of African American Socialists in opposing Wilsonian foreign policy in 1918 and 1919, is taken up in chapter 7.[6]

Particularly important in early national Socialist Party policy formulations as well as foreign policy debates were Morris Hillquit, centrist Socialist leader from New York who was on the National Executive Committee throughout the war; Victor Berger of Milwaukee, whose electoral success and strong interest in the war due to his German-American background put him at the front and center of many antiwar campaigns; Meyer London, Socialist Congressman from New York; Charles Ruthenberg, the unofficial spokesman for the Left within the National Executive Committee; Mary Marcy, editor of the left-wing Socialist publication the *International Socialist Review*; and Eugene Debs and Kate Richards O'Hare—the party's most popular stump speakers. Also important were a core group who would later become prowar Socialists, including John Spargo, Upton Sinclair, Allan Benson, and William English Walling.

Utopian thinking emphasizing both international labor solidarity and American exceptionalism perhaps found its clearest manifestation in initial efforts by the U.S. Socialist Party to stage a conference of Socialist movements from all the warring countries in Washington, D.C., in the fall of 1914 in the hopes that it could broker a Socialist-led peace. These efforts preceded the formulation of a party program on the war as well as the extended debate that developed in the Socialist press over the roots of the war, national preparedness, and Wilson's foreign policies. Undergirding the efforts to stage a conference was a belief that, in the new world, Socialists from the old world could set aside their differences and untangle the complex web of secret diplomacy woven by the ruling and capitalist classes of Europe. Assisting them would be American Socialists of diverse nationalities. Yet from the beginning some within the Socialist Party leadership opposed the conference as unrealistic. Socialist Party chairman Morris Hillquit argued that the idea was "fantastic" and would make U.S. Socialists look "ridiculous in the eyes of the International Socialist Movement." That Hillquit was so concerned with the national reputation of the American Socialist movement was in itself paradoxical and at odds with ideas of international Socialist solidarity. Yet Hillquit also emphasized pragmatic concerns, suggesting that the "Socialist parties in Europe are completely stunned by the sudden and catastrophic events of the war." They were neither ready to talk nor even likely to receive passports to leave their countries. He insisted that "this is not the time and Washington, D.C., is certainly not the place."[7] At the request of the National Executive Committee, cables nonetheless went out to the major European Socialist movements, with the expected noncommittal replies. As Hillquit later commented, "[t]he Socialists of the belligerent countries had neither the facilities nor the desire to meet for a general peace confab one month after the outbreak of the war."[8]

The next efforts came in January of 1915 with a proposal for a conference of neutral powers to be held in one of the neutral Scandinavian countries or Switzerland. Here too, pragmatism wrestled with utopianism among the Socialist Party leadership. Initially, Victor Berger and Morris Hillquit favored the conference and sought passports. Berger wrote President Wilson and Honorable William Redford seeking the administration's approval to travel through Austria and Germany to attend an international Socialist meeting because "[e]verybody from the crown prince of Germany down to the last private seems to agree that this war is unnecessary, wanton and inexcusable."

Long known as a realist, Berger argued that a Socialist-driven peace was not "utopian" given the large Socialist vote in Europe. Similarly, Hillquit, although not thrilled at the idea of losing four or five weeks work as a successful attorney, supported the conference and initially planned to attend because he believed it would "contribute very materially to the establishment of a harmonious and sympathetic understanding of the situation among the Socialists of all countries and lay the foundation for the rebuilding of the international."[9]

Yet when a number of neutral powers decided not to attend the conference, leaving only Sweden, Norway, Denmark, and Holland as likely participants, Hillquit doubted whether it could have much effect due to its "local" composition. Noting that neutrality did not mean the same thing in Europe as in the United States, he suggested that participation in the conference might harm future U.S. efforts to hold an international conference. Hillquit insisted that it would be the Socialists of America to whom the initial work of "reconstructing the shattered International of the workers" must fall. Berger similarly reversed course, suggesting that at the planned conference in Northern Europe there would be no large power except for the United States. The U.S. Socialist Party therefore chose not to join in efforts to arrange a conference of neutrals.[10] However, when representatives of forty Socialist movements met in Zimmerwald, Switzerland, in September 1915 and developed a program opposing the continuation of the war, the U.S. Socialist National Executive Committee supported the program. But the Zimmerwald meeting did not put an end to the hope that the U.S. Socialists would lead in bringing peace among European Socialists. In January 1917, the U.S. Socialist Party again tried to arrange an international conference of Socialists, setting the date and location for June of 1917 at the Hague. By this time, however, the United States was at war and the Socialists were denied passports.[11]

Although Socialists directed most of their early peace efforts toward trying to plan an international Socialist peace conference, centrists in the party leadership also tried to encourage President Wilson to stage a conference of neutrals in an effort to mediate an end to the war. Socialist Congressman Meyer London introduced a resolution in Congress on December 6, 1915, asking the president of the United States to "call a conference of the neutral nations of the world with the purpose, if possible, to bring or hasten the coming of peace in war-distracted Europe." The Socialist Party then initiated a petition drive in support of the resolution at mass meetings and within sympathetic labor unions as well as publicizing the resolution in the Socialist press. Perhaps most importantly, the Socialist Party created a committee to meet with the president and enlist his support for the resolution. Initially, the party asked Eugene Debs, James Maurer of the Pennsylvania State Federation of Labor, and Morris Hillquit to serve. Debs, however, refused, arguing that he could "see no possible good in us as socialists calling on a capitalist president and asking him to do a thing he is committed not to do and has refused to others." In Debs's place, the party substituted Meyer London.[12]

When the committee met with Wilson on January 25, 1916, he suggested that he had a similar plan under consideration. However, Wilson worried about the participation of other neutral countries because they were practically all dependent on one of the belligerent powers. He was instead considering direct mediation by the United States. Wilson assured the committee, however, that he would give their plan serious consideration. Upon leaving, Maurer reportedly told Wilson that "Your promises sound good Mr. President but the trouble with you is that you are surrounded by capitalist and militarist interests who want the war to continue; and I fear you will succumb to their influence." According to Hillquit, Maurer's "Pennsylvania Dutch bluntness" evoked an "amused smile on the pale and intellectual face of Woodrow Wilson." Wilson claimed that he was "more often accused of being influenced by radical and pacifist elements than by the capitalist or militarist interests." But Hillquit, recounting the episode in his memoirs over a decade later, thought that subsequent events had borne out Maurer rather than Wilson.[13]

Two other efforts to bring a quick end to the war also enjoyed temporary popularity in Socialist circles: the embargo movement and the left-wing movement for general political strikes. Efforts to win public support for an American embargo went through several stages and embodied multiple goals. By 1917 most of those who favored an embargo did so primarily to prevent German submarine attacks on the United States and thereby keep the country out of war. But in 1914–1915 many seriously countenanced an idea that may first have been propounded at the 1914 New York meeting: by starving the war the United States could bring an early end to it. The faith placed by some Socialists in this proposal was evidenced in a speech by Kate Richards O'Hare, who argued that "The Congress of the United States has the power to stop the war in Europe almost instantly by forbidding the exportation of food and ammunition."[14] Similarly the *Appeal to Reason* called on Wilson "to prohibit the shipment of all food from the United States until this war is ended" so as to "starve the war and at the same time provide food for the hungry here."[15]

Walter Lanfersiek, acting in the name of the Socialist Committee on Immediate Action, demanded that the U.S. government seize "packing plants, cold storage houses, grain elevators and flour mills" as well as the means of transportation. If the United States stopped food exports to Europe, Lanfersiek insisted, the "rulers of Europe, unable to secure foods for their armies, will be forced to call off their soldiers." The proposal also called for prohibiting money and munitions to the European belligerents. Lanfersiek's ideas were then included in an antiwar petition of the Women's National Committee of the Socialist Party that called for a ban on the exports of food, money, and armaments to belligerents. The Women's Committee ultimately gathered over 100 thousand signatures for their petition and it was introduced in Congress in February of 1915. But the petition was subsequently referred to the House Committee on Interstate and Foreign Commerce; this group, according to Philip Foner, quietly "buried" it.[16]

The failure of Congress to act on the embargo initiative in turn gave new momentum to left-wing activists who sought to use general strikes in the United States, both to stop continued shipments of war goods to Europe and to serve as a catalyst for general strikes throughout the world that would finally achieve the international labor solidarity necessary to end the war. The failure of European Socialists to use general strikes to stop governments from warring against each other in 1914 perhaps inspired more discussion in the U.S. Socialist press during the early years of the war than any other subject. The left-wing paper, the *International Socialist Review*, in particular, devoted significant attention to the issue and encouraged a dialogue within its pages among IWW activists such as Big Bill Haywood and left-wing Socialists such as Henry Slobodin and Mary Marcy about how general strikes to achieve political ends might be implemented in the United States. Yet these discussions never moved beyond a theoretical stage, with a majority within the IWW leadership ultimately concluding that industrial organization was not yet sufficiently advanced to ensure the success of general strikes either in the United States or Europe. These conclusions in turn led the main body of the IWW to repudiate political action and to focus on industrial organizing even while continuing to declare its opposition to all war. Left-wing Socialists, by contrast, continued to champion the tactic of general strikes for purposes of ending the war in Europe and preventing U.S. involvement in the war, but they lacked any effective means of implementing these plans. Absent access to any real organizational infrastructure that would sustain a strike, left-wing Socialists like Mary Marcy instead devoted their efforts to trying to undercut support for capitalist morality in the pages of the Socialist press in ways that would encourage spontaneous rebellions by workers against both their industrial masters and the government.[17]

Early Socialist efforts to bring peace to Europe thus enjoyed little success. Yet this early peace work demonstrated that for a fleeting moment U.S. Socialist leaders believed that they might have a unique role to play in both revitalizing international Socialist and labor solidarity and in encouraging the U.S. government to use its international power wisely. Although U.S. Socialist beliefs in their own exceptionalism were not borne out by their efforts to broker a Socialist or U.S.-negotiated peace, or to encourage a rolling wave of general strikes throughout the world, the U.S. Socialist Party did arguably prove exceptional in its persistent and initially successful campaign to keep the United States out of the war.

SOCIALIST ANALYSES OF WAR AS AN IMPORTANT ANTIWAR ACTIVITY

In his memoirs, Morris Hillquit highlighted the May 1915 peace program adopted by the National Executive Committee as one of the most remarkable aspects of the Socialist Party's antiwar work. He suggested that the program was the "first formulation of a comprehensive program of what later came to be known as a 'democratic peace.'"[18] Yet more important than the proclamations of the National Executive Committee in preventing U.S. involvement in the war between 1914–1917 were the day-to-day work of the Socialist press and Socialist speakers in analyzing the roots of the war and war developments, in counteracting the propaganda of preparedness activists, and in critiquing Wilson's foreign policies. These activities not only limited Socialist and labor support for U.S. intervention in the war but also provided a basis for the official peace programs that would be formulated by the party between 1915 and 1917.

The Socialist press played a particularly important role in the antiwar activities of the party because, in a day before the widespread use of radio, it was through its newspapers that the party most regularly communicated with its members and sympathizers.[19] Socialist papers like the *Appeal to Reason, American Socialist,* and the *International Socialist Review* boasted national circulations that rivaled the mainstream press.[20] Others, such as the *Milwaukee Leader, New York Call,* St. Louis–based *Rip Saw,* and the *Rebel* of Hallettsville, Texas, enjoyed wide circulation within particular cities and regions and were often the primary source of news for their readers. Some Socialist writings not only appeared in newspapers but became part of collected volumes that were used as the essential textbooks for Socialists in the formulation of policy. One example of this type of source was William

English Walling's, *The Socialists and the War*, published in 1915, it became the definitive record used by Socialists in explaining early Socialist responses to war in both Europe and the United States.[21]

Although some criticized the U.S. Socialist press for being "pro-German," Socialist counterclaims that the mainstream press was pro-British were probably more accurate because Britain successfully cut the transatlantic cable lines between the United States and Germany only a week after it declared war.[22] As a consequence, most U.S. newspapers relied heavily on British news sources in covering the war. By contrast, the Socialist press used their transnational ties with European Socialists to publish a wide range of Left perspectives in their papers, including those of German Socialist leaders like Conrad Haenisch, Irish rebel leader James Connolly, and British Socialist James Ramsey McDonald. They also sought to encourage controversy about these perspectives by inviting a dialectical form of rebuttal in which responders questioned some of the underlying precepts of these articles and offered a new synthesis.[23]

In the early stages of the war, however, it was the U.S. Socialists who dominated the headlines and pronounced their judgment on the war. Many analyses came from staff reporters and grassroots activists, but others were contributed by the party's intellectual elite, ranging from literary figures such as Upton Sinclair and Jack London, to the coolly analytical and highly successful lawyer Morris Hillquit, to the passionate political and social crusaders Eugene Debs, Kate Richards O'Hare, and Victor Berger. Sinclair, Hillquit, and Berger figured more prominently in the debates over the roots of war, while Debs and O'Hare played a more important role in attacking Wilson's neutrality and preparedness policies. In a league all of her own was left-wing Socialist Mary Marcy, who scathingly attacked bourgeois gender morality in an effort to encourage a spirit of rebellion among both men and women workers that might lay the groundwork for a general strike. Also not to be overlooked were brilliant Socialist cartoonists like Robert Minor who encapsulated in engaging visual form many of the essential arguments of Socialist writers and speakers.

Like writers for the mainstream press, Socialist writers at first attributed some of the blame for the war to the incompetence of the rulers of Europe. Yet they took care to distinguish themselves from both mainstream journalists and naive "bourgeois pacifists" by emphasizing the economic and class roots of the war.[24] As the sharp-penned Upton Sinclair commented, the three nations that began the war—Austria, Russia, and Germany—were governed "first by a doddering imbecile, the second by a weak-minded melancholic, and the third by an epileptic degenerate drunk upon the vision of himself as the war lord of Europe." But Sinclair also emphasized that behind each of these men was a clique of capitalists and aristocrats seeking to enrich themselves. Although more sympathetic to the British, he also assessed some blame to the English capitalists who had "grabbed up everything in sight and being jealous of the capitalists of Germany looked towards Germany with an attitude which caused hatred of England among the people of Germany."[25]

Hillquit sounded similar themes, arguing that the "[t]he murder of the Austrian archduke," was a "pretext." The subsequent diplomatic negotiations between "Austria and Servia, Germany and Russia, France and England. . . . precipitated and fashioned the outbreak of hostilities but . . . the war of today was foreordained when the nations of Europe went out to steal slices of the remaining globe for their merchants and manufacturers." Other writers, such as William Bohn, filled in the details by noting that the war was really about the issue of whether the Germans and Austrians or British and Russians would control the economic resources of Southeastern Europe and "Asia minor." William English Walling pointed out that "London and Paris financiers" controlled "twice the capital of Germany" and argued that they sought to bring U.S. capitalists into a "trust of nations" that would soon control 75 percent of the world's wealth. In his collected volume, Walling argued that Hillquit probably spoke for majority opinion within the party in emphasizing that "[t]he Socialist diagnosis of the causes of modern wars may be summed up in one sentence. The basic cause is capitalism. The contributory causes are imperialism, militarism, social unrest, international grudges and pseudo patriotism."[26]

But Victor Berger reversed the order. Berger proved unique among Socialists in arguing that race hatred was the major cause of the war and that capitalism played only a contributory role. The Balkan Peninsula, he suggested, seethed with nationalist and racial antagonisms. A Greater Servia meant the breakup up of Austria-Hungary; Pan-Slavism posed a threat to the Russian Czar. Berger also insisted that the "ruling element in Germany" was still the "old feudal landed nobility—the Junker class," a hereditary aristocracy that supplied most of the military officers, rather than the capitalist class. In contrast to most of the German-American press, he argued that Junkerdom was quite definitely a "standing menace to the peace of Europe, because Junkerdom is the personification of German militarism." But Berger insisted that "German Social Democracy" was among the most advanced in the world and constituted a force for "aggressive democracy" that had aroused great fear in the Kaiser. Although disappointed that German Socialists had failed to stop the war, he believed that their support for the German government resulted from a fear of invasion by imperial Russia. When Karl Liebknecht declared his opposition to a new war loan, Berger announced his support for this antiwar faction within the German Socialist movement. But significantly, Berger remained convinced that the war had demonstrated that Socialists were not "antinational" but rather "international"; at war's end, the new Socialist International would need to be rebuilt with full cognizance of the strong pull that national ties continued to exercise on Socialists and workers.[27]

Joining Berger in an effort to absolve German Social Democrats of war guilt in the American press was German Socialist leader Conrad Haenisch, who decried the "mud-slinging on all sides against the German Social Democracy." He argued that Socialists needed to remember that it was the "theoretical and organizing genius of the German people" that had accomplished "wonderful things in the upbuilding of the German labor movement and in the upbuilding of the International." Haenisch insisted that the war had shown that the "labor parties of all the countries are interwoven with the inner life of the national states and with the national culture of their countries." Therefore, "If the German Social Democracy through its attitude to the world has betrayed the International, then, the labor parties of other countries have committed treason a thousand times over." Others strongly disagreed, however, arguing that the German decision to support their government was more inexcusable because the danger of an invasion of Germany was remote. By contrast, French and Belgium Socialists found it necessary to form alliances with their governments in an effort to protect them from an actual German invasion.[28]

Hillquit, as was common, sought to play the role of mediator and to prevent a cleavage within the Socialist movement on the issue by emphasizing that it was not in the best interest of U.S. Socialists to take a position favoring either side in the conflict. He emphasized that the Socialists of Europe "nearly unanimously" supported their governments because they were "threatened with foreign invasion." England and Russia, on the other hand, faced no invasion and Socialist opinion was therefore more divided. Hillquit drew the conclusion that the "differing attitudes of the Socialists of the various countries is to be accounted for not on ideological grounds, not on the theory that one part of the Socialist International has remained true to its principles while another large portion has betrayed them overnight, but by the much simpler explanation that the Socialists of each country have yielded to the inexorable necessities of the situation."[29]

Yet Irish Socialist and revolutionary leader James Connolly helped reignite the controversy in a series of poignant articles written for the Socialist and IWW press during a one year period prior to the Irish Easter Rebellion in

April 1916. Connolly would play a leading role in the rebellion and would be executed by the British for his revolutionary activities. In contrast to German-American Socialists and their supporters, Connolly felt no compunction to toe a neutral line. He noted that although he wished the Socialists could have prevented war, this had failed due to the "divorce between the industrial and political movements of labor." Since war was now a reality, Socialists needed to realize that there could be no hope for peaceful development in Europe when the "British fleet" held a "knife" at the "throat of Europe." He therefore asserted that he wanted to "see England beaten so thoroughly that the commerce of the seas will henceforth be free to all nations—to the smallest equally with the greatest."[30] Others, of course, hotly insisted the opposite. Concurring with President Wilson, they argued that German autocracy posed the greater threat to world peace. George Herron, an American Socialist living in Europe, wrote Hillquit insisting that his "neutrality" was a delusion. He argued that "German victory would mean the end of socialism for a long time to come" and that "American socialists as a whole are as innocent of any understanding of the real situation as a parcel of new born babes."[31]

If American Socialists disagreed enormously about the relative war guilt of Britain and Germany, the very diversity of opinion exposed by Socialists served as an important counterweight to the generally pro-Allied views of the mainstream press and preparedness activists. In concert with the immigrant press and a host of local labor papers, they helped to undercut efforts to portray the war in simple terms as one between English democracy and German autocracy. In highlighting the importance of the capitalists of all nations in contributing to the outbreak of the war, American Socialists also hit upon a common theme: ultimately true peace and security for workers would be guaranteed only when industrial democracy was achieved throughout the world. As Eugene Debs explained, "Permanent peace . . . will never prevail until national industrial despotism has been supplanted by international industrial democracy. The end of profit and plunder among nations will also mean the end of war and the dawning of the era of 'Peace on Earth and Good Will among Men.'" A demand for industrial democracy thus became one of the most important and agreed-upon planks in the peace programs adopted by the party in 1914 and 1915, even while Socialists continued to diverge about the best methods for ensuring the triumph of industrial democracy.[32]

Until industrial democracy was achieved, Socialists of diverse views signaled that it was important for American workers to be on the alert against the efforts of the U.S. capitalist class, in combination with its political handmaidens, to drive the country into war. When the preparedness movement

gained ground in the second year of the war, Socialists and their labor supporters were prepared for battle. Preparedness activists, bowing to popular
opposition to U.S. involvement in the war, at first concentrated primarily on
the need for higher levels of defense spending and universal military training as preventative measures that would also have positive social repercussions. A stronger military might prevent an invasion of the United States
and continued attacks on U.S. shipping that might otherwise catapult the
country into war. Military service, preparedness activists emphasized, was
a duty of male citizenship that would also help to improve male virility. Yet
both the centrist and left-wing Socialist press devoted extensive attention to
deconstructing preparedness ideas about military readiness and the gendered
duties of citizenship, providing influential counter-hegemonic ideologies
upon which opponents of war and militarism could draw.

CONTESTING PREPAREDNESS

Leading the charge in the early campaigns for better military preparedness
and military training were Army Chief of Staff General Leonard Wood and
former President Theodore Roosevelt.[33] Wood, a strong believer in the value
of the strenuous military life in building manly character, derided pacifists as
"emasculated traitors" who helped cause wars by preventing effective military
preparedness. Concerned about alleged U.S. military weakness even before
the onset of the European War, Wood instituted a volunteer military training
camp program for college students in 1913. Following the outbreak of war
in Europe, Wood expanded the program to include camps for prominent
businessmen, the most well-known of which he established at Plattsburg,
New York. Wood, as well as many participants in the camps, promoted them
as useful models for implementing universal military training for all young
men in the United States, who would then become conscripts in a reserve citizens' army. Proponents of universal military training argued that the camps
promoted physical well-being and fostered the development of "good manly
men and gentlemen," broke down class divisions, and encouraged a spirit of
democracy. Wood and his colleagues also used the camps to popularize the
notion that military duty, like taxation, was an obligation of male citizenship.[34] Men earned their right to suffrage, insisted Wood, by virtue of their
willingness to militarily defend their country.[35]

Theodore Roosevelt frequently visited the camps and used them as a pulpit
from which to promote his preparedness message and attack pacifists. In an
address at Plattsburg, Roosevelt lauded those in attendance for "fulfilling the

prime duty of free men."[36] In subsequent talks on military training, Roosevelt emphasized his belief in universal military training for rich and poor alike, arguing that it broke down class barriers, promoted manly citizenship, and strengthened democracy. "The man who isn't fit to fight for his country," insisted Roosevelt, "isn't fit to vote."[37] While lauding the manliness of those who volunteered for military training and service, Roosevelt employed a seemingly endless supply of scornful terms for male pacifists, variously labeling them "mollycoddles, sissies, and sapheads" and characterizing them as "fat," "flabby," and opposed to democracy. Roosevelt reluctantly supported female suffrage but argued that women had their own special citizenship duties. The woman who did not "bear at least four children," he believed, should "be tried as traitors to America, much the same way as soldiers who refused to fight." Roosevelt reserved particular venom for feminists who approved the song "I Did Not Raise My Boy to Be a Soldier," insisting that such women belonged in harems in China because, by opposing military preparedness, they made other women vulnerable to sexual attack from invading armies.[38]

Roosevelt's and Wood's goals of universal military training and an enlarged military were popularized by an imposing array of preparedness organizations, including the National Security League, the Military Training Camps Association, the National Defense League, and the Navy League. Such groups, suggests John Whiteclay Chambers, were not dominated by men from the military but by a corporate elite. The Wall Street lawyers, bankers, and businessmen who joined preparedness organizations favored a stronger military in part because they were commercial expansionists and sought to promote a more aggressive role for the United States in international affairs. Some may also have feared a German or Mexican invasion. But these American "aristocrats" suggests Chambers, were also "guided by a spirit of class leadership" and a "personal need for physical challenge and self-sacrifice." Before the industrial revolution, most men had worked jobs that involved at least some physical labor. The managerial middle- and upper-class group of men that emerged in the wake of industrialization, however, often enjoyed comfortable office jobs. Yet this comfort came at a price; many expressed concerns that American men were losing their virility and masculinity due to their lack of physical exercise. Flagging masculinity in turn eroded male authority and paved the way for uppity women suffragists to demand equality and the vote. Preparedness activists emphasized that the new class of white-collar men could improve their physical fitness and manliness through military training and, possibly, prowess on European battlefields.[39]

Democratic rhetoric notwithstanding, such men clearly envisioned themselves as officers, and working-class men as foot soldiers in any future military endeavors. Thus while military training and service would allegedly afford middle- and upper-class men a theater in which to demonstrate their virility and leadership skills, it would benefit ordinary working men by teaching them obedience, hard work, persistence, and efficiency. A leading economist and preparedness activist explained that American workers had imagination in abundance but lacked discipline. Military training, he asserted, would give American men the capacity to "stick to a definite job and do it under any conditions," thereby making them "far more desirable citizens and far more productive laborers." The National Defense League boasted that military training inculcated "cheerful and immediate obedience to orders and superiors." Others lauded the role of military training in Americanizing immigrants and disabusing them of radical foreign ideologies. For many corporate officials, universal military training and a larger military offered hope both to strengthen America's position in the world and to create a more docile and obedient workforce.[40]

Preparedness activists also enlisted women in their cause, insisting that "patriotic mothers sacrificed their sons to war not only in defense of their country but also in defense of the characters of their sons."[41] Patriotic mothers believed that protecting their homeland from foreign invasion was a logical extension of their role as homemakers. The Woman's Section of the Navy League obtained one hundred thousand signatures to "urge upon Congress the necessity of providing adequate means for defense for America's homes and shores."[42] Women preparedness activists usually came from the same upper-class backgrounds as men in the movement and typically remained neutral on questions of women's suffrage, at least when they were working for the preparedness cause. In addition to helping men organize lobbying campaigns and parades, women particularly publicized the ways in which German soldiers brutalized women and children, helping to affirm the powerful metaphor of the "rape" of Belgium. This metaphor was in turn used to imply that military preparedness was necessary to protect the virtue of American womanhood and the sanctity of U.S. family life.[43]

But the early propaganda of preparedness advocates made easy fodder for the Socialists. Much as U.S. Socialists blamed European capitalists for the war in Europe, so also they insisted that it was the business class in the United States that was working in collusion with a few politicians like Roosevelt to expand the military as a prelude to U.S. involvement in the war. The goal of business in pushing the country toward war, according to Socialists, was clear: profits. They pointed to the lucrative munitions trade that had developed between the United States and Britain since the war as evidence. Cartoonist Robert Minor of the *New York Call* engagingly captured Socialist perceptions of the class backgrounds and interests of preparedness activists in a cartoon entitled "The National 'Security' League," which showed two cynical-looking businessmen waving American flags as they rested upon stacks of security bonds and bags of money.[44] Socialist journalists, for their part, regularly investigated the backgrounds of the leading officials of preparedness organizations and concluded that most of them came from big business backgrounds.[45] Reversing the gender ridicule of preparedness activists, Socialist writers derided militarist interests as part of the "silk-stocking, French novel–idle rich" set whose masculinity compared quite unfavorably with that of the "husky, hard-working, farming and working class."[46]

The Socialist press also devoted itself to debunking two arguments that lay at the heart of preparedness propaganda: first, the notion that the United States was in imminent danger of invasion and second the idea that a stronger military would prevent such an invasion or the need for future involvement in the war. In a series of debates in New York City, Morris Hillquit suggested that due to logistical difficulties the possibility of a European invasion of the United States was extremely remote. There never was a country, he argued, "economically, geographically, or ethnologically and historically" that was better situated to escape war than the United States. He insisted that what American businessmen really feared was not an invasion but a loss to their profits if U.S. trade with Europe continued to be interrupted by the war.[47] Similarly, Eugene Debs argued that "I have not the least fear of invasion or attack from without. The invasion and attack I want the worker to prepare to resist comes from within, from our own predatory plutocracy right here at home. I do not know of any foreign buccaneers that could come nearer skinning the American workers to the bone than is now being [done] by the Rockefellers and their pirate pals."[48]

To attack the notion that a strong military would help to prevent an invasion, Socialists resorted to their own gendered arguments. The editors of the *Appeal to Reason*, for example, responded to a question from a reader about whether a larger military establishment might be the best means of assuring peace by citing an example from civilian street life. "It is well known," wrote the editors, "that when an individual is by long training equipped for a fight and is armed with a revolver and a knife and a black-jack, he is more likely to be overbearing, insolent and offensive . . . [and] to pick a quarrel. The same is true of nations."[49] When another reader queried, "[w]hat shall we do if our country is in actual danger from a foreign foe[?]," the editors retorted that Socialists should first try to get the working classes of each country to negotiate with one another. But if this didn't happen, workers should have "good manners" and "stand back courteously" to let the businessmen and their sons enlist because "the country belongs to them chiefly."[50]

A broad spectrum of Socialists also objected to claims that military service built manly character and should be a prerequisite for the exercise of the franchise in a democracy. One of the first Socialists to attack efforts to conflate military service and manliness was ironically Jack London, a prominent writer of manly adventure stories who would later support U.S. intervention in the war. Yet during the early months of the war, London became famous for a treatise called "The Good Soldier" that indicted military service for turning a man into a "blind, heartless, soulless murder machine." London asserted that a soldier was "not a man . . . [because] all that is human in him has been sworn away when he took the enlistment roll." London's treatise was viewed as so subversive that it was barred from the mails by the end of 1915. For his part, Debs insisted that "working men are forced into war as working women are forced into prostitution." Soldiers became part of a "crimson carnival where the drunken devils are unchained and the snarling dogs are 'sicked' upon one another by the brutal masters."[51]

Other Socialist writers tried to substantiate London's and Deb's arguments by publicizing examples of how war caused moral degeneracy in men. Some cited examples of the use of torture and indiscriminate murder by American troops during the U.S. war in the Philippines.[52] Those who had been to Europe since the outbreak of war documented the "moral and mental disintegration" of former acquaintances and soldiers they encountered there. William Gunn Shepard, for example, wrote of a British journalist friend who became so disillusioned after being sent to the front that he "wished he were dead." The man insisted that "everything that was good in him . . . [was] dead already." Shepard described the soldiers he encountered in Belgium as "herded unthinking beasts" whose characters had "fallen apart since the binding support of their home environment" had been taken away. He insisted that "to be turned into such a man . . . [was] worse than death."[53]

Other Socialists focused on the effects of universal military training on the home front. In contrast to Roosevelt and others who insisted that the dog tent was the cradle of democracy, Socialists argued that freedom from military compulsion was one of the touchstones of American liberty. Universal military training, they argued, would "take the flower of the nation's youth and pervert their minds with military ideals," molding "their characters in the ways of blind obedience." Blind obedience, they suggested, was absolutely incompatible with democracy because exercising the franchise required the ability to reason independently. The only ones who would benefit from inculcating youth with a spirit of blind obedience were employers who—as they readily admitted—hoped to use military training to create a more docile and compliant workforce. Such employers also hoped to use the enlarged militia to suppress strikes and to pursue commercial expansion into areas as diverse as Mexico, China, and Europe.[54] Socialists even disputed the argument that military training promoted the physical vigor of men, arguing that physical education classes, recreation, and healthier conditions in industry were more effective ways to inspire health among both men and women.[55] In his debates with preparedness activists in New York, Morris Hillquit summarized the views of many Socialists in asserting that preparedness propaganda emphasizing the "ennobling influences of military discipline" would be "amusing if [it] . . . were not so serious and dangerous." He insisted that "the barracks of professional soldiers reek with brutality, vice and degeneracy" and had a "demoralizing effect on the youth of the country."[56]

As an alternative to the false manly ideals embodied in the image of the American soldier, centrist Socialists offered their vision of "social man." Social man was guided not by the herd instinct or by blind obedience but by reason and by a vision of a better world. Judging by Socialist cartoons, social man was apparently as large-muscled as his military counterparts. His heroism, however, lay not in his courage in battle but in his poise and capacity for calm deliberate thinking during times of crisis. These Socialists believed that social man would eventually become the bedrock of all democratic governments and would lead in the quest for industrial democracy and public ownership of the means of production through peaceful political means. Social man also scorned "narrow-visioned and nefarious nationalism" and was destined to become the champion of a new and "true internationalism based on social justice." Needless to say, social man was not afraid to oppose unnecessary wars. From a Socialist perspective, social man clearly served as a more ideal model for male citizens than the soldier. The personification of this form of manly citizenship was arguably the lawyerly Morris Hillquit or successful politicians such as Victor Berger or Meyer London.[57]

By contrast, the left wing of the party encouraged workers to reject notions of bourgeois citizenship altogether because workers had "no country." Rather than counsel the need for calm, deliberative action in working-class men, Mary

Marcy emphasized the need for men to engage in active rebellion against authority in both its political and industrial forms. Men's fighting instinct should not be repressed but rather redirected to serve the goal of the class struggle and to bring about the kind of mass action that would be necessary to prevent U.S. involvement in war.[58] Reading Marcy's tracts likely evoked images of Big Bill Haywood rather than Morris Hillquit. Occupying a perhaps deliberately ambiguous position between the two camps was Eugene Debs, the quintessential icon of American socialism in the early twentieth century, who seemed to embody elements of both group's visions of manliness.[59]

Similar disagreements emerged over women's citizenship roles. As an antidote to the patriotic mother, some leading women Socialists offered an alternative vision of the redemptive mother who used her nurturing instincts and feminine sensibilities to preserve life and create a better world for her children. In contrast to anarchist and antiwar activist Emma Goldman, who questioned conventional constructions of motherhood, these Socialist women embraced the transformative power of motherly values in reforming government and in inspiring a cooperative rather than competitive ethos in international affairs. Women and mothers, suggested Meta Stern of the *New York Call*, had long been the "conserving, producing, peaceful element of the human species." But in the past most women's energies had been consumed in household tasks. The time had now come for "a new motherhood," which "reaches beyond the one little cradle, beyond the personal family and individual home. . . . [to] the children of city, state, nation, and world." She optimistically predicted that once women gained the vote and "the mother voice [was] . . . raised in international relations," war would end because "women will refuse to send their loved ones forth to murder and be murdered."[60]

Such sentiments were widespread among Socialists, who regularly urged women to "bring all your womanliness" and "all your motherliness" into "the war against wars." Socialist women were also encouraged to join the Woman's Peace Party or Anti-Enlistment League and to work for women's suffrage so that women could vote to end war.[61] When such activities provoked attacks by Theodore Roosevelt, Socialist women labeled him an "idiot" and particularly denounced his degradation of women as mere breeders. That many Socialist men shared this disgust was evidenced in their writings and in a cartoon of Robert Minor's dedicated to Roosevelt and entitled "Breed, Mother, Breed," which showed a woman releasing younger and younger sons into battle only to have them wind up as skulls and bones at the bottom of a dung heap (Figure 2.1).[62]

BREED, MOTHER, BREED! ROBERT MINOR

Dedicated to Theodore Roosevelt

Figure 2.1. *New York Call* (Socialist), August 8, 1915, s 2, 1. Preparedness activists like Theodore Roosevelt insisted that women's duty during wartime was to patriotically support the government and to bear and raise sons to be soldiers. Socialist cartoonist Robert Minor responded by offering this stinging visual satire and dedicating it to Roosevelt.

If in most respects this Socialist view of woman and her relationship to war was comparable to that of feminist pacifists, it also differed in some important ways. In particular, Socialists castigated leading women activists like Jane Addams for their naïveté about the economic roots of war and for being unprepared for the level of opposition they would face from economic interests as a result of their peace work. Because of the economic powers arrayed against peace, argued Socialists, women could end war only in co-operation with men from the Socialist and labor movements.[63] Kate Richards O'Hare underscored these themes in a play she wrote and performed with her husband on the Socialist lecture circuit throughout 1915–1916. The play commenced with a group of peasant women from a number of belliger-ent countries traveling to the United States in an attempt to convince the American government that it must cease sending gold and munitions to European powers because it was fueling the war. But the imposing figures of the American businessman, banker, and speculator dismissed the pleas of the women. The women, however, received assistance from a character called "Columbia" who represented American women. But Columbia could not reverse the wayward course of the country on her own; she sought help from a character named "America" who represented the male citizen. His sup-port was necessary, Columbia asserted, because "a government, like a home, must have both a father and a mother to be complete." Together, Columbia and America brought peace to Europe.[64]

O'Hare, a mother of four, thus emphasized the need to update, and to make more egalitarian, the traditional values of the Victorian family rather than to repudiate them. With some modification, family values could serve as an effective bulwark against the new militarist citizenship roles that prepared-ness activists were attempting to foist on the American people.[65] By contrast, the critiques of left-wing Socialists raised more fundamental questions about gender roles within the family, their suitability as models for a future society, and their relationship to war. Mary Marcy insisted that marriage was rooted in the property rights of men, who wanted sons to inherit their property. Because of the historic male interest in passing on their property to sons, unmarried mothers had typically been shunned while married women had too often been treated as the absolute property of their husbands.

But because of the need for soldiers created by the Great War, Marcy sug-gested, the "*morals* of the Capitalist Class changed overnight." Both mar-ried and unmarried women in Europe were now being urged to become "impregnated" by soldiers before they went to the front so as to ensure that they became "mothers of future sons for future armies." The "chastity of women [had] ceased to be a virtue" and child-bearing for both married and unmarried women was now viewed as the "noblest profession." She noted that European states had recently implemented a number of provisions for mothers' pensions that were available to both unmarried and married women. Rather than counsel women to return to the old values, Marcy suggested that working women needed to create a new morality that would ensure that they ended their subservience to either their husbands or the state. But they must also join with working men in the general wave of industrial strikes that would overthrow the bourgeois state and bourgeois morality, and end the perpetual state of war that the bourgeoisie encouraged.[66]

Mary Field, another regular writer for the *International Socialist Review*, argued that the war had clarified for women the "real meaning of their lives to the state." Women were viewed by state leaders as "breeding machines for soldiers" whose "bodies and their children belong no more to themselves than do the pigs in the stockyards." This revelation led Fields to the radical conclusion that women who hated war should demand "abortion as a right" because all military governments ultimately relied upon "fruitful and obedient women" to breed armies. For Field, female suffrage alone would not empower women or end war; women also needed control over their reproductive rights, the right to divorce, and the ability to support themselves economically without reliance on male relatives.[67]

If left-wing Socialists tended to diverge from the main body of Socialists in rejecting elements of the Victorian family, both groups nonetheless played an important role in attacking the gendered propaganda of preparedness activists. Yet the practical applications of their ideas led in different directions. Left-wing Socialists continued to promote the idea of general strike, and sought to encourage spontaneous worker rebellion through their efforts to discredit bourgeois morality. Those emphasizing political action, meanwhile, rallied behind the plans of Socialist Allan Benson, who sought to make foreign policy more subject to democratic checks and balances.

ALLAN BENSON AND THE CAMPAIGN
FOR A NATIONAL REFERENDUM ON WAR

A columnist for the Socialist paper, the *Appeal to Reason*, Benson enjoyed relatively little clout within Socialist leadership circles on the eve of the war. But Benson's plans for making foreign policy more democratic soon gained him temporary fame and the 1916 Socialist Party presidential nomination. A strong believer in women's suffrage, one aspect of Benson's plans emphasized the need for Socialists to push for the immediate enfranchisement of women so as to capitalize on their allegedly more pacifistic tendencies. Second, Benson championed a far-reaching plan for taking the power to declare war away from Congress and putting it directly in the hands of the American people. The best way to protect American working families, he ultimately believed, was to put the decision over peace or war directly in the hands of working-class men and women. "To strip the owning class of the war-making power would leave the world at peace," he argued, "though the private ownership of industry gave the owning class the desire for war." Concerned about the possibility of U.S. war both with Mexico and Europe, Benson began promoting his ideas in the Socialist press in the autumn of 1914. He first proposed an amendment to the Constitution that would replace Congress' power to declare war with a provision mandating that questions of U.S. involvement in war be determined by a direct referendum of all American citizens—men and women. Congress and the president, however, would retain the right to mobilize troops in the event of an invasion of the United States. Benson argued that "[t]he responsibility of making war is so great that it should be borne only by the people." Although some viewed the idea of a national referendum on war as impractical, Benson's supporters argued that it was in accord with widely held democratic ideals and would likely garner more widespread support from American workers than a general strike that would provoke widespread violence and threaten workers' livelihoods.[68]

Unsurprisingly, Benson's proposal was largely ignored by left-wing Socialists, but it won quick support from over one hundred Socialist locals. Other opposition, however, soon emerged from an unexpected source. The ever cautious Morris Hillquit thought the idea "wild" and unrealistic, arguing it would "only serve to embarrass the party." Benson in turn complained to Eugene Debs that Hillquit had "trained eels" on the Central Committee who were hindering the advancement of the war referendum motion. Debs publicly supported the referendum idea, arguing that it was "absolutely logical and unassailable," but he also privately warned Benson that he was becoming "splenetic . . . toward those who do not agree with your program."[69]

Armed with Debs's endorsement, Benson continued to promote his proposal, mostly by responding to criticisms of it in the Socialist press. Some, for example, wondered what would happen if the general population proved more hawkish than Socialists anticipated and voted for war. Would antiwar activists then be obligated to support the war and give military service to their country? And if women were given the franchise on such an important issue would they be required to serve militarily alongside men? At first, Benson argued that both men and women who voted for war would be responsible for fighting it, and would be the first conscripted. But he then reassured people that he had not "the slightest idea that there are or ever will be a thousand such women in the United States." Shortly thereafter, chivalry got the better of Benson and he proposed a new plan in which only men would be at the front of the line when it came to military service. Men who voted for war, argued Benson, would be automatically enlisted in the military. If men were still needed, then the ranks of the military should be filled with men who voted against war by "lot and muster." Third in line for military service would be women who voted for war, but they should be conscripted only if "war would not have been declared without their votes." Finally, Benson insisted that under "no circumstances should a woman who voted against war be required to perform military services."[70] Benson's tortured thinking on the issue was quite revealing for it demonstrated that—despite supporting women's enfranchisement—he continued to view women's citizenship roles as different than those of men's. In an ideal world, strong working-class men and nurturing working-class women would prevent war. But in the event that a country's citizens democratically voted for war, men still had greater military responsibilities than women. Indeed, Benson implied that the future sanctity of the family might depend upon protecting pacifistic women from military duty.

Benson, suggested James Weinstein, "so caught the mood of the [Socialist Party] membership" with his war referendum proposal that he won the nomination for the Socialist candidate for president in 1916 over James Maurer and Arthur Le Sueur, "both of whom were better known and better qualified for the honor."[71] That Benson's war referendum proposals proved so popular and became such an important part of the 1916 Socialist Party platform must be understood against the backdrop of the increasing tensions between Wilson and Socialists over the administration's neutrality and preparedness policies.

CONTESTING WILSON

Since Wilson declared U.S. neutrality only shortly after the outbreak of war, Socialists at first found little to criticize about the president's foreign policies apart from his failure to be more proactive in promoting peace. Yet two interrelated aspects of Wilson's foreign policies increasingly concerned Socialists. First, they complained that Wilson was allowing un-neutral patterns of trade and credit to develop between the United States and the belligerents.

Specifically, U.S. trade and credit to Britain increased exponentially after the outbreak of war, while exports of both goods and capital to Germany plummeted. Second, they increasingly criticized Wilson's responses to submarine warfare as both pro-British and procapitalist. These concerns in turn led many Socialists to define preparedness and national security in significantly different ways than Wilson.

From Wilson's perspective, the un-neutral trading patterns that developed between 1914 and 1916 were justified both by international law and by the realities of the wartime situation. Under international law, a belligerent could buy military and commercial goods as well as foodstuffs from a neutral power at its own risk. The lion's share of American trade, credit, and loans went to Britain after the outbreak of war because Britain had successfully established an informal but highly effective blockade of continental Europe. Wilson's own Secretary of State, Williams Jennings Bryan, tried to discourage at least the loans to Allied countries on the grounds that "money is the worst of all contrabands because it commands everything else." Wilson, however, argued that for the United States to ban loans to the Allies, or to curb the trade with Britain artificially, would in itself be an un-neutral act. Although Britain committed many violations of neutral law by seizing contraband from U.S. ships, halting American trade with neutral Denmark and Holland, arming British merchant ships, mining the North Sea, and flying neutral flags (including that of the United States) on its ships to avoid attack, Wilson ultimately believed that these violations were less serious than the ones committed by German submarines.[72]

Germany first began using its new fleet of U-2 submarines in retaliation for the British blockade of Europe. On February 4, 1915, German leaders declared a war zone around Britain and urged all neutral ships to stay out of the zone because of the danger of mistaken identity. Neutral passengers were also warned to stay off enemy ships. But Wilson proclaimed that Germany would be held to strict account for any loss of American life or property. Under international law, most of it written before the invention of the submarine, attack ships were required to warn commercial vessels of an impending attack so that civilians could be evacuated. Submarines found it difficult to adhere to this law because they were so slow-moving above the water; once they surfaced, armed British merchant ships rammed and sank them. Critics argued that international law governing freedom of the seas was outdated and failed to take into account the special needs of submarines. Secretary Bryan suggested a compromise whereby Germany would abandon unannounced submarine attacks and the British would disarm their merchant vessels. But when Britain refused to seriously consider the proposal, Wilson abandoned the compromise and even accepted the British claim that its armed merchant ships were not in violation of international law because they were only "defensively armed." Even more surprisingly from the perspective of its critics, the Wilson administration chose not to ban American citizens from traveling on "defensively" armed British merchant ships despite widespread claims that such ships regularly carried munitions in their holds.

German U-boats sank over ninety ships in early 1915, but killed only one American passenger. The stakes for Americans dramatically increased, however, when on May 7, 1915, a German U-boat sunk the British luxury liner the *Lusitania*, killing 1,198 passengers, 128 of them American. In the wake of the disaster, Wilson demanded that Germany renounce submarine warfare, something it was clearly unprepared to do. When German leaders argued that the *Lusitania* carried munitions, Wilson dismissed this information as unimportant and began promoting the need for an expansion of the U.S. Navy. Germany expressed regret and offered to pay indemnities for the *Lusitania* disaster, but the issue of submarine warfare remained an open source of contention between the two countries. Historians suggest that the *Lusitania* affair marked a turning point in the war, because after this date public opinion shifted toward the Allies.[73]

Yet for Wilson's opponents on the Left, the *Lusitania* marked another kind of turning point: they became convinced that Wilson's policies were insufficiently neutral and were unnecessarily driving the country toward war. For the German-American and Irish-American immigrant Left press, Wilson's handling of the incident demonstrated that the president was pro-British. As the *Irish World and American Industrial Liberator* explained, "A British ship, which as an auxiliary of the British navy, is virtually a warship, is sunk by a German submarine as she is carrying war material to the British army. Some Americans who are on board of her after having been warned of the danger to which they are exposing themselves lose their lives. . . . No one outside of a lunatic asylum would consider the killing of such citizens sufficient justification to plunge the nation into war." Yet by demanding that the Germans renounce submarine warfare, suggested the *Irish World*, the president was following just such a path. "The supreme duty of the hour," the editors insisted, was "to frustrate the pro-British attempt to stampede the country [into war]." The *Gaelic American* argued that the *Lusitania* constituted a "floating arsenal" and placed blame for passenger deaths on both the British and U.S. governments who should never have put "non-combatants and children on board an auxiliary cruiser of the British navy." German Americans reacted in a more muted fashion due to concerns about charges of disloyalty, but they also emphasized that German actions were justified by the long-standing starvation blockade of Europe. Both the German- and Irish-American press urged the president to be more evenhanded in his policies toward Britain and Germany.[74]

The Socialist press incorporated these perspectives but added another dimension; it claimed that Wilson's policies both before and after the crisis revealed not only that he was pro-British but also that he was procapitalist. Morris Hillquit, for example, expressed admiration for the president's initially calm handling of the *Lusitania* situation but emphasized that submarine warfare was not really a threat to U.S. workers; rather it was the "parasitic classes" who traversed the seas during the war, either for purposes of profit or for their own leisure, who were vulnerable to U-boat attacks. The *Appeal to Reason* puzzled, "Why, except for the sake of precedent, should Mr. Wilson have insisted upon the right of American citizens to travel through the war zone upon British ammunition ships?" In an opinion piece in the *Appeal*, C. B. Hoffman asked his readers, "Are you going to die in a trench or rot in a hospital because a few American nabobs counting on your stupid patriotism, braggingly risked their lives in the pursuit of their private pleasures?" Cartoonist Robert Minor of the *New York Call* perhaps best captured this mood of class dissonance among Socialists with a cartoon that showed Wilson conferring with an overweight munitions shipper while telling a muscular and concerned worker to "Be Prepared to Go to War to Defend Your Right to Travel in Europe This Summer"—a leisure pursuit clearly reserved for the wealthy during this era (Figure 2.2).[75]

Yet *New York Call* writers were not as tough on Wilson and praised him for having a cooler response to the crisis than "fire eaters like Roosevelt" and the "hysterical war-mad capitalist press." They even defended Wilson's widely derided remarks, issued shortly after the *Lusitania* incident, about being "too proud to fight" a war with Germany over submarine attacks. The editors suggested that those in the mainstream press who sneered at the comments apparently favored descending instead to "the level of saloon brawlers" when it came to international affairs. To the editors, Wilson's vacillation in the wake of the affair was consonant with their ideas about "social man." The president demonstrated a capacity for calm, deliberate reasoning during times of crisis that had helped prevent immediate U.S. intervention in the conflict. Responding to calls on the political right demanding that the president defend "national honor," women writers of the *New York Call* commented that "[w]e consider national honor a pompous, empty phrase since we know how our

WOODROW SAYS: By ROBERT MINOR

"Be Prepared to Go to War to Defend Your Right to Travel In
Europe This Summer."

Figure 2.2. *New York Call* (Socialist), July 25, 1915, s 2, 1. This cartoon poked fun
at the idea that U.S. national security interests were really at stake in the German
sinking of the British ship the *Lusitania*. It is also a good example of how
Socialists reversed the gender ridicule of preparedness activists. The skeptical
worker is portrayed as more large muscled and masculine than either Wilson or
the munitions shipper.

nation and every warring nation is and was before the war steeped in national dishonor." They suggested that "there is no thinking woman who does not know that to let the sinking of the *Lusitania* plunge us into war is a fearful ... crime."[76]

Yet if Socialists were understandably happy that Wilson rather than Roosevelt was in office at the time the *Lusitania* was sunk, they nonetheless worried that Wilson was also increasingly falling prey to efforts by big business interests to drive the country into war. Individually, Socialists proposed policies that they believed were more neutral than those of the president. Victor Berger, for example, argued that true neutrality called for strong rules against the food blockade of continental Europe as well as an embargo of arms and munitions to all parties. Benson supported proposals to prevent Americans from traveling on belligerent ships.[77] Against this backdrop, the Socialist Party National Executive Committee met to formally adopt an antiwar program.

Much dissension reigned at the committee meeting, held in May 1915, but the committee finally passed both an Anti-War Manifesto and a Peace Program. The manifesto clearly reflected the tenor of the hour, emphasizing that "No disaster, however appalling ... justifies the slaughter of nations and the devastation of countries." It called upon the "people of the United States" to "throttle all efforts to draw this country into the dangerous paths of international quarrels, imperialism, militarism and war." The peace program included many of the ideas that Socialists had promoted widely during the preceding months, albeit sometimes in muted or altered form. For example, the program emphasized industrial democracy as a major goal on the grounds that achievement of worker control over the means of production would eliminate the economic causes of war. Following the lead of Allan Benson, it called for more democratic controls over foreign policy. The extension of the franchise to women and universal disarmament "as speedily as possible" were also important components of the program. A related amendment decreed that any Socialist elected to public office who voted for war or war appropriations would be expelled from the party. The plan also recommended peace terms without annexations or indemnities, as well as calling for the self-determination of colonies and an international parliament, planks that preceded similar proposals by Woodrow Wilson and the Bolsheviks.[78]

Yet if some of the Socialist Party goals delineated in the 1915 program anticipated those of Wilson, the party proved distinctive in its emphasis on the economic causes of war, its insistence on industrial democracy as essential to guaranteeing peace and the future security of workers, its demand for total international disarmament as "speedily as possible," and its platforms for democratic controls over foreign policy. The emphasis on these demands signaled that for Socialists the major threat to U.S. national security was internal rather than external. It came from the business and militarist classes who unnecessarily sought to drive the country into war rather than from German U-boats. In this respect the comprehensive peace agenda of the party differed significantly from that of Wilson.

The chasm between Wilson and the majority wing of the Socialist Party widened when Wilson announced his support for a modest preparedness program in early November 1915. Opposed to a "great standing army," on the grounds that it was "undemocratic," the president nonetheless asked for a $500,000 naval expansion and an increase and reorganization of ground forces. To Edith Galt Wilson he confided that he believed such a program was necessary because the U.S. armed forces were so "tiny" and "so scattered" they would be "unable to do anything effective" to meet a German threat. Wilson also expressed concern about the ability of the United States to defend the Western hemisphere and to protect the integrity of the Monroe Doctrine from foreign aggression. Yet in publicly promoting his preparedness package, suggests Ross Kennedy, the president emphasized not so much the immediate threat of German submarine warfare but American exceptionalism. The United States, argued Wilson, had been "born into the world to do mankind service" and to act in the cause of "justice and righteousness and peace." In the case of World War I, this meant defending the rights of neutrals to trade peacefully. By arming to defend its shipping and "honor," the United States would also be "standing for the rights of mankind."[79]

Apparently swayed by Wilson's exceptionalist rhetoric, a few Socialists chose to support Wilson's preparedness program. For example, Upton Sinclair and Charles Edward Russell embraced some of the president's proposals, arguing that the time had come for the United States to develop a democratic and pragmatic preparedness program that would protect the country from German autocracy. Yet the majority of the party remained strongly opposed to military preparedness. Eugene Debs argued that a "large standing army, a powerful navy, and a stupendous military armament such as President Wilson with the backing of Wall Street proposes, means a military autocracy . . . and if the American people acquiesce in such an obviously plutocratic program they must not be surprised if other nations treat it as a challenge to war." When Upton Sinclair solicited Debs's signature for a petition demanding a "democratic defense," Debs refused to sign, arguing that "any kind of a military establishment that may be instituted under the prevailing system and under the present government will be controlled by the ruling class and its chief function will be to keep the working class in slavery."[80]

Others emphasized the economic costs of Wilson's preparedness program for workers. "Mr. Workingman," suggested the *Appeal to Reason*, "Get Ready to Pay the Bill." It suggested that the government would soon "rivet" on workingmen a "burden of debt and taxation" to pay for the increase in military expenditures. Although the paper conceded that the prosperity of the Wilson years had been created in part by increased military orders from both Britain and the U.S. government, they argued that war profits never trickled down to the workingman but were instead enjoyed only by a few business leaders. True prosperity for workers could be achieved only through democratic control of the means of production.[81] When a wave of preparedness parades rolled across the country and inspired a creative flourish of patriotic spectacle in the spring of 1916, Socialists denounced them as "monstrous fraud[s]," arguing that many employers forced their workers to participate.[82]

Despite continued widespread opposition from Socialists and other pacifists to preparedness, Congress passed the National Defense Act in May 1916 granting Wilson most of his requests, including an increase in the size of the regular army and the creation of training camps similar to those used by General Wood in Plattsburg. Significantly, however, the bill did not mandate universal military training. Another bill dramatically increasing naval appropriations passed in August.[83]

With preparedness now the law of the land, attention shifted to the presidential election. Not surprisingly, foreign policy issues played a dominant role in the campaigns of all the presidential candidates. Wilson's campaign team coined the slogan "He Kept Us Out of War," even while Wilson emphasized that he was now prepared, if necessary, to use military force to defend "national honor" and to protect the rights of neutrals to trade. Wilson's frequent use of the phrase national honor led the *Appeal to Reason* to query "What is this honor, anyhow?" The question was a good one for it was not always clear what Wilson meant by the term. In the wake of the *Lusitania* incident, national honor had meant being "too proud to fight." But now Wilson implied that national honor, and implicitly national security, meant a "moral obligation" to protect the capitalist profits not only of American businessmen but of capitalists throughout the world.[84]

The Socialist Party platform of 1916 demonstrated how significantly the party now diverged from Wilson in its approaches to both preparedness and national security. The section of the platform on foreign policy began with an analysis of the war, claiming that "[f]undamentally, it was the desire and effort of competing national groups of capitalists to grasp and control the opportunities for profitable investment" that caused it. Similarly, the present preparedness effort in the United States was fueled by U.S. capitalists who "sought to fasten upon this country the crushing burden of militarism" for the sake of their own profits. The platform insisted that "Not until the capitalist system of production is destroyed and replaced by industrial democracy will wars for markets cease and international peace be securely established."[85]

Denouncing military preparedness as based on the false premise that the United States faced a foreign invasion, the platform instead called for "that sort of social preparedness which expresses itself in better homes, better bodies, and better minds," all of which were vital to real national defense. The greatest threat to national security, it again insisted, was not internal but external. The capitalist class, the party predicted, would try to drive the country into war for the sake of its own profits. The best way to prevent war was to oppose increased military expenditures and to instead focus on making foreign policy more democratic. The platform not only endorsed Benson's call for a national referendum vote on questions of war and peace but also asked that the power to create foreign policies and conduct diplomatic negotiations be lodged in Congress rather than the office of the president. The platform also called for independence for the Philippines and, as discussed previously, demanded the abandonment of the Monroe Doctrine because it had changed from a "safeguard to a menace." Capitalists, they insisted, used the doctrine to promote interference in the Caribbean.[86]

Although Benson fared poorly in the election, historians of the Socialist Party caution against seeing his vote tallies as a mandate on the Socialist Party's antiwar program. In contrast to Debs, who tallied over 900,00 votes in 1912, Benson totaled only 585,113 in 1916. But historians cite several reasons for doubting that these tallies demonstrate opposition to the party's antiwar programs. First, Benson was a relative unknown by comparison with Debs and was disliked among many in the party leadership. Second, some who fervently believed in the party's antiwar agenda nonetheless switched their vote to Wilson because they doubted that Benson could win and believed that Wilson was more likely to keep the country out of war than Hughes. Third, historians point out that Socialist vote tallies in local elections remained high throughout the war and often surpassed prewar vote tallies. Finally, they note that party membership was on the rise throughout the period from 1916–1919, suggesting that the rank and file supported the party's antiwar agenda even while failing to embrace Allan Benson.[87]

CONCLUSION

Historian Thomas Knock, in his classic book *To End All Wars*, emphasized the overlap between the foreign policy programs of the Wilson administration and American Left groups such as the Socialist Party. Similarly he highlighted the decisions of a small group of prowar Socialist leaders to support Wilson's policies, as well as illuminating the likelihood that many Socialists voted for Wilson in 1916.[88] Yet it seems equally important to recognize how fundamentally the platform and programs of the majority wing of the Socialist Party diverged from those of the Wilson administration by the time of the presidential election in 1916. By this date, Wilson's sense of American exceptionalism had led him to adopt a quite broad definition of U.S. national security that included defending not only American but apparently all neutral shipping, upholding international law, and protecting the Western hemisphere from foreign invasion. Wilson had also begun to promote the idea that an international organization of nations could uphold peace through collective security. Although the president did not embrace conscription until after the United States entered the war, his support for the National Defense Act signified that he supported military training for American men and agreed with preparedness activists that military service was an obligation of male citizenship.

To some degree, U.S. Socialists shared Wilson's sense of American exceptionalism, as was evidenced in their ambitious 1915 comprehensive peace program that anticipated Wilsonian concepts such as no annexations and no indemnities, self-determination for colonial peoples, and peace through international organizations. But perhaps what was most exceptional about American Socialists when compared to their European counterparts was not what they shared in common with Wilson but the way they stayed the course in opposing Wilson's drift toward U.S. involvement in the war. No doubt this was due in part to the relative geographic isolation of the United States, which in turn afforded American Socialists the luxury of endlessly debating the war in a way that had not been possible for European Socialists. But collectively U.S. Socialists also developed a compelling critique of Wilson's ideas about national security that strengthened their resolve to oppose the war. From the perspective of American Socialists, Wilson's definition of national security was not class-neutral but rather was predicated on the interests of the capitalist class. If U.S. workers were placed at the center of the analysis of U.S. national security interests, then it became clear that U.S. intervention in World War I would not serve the interests of the majority of Americans. Most Socialists supported war in the event of an invasion but, in contrast to Wilson, they were fundamentally opposed to becoming involved in the war for the sake of neutral shipping. Workers, they argued, had no responsibility to die in order to protect capitalist profits or wealthy travelers. Following from this, workers had very little stake in defending the sanctity of international law because this law had been written by the ruling classes of the major imperialist nations to serve their own financial needs. Although Socialists acknowledged that workers sometimes benefited economically from the expansion of munitions industries, they insisted that only democratic control of industry would ensure workers the just fruits of their labor and prevent the endless cycle of wars caused by the capitalist pursuit of profit.

This line of thinking in turn led Socialists to the conclusion that the greatest threat to U.S. security was not German U-boats but U.S. militarist and business interests. To counteract this threat, U.S. Socialists not only rallied against preparedness but also promoted far more direct forms of democratic control over foreign policy than did Wilson. Absent these kinds of democratic controls over governments, they believed, international organizations of nation-states would make very little real difference in ensuring the security of the world's workers. Socialist ideas about democratic controls over foreign policy in turn linked to their ideas about both male and female citizenship obligations. In contrast to preparedness activists, most Socialists vehemently denied that military service was an obligation of male citizenship and that breeding sons for war was a prerequisite for female citizenship. Only in cases of invasion or in the event that workers were allowed to vote on the decision for war, they argued, were men required to militarily serve their country and women to sacrifice their sons for it. In these ideas lay the roots of the Socialist Party's later insistence that dissent during wartime was patriotic. These critiques also underlay the later insistence by the party that conscription was unconstitutional because it violated the Thirteenth Amendment that prohibited involuntary servitude.

Given its minority status in American politics, the Socialist Party possessed little power to unilaterally hold back the tide pushing for war in American society. Yet Socialist ideas about citizenship responsibilities, preparedness, and national security became an important component of antimilitarist and often anti-imperialist working-class subcultures that made it difficult for either Wilson or Samuel Gompers to align labor solidly behind the war effort, as we shall see in the following chapters.

3 Antiwar Cultures of the AFL, the Debate over Preparedness, and the Gompers Turnabout

IN THE AUTUMN OF 1915, the Seattle Central Labor Council (SCLC), an AFL affiliate, considered an unusual issue at its weekly meetings. Ordinarily such meetings were dominated by discussions of how to promote union organizing campaigns, resolve jurisdictional disputes between local unions, or assist in area strike activities. But during September, students from the University of Washington testified before the council on the introduction of compulsory military training into the university curriculum. E. P. Marsh, president of the Washington State Federation of Labor, argued that the issue fell within the purview of the SCLC and state labor movement because state universities were "for the great masses" and must be "democratic in fact as well as in theory if we are to have a citizenry worthy of its name." In part, Marsh objected to compulsory military training because it was an unfair burden to working-class students, who had to pay for uniforms as well as incur the cost of the extra course. But more importantly, he argued that military training instilled "a spirit of blind obedience," deadened the "initiative faculty," and bred "the spirit of militarism." The current European war, he argued, might have been prevented if past generations of European men had not been made "compulsory students of the grim god of war." Reiterating arguments made by other area labor activists and Socialists, Marsh insisted that the need for military preparedness in the United States was mostly "bunk," inspired by businessmen who stood to gain from increased munitions sales.[1]

Seattle Central Labor Council President Hulet Wells added another dimension, emphasizing that compulsory military training would result in a standing army "trained in the science of destroying life, ready to the hand of the employing class if ever an industrial crisis comes." Europe, he insisted, posed no real threat to national security. Rather, "[o]ur enemies are here in the land we live in—the country that ought to be ours but is not." Business groups sought a larger military under the guise of preparedness in order to perpetuate more crimes like the Ludlow massacre and to take the "fruits of industry" from labor which "produces all."[2]

Reinforcing Marsh's and Wells's viewpoints in the local labor press were the comments of Irish labor leader James Larkin who visited Seattle in September at the invitation, and with the sponsorship, of the Seattle labor movement. Under a banner headline announcing "Irish Orator Flays 'Em All," the *Seattle Union Record* highlighted Larkin's belief that the "high state of armed preparedness" within European countries ensured that they would "fly at each others' throats when the contending capitalists gave the word." By contrast, Irish workers had refused to go to war on behalf of imperialist Britain and had issued a proclamation encouraging all workers to "lay down their arms and refuse to fight." Workers in the United States, Larkin insisted, should use the current favorable situation to launch a general strike rather than supporting the war campaigns of the capitalist class.[3]

Although the debate over military training at first engaged mostly male trade unionists and labor leaders, women's auxiliaries such as the Label League joined the discussion when city officials proposed compulsory military training for boys and nurses training and a course in hygiene for girls, both at the high school level. At meetings and on the women's page of the *Seattle Union Record*, affiliated women disputed claims that military service encouraged male fitness and instead insisted on outdoor games and athletic activities in the gymnasium as essential to the health of both boys and girls. Dr. Anna Louise Strong of the school board addressed the women's auxiliary of the Carpenters Union and highlighted studies demonstrating how military training allegedly encouraged a one-sided kind of development that promoted both physical and mental defects. In an effort to refute the arguments of women who had written to mainstream papers supporting military training, contributors to the *Seattle Union Record*'s women's page emphasized that military training was a moral danger because it placed an emphasis on "might and not right" and violated the commandment "Thou Shalt Not Kill." True patriotism, they argued, was bred of good character rather than military training. Compellingly, contributors also emphasized that "We should be unalterably opposed to military drill in our public schools because it would join in close partnership the finest thing that American civilization has given to humanity—our free public schools, the hope of democracy—with war, the most barbaric, inhuman and un-Christian system ever foisted upon a struggling world."[4]

The campaign against military training in the schools was but one part of an ambitious antiwar and anti-preparedness program promoted by the Seattle Central Labor Council that often seemed to displace more traditional trade union issues on the council's agenda from 1914–1917. Far from unique, the SCLC cooperated with a host of other municipal labor councils as well as national AFL unions in an effort to thwart what it viewed as a headlong rush toward war promoted by the business class and, to some degree, by the Wilson administration.[5] Such activities shed critical light on a neglected dimension of public opinion during the Great War. In particular, they illuminate the strong antimilitarist and antiwar impulses coursing through diverse working-class subcultures and institutions in the period prior to U.S. belligerency. The alternative forms of "working-class Americanism" promoted by local and constituent AFL trade unions in turn posed a challenge to Gompers's efforts to align the AFL behind Wilson's foreign policies.[6]

This chapter explores the debate within the AFL over Wilson's policies toward the European war between 1914–1917. Initially, the AFL leadership joined a chorus of other groups in opposing both U.S. involvement in the European conflict and the preparedness movement. But Gompers's position on the war shifted seemingly in sync with that of the Wilson administration and, by 1916, he had emerged as an advocate of preparedness and voluntary military training as well as a strong supporter of the president's neutrality policies. Yet antiwar cultures within the AFL continued to flourish in 1915–1916, as four case studies of the Seattle Central Labor Council, Chicago Federation of Labor, United Mine Workers, and International Ladies' Garment Workers' Union demonstrate, setting the stage for a showdown between the AFL leadership and dissidents.

INITIAL RESPONSES OF THE AFL LEADERSHIP TO THE WAR IN EUROPE

Following the outbreak of war in Europe in the summer of 1914, the AFL Executive Council joined other labor groups and trade unions throughout the country in issuing a strong condemnation of the conflict that emphasized its class roots. The official AFL proclamation emphasized that the "greed and commercialism" of the business class caused the war; yet it was working people who inevitably bore the "brunt of war" since they were the ones who did most of the fighting, paid most of the war taxes, and "suffered most from the disorganization of industry." Soldiers, insisted AFL leaders, should be pitied rather than admired because they were mere "pawns" in the games of military leaders. AFL leaders emphasized strict neutrality on the part of the U.S. labor movement so that it could serve as an effective mediator among

European labor movements and play a leading role in reviving labor international after the war.[7]

Yet AFL President Samuel Gompers reversed himself and began advocating a limited form of preparedness in the aftermath of the *Lusitania* affair. In part, Gompers's embrace of preparedness reflected his changing ideas about the war. A British immigrant with pro-British sympathies, he agreed with Wilson that German submarine attacks were a crime against humanity and a greater threat to U.S. national security than Britain's blockade of the European coast. The United States, he argued, might ultimately be forced to respond to German attacks. As his devoted personal secretary Florence Thorne explained, Gompers "recounted vividly damages to our shipping and losses of lives by German submarines" but was "quite oblivious to Great Britain's invasion on the high seas." She believed that the AFL president was "personally committed to aid Great Britain." Gompers was also likely influenced by his long-standing procapitalist belief that exports were vital to the economic well-being of U.S. workers, an assumption that led him to support limited forms of U.S. imperialism in the early twentieth century. Since Britain was the most important trade partner of the United States, it was vital that trade between the two continue even during war. Finally, Gompers was also influenced by his close observation of the growing partnership between labor and the government in Britain in promoting the war effort. Gompers watched the evolution of this partnership with interest and increasingly believed that U.S. labor would be better served by cooperating with the Wilson administration in its preparedness efforts rather than by opposing them.[8]

One of the first public signs that Gompers's thinking about the war was undergoing a transformation came in the autumn of 1915, when Secretary of War Leonard Wood invited Gompers to attend a Plattsburg training camp. Gompers declined to attend but not for the reasons one might expect. He concurred with Wood that "many indications" marked a "decline in national virility" and the need for improved military training for American men, but he objected to the camps because of their educational qualifications and elitist character. He hinted, however, that he might be more supportive of the camps if they were reorganized on a democratic basis. Wood subsequently met with Gompers several times and worked out broader qualifications for camp attendance. Gompers, in return, gave his support for a campaign to gain increased appropriations from Congress for the training camps.[9]

By the winter of 1916, Gompers had fully shifted his public pronouncements about preparedness from that of opposition to that of support. In a series of articles in the *American Federationist* in the winter of 1916, the AFL president publicly embraced the preparedness cause, insisting that preparedness was something very different from militarism. Preparedness, argued Gompers, "must be the attitude of a nation toward all relations of life and all lines of action and development"—including both industrial and military development. He insisted that while preparedness was designed to serve the needs of the people, militarism developed when special interests seized control of national preparedness movements and used them for their own narrow purposes. Labor, he suggested, must participate in all preparedness agencies and campaigns in order to ensure that they were in accord with "democratic ideals." Labor should welcome military preparedness and military training so long as they were administered in a voluntary and democratic fashion, because "war is a test of physical fitness and the organization of material resources. The nation that has failed in these will pay dearly in the perils of war."[10]

Gompers's decision to embrace preparedness was doubtless one reason why the Wilson administration chose to appoint him to the Council of National Defense—an organization created to prepare the country for possible intervention in the war—in October of 1916. But also important was the paradoxical growth in antiwar sentiment within the ranks of the AFL during this same period. The strong oppositional currents within labor in turn made efficiency experts like Howard Coffin as well as Secretary of Labor William B. Wilson worry about industrial unrest and opposition to conscription in the event of war.[11] Antiwar and antimilitarist activism within the AFL could gain momentum even at a time when Gompers and other AFL leaders were promoting preparedness because of its decentralized and federated structure.

Although Gompers generally controlled the executive council of the AFL and usually succeeded in pushing his agenda through the AFL conventions, constituent unions and AFL municipal bodies had traditionally maintained a good deal of independence within the Federation. In the late nineteenth century, many municipal trades councils were affiliated with the Knights of Labor. Since such councils were composed of workers from a variety of industrial fields, they often manifested a strong class as opposed to craft consciousness that resonated well with the goals of the Knights of Labor. When the Knights declined, municipal councils often affiliated with the AFL, but frequently found themselves in conflict with the leadership of the AFL, which gave more powers and voting weight to the national and international unions. Most national and international unions enjoyed proportional voting power within the AFL based on their membership. By contrast municipal and state bodies received only one vote each in the AFL convention. Yet municipal labor bodies compensated for their lack of voting power within the AFL by building strong bases of local support and becoming centers of working-class community and political activity. The AFL leadership enjoyed little control over the political and antiwar activities of these groups and until late 1916 seemed to pay little attention to them. AFL leaders were more concerned with antiwar activism within the leading national and international unions, but until early 1917 allowed these unions the same independence on the war question that they exercised on most issues.[12]

Dozens, and perhaps hundreds, of municipal labor councils became active in antiwar agitation during the years from 1914–1917, and no single account can adequately convey the richness and diversity of the political subcultures that developed surrounding these activities. The Seattle Central Labor Council offers an example of a small and relatively homogenous local AFL affiliate whose pacifist agenda was shaped, at least in part, by Socialists who were active in the council. The Chicago Federation of Labor, by contrast, was dominated by Irish-American activists who were mostly non-Socialist. It represented a large and diverse, as well as multiracial and multiethnic, population. The United Mine Workers and International Ladies' Garment Workers' Union offer examples of two contrasting types of national unions active in antiwar politics.

THE SEATTLE CENTRAL LABOR COUNCIL

Among the striking features of the Seattle Central Labor Council during the World War I era was the fluctuating nature of its membership; the council represented between nine thousand and sixty thousand workers depending on the ebbs and flows of local organizing efforts. Since Seattle was a major shipping center for the natural resources of the Northwest, shipyard unions were disproportionately represented within the Seattle Labor Council, along with lumber workers and workers from the metal and building trades. The SCLC competed vigorously with the IWW for the loyalty of many of these workers. Many of the council's leaders dabbled in Socialist politics, including SCLC presidents Hulet Wells and Thomas Bolton and secretaries James Duncan and Robert Bridges. Many women active in the council, such as Dr. Anna Louise Strong, also participated in local Socialist politics.[13]

By contrast, although foreign labor leaders and revolutionaries often visited the council, immigrant Left activists did not play a dominant role in the leadership of the Seattle council because the labor movement was not as ethnically diverse as in Chicago. About two-thirds of the white population of

Seattle was native-born or British Canadian, while the other one-third was predominantly comprised of "second stage" Scandinavian immigrants who had first settled in the Midwest before moving to Seattle. African Americans made up only about 1 percent of the population. Seattle was also home to a substantial but isolated Japanese population that was systematically excluded from the union movement. Indeed, the Seattle labor movement originated in the Chinese exclusion movement of the 1880s and subsequently made Asian exclusion one of its keystones, arguing that the immigration of "coolies" would undermine white labor standards.[14]

The homogenous nature of the membership of the Seattle Central Labor Council, and its exclusionist traditions, encouraged a somewhat "herrenvolk" vision of its trade union mission that sometimes bled over into its work in advancing democratic rights for workers and in promoting a worker-centered foreign policy. U.S. labor historian David Roediger has used the term "herrenvolk republicanism" to describe the effort of nineteenth century white male workers to claim democratic rights and privileges for themselves while denying it to African Americans. "Whiteness," suggests Roediger, became a critical component of white working-class identity.[15] To some extent, this generalization also holds for World War I–era Seattle. Although the SCLC was more open to the participation of women than most labor groups, Asians were clearly defined as the "other," against which the interests of white labor must be defined. For example, the Label League, one of the women's groups cited above who rallied against militarism, was primarily charged with the task of visiting area businesses and determining whether they deserved to be assigned the union label and frequented by area unionists. Race clearly became a category of exclusion undergirding their work. In a report on area laundries, the league noted that union laundries not only demonstrated superior working conditions but used "a hose with a tiny automatic sprinkle" in place of the "Chinamen's mouth-squirting process to dampen the laundry." The council also continued to favor immigration restriction during the World War I era, arguing that the United States had "long ago ceased to be a haven of refuge for anyone." Far better, suggested the editors of the council's paper, to "Let the Europeans and Asiatics stay in their own countries and solve their problems of proper distribution of the world production there while we are trying to do the same thing here."[16]

This kind of racialized and defensive thinking could in turn sometimes lead to conspiracy theories when it came to U.S. war policies, as when the Seattle Council passed a resolution shortly after the United States entered the war claiming that conscription had been enacted primarily to ensure that businessmen could replace union workers with "coolie labor." Significantly, the resolution did not—in contrast to past measures—oppose all military conscription but instead demanded guarantees that there "shall be absolutely no relaxation of the present restrictions on Oriental immigration."[17]

But if the long tradition of Asiatic exclusion in the Western labor movement sometimes led Seattle labor activists to direct their anger over the war at Asians, in most cases they reserved their venom for the business class and for Wilson, whom they believed lay behind the preparedness effort and push for U.S. intervention in the European war. When war first broke out, the Seattle Council called it an "international crime" and, using arguments that paralleled those of some leaders of the national Socialist Party, argued that "one reason for the suspicious eagerness with which the rulers of all these nations have entered into hostilities is because of the universal industrial unrest and the growing spirit of working class solidarity which, if unchecked, threatens the present ruling class." The council insisted that the war could be of no possible benefit to workers "whose enemies are not the workers of other nations, but the exploiting class of every nation." The council pledged its full "efforts against any attempt to draw our country into a foreign war."[18]

As preparedness activists began to mobilize in late 1914 and early 1915, the SCLC rallied against them. Their efforts included not only opposing military training in the schools but also rallying against increases in the state militia and national defense budgets. Headlining these activities, the local labor paper noted that "Sane Men and Women Unite in Decrying Strident Howling for Larger Army and Navy—If European War Teaches Anything It Teaches That the Armed Nation is the Attacked Nation—Sanity Needed."[19] At first, the council primarily blamed the business class, whom they later dubbed "paytriots," for promoting unnecessary preparedness programs and seeking to drive the country into war for the sake of their own profits. But in the aftermath of the *Lusitania* affair, SCLC leaders and the local labor press, in contrast to Gompers, became increasingly critical of the Wilson administration. Comparing Wilson with his Secretary of State William Jennings Bryan, they argued that Bryan deserved praise for emphasizing arbitration rather than ultimatums following the sinking of the *Lusitania*. Wilson, by contrast, was "too much the schoolmaster to sense the possibilities of new methods and has held to the time dishonored methods of the application of force to international misunderstandings" while putting false notions of "national 'honor'" before "the lives of the nation." The council passed a resolution emphasizing that they would "resist in every possible way any attempt made to compel us, the working class of this United States, to murder our brothers of any other portion of the earth. . . . [W]e take as our watchword, not one man nor one dollar for war."[20]

By January of 1916, at just about the time that Gompers began publicly proclaiming his support for preparedness, the council created an antimilitarism committee to coordinate its many antiwar activities. Among its first duties was a campaign to prevent local unions from participating in a planned preparedness parade. The council also arranged an alternative mass antiwar rally for those wishing to boycott the parade and worked with other groups, ranging from the Socialist Party to the Emergency Peace Federation and Union Against Militarism, to support their antiwar activities.[21] After the Pershing raid into Mexico in the summer of 1916, the SCLC drew links between the preparedness crusade and the Mexican crisis, suggesting that some business "parasites" were trying to increase the size of the military primarily because they sought U.S. military intervention in Mexico in order to protect their properties there. In September, a representative from the Carranza government spoke to a meeting of the Seattle Central Labor Council for over two hours and reportedly held the audience "spell-bound."[22]

Although not an official antimilitarist activity, the SCLC—like the national Socialist Party—also devoted significant time to deconstructing propaganda regarding the gendered duties of citizenship during wartime. SCLC president Hulet Wells, for example, utilized the pages of the *Seattle Union Record* to lambast a local actor for perverting the meaning of the popular antiwar song *I Didn't Raise My Boy to Be a Soldier* by adding a verse "but if his country needs him he will go." Wells accused the man of falling prey to "'preparedness' propaganda" and argued that behind this propaganda was "the same old militarist crowd—the professional soldiers, big business, and the blood baiters, like Roosevelt. But they are greatly strengthened now by the people whom they have succeeded in frightening with the bogie of a foreign invasion, until these timid souls have begun to see things in the dark."[23] Another writer summarized the views of many in emphasizing that American men had a responsibility to protect their country in the event of invasion but not to go abroad in the defense of the interests of the capitalist class. In a likely reference to the song *I Didn't Raise My Boy to Be a Soldier*, he suggested that he could not imagine any boy's mother saying to him "Go, Son! Somewhere in Europe you will find other women's sons, hunt them up and kill as many as you can until they kill you."[24]

Such exchanges were revealing for they demonstrated that many male labor activists in Seattle, in contrast to preparedness advocates, believed that their military obligation to their country was limited to defending the physical boundaries of the United States. They equated warfare for any other purposes with murder and argued that it was at odds both with true manliness and with genuine patriotism. Similarly they believed that women who promoted war for purposes other than self-defense betrayed their maternal instincts. Significantly, the attitudes of Seattle labor activists did not change when Germany announced its policy of unrestricted submarine warfare in January of 1917. Instead, local activists increased their volume of antiwar work. For example, in February, the SCLC worked with the Emergency Peace Federation in promoting a campaign to send telegrams to Congress supporting the Socialist proposal for a referendum vote on the question of declaring war. They also continued their work against compulsory military training and military service.[25] In late March 1917, only shortly before President Wilson's declaration of war, the SCLC unanimously passed a resolution denouncing the "hysterical preparation for war," and declaring that "true patriotism is best shown by avoiding rather than seeking cause for a sacrifice of the lives of our citizens."[26]

THE CHICAGO FEDERATION OF LABOR

Chicago-area labor activists replicated some of the antiwar activities pursued by the Seattle Central Labor Council. Yet in other ways, the Chicago Federation of Labor hewed a different path, reflecting the diverse concerns of its membership and leaders. A center for both the meatpacking and steel industries, Chicago attracted a diverse assortment of northern and southern European immigrants in the late nineteenth and early twentieth centuries, including sizable populations of Irish, Germans, Poles, Italians, and Slovaks. Some estimate that by the eve of World War I, 70 percent of the population of Chicago was immigrant or the children of immigrants. Chicago was also home to a small African American community that expanded rapidly during the war.[27]

Longtime Chicago Federation of Labor President John Fitzpatrick, an Irish immigrant known for his personal integrity, commitment to union democracy, and his sympathy toward the Irish nationalist movement, eschewed the harsh Americanization rhetoric of the AFL and recruited immigrant and African American organizers to lure workers from these communities to the labor movement. Tactics for promoting union organizing in these communities varied, but by the eve of the war the federation had become a community center for diverse types of political and cultural activities. Speakers at CFL meetings included not only local immigrant and African American leaders but also a heterogeneous array of visitors from other countries, ranging from Irish labor leaders, to Polish and Indian nationalists, to Mexican and Russian revolutionaries. Fitzpatrick also practiced an open-door policy toward progressive reformers, Socialists, and syndicalists, welcoming them so long as they were willing to support local AFL efforts. Among those progressives who rallied around Fitzpatrick and sought to use the Chicago Federation of Labor as a base to reform the union movement from within was Robert Buck, former alderman and future editor of the CFL's newspaper, the *New Majority*; Edward Nockels, the CFL's secretary; and Lillian Herstein and Margaret Haley—both of the Chicago Teachers' Federation. Also critical to the CFL's organizing campaigns during the war years was William Z. Foster, a syndicalist who eventually embraced communism. By making the council a magnet for area immigrants, progressives, and radicals, Fitzpatrick helped transform the CFL into one of the most powerful councils in the country, boasting the allegiance of 350 locals and a membership of 350,000 workers.[28]

The antiwar activities of the CFL bore the strong imprint of Fitzpatrick's Irish nationalist and anti-imperialist thinking. Although nationalist loyalties and labor internationalism are often viewed as incompatible tendencies, Fitzpatrick and other Irish-American labor leaders within the CFL linked their sympathy for Irish freedom to a broader critique of international capitalism, emphasizing that the struggle for Irish independence was at its roots a class struggle. "The same imperialistic British capitalists who are grinding down the Irish workers into subjection," wrote Fitzpatrick, "through alliance with the pro-British New York House of Morgan Company and other supposed American money concerns are exploiting the workers of the United States."[29] Similarly, they supported other anticolonial rebellions from Mexico to India because imperialism buoyed the power of the owning classes and hurt workers in both industrialized and predominantly rural societies. Yet even while emphasizing the class roots of anti-imperialist struggles, the CFL's leaders also betrayed a sense of ethnoracial consciousness. Following the Easter Rebellion in Ireland, the Chicago Federation of Labor passed a resolution "asserting the inherent injustice of the domination of the *Celtic* people of Ireland by *alien people and powers* and therefore as protesting against the consequent unjust and illogical appeal to the doctrine of treason as a ground for the summary execution of *Celtic* persons taken as prisoners of war" [emphasis added]. The resolution seemed to suggest that CFL leaders believed imperialism to be a particularly egregious form of class oppression because it involved the domination of one ethnoracial group by another.[30]

Irish-American labor activists argued that they were opposed to U.S. intervention in World War I on the side of the British because it would strengthen the forces of British imperialism in ways that would harm both U.S. workers and workers throughout the British Empire, including Ireland. Convinced from the outset of hostilities that British and American capitalists would try to drive the country into war, the CFL advocated even stronger tactics than did the Seattle Labor Council in an effort to prevent U.S. intervention in the conflict. In August 1914, in addition to passing a strongly worded anti-war resolution, the CFL joined Irish-American groups, German-American groups, and the Socialist Party in demanding an embargo on American shipments traveling to Europe in order to prevent incidents between American sea captains and European belligerents. Initially both the AFL and President Wilson failed to respond to the proposal. But in 1915, the AFL Executive Council announced that it did not support the embargo proposal because they believed it would have "disastrous effects" on U.S. workers. They also defended the right of nations to be free and independent in seeking goods during wartime. This statement clearly put the AFL Executive Council in Wilson's camp on the question of international law and free trade.[31]

By contrast, Irish-Americans from across the political spectrum—as discussed in chapter 2—denounced Wilson for relying on "old worn out practices of naval warfare" to protect American trade during war time. International law they insisted, was not inherently neutral; Britain, as a prominent naval power throughout the nineteenth century, had played an important role in establishing the precedents upon which international law was based, and later in codifying it at international conferences. International law therefore unfairly favored countries with large battleship fleets like the British. Following the sinking of the *Lusitania*, Irish-American editors complained that Wilson was unrealistic to expect German submarines to adhere to the rules of international law by surfacing to warn vessels carrying civilians of an impending attack; if submarines surfaced, they were inevitably rammed and sunk by British naval vessels. They also insisted that it was wrong to demand that the Germans renounce submarine warfare if they could not adhere to these terms.[32]

For its part, the CFL met only shortly after the *Lusitania* incident to reaffirm its opposition to U.S. intervention in the European conflict for the purpose of "advancing the position of large capitalists" and urged the AFL Executive Council to call a congress of labor groups in the United States for the purpose of arranging a referendum of all trade union members on the war. If the vote was against American involvement, argued CFL activists, then the

AFL should develop effective means for resisting the U.S. government's war policies. Significantly, a visiting representative from the Irish Federation of Labor was at the meeting and urged CFL delegates to support the measure. "Stand for your class," he argued, "and if needs be, fight for your class and help the men and women of Ireland to destroy the master class of Europe." The Irish representative's comments clearly demonstrated the ways in which Irish nationalists tended to conflate class and national identities. According to the CFL "Minutes," the delegate was wildly cheered and the resolution subsequently passed unanimously. Gompers responded that he would submit the resolution to the AFL Executive Council "if it becomes necessary," but refused to take any immediate action.[33]

The differences between the AFL and CFL on a host of war issues as well as matters of union democracy helped inspire an ambitious plan on the part of the CFL to alter the basic structure of the American Federation of Labor. In January of 1916, the CFL proposed to create two separate organizations within the AFL, one comprised only of municipal labor bodies and state federations of labor and the other comprised of trade unions. Each coalition would be independent of the other but would exercise equal rights and power within the AFL. The CFL cited as a precedent the French Confédération Générale de Travail, which embodied a two-tiered structure consisting of a national alliance of central bodies and a national alliance of trade unions. The *Seattle Union Record*, commenting favorably on the proposal, noted that "[t]he Chicago Federation of Labor finds intolerable the prevailing corruption that the central bodies are a sort of children in the labor movement—minors entitled to no particular respect or rights—and is setting about legally to change it." Advancing the proposal in the face of the combined opposition of the trade unions and AFL leadership, however, proved impossible.[34]

With little possibility of changing national AFL policy toward the war, the CFL instead redirected its efforts locally. Shortly after Wilson announced his preparedness program, the CFL developed an imaginative alternative preparedness program. The best way to prevent U.S. involvement in war, the CFL claimed, was not to be militarily prepared but to develop a humane world society. In a well-educated society where all were adequately fed and clothed, workers would refuse to participate in war. The CFL's alternative preparedness program included passing the Keating Child Labor Bill, supporting legislation abolishing strikebreaking, eliminating the tenement system, putting the "power of the nation back of the home" by granting pensions to mothers and protecting children, building the strength of the trade union movement, opposing military training in the schools, opposing a standing army, and creating a democratically controlled military system.[35] Surprisingly, in defending their program, the leaders of the CFL sounded more of an internationalist note than the Socialist leaders of the SCLC. "We feel" wrote the authors of the executive council report on preparedness, "that the labor movement of Chicago, situated as we are in the very center of America feeling the life of both the East and West, should help to . . . counteract the hysteria and speak for the international spirit of labor which we hope will revive when the guns of Europe have been stilled and we are able to start to build upon the ruins of a better civilization."[36]

Following release of the committee report, the CFL joined the SCLC in staging boycotts and counterdemonstrations of preparedness parades at which they especially denounced the prowar activities of groups like the Illinois Manufacturers Association. They also began to advocate on behalf of public ownership of war-related industries, arguing that this was the only way to prevent private profit-mongering from driving the country into war. John Fitzpatrick personally led the campaign against the introduction of military training in the schools.[37] The CFL also took a strong stand against British atrocities committed during the suppression of the Irish Easter Rebellion in April of 1916. Reasserting its long-standing opposition to British imperialism, council activists argued that British actions during the Irish rebellion were legitimately the concern of the labor movement because "the Celtic population of Ireland has been dominated and governed against its consent by that same ruling class which, for a still greater period of time, has dominated and exploited the working class of England and has made use of the working class of England to hold Ireland in military and political subjection."[38]

Following the Easter Rising, John Fitzpatrick and other Irish-American labor activists became active in the newly formed Friends of Irish Freedom, created to help advance the cause of Irish independence.[39] Bitter feelings toward the British in turn intensified the desire of Fitzpatrick and others to keep the United States from entering the war on the side of Britain. The CFL leadership became convinced that the mainstream press was both pro-British and procapitalist and endorsed plans for a labor paper and public ownership of the cable, telegraph, and telephone lines. Following the German decision to commence unrestricted submarine warfare, the CFL renewed its efforts to provoke AFL action on the war. On February 4, 1917, it called on Gompers to demand that American citizens be prevented from entering war zones and also joined the Socialist Party as well as the SCLC in asking for a referendum vote of the people on the issue of the war.[40]

Joining the SCLC and Chicago Federation of Labor in their efforts to prevent U.S. involvement in the European conflict were municipal labor councils as diverse as the Cleveland Federation of Labor; the Industrial Council of Kansas City, Missouri; the Minneapolis Trades and Labor Assembly; the San Francisco Central Labor Council; and the New York Central Labor Union. Some modest efforts were even made by the leaders of central labor federations to develop a network of central federated unions to work against U.S. involvement in the war. The New York Central Labor Union proved especially important in these efforts.[41] Also attempting to channel dissenting municipal labor bodies in ways that might inspire united action was Illinois Congressman Frank Buchanan, who created Labor's National Peace Council in 1915. Yet given their lack of real power within the AFL, central labor leaders needed the support of the constituent national and international unions if the labor movement was to successfully prevent U.S. involvement in the war. It was this concern that led municipal labor leaders to support a labor conference on the war. At first, united labor action by AFL affiliates seemed a real possibility because antiwar and/or antimilitarist sentiment was also strong within many major national and international unions—among them, the United Mine Workers and International Ladies' Garment Workers' Union.

THE UNITED MINE WORKERS OF AMERICA

By the eve of World War I, the United Mine Workers of America (UMWA) was one of the largest and most powerful AFL unions. In contrast to most AFL unions, it was organized on a semi-industrial basis, meaning that it unionized all workers within and surrounding mines without respect to their craft. The union's constitution was unique in that it barred discrimination based on race, national origin, or religion. The UMWA membership was thus highly diverse by 1914, and included large numbers of first- or second-generation immigrants from Britain, Ireland, Italy, Germany, Mexico, and Eastern Europe, as well as a significant number of African Americans. By 1914, the *United Mine Workers Journal* was published in three languages: English, Italian, and what they termed "Slavish," a written form of various Slavic dialects. The UMWA leadership included many prominent Socialists, but the president of the organization for most of the war was John White, a non-Socialist miner from Coal Valley, Illinois, who was more closely allied with Irish-American progressive Frank Walsh. Although the Socialists and non-Socialists who allied behind White feuded over a number of financial and organizing issues, both groups were strongly antiwar.[42]

Four factors proved especially important in stimulating strong antiwar sentiments within the United Mine Workers. First, both Socialist and non-Socialist

UMWA leaders charged that the U.S. business class was trying to drive the country into the European war, and perhaps a war with Mexico, for the sake of its own profits. Businesses, UMWA leaders believed, would not likely share any future profits with U.S. workers, despite the fact that workers would disproportionately fight and die in wars. Any temporary increases in jobs in the mining industry due to wartime profits were not worth the cost of miners' lives. Second, fresh from the so-called "coal wars" between miners and mining companies that had produced tragedies like the Ludlow massacre, most miners and their representatives were imbued with a strong antimilitarist ethos and sought to prevent any build up of U.S. military forces. One the one hand, as repeated experiences demonstrated, such forces might be used against workers. On the other hand, military service instilled a spirit of blind obedience that was at odds with the "manly" values that miners associated with standing up to the boss on their jobs and through their trade unions. So strongly did most UMWA activists feel about the negative influence of military values on workers that some locals banned members from joining state militias, a policy opposed by Samuel Gompers. Even more tellingly, the international executive board under the leadership of John White also barred from UMWA membership all Boy Scouts, a group they viewed as a paramilitary organization.[43]

Third, both the White contingent and Socialists within the UMWA appeared influenced by currents of Irish nationalist thought that had been influential in mining circles since the days of the Molly McGuires. In particular, UMWA activists joined Irish-American labor activists like John Fitzpatrick in charging that international law did not provide a truly neutral mechanism for resolving disputes between nations. Instead, many rules of warfare favored Britain and other leading imperial powers, or were outmoded and failed to take into account new technologies such as submarines that were favored by nations without strong naval fleets. In contrast to Wilson, UMWA leaders strongly doubted that American interests would be served by going to war to protect and promote principles of international law. Finally, leading UMWA leaders and journalists from both camps insisted that the U.S. soldiers should also not be going abroad to spread American "blessings" such as democratic rights and privileges to other peoples until everyone enjoyed them in the United States.[44]

UMWA President John White ably captured elements of all of these concerns in a courageous speech given before a group of preparedness advocates in May of 1916. White emphasized that two major groups supported preparedness. One group consisted of bankers and munitions makers who stood to reap significant profits from increased U.S. military spending as well as U.S.

involvement in the war. But he insisted that they weren't the only danger. Equally worrisome was a "well-to-do and wealthy leisure class" that "rests under the delusion that American ideals have already been completely realized." This group believed that their country was already "so perfect that nothing remained but to raise great armaments" in order to help others solve their problems and bring American "blessings" to them. Specifically, with respect to World War I, the leisure classes proposed to "sacrifice" U.S. workers for "a code of conduct between nations as outworn and criminal as the dueling code between individuals."[45]

By contrast, White emphasized that from the perspective of U.S. workers ideals like "liberty, justice, education, [and] equality of opportunity" had not yet been achieved for the vast majority of Americans. Workers believed that the "great sacred struggle to conquer America for its own people" took precedence over spreading alleged American blessings abroad. For these reasons, White told the mostly hostile audience, workers will have none of "your war of gold lace and cannon; a war in which great masses of men in uniform are led to slaughter by leaders . . . who regard it as the road to glory and the king of sports." He also emphasized that workers would oppose compulsory military training and military service, which they viewed as "the saddest most abject surrender of American ideals ever proposed in this country."[46]

Joining White and other UMWA leaders in their indictment of preparedness and of the effort to drive the United States into the European War was the highly popular *United Mine Workers Journal*. In addition to offering a steady barrage of articles critical of preparedness and Wilson's neutrality policies, the journal's cartoons often ably encapsulated in visual form the antiwar messages of UMWA leaders. One cartoon in the English language section, for example, pictured a "war monster" into whose mouth thousands of workers with foodstuffs and munitions marched. The captioned warned, "It will grow as long as the workers will continue to feed it" (Figure P.2). Another showed Uncle Sam under a military recruitment sign offering a worker in blue collar clothes a military uniform. The worker responded, "Nix of that Stuff Uncle: This Suit is Good Enough For Me."[47]

The editors of the Italian language section of the *United Mine Workers Journal* supplied its readers with a steady stream of antiwar articles and cartoons even after Italy officially joined the Entente powers and declared war against Austria-Hungary in the spring of 1915. One Italian cartoon from January of 1916 aptly summarized White's point that many workers would likely be reluctant to fight for the American dream abroad when it remained elusive for them in the United States. The cartoon showed Italian-American miners standing

Zio Sam:—Bisogna prepararsi alla guerra ed essere pronti a morire per la patria.
Minatore:—Caro zio, la patria non può lamentarsi di noi. Dà un'occhiata a quel cimitero, e vedrai quanti di noi sono già morti per lei!

Figure 3.1. *United Mine Workers Journal*, January 27, 1916, 19. This Italian language cartoon shows Uncle Sam lecturing Italian-American miners on the need "to prepare for the war and be ready to die for the homeland." They respond by urging Uncle Sam to "Look at that cemetery and . . . see how many of us have already died for her" in mining accidents (translation by Alex Grab, University of Maine).

with Uncle Sam in a graveyard filled with headstones containing the numbers of miners who had died in each of three recent years from mine accidents or violence at the hands of militias like those in Ludlow. When Uncle Sam told the miners that there was a need to "prepare for the war and be ready to die for the homeland," the miners responded, "Dear uncle, the homeland cannot complain about us. Look at that cemetery and you will see how many of us have already died for her" (Figure 3.1). In another cartoon, the editors portrayed a fat capitalist waving an American flag filled with dollar signs against the backdrop of both Mexico and Europe, which were pictured in flames and littered with the debris of war. The "shrewd" U.S. capitalist chanted "Long Live the Homeland" as he crushed a worker underfoot. Still other cartoons expressed an old-world skepticism about Wilson's efforts to bring peace to Europe. One such cartoon showed Wilson sending a dove into Europe looking for an olive branch (Figure 3.2). The caption, however, explained that the dove would need to "escape quickly" from the "slaughterhouse" or "risk . . . being eaten alive."[48]

Povera Colomba!

Noè Wilson Ha Mandato Quell Uccello
A Cercare la Fronda dell Olivo,
Ma se Non Sfugge Presto a Quel Macello,
Corre il Rischio di Farsi Mangiar Vivo.

Figure 3.2. *United Mine Workers Journal*, January 4, 1917, 19. "Poor Dove."
President Wilson, suggests this cartoon, sent a dove to look for an olive branch
in Europe. But the caption warns that if the bird "does not escape quickly from
[the European] slaughterhouse," it "runs the risk of being eaten alive." The
cartoon suggests an old world skepticism regarding the prospects for a U.S.-
brokered peace and seems to warn against U.S. involvement in European affairs
(translation by Alex Grab, University of Maine).

But antiwar activism in the UMWA was not limited to cartoons, writings, and speeches opposing preparedness and U.S. intervention in the war.
UMWA officials also took the lead in organizing a conference of several AFL
unions on the question of how labor could prevent U.S. involvement in the
war following the sinking of the *Lusitania*. At a UMWA International Executive Board meeting, John White argued that such a meeting was necessary

because there was a "grave danger" of the United States being brought into the war and "every honorable effort should be made to emphasize labor's protest and opposition to war." He suggested that whether UMWA members were personally "pro-Ally or pro-German," they were almost "unanimous" in their opposition to U.S. involvement in the conflict. The United Mine Workers, he argued, as "one of the foremost labor movements of the world . . . [can] well afford to emphasize our position on this most vivid question and contribute in every way we can to the prevention of war such as is now destroying the greater portion of Europe and sacrificing millions of souls." He therefore successfully urged the international executive board to pass a resolution urging that American labor do everything in its power to prevent U.S. intervention in the war. The resolution was then sent to the president of the American Federation of Labor.[49]

Since Gompers proved uninterested in staging a meeting, the UMWA moved quickly to plan its own conference of select national unions at its headquarters in Indianapolis. In addition to the UMWA, the Teamsters, International Typographical Union, Stone Cutters, Bricklayers, Carpenters, Book Binders, Barbers, and Structural Iron Workers sent representatives to the meeting, held on May 27, 1915. Daniel Tobin of the Teamsters chaired the meeting, while William Green of the UMWA acted as secretary. Although the meeting reportedly encouraged an open exchange of ideas about the war, only a few details were released to the press. One was a statement declaring that all unions represented at the meeting declared their opposition to war. Another was an adopted motion that asked representatives at the meeting to encourage their unions to adopt suitable resolutions regarding the war and send them to Gompers. Yet the meeting refused to endorse more radical measures such as the call for an embargo on arms shipments or exports to Europe endorsed by Labor's National Peace Council and the Chicago Federation of Labor. Instead, the meeting closed with an agreement that Secretary Green would communicate with President Gompers about the desirability of calling a "conference of the representatives of all labor organizations if the situation regarding war would seem to justify such action." Daniel Tobin of the Teamsters also directly telegrammed Gompers with this demand.[50]

Gompers, however, failed to act on the issue, leaving arrangements for a labor conference on the war in a state of limbo. In the aftermath of the conference, the UMWA therefore joined other trade unions throughout the country in opposing compulsory military training, criticizing and protesting against preparedness parades, and demanding that the government seize control of armament factories in order to take the profit motive out of the quest for preparedness. The *United Mine Workers Journal* commented that it was "almost unbelievable" that Americans could support universal training and a vast increase in armaments when it was so clearly the "rivalry in armaments" that was responsible for devastating the "whole of the Eastern hemisphere." They also warned that a larger army and a growing stockpile of armaments might be used to establish a protectorate over Mexico. Rather than use humanitarian reform as a pretext for intervening in Mexico, UMWA leaders joined the PLM in arguing that the president ought to address starvation in the United States. By the spring of 1917, The UMWA, like the SCLC and Chicago Federation of Labor, remained fundamentally opposed to a U.S. declaration of war against either Mexico or Germany.[51]

INTERNATIONAL LADIES' GARMENT WORKERS' UNION

The fourth group to be considered here, the International Ladies' Garment Workers' Union (ILGWU), was in many ways the most unique. One of the few unions in the AFL whose membership was predominantly female, the union was nonetheless led primarily by Jewish men. A talented cadre of women organizers at the grassroots level, however, infused the organization with a feminist ethos. In particular, this group consistently advocated suffrage for women and also pushed the case for more women in leadership positions within the labor movement.[52] Headquartered in New York, the union drew the bulk of its membership from among women, children, and some men who labored in small to midsize shops that produced women's clothes and accessories in the garment district of the city. A majority of these workers were first generation immigrant Jews from Russia or Eastern Europe, but the industry also boasted a significant Italian population. Not surprisingly, given its diverse composition, the leaders of the ILGWU strongly advocated more lenient immigration policies, placing them at odds with labor groups like the Seattle Central Labor Council on this issue. The New York–based locals within the ILGWU became particularly famous for their success in creating solidarity among diverse groups of immigrant workers during the strike against New York shirtwaist companies in 1909. Yet this victory would be overshadowed by the tragic Triangle Shirt Waist Factory fire of 1911 that took the lives of many young Italian and Jewish women active in the strike.[53]

Although headquartered in New York, the ILGWU had also expanded to major cities such as Chicago, Philadelphia, and Montreal by the eve of World War I. This even further increased its ethnic diversity and contributed to factionalism within the organization between anarchists, Socialists, and moderates. As a consequence, the New York–based male leadership of the ILGWU often relied on local Socialists to advance their antiwar agenda rather than using the union or the union newspaper, the *Ladies Garment Worker*. Women organizers for the ILGWU, for their part, more frequently became involved in the peace activities of the Women's Trade Union League (WTUL). A mixed-class organization created around 1903 by Socialists and reformers, the WTUL included within its ranks both trade union women and wealthy female patrons dedicated to improving conditions for working women. It developed close, but sometimes tense, relations with both the male-dominated AFL and the "middle-class–dominated feminist movement." The League's twin loyalties, suggests historian Robin Jacoby, ensured that it contained within its "very structure the contradictions inherent in the concepts of class and female solidarity."[54]

Women like Rose Schneiderman and Leonora O'Reilly, who began their working lives as garment workers in New York at quite young ages and at various times served as organizers for the ILGWU, became active in the WTUL in part due to conflicts with male trade union leaders. For these women, the WTUL provided important moral and economic support, even though O'Reilly sometimes found it necessary to admonish middle- and upper-class elements within the WTUL not to treat working women in a condescending way.[55] Schneiderman and O'Reilly believed that working women's lives could be improved not only through the labor-organizing campaigns conducted by the WTUL but also through its women's suffrage and feminist peace work. In an effort to be inclusive, the Women's Peace Party created by Jane Addams and Carrie Chapman Catt following the outbreak of war invited O'Reilly to travel on the women's peace ship to Europe in 1915 and to represent the WTUL at the women's peace meeting at the Hague. Yet as O'Reilly's speech before the Hague meeting made clear, the perspective of WTUL women on peace issues was in some ways unique. Upset that women trade unionists were not better represented at the meeting, O'Reilly insisted that the labor movement had done more to advance the cause of peace over the past fifty years than "all the capitalist peace movements put together." Since women were increasingly moving into industry, she argued, they could prove a particularly important voice for peace within the labor movement. Working women's votes could also be critical in turning the tide against war. In other writings after the Hague meeting, O'Reilly predicted that peace between nations would prove impossible without industrial democracy because the business pursuit of profit drove wars. And the cooperation of working women, both economically and politically, was necessary to the achievement of industrial democracy.[56]

Such views were not confined to working women within the WTUL. Wealthy patron and WTUL leader Margaret Dreier Robins opened the WTUL national convention in 1914 by insisting that "peace between nations can come only as the result of peace within nations" and through the achievement of "economic justice to the workers." She therefore sponsored a resolution resolving that "we work increasingly to build up our own labor movement so as to stand ready to further that international solidarity of the workers at present so disastrously interrupted." By contrast, the Women's Peace Party included within its platform only a tepid and vague commitment to eliminate the economic causes of war; no mention was made of labor. The international women's meeting at the Hague meanwhile, overwhelmingly stressed that women were the greatest potential source for peace work and shaped their program accordingly, despite O'Reilly's suggestions that they develop closer relations with the labor movement.[57]

Although women organizers from the ILGWU became quite active in the WTUL's peace work, this activity was initially largely ignored by the male dominated leadership and press of the AFL union. The ILGWU journal, the *Ladies Garment Worker*, never officially took a position on the question of whether the United States should intervene in Mexico or Europe and largely neglected the issues of preparedness and peace activities. Following the outbreak of World War I, the journal simply noted that "our hearts go out to the suffering toilers of Europe in general and those of our own trade in particular," noting that "there are few of us who have not some relatives in the affected countries." The journal emphasized that it was "useless to apportion blame or try to fix responsibility" because the war was "inevitable and had to come: the belligerent nations were armed to the teeth for several decades, and it was feared and expected all the time."[58] Rather than emphasizing the need for a labor congress to oppose the war, the ILGWU in 1915 instead officially supported the AFL's call for a labor conference at the same time and place as the peace negotiations. Reflecting the concerns of its Jewish leadership, the ILGWU did introduce a resolution at the AFL convention asking the labor movement "to espouse the cause of the hunted Jewish people in foreign countries, particularly Russia, who are just at present suffering cruel and frightful discrimination at the hands of callous civil and military authorities." The resolution was unanimously adopted by the AFL convention.[59]

Yet Russian Jews, in particular, initially opposed the United States entering the war on the side of the Entente because they were loathe to see the United States allied with Tsarist Russia, a land—as the above resolution suggested—famous for pogroms against Jews and forced conscription. In

New York the leadership of the union therefore became highly active in campaigns on behalf of antiwar Socialists like Meyer London and Morris Hillquit. When London emerged victorious in the New York race for the Twelfth Congressional District, the *Ladies Garment Worker* announced that it was a "victory for Socialism and the worker."[60] The linkages between the Socialist Party and the ILGWU grew stronger as the war progressed; ILGWU delegates sponsored a resolution at the AFL convention in 1916 that had first been introduced by Meyer London in the House of Representatives. The resolution called on the United States to "convene a congress of neutral nations with the object of terminating the fratricidal war in Europe and establishing a durable peace upon just terms which shall include effective machinery for the peaceful settlement of international disputes in the future and ample provisions for the political independence and self government of the oppressed nations and removal of all political, national, and civic disabilities of the Jewish people." The American Federation of Labor was asked to render "moral and material assistance to the full extent of their means to their suffering fellow-workers, the victims of the war and of political, religious and racial persecution."[61]

The resolution clearly suggested that Wilson's proclamations about the need for a League of Nations and a desire to help oppressed nationalities in Europe had influenced the group and that, in contrast to Irish Catholic labor leaders like John Fitzpatrick, they were apparently less suspicious of the president's motives. Indeed, many read race into the president's proclamations and assumed that he would also champion the efforts of the Jewish race to end its persecution at the hands of European states. For these reasons, the ILGWU leadership appeared to welcome a future role for the United States in postwar international affairs in a way that groups like the Seattle Central Labor Federation did not. Yet the ILGWU emphasized that the United States would have more bargaining power as a neutral nation than as a belligerent. The ILGWU's other action at the AFL convention was therefore to strongly lobby on behalf of an AFL resolution of 1916 opposing military training in the schools that was sponsored by the Brotherhood of Painters and Decorators and earned accolades from the Seattle Central Labor Council. Significantly, the resolution won the strong support of both feminist and Socialist activists within the ILGWU.

The resolution came in response to an effort by the secretary of war to communicate with public schools throughout the country to inquire whether they were willing to introduce military training for boys into their schools. If the response was affirmative, the war department offered to provide instructors, rifles, and ammunition. The sponsors of the AFL resolution opposed this policy and requested that the executive council of the AFL contact President Wilson to request that he prevent any further attempt to "militarize the public schools." As was often the case with controversial resolutions, the AFL leadership referred the resolution to a subcommittee that recommended nonconcurrence and offered a substitute resolution supported by Samuel Gompers. The substitute resolved that the AFL opposed "any increase in the standing army" and asked that the constitutional provisions that guaranteed the right to bear arms "be respected." But the supporters of the Brotherhood of Painters resolution, in a rare challenge to parliamentary procedure, complained that the substitute had "absolutely nothing to do with the original resolution."

A vigorous debate followed in which many delegates announced their strong opposition to military training in the schools and defended the original resolution. Among these was one of the few female delegates at the convention, Sara Shapiro of the International Ladies' Garment Workers' Union. Strongly imbued with the feminist as well as antimilitarist ethos of her union, she announced that she desired to speak on behalf of "the women not directly represented in the convention, the mothers and sisters of trade unionists." Such women in New York, she argued, were "bitterly opposed to military training in the schools." The substitute committee resolution was resoundingly defeated by a vote of 185 to 84, and the original resolution adopted instead, prompting the Seattle Union Record to report that for the "First Time in History Democracy [was] Winning in the [AFL] Convention."[62]

The vote clearly signaled the strength of antimilitarist sentiment within the AFL. Although no breakdown is available on who voted for the antimilitarist resolution, it likely included representatives of all four of the groups considered here: the Seattle Central Labor Council, Chicago Federation of Labor, United Mine Workers of America, and International Ladies' Garment Workers' Union. All of these groups strongly opposed military training in the schools as well as compulsory military service in 1916. All of these groups likewise remained opposed to U.S. intervention in the war at the end of 1916, although their reasons differed. At one end of the spectrum lay the SCLC and United Mine Workers; they adopted a kind of working-class isolationism in response to the war. The two groups argued that only a physical invasion of the United States constituted reasonable grounds for U.S. intervention in the war. In the absence of a genuine physical threat to U.S. soil, policymakers should—as John White put it—focus on conquering America for its own citizens. Increasing the size of the American military was bound to play into the hands of the business class at the expense of workers. At the other end of the spectrum lay the immigrant leaders and feminist organizers of the International Ladies' Garment Workers' Union, who sought an expanded international role for the United States but believed that the best way to realize this goal was for the Wilson administration to remain neutral during the war. Occupying its own unique position somewhere in the middle of the spectrum was the Chicago Federation of Labor. CFL leaders clearly distrusted Wilson's pro-British and imperialist tendencies and for this reason never embraced a stronger international role for the U.S. government. On the other hand, they believed that U.S. labor might serve as an effective force for reviving the international labor movement, which in turn might one day permanently alter international relations and bring an end to both imperialism and the capitalist exploitation that accompanied it. In the interim, however, U.S. labor must strongly oppose U.S. intervention in the war on the side of Britain; this development would serve only to buoy the forces of imperialism and militarism in ways that would make achieving the goals of the international labor movement much more difficult.

Unfortunately for antiwar forces within the AFL, the vote on the Brotherhood of Painters resolution against military training in the schools marked the high tide of antimilitarist influence within the AFL. Over the next few months, Samuel Gompers, with the assistance of other Council of National Defense members, devised a plan for securing a pledge of labor loyalty in the event of war.

THE GOMPERS TURNABOUT

Although Gompers chose to renounce pacifism and support preparedness early in the war, his most significant turnabout came when he reversed the de facto AFL policy of noninterference in the antiwar activities of AFL unions and chose to try to align them behind a pledge of labor loyalty to the government in the event of war. Several factors likely influenced Gompers's change in policy. The press at the time reported that the Council of National Defense, worried about continuing labor opposition to the war, pressured Gompers to develop a strategy for securing trade union cooperation in preparing the country for possible intervention in the war. But Gompers was doubtless a willing partner with the Council of National Defense in developing such a strategy due to his own evolving views on the war. Pro-British from the outset of the conflict, Gompers had become convinced by 1917 that the war was fundamentally one between German autocracy and British democracy. Unless the United States accepted "the challenge" to fight on the side of democracy, he argued, "autocracy would run rough-shod over the peoples of the whole world."[63] Absent from any of Gompers's addresses or articles on the war, in contrast to those of labor dissidents, was an analysis of British imperialism as a source of international injustice and repression. Gompers, like Wilson, also expressed doubts about maintaining "neutrality when international guarantees for human life and rights were denied and outraged" by the Germans. The AFL president largely accepted Wilson's interpretation of international law and strongly opposed a U.S. embargo of goods to Europe because, like Wilson, he thought it would be an un-neutral intervention in trade and would hurt the economic interests of the United States.[64]

Through his work on the Council of National Defense, Gompers had also become convinced that the United States was not adequately prepared for war. By March of 1917, Gompers concurred with General Leonard Wood that there were many threats to U.S. democracy but that an "armed people cannot have their liberties taken away from them"—a stark contrast with the thinking of AFL antiwar activists who believed that U.S. military forces constituted the greatest threat to their democratic rights. Perhaps even more importantly, Gompers assumed that by cooperating with the government on national security policy the AFL would help to secure more representation for itself within executive branch committees like the Council of National Defense. Labor representation in such committees, he optimistically predicted, could bring about the "democratization of all governmental institutions." Standing in the way of this democratization, however, were those Socialist and labor dissenters agitating on behalf of a referendum vote on the question of war. To Gompers, such a vote would be unconstitutional; in a representative democracy only elected representatives had the right to declare war. On the other hand, by supporting the U.S. government's military policies, labor would be accorded an important advisory position within government councils that would allow it to protect its interests. The AFL would also be well situated to demand a democratization of the army as well as democratic representation for labor in future peace councils.[65]

Convinced that a pledge of labor loyalty in the event of war would constitute a service both to his country and to labor, Gompers arranged for meetings of both the AFL Executive Council and representatives of national and international unions to consider the issue of labor preparedness for war in mid-March of 1917. Significantly, Gompers excluded central labor bodies from his invitation, noting that he would send representatives around after the meeting to educate them about the AFL's war policies. The short notice also precluded national and international unions from holding referenda of their membership on the question of labor policy toward the war. Sensing that Gompers sought an affirmation of his own pro-preparedness views, several antiwar unions—including both the United Mine Workers and the Ladies Garment Workers—refused to send delegates. UMWA President John White wrote directly to Gompers to decline the invitation, suggesting that he was "personally against the whole scheme of war and preparedness." He disputed the notion advanced by Gompers that humanitarian issues lay behind Wilson's decision to break diplomatic relations with Germany and argued instead that the war was a distinctly "commercial one." White insisted that "in his broad travels" he had "found very little sentiment among the working people in favor of this terrible war." The United Mine Workers, he emphasized, opposed military training and believed that "the great masses of people should determine whether or not they should engage in this unjust and uncalled for war." White therefore begged to be excused from the conference.[66]

Gompers faced strong opposition even from within the AFL Executive Council. The council met on March 9, three days before the meeting of national and international trade unions in order to consult on a statement to be presented to the larger body. Gompers began the meeting with expert testimony from efficiency expert Howard Coffin and Secretary of Labor William B. Wilson. Coffin claimed that the country was woefully unprepared for war, and emphasized that it was particularly vulnerable in the event of an invasion of the Northeast, since this was where virtually all U.S. munitions plants lay. Both the Germans and British, suggested Coffin, could quickly defeat the U.S. Navy and overrun the Northeast in less than thirty days, with the result that the United States would "pretty much be at their mercy." The solution, from Coffin's perspective, was to support universal military training, increased expenditures on military production, and schemes for assuring adequate control of natural resources as well as industrial procurement in the event of war. He implied that if labor were to assist in preparedness efforts before the war, it might prevent some of the "half-baked" emergency legislation to which Britain resorted after the outbreak of war.[67]

Yet several at the meeting expressed skepticism, among them AFL Vice President James Duncan (no relation to James Duncan of Seattle) and William D. Mahon, president of the Amalgamated Association of Street and Electrical Railway Employees of America. In reference to the Northeast invasion scenario envisioned by Coffin, Duncan commented that "[w]e would have to be asleep for all of those things to happen." He insisted that Coffin's assessments were highly flawed because they relied on military data and reports and presumed no resistance on the part of local populations. "To a military man," suggested Duncan, "nothing is right except a uniform and a gun and anyone who does not appreciate it is a witless creature whose education has been sadly neglected." Yet much as Confederate soldiers fought valiantly to defend their homes and families during the Civil War, so too would American citizen soldiers "rise to the occasion" in the event of a foreign invasion. For his part, Mahon questioned whether anyone wanted to invade the United States. Until evidence existed of a genuine security threat to the United States, he argued, the position of the labor movement should still be that it was unalterably opposed to war.[68]

But Secretary of Labor Wilson expressed fear that if labor did not illustrate its willingness to cooperate with the government in the event of war, "it would be crushed; it would be run over as with a juggernaut." For his part, Gompers argued that the threats to American security were real; some 250,000 reservists from the German army were in the United States and/or poised on the borders of Mexico and Canada to launch an invasion of the United States. Mahon, by contrast, regarded information pertaining to a German-Mexican alliance as purely speculative and little more than a "myth."[69]

Yet ultimately, Gompers persuaded the council to give its approval, after some amendments, for a statement on the war entitled "American Labor's Position in Peace or in War" that was in turn to be submitted to the meeting of national and international trade union movements for endorsement. In an apparent nod to antiwar sentiment, the proclamation did not endorse U.S. involvement in the war but declared that "[w]hether we approve it or not, we must recognize that war is a situation with which we must reckon. The present European war, involving as it does the majority of civilized nations and affecting the industry of the whole world, threatens at any moment to draw all countries, including our own, into the conflict." The document argued that past wars had provided new opportunities for labor to be exploited. It therefore demanded that the government cooperate with U.S. organized labor in upholding trade union standards in the event of any future war and asked that "in order to safeguard all the interests of the wage-earners, organized labor should have representation in all agencies determining and administering policies of national defense." In return, "the National and International Trade Unions of America in national conference assembled in the capital of our nation, hereby pledge ourselves in peace or in war, in stress or in storm, to stand unreservedly by the standards of liberty and the safety and preservation of the institutions and ideals of our Republic."[70]

The trade union conference, which met on March 12 and included 148 labor representatives from 79 affiliated organizations, as well as some AFL departments, was asked to endorse the statement already prepared by Gompers and the AFL Executive Council. Since the conference deliberated in secret, little is known about discussions during the session. Several amendments were apparently suggested, but they failed to achieve sufficient backing and "Labor's Position in Peace and War" was brought up for a vote unchanged and passed unanimously.[71] Daniel Tobin of the Teamsters, who had attended the Indianapolis antiwar conference staged by the UMWA, complained bitterly about the way Gompers conducted the Washington trade union meeting. "When I arrived there," he complained, "I found you had a program already prepared: cut and dried . . . and that we would not be allowed to change one word of that document." Tobin also argued that the group had no real authority to pass the resolution because none of the constituent unions represented had been given time to submit the proposal to their unions. Yet Tobin, like others who suggested amendments at the meeting, voted for the final proposal, as did others who voiced some criticism of it during the gathering.[72]

Municipal labor bodies and local chapters of national and international unions, for their part, expressed puzzlement over "Labor's Position in Peace and War." Excluded from the meeting, many simply wondered how national and international unions could have voted to pledge their loyalty to the government in the event of war without consulting either their membership or central labor unions. Others wrote to Gompers angrily condemning his actions, while some simply ignored the proclamation. In Seattle, over two weeks after the conference, 250 delegates from the SCLC representing twenty-five thousand unionists held a "Patriotic Discussion" on the war lasting over one hour, after which they voted unanimously against the war and pledged their united support to combat the "jingo press." The minutes of the meeting claimed that straw votes all over the city showed that Seattle working people were ten to one against the war. Yet one week after Wilson's declaration of war, clearly hoping to avoid repression, the council held another meeting at which they saluted the flag "in a dignified manner" and pledged their loyalty to the government. Perhaps following Gompers's lead, they also discussed "measures to be taken by labor to conserve the conditions which have been built with years of effort by the organized workers."[73]

In Chicago, local activists inquired at weekly CFL meetings how their national representatives could have voted to support the war without consulting them. In response, the CFL created a committee to investigate the issue. In the meantime, it continued to vigorously oppose the war and sent a telegram to President Wilson informing him that "The common people do not want war." It suggested that "no nation that allows itself to be driven into War by the reactionary elements is acting along the lines of real courage." Not until mid-May, two months after the Washington Conference and over one month after Wilson's declaration of war, did the CFL committee created to investigate the conference's decisions finally release its report. The authors argued that "some criticism of Labor's position as enunciated [in "Labor's Position in Peace and War"] might have been made inasmuch as it was in recognition of war in place of a protest against war and that a demand for peace should have been made." But they suggested that there was nothing "detrimental" to the current interests of organized labor in the document and therefore recommended endorsement. After much debate, the CFL finally voted 140 to 59 to endorse "Labor's Position in Peace and War."[74]

CONCLUSION

Gerald Horne, in a 1996 commentary on African Americans and U.S. foreign policy during the early Cold War, raised the question of whether African American leaders of the era "played a strong hand weakly." He argued that the NAACP leadership, in particular, unnecessarily supported the Cold War foreign policies of the Truman administration at a time when Jim Crow was already in retreat at home and when African Americans could have played an important role in advancing an agenda in support of international racial equality.[75] Given the breadth of antiwar sentiment within labor on the eve of World War I, one may similarly ask whether antiwar activists within labor played a strong hand weakly. Although a nationwide general strike was likely beyond the organizational capabilities of the AFL or its leading unions on the eve of war, a labor conference staged to demand a referendum vote on the question of war and peace within labor seemed more than feasible. A democratic verdict rendered by AFL members against participation in the war might in turn have altered working-class politics surrounding the war in ways—and with repercussions—that can scarcely be imagined.

But the same federated trade union structure that nurtured strong antiwar subcultures also made coordinated action on the war difficult. Central labor bodies were allied against national and international bodies; Socialists feuded with non-Socialists; the international agendas of diverse immigrant groups were in conflict with one another; Gompers schemed against his political enemies. Against this backdrop, no one proved willing to step forward and attempt to forge a cohesive campaign within the AFL against U.S. involvement in the war. The AFL leadership thus gained an inside advantage in the battle for position between pro- and antiwar labor activists over who would influence Wilson's foreign policies. Yet the battle was not over. As the CFL's comments on "Labor's Position in Peace for War" hinted, the statement was so vague and amorphous that it left much about labor's loyalty to the government in the event of war still to be defined. A battle would soon ensue between labor and Socialist loyalists who were incorporated into government bureaucracies during the war and their antiwar rivals over just these issues.

Figure P.3 *Seattle Union Record*, May 12, 1917, 1. After Wilson declared war, labor dissidents devoted particular attention to trying to stop conscription. An extended explanation underneath this cartoon emphasized that the capitalist elite sought a permanent standing army under their control to protect their businesses within the United States from labor unrest as well as to promote "American financial imperialism abroad."

PROLOGUE: WILSON AND U.S. BELLIGERENCY

Although Wilson was reelected in late 1916 in part on the strength of his antiwar platform, he declared war against Germany less than six months later. Two developments precipitated his decision. On January 31, 1917, Germany announced unrestricted submarine warfare against all vessels found in British waters. Wilson responded by severing diplomatic relations with Germany. Yet German leaders, convinced that they could win the war in six months by unleashing their U-boats, failed to alter course; multiple American ships were sunk in British waters over the next few months. Second, in late February, British officials gave to the Wilson administration a memo they intercepted from German foreign minister Arthur Zimmerman to the Mexican government. It proposed a military alliance between Germany and Mexico and suggested that, in the event that the United States entered the war, Germany would help Mexico "reconquer" the land it had lost in 1848. Although the Mexican revolutionary government of Venustiano Carranza never demonstrated any interest in a proposal that might have again inspired a U.S. military invasion of Mexico, to Wilson the combined German initiatives constituted grounds for war.[1]

Wilson's war message, delivered to Congress on April 2, 1917, perhaps more thoroughly conflated the international needs of capitalism with those of democracy than any other presidential speech. Wilson began by highlighting the damages to American shipping and trade caused by the "cruel and unmanly business" of submarine warfare. Yet Wilson insisted that it was not "selfish" economic interests that led him to seek a declaration of war against Germany. Rather, the interests of all humanity were at stake in the defense of international law; this law protected the "free highways of the world" upon the seas. Yet these highways could never be safe so long as autocracy prevailed. The president therefore called for a "concert for peace" among democratic nations designed to defeat autocracy and to ensure the vindication of principles of "peace and justice" that lay behind international law. In perhaps his most memorable statement, Wilson insisted that "the world must be made safe for democracy."[2]

Although Wilson's words were credited with igniting the hopes of reformers and revolutionaries around the world, in the United States they received a more mixed reception. On the one hand, many on the political right criticized Wilson's statement of war aims as excessively inflated and wondered about the potential commitments they might involve. For example, Theodore Roosevelt dismissed the idea that the United States had gone to war "to make democracy safe." Instead he insisted that the United States intervened in the European conflict because it had a "special grievance" with Germany and needed to "make the world safe for ourselves." On the other hand, many antiwar Socialists and labor activists also doubted Wilson's commitment to democracy. Moreover, they insisted that even if the president was sincere, democracy could not be exported from one nation to another.[3]

AFL leaders, however, had already pledged their commitment to the president in the event of war, and his speech served only to reaffirm this commitment. Over the next several months, they would be systematically incorporated into government bureaucracies and serve on several diplomatic missions. Joining AFL leaders in governing circles were those few leading Socialists who announced their support for Wilson's programs in the aftermath of his announcement of war. By contrast, the Wilson administration systematically crushed Socialist and IWW dissent, reaffirming doubts about the president's commitment to democracy even at home. Despite criticism, President Wilson increasingly relied on AFL leaders and prowar Socialists as he struggled to cope with high strike levels that hindered economic mobilization for war and to respond to the rising tide of Socialist and labor unrest in Europe in the aftermath of the Bolshevik Revolution in October of 1917.

On January 8, 1918, partly in response to the Bolshevik challenge, Wilson gave his famous "Fourteen Points" speech in which he outlined his peace proposals as well as his plans for the League of Nations. Contrary to popular and even historical belief, Wilson did not use the term self-determination in the speech, but instead spoke of the need for "impartial adjustment of all colonial claims" with due consideration to "the interests of the populations concerned." In this respect, Wilson's goals for international self-governance and democracy proved far more evolutionary than those of the Bolsheviks, who embraced *self-determination* for oppressed nationalities without qualification in December of 1917. Yet because Wilson would subsequently appropriate from the Bolsheviks the term self-determination in explaining U.S. wartime goals, he also became associated with the term.[4]

Probably more important to Wilson, however, were his plans for using the League of Nations to build a concert of powers that could establish an international rule of law and, in so doing, help to develop peaceful mechanisms for the gradual evolution of democratic forms of government throughout the world. That Wilson continued to view the fates of democracy and capitalism as intertwined was evident in points three and four of his speech, which called for international recognition of freedom of the seas and the "removal, so far as possible, of all economic barriers" that limited "equality of trade conditions among all the nations." These provisions were aimed not only at imperial trade preference systems but also at revolutionary regimes like those in Mexico and Russia that might seek to restrict the free flow of capitalist trade and investments. As revisionist diplomatic historians have long argued, Wilson's Fourteen Points constituted a reaffirmation of long-standing ideas about an "Open Door" approach to the health of world capitalism.[5]

Despite the capitalist undertones, the president's speech elicited considerable enthusiasm among moderate British and European labor leaders and Socialists disillusioned by the war policies of their own governments but wary of Bolshevism. Yet when Allied labor and Socialist leaders began promoting an interbelligerent labor conference designed to negotiate an end to the war using Wilson's Fourteen Points as well as the spring 1917 Soviet Petrograd formula of "no annexations and no indemnities" as the framework, Wilson balked. In part, Wilson's opposition stemmed from his assumption that diplomacy must remain the preserve of governments, albeit democratic ones. Equally important, Wilson backtracked in late 1917 and early 1918 on his belief in a "peace without victory" and on his former commitment to the Soviet Petrograd formula. Aggressive German actions, such as the harsh peace imposed on Russia in the Brest Litovsk treaty, convinced him that the German empire in Central Europe must be dismantled if peace were to prevail. Germany must also be forced to pay indemnities to those countries that it had occupied and must be thoroughly democratized. An interbelligerent labor conference, he feared, would play into the hands of the Germans, especially since so many German Socialists seemed largely supportive of their government's war aims.[6]

By contrast, Allied labor and Socialist repugnance for German foreign aggression and the German Socialists was offset by their disgust for the imperialist plans of the Allies as they were revealed in the "secret treaties" between the major Entente powers published by the Bolsheviks shortly after they assumed power in November of 1917. Disillusioned with the "secret" and aggrandizing diplomacy practiced by all the major European powers but inspired—if a bit frightened—by the revolutionary unrest spreading throughout the globe, Allied labor and Socialist leaders continued to promote plans for an interbelligerent labor meeting at Stockholm despite Wilson's, and AFL President Samuel Gompers's, opposition. Only labor, they believed, could achieve a "people's peace" and give birth to a "new diplomacy" that would serve the needs of ordinary people.[7]

Antiwar U.S. Socialist leaders, in contrast to Gompers and the prowar Socialists, proved generally supportive of Allied labor and Socialist diplomacy in 1918 and tried but failed to obtain passports from the Wilson administration to attend European labor meetings and the planned interbelligerent labor conference. In the meantime, they remained preoccupied with fighting the imminent imprisonment of dozens of Socialists throughout the country. By war's end, Wilson's relationship with the U.S. Left lay in tatters, while the Allied Left increasingly viewed him with suspicion. These developments in turn set the stage for Wilson's efforts to win their renewed loyalty at Versailles through the labor provisions incorporated into the treaty and the creation of the International Labor Organization.

4 Dialectical Relationships
Collaboration and Resistance in Wartime

IN THE SPRING OF 1917, AFL Vice President James Duncan, a former granite cutter of humble Scottish immigrant origins, took the trip of a lifetime at U.S. government expense. Appointed by President Wilson as an "envoy extraordinary" to a diplomatic mission that visited Russia in the wake of the March revolution that overthrew the Czar, Duncan and other members traveled by ship across the Pacific to the port of Vladivostok, and then by train across Siberia to Petrograd and Moscow. Chaired by "Broadway" capitalist and longtime statesman Elihu Root, the commission represented a cross section of prominent Americans supportive of Wilson's war aims, including leading businessmen, social reformers, and military officials, as well as Duncan and prowar Socialist Charles Edward Russell. The goal of the mission was officially to cultivate Soviet-American friendship and discuss war aims with America's new ally. But informally the commission was also charged with collecting information on Russia's commitment to remaining in the war, its war-making capabilities, and its current precarious financial and industrial situation. The dry official report of the visit, written by Root, expressed confidence that Russia could be kept in the war if it received sufficient economic and military aid from the United States. Root particularly commended Duncan and Russell in the report for establishing "relations of confidence and esteem with the Council of Workmen's and Soldiers' Deputies," and for counseling workers and factory managers in munitions plants on how to increase industrial efficiency.[1]

Duncan's far more ebullient and lengthy report, published in full in the *Proceedings of the Convention of the American Federation of Labor*, was part travelogue, part political treatise, and part AFL advertisement. In a compelling and lucid style, Duncan wrote of Siberian farmlands that compared favorably to the fertile plains of the American Midwest, rugged forests similar to those of Vermont, and plateaus like those of Nebraska. He described Siberian men as "poor" but "big, strong and healthy, with perhaps a smattering of indolence which might be excused because, where returns or wages for labor performed are meager, ambition to earn is not keenly in evidence." Duncan expressed particular compassion for Siberian women, whom he described as "agile, docile, perhaps underfed, [and] poorly clothed" with "regret and despair evident in their soft blue eyes." Yet he emphasized that a new spirit of hope was germinating in Russia due to the recent birth of democracy there. Although the Bolsheviks made the most "noise" at local meetings, Duncan expressed faith that moderate Socialists and pragmatic workingmen were in the majority in the workmen's councils he encountered in Russia. Such men remained committed to helping the other Entente democracies win the war and to strengthening democracy and industry in Russia. Duncan sought to help them in their pursuit of democracy and prosperity by educating them about AFL trade union and industrial practices.[2]

Duncan also symbolically emphasized that he had scored a victory for democracy and for U.S. labor by holding his own in ongoing social engagements with the business and military elites who dominated the commission. In particular, Duncan recalled fondly a particularly long train ride in a luxurious railroad car previously reserved for the Czar that contained a cribbage set. He challenged the "military men" to a cribbage game to "settle for all time whether now that democracy was in the ascendancy, any form of militarism or the benign influence of industrialism were to be paramount." Although the military men on the commission chose Duncan's opponent for his "constructive and calculating mind," Duncan won the game and "militarism" abdicated to "industrialism."[3]

Upon the commission's return to the United States, AFL leaders praised Duncan both for the "eminently successful manner in which he discharged the obligations resting upon him" and for ensuring that "full recognition was given to the trade union movement, to the workers, [and] the masses" in the previously elite world of diplomacy.[4] By serving his country so nobly, they believed, Duncan had paved the way for the appointment of other AFL representatives to government agencies and diplomatic missions, thereby advancing democracy, the trade union movement, and international peace.

Yet critics of the AFL saw the Root commission quite differently. Even before commission members sailed for Russia, the Socialist Party characterized Root as a "corporate lackey" and complained that "If Root is sent to Russia, his mission will be to represent the American money lords." Party leaders insisted that "[n]o socialist, no representative of the working class of America" should join the commission and specifically asked Russell to decline his invitation, since he did not represent the antiwar majority within the Socialist Party. When Duncan and Russell accepted their positions anyway,

Victor Berger characterized them as "hot patriots in the capitalist sense of the word" and implied that they would doubtless do the bidding of the capitalist war machine.[5]

IWW activists on the West Coast also took an interest in the mission, which received much publicity as it departed and returned through Seattle. Local radicals attempted to deflate the positive local press coverage by criticizing Gompers, Duncan, and Russell for their "puffed-up" arrogance in assuming they represented American labor on the commission, for hobnobbing with military and business elites as if they were "born and raised in the club house," and for their inaccurate understanding of the Russian Revolution. When the Russian ship the *Shilka* landed in Seattle several months after the Root commission returned, IWW activists seized the opportunity to interview Russian sailors firsthand. The local IWW press gleefully reported that, according to the Russian sailors, the Root commission had to wait several weeks to get a hearing with the Workers, Soldiers, and Peasants Council because the Council's representatives were "so busy with the affairs of workingmen that [they] had no time for bourgeois representatives of American capitalism." The editors wondered whether, given the repression of free speech and dissent in the United States during the war, the Russians would soon take it upon themselves to make America "safe for democracy."[6]

Although the Socialist Party and IWW voiced the strongest concerns about the Root mission, even many within the AFL fold had their concerns. UMWA organizer Mother Jones, for example, described the commission as the "slickest rottenest," Russell as an "intelectual [sic] socialist," and Duncan as an "ultra conservative." She decried the fact that honest and thoughtful men like John Fitzpatrick and Edward Nockels of the Chicago Federation of Labor were never appointed to government missions or committees and argued that "We have not had what I term a good watch dog in all of Washington to keep an eye on what these pirates are doing." The AFL press in Seattle raised similar concerns about the Root mission and joined the IWW and Seattle Socialist Party in vying for interviews with the *Shilka* sailors in trying to uncover the "real truth" about the Russian revolution.[7]

The controversy over the Root mission represented in microcosm the debate that would surround the AFL's and the prowar Socialist's collaborationist strategies throughout the war. The AFL leadership assumed that by loyally pledging their support to the government in March 1917, they had earned their right to plum assignments like that enjoyed by Duncan on the Root commission. They also argued that by participating on government committees and missions—even those led by businessmen—they were offering the government invaluable advice and paving the way for more democratic input by labor on both domestic and international issues in the future. Yet opponents of collaboration charged that the AFL leadership and prowar Socialists increasingly behaved as toadies of the Wilson administration. Collectively and individually they asked incisive questions about whether the AFL's policies—both domestic and international—served the interests of the working class. Building on the national security and peace platforms they developed during the Mexican and preparedness debates, dissidents offered promising and imaginative alternative strategies for ending the war and promoting international labor cooperation that differed markedly from those of Wilson and drew striking popular support.

Although the wartime critiques of AFL and Wilsonian diplomacy offered by Socialist and labor dissenters were in many ways insightful, in one respect they proved wrong. The AFL and prowar Socialists, far from serving as mere errand boys for the Wilson administration, exercised significant power within it. They used this power in ways that encouraged the campaign of repression against American Socialist and labor dissidents and undercut efforts by the international labor and Socialist movements to encourage a labor-negotiated end to the war. Yet despite government repression, American Socialist and labor opponents of Wilson's policies continued to exercise surprising influence both at home and abroad, helping to ensure an escalating dialectic of response and counterresponse.

THE WILSON ADMINISTRATION AND THE SPLIT WITHIN AMERICAN SOCIALISM

In a letter written to presidential advisor Edward House in October of 1917, the liberal journalist Walter Lippmann complained about the administration's denial of mailing privileges to antiwar Socialist publications and argued that it would create far more support for the Socialists than they would otherwise enjoy. "A great government" he argued, "ought to be contemptuously uninterested in such opinion and ought to suppress only military secrets and advice to break the law or to evade it." Historian Thomas Knock blamed Wilson's failure to follow such advice on his "acquiescence" in the policies of underlings like Postmaster General Albert Burleson and argued that the administration's suppression of civil liberties played a major role in unraveling the "left-of-center coalition" he had built for himself before 1916.[8] Yet this interpretation confuses cause and effect. To the extent that a left-of center coalition still existed in 1917, it unraveled because the wartime program of the Wilson administration was so fundamentally at odds with the antiwar politics of many on the left, particularly the Socialists. Wilson, in turn, consciously chose to suppress Socialist opinion in 1917 because he realized that the antiwar message of the Socialist Party had appeal both abroad and at home. Since his own administration was divided on whether to pursue a conciliatory or repressive policy toward the antiwar Socialist majority, Wilson relied to a surprising degree on prowar Socialists and AFL leaders in assessing the Socialist threat.

The first sign of trouble for Wilson came only four days after he asked Congress for a declaration of war, when the Socialist Party staged its Emergency Convention in St. Louis. Defying the trend set by Socialist parties in other belligerent countries, the American Socialist Party voted overwhelmingly to continue its opposition to the war. In his opening address, Morris Hillquit asserted that "We have been violently, needlessly, criminally drawn into this conflict." The American people, he argued, were overwhelmingly opposed to the war, and the Socialist Party was responsible for continuing to lead the crusade against it. He admitted that Socialist Party membership had declined since 1916, but dramatically emphasized that the convention and subsequent antiwar policies of the party would "make or unmake the Socialist movement in the United States." Charging Wilson with hypocrisy, Hillquit lambasted the president for claiming to war in the name of democracy when he had not even "consulted the American people" about whether they wanted war, a clear allusion to the president's opposition to Benson's proposals for a national referendum vote on the war.[9]

The majority report of the convention, prepared by a committee chaired by Kate Richards O'Hare, famously declared that "[a]s against the false doctrine of national patriotism, we uphold the ideal of international working class solidarity." Less quoted but more impressive was the report's point-by-point renunciation of the rationale for war outlined by Wilson in his address to Congress. German autocracy, it argued, had not caused the war as the president claimed. Rather, the "[c]apitalism, imperialism and militarism" practiced by all the major belligerents had "laid the foundation of an inevitable general conflict in Europe." The war was also not one for national honor because "ruthless as the unrestricted submarine war policy of the German government was and is, it is not an invasion of the rights of the American people as such, but only an interference with the opportunity of certain groups of American capitalists to coin cold profits." Repudiating Wilson's claim that the war was being waged for unselfish purposes, the report cited statistics that American manufacturers of munitions and war supplies had made over seven billion dollars in profit from the war trade and sought a U.S. declaration of war to ensure even greater profits. It was also "cant and hypocrisy," charged the authors, to declare that the war was not one fought against the German people because it was they who would be "mowed down" in the event of American military mobilization.[10]

Finally, the report insisted that the war was not waged to "make the world safe for democracy" because "[d]emocracy can never be imposed upon any country by a foreign power by force of arms." Democracy, moreover, would suffer in the United States as a result of the war. The authors noted that already the decision for war had been made in an undemocratic fashion without consulting the people of the United States. Prophetically, they predicted that in the near future the war would be used as a "pretext for an attempt to throttle our rights and to crush our democratic institutions, and to fasten upon this country a permanent militarism." The report concluded by emphasizing that the declaration of war was "a crime against the people of the United States and against the nations of the world."[11]

The convention produced two minority reports, the first written by Louis Boudin of New York, Kate Adler of Washington, and Walter B. Dillon of New Mexico. This report also declared "unalterable opposition" to the war but made a point of warning as well against apparently defensive wars, since German Socialists claimed they supported the war program of their government only because of the imminent threat of Russian invasion. The other report, written by John Spargo, made the case for those Socialists who believed that the Socialist Party should throw its support behind the government war effort. Spargo insisted that, while it was true that the American capitalist class had taken "too great an interest in the war," this should not obscure the fact that fighting on one side in the conflict were "the greatest autocracies in the world, the most powerful reactionary nations, while on the other side are ranged the most progressive and democratic nations in the world." It would be "treachery to the principles of international socialism," he argued, as well as "treachery to the democratic principles and institutions of America" not to support the Entente cause. On a practical level, he insisted that "disloyalty to the essential principles of Americanism would destroy hope of ever winning the great masses of the American people to our cause." Although Hillquit applauded Spargo for advancing an unpopular position, the convention overwhelmingly adopted the O'Hare report; it received 140 votes, Boudin's report received 31, and Spargo's only 5. In a subsequent referendum, the party membership adopted the majority report by a vote of about three to one.[12]

Despite the strongly antiwar tone of the majority report and its overwhelming endorsement by the party membership, officials within the Wilson administration initially disagreed about how to respond. Many liberals within the Wilson administration initially sought to pursue a conciliatory policy toward the antiwar Socialists in the hope that they might be enlisted to help with diplomacy toward the European Left. Secretary of War Newton Baker, for example, recommended Morris Hillquit for the Root commission after the St. Louis convention. Baker's recommendation came amid concerns that Duncan, or any other appointee recommended by the AFL leadership for that matter, would receive a tepid welcome among Russian Socialists due to Gompers's well-known anti-Socialist politics. Yet when Secretary of State Robert Lansing, a more conservative force within the administration, met with Hillquit, he found him to be a "natural intriguer and utterly unreliable" and worried that he was in favor of any means possible of "forcing peace."[13]

With his advisors divided about Hillquit and other leading antiwar Socialists, Wilson chose to trust the advice of prowar Socialist William English Walling, who wrote a letter to Secretary of Labor William B. Wilson forwarded to the president by Lansing. Walling argued that "none of the official leaders of the majority now in control of the American party can be trusted. On the contrary, all of them are in bitter opposition to the American government and American people." He argued that this included the "rabid" foreign-born Socialists such as Hillquit and Victor Berger who had proven "notoriously pro-German throughout the war" and the "small ultra-pacifist group" composed of such men as Debs and Benson who had been "won over absolutely to the program of immediate peace . . . at any price." The St. Louis convention resolutions, suggested Walling, if passed by the membership, were "treason."[14] So impressed was President Wilson with Walling's warnings that he at first insisted that Walling should represent the Socialist Party on the Root commission. But when Walling declined, Wilson chose to extend the invitation to one of the prowar Socialists recommended by Walling: Charles Edward Russell.[15]

Yet the appointment backfired because, by the time the commission arrived in Russia, news had spread that the bona fide Socialist Party in the United States did not consider Russell their representative. Throughout their trip, Russell and Duncan were dogged by questions and protests about the failure of the administration to include someone on the committee who represented the antiwar Socialist majority or antiwar components of the labor movement. So hostile were many Russian Socialists to Russell that some even tried to prevent him from proceeding to Petrograd. Indeed, Russell claimed that the American Socialist Party was engaged in a conspiracy to sabotage the mission by deliberately channeling negative information about him to Russian Socialists. He charged that a particularly close relationship existed between "East Side" New York Jewish Socialists like Morris Hillquit and "certain Russian extremists."[16] Although Duncan and Root nonetheless reported that the commission had been well received by Russian workers and Socialists, even the U.S. consul at Petrograd, North Winship, had his doubts. In his briefings to the State Department he argued that the activities and proclamations of Russell and Duncan, as well as letters of greeting sent by Gompers and prowar Socialists to coincide with their trip, had been largely ignored by the Socialist publications in the city. *Pravda*, on the other hand, published a protest letter from the Lettish Federation of the American Socialist Party charging that Russell was a "bourgeois renegade and traitor of the working people" as well as a "lackey" of American imperialists. Winship also noted that the "ovations" that greeted some of Duncan's speeches in the city had largely been made by "middle-class" audiences, since few workers turned up for events at which commission members spoke.[17]

Even as the Root mission met with mixed receptions in Russia, a new issue surfaced that caused further tensions between the U.S. antiwar Socialist majority and the Wilson administration. European Socialists began inviting Socialist and labor leaders from all belligerent countries to a conference in Stockholm tentatively set for June. The goal of the conference was officially to encourage Socialist and labor leaders to frame peace terms that might bring an early end to the war. But Gompers, Walling, and Russell quickly charged that the Germans were the driving force behind the conference and sought to use it to promote pacifism in Europe in ways that would undermine the Entente war effort. Gompers sent a telegram to multiple European labor leaders as well as the State Department and Duncan in Russia declaring that the planned conference was "premature and inappropriate" and could lead "to no good purpose." Only governments, he argued, had the right to frame peace terms. In the unlikely event the representatives to the planned Stockholm Conference succeeded in agreeing upon peace terms, it might undermine the national diplomatic agendas of Entente nations, weaken efforts "to democratize the institutions of the world," and "hazard the liberties and opportunities for freedom of all peoples."[18] Gompers clarified his remarks in public speeches, arguing that there was no foundation for a just peace until German militarism was crushed. In his autobiography, Gompers later recounted that "[a]t no time in my life did I have to work harder to prevent the labor movement from chasing a rainbow than when the international Socialists began sending invitations for wartime conferences of the workingmen of all countries."[19] Russell and

Walling, meanwhile, argued that the conference was being "engineered by Berlin" to promote a separate peace between Russia and Germany. On these grounds, as well as the disloyalty shown by American Socialists to the government, Walling recommended denying passports to Hillquit and Berger.[20]

Morris Hillquit, responding to press releases by Russell and Walling about the alleged German plot that lay behind the Stockholm Conference, wrote Lansing and insisted that as a member of the International Socialist Bureau, he knew there was not the "slightest foundation" to the charges. The conference had first been proposed by the American Socialist Party before the United States entered the war. In this sense it could hardly be considered a pro-German plot: rather it was a pro-American proposal designed to promote the Wilsonian aims of no annexations and no indemnities in a way that would help bring about an early peace. Yet the State Department chose to deny passports to American Socialists seeking to attend the conference, provoking further outrage from the Socialist press, which called it "despotic" and lamented the influence of a "handful of ex-Socialist and pork chop patriots" in determining the policy of the government toward international socialism. Other Allied countries in turn followed suit, preventing the Stockholm meeting from taking place in the summer of 1917, although efforts would continue to promote a similar type of conference in the future.[21]

With its international efforts to help plan and attend an interbelligerent labor and Socialist conference at least temporarily blocked, the Socialist Party devoted itself to grassroots antiwar activities. At its St. Louis convention, the party had outlined several potentially important lines of action, including promoting public opposition to war through both educational efforts and demonstrations, "[u]nyielding opposition" to military and industrial conscription as well as military training in the schools, "[v]igorous resistance to censorship and restrictions to free speech," and aggressive lobbying for the socialization and democratic management of large industries and natural resources because the "end of wars will come with the establishment of socialized industry and industrial democracy the world over." Building on his campaign proposals in 1916, Allan Benson also proposed that, if conscription appeared likely to be passed into law, the Socialist Party demand a national referendum on the issue. Benson's proposal proved quite popular and the party launched a petition drive almost immediately to gain enough signatures to force the issue on Congress. The petition drive, along with a more far-reaching campaign against conscription, quickly became the focal point of most Socialist Party antiwar activities in the spring of 1917.[22]

When Congress chose to ignore the petitions and passed conscription into law without a democratic referendum on May 18, the Socialist Party not only continued its petition drive but also joined in legal challenges based on the argument that conscription violated the Thirteenth Amendment prohibiting slavery and involuntary servitude (Figure 4.1). The party also played a vanguard role in exposing what it viewed as disinformation about the draft. On Registration Day in June, when all men of eligible age were required to register for the new "selective service system," most papers reported on the peaceful and orderly way in which men in the required age group fulfilled their legal and patriotic duties. The Socialist press, in its typical muckraking style, not only emphasized extensive draft resistance but also uncovered the fact that two-thirds of those who registered claimed exemptions. Historians of the draft who have focused on different regions of the country, from the deep South and Southwest to the Midwest and New England, have largely verified these statistics. They have also demonstrated that requests for draft

Figure 4.1. *Seattle Union Record*, April 28, 1917, 1. Labor dissidents emphasized that conscription violated the Thirteenth Amendment, which prohibited involuntary servitude. As this cartoon makes clear, many believed conscription to be both un-American and undemocratic.

exemptions and draft evasion were common among all ethnic and racial groups. Men, of course, sought exemptions for many reasons, but to Socialists it clearly demonstrated a lack of patriotic enthusiasm for war. As one headline explained, "Registration Day Shows Overwhelming Vote Against War By Men Of Draft Age." The information clearly placed prowar forces on the defensive, as Provost Marshall General Crowder spent the week following Registration day struggling to explain to the mainstream press why so many men were seeking exemptions.[23]

In addition to highlighting uncomfortable facts about the draft, the Socialist press also continued to play an important role in debunking militarist propaganda that conflated manliness with military service and womanliness with breeding sons to be soldiers and keeping the home fires burning. In this campaign the Socialist press faced a formidable new foe: the Committee on Public Information (CPI), created by President Wilson only a week after he declared war and led by progressive journalist George Creel. The CPI, using many of the techniques of the newly developing advertising industry, promoted the war effort through films, posters, magazine advertisements, and by sponsoring seventy-five thousand "Four Minute Men" to speak at community gatherings about war aims in simplified terms that everyone could allegedly understand. According to Steven Vaughn, the most pervasive theme in CPI propaganda was that the United States entered the war on the side of the Allies to promote democracy. Yet CPI propaganda also drew heavily on the gendered images and arguments that had earlier been promoted by preparedness activists. In advertisements and posters, manly American soldiers fought bestial Huns and won the adoration of proud mothers and girlfriends who were in turn supporting the war effort through Red Cross work and other voluntary activities. Combat, suggested captions under such visual propaganda, made boys into men—cultivating both physical and mental stamina. Similar themes dominated movies produced by the private sector in cooperation with the CPI, such as *The Slacker* and *The Man Who Was Afraid*. These visual representations sent subtle and not-so-subtle messages about the respective gender duties of male and female citizens during wartime.[24]

Yet the Socialist press soon utilized their own arsenal of gender stereotypes, first developed during the preparedness debates, to emphasize the attractiveness and value of patriotic dissent. Among these were the stock image of "social man" whose manliness was based on the power of reason rather than military prowess and who demonstrated his courage by opposing the "narrow-visioned" nationalism caused by wars. The redemptive working-class mother also played a continuing role in Socialist propaganda; she used her maternal instincts to defend men from needless military service and possible death on the battlefield and offered a stark contrast to the submissive patriotic mothers idolized by Theodore Roosevelt who knit socks for the Red Cross and bred sons to be used as cannon fodder. In the spring of 1917, the propaganda battle between the Socialist press and government reached white-heat level as Socialist newspapers coined the slogan "Pacifist Brawn and Silk-Stocking Militarism" to convey their belief that it was hard-muscled working people—both male and female—who opposed the war, while the effete idle rich aggressively promoted the war effort because it garnered them huge profits that they could use to continue their profligate lifestyles. Adding fuel to these arguments in the rural South was a cogent slogan resurrected from Confederate draft protests of the 1860s; the war was a "Rich Man's War and a Poor Man's Fight."[25]

In an effort to draw further support for its expanding range of anticonscription and antiwar activities, the Socialist Party cooperated with other peace groups in staging the "First American Conference for Democracy and Terms of Peace" in New York City on May 3, 1917. Among the most prominent of the many Socialists who played a leading role in the conference were Morris Hillquit and Victor Berger. The conference created the People's Council of America as a populist alternative to the Council of National Defense created by President Wilson. Although Gompers liked to believe that the Council of National Defense had helped to democratize policymaking, Socialists charged that it "abrogated the functions of Congress" and placed them in the hands of appointed officials who were mostly from the class of "hereditary junkers" that stood to reap enormous profits from the perpetuation of the war. The People's Council, by contrast, was conceived to be democratic in structure and open to anyone who wished to join. The group pledged itself to the Bolshevik (and U.S. Socialist Party) peace demands of no annexations, no indemnities, and self-determination for all peoples, and demanded a quick negotiated settlement to the war. It also opposed conscription and condemned the suppression of free speech. The group made use of the extensive infrastructure of Socialist locals to create local People's Councils modeled on the Workers' Councils in Russia, and soon the organization boasted affiliates across the country. Many of President Wilson's advisors, alarmed by the rapid-fire growth of the People's Council movement, as well as by the spread of antidraft protests often inconclusively blamed on the councils, advised him to address the rising tide of disloyalty. In his Flag Day speech on June 14, the president took their advice, emphasizing that the aims for which the United States fought were just and warning against seditious behavior.[26]

The Espionage Act, passed into law on June 5, gave the government a powerful tool with which to attempt to crush the dissent emanating from both the People's Council and Socialist Party. It provided for substantial fines and imprisonment for up to twenty years for obstructing military operations in wartime and also made it a crime to use the mails for these purposes. As David Kennedy has demonstrated, Postmaster General Albert Burleson used his power under the act in a conscious effort to "break the backs of groups dependent on the mails to circulate news among their members, including ethnic communities, radical labor organizations, and minority political parties." During the summer months of 1917, the post office department banned at least twelve Socialist publications from the mails. Among the first Socialists to be arrested under the provisions of the Espionage Act was Kate Richards O'Hare, for giving a speech in Bowman North Dakota on July 17 in which she allegedly claimed that the women of the United States were being treated as "brood sows to raise children to get into the army and [be] made into fertilizer." O'Hare vigorously denied the claim but she was convicted in December to five years in prison for obstructing military recruitment. A string of convictions of high-profile Socialists, including Eugene Debs, followed, along with those of innumerable Socialists active at the local level, such as Hulet Wells, former president of the Seattle Central Labor Council.[27]

Although the Espionage Act was implemented and enforced by federal officials like Burleson working in cooperation with state and local authorities, Wilson clearly had the power to stop the persecution had he chosen to do so. Indeed, a striking number of prominent liberals joined Walter Lippman in encouraging him to curb the suppression of free speech in the spring and summer of 1917. Yet Wilson, while expressing some concerns about the way Burleson interpreted his orders, never disavowed censorship or restrictions on free speech during wartime. Indeed, to a surprising degree, Wilson followed cases involving Socialists carefully and urged government monitoring. Of particular concern to Wilson was Morris Hillquit's New York mayoral campaign. Walter Lippmann, in concert with other liberal allies of the president, warned early in the autumn of 1917 that Hillquit would likely receive a "very large vote" and that it might "let loose pacifist feeling throughout the country." Lippmann's advice was for the president to make some kind of public statement extolling the virtues of the Democratic candidate in the race while eschewing any kind of censorship that would give the Socialists more political ammunition. Wilson subsequently wrote Attorney General Burleson directly urging him not to suppress the Socialist paper the *New York Call*, "until *after* the election in New York City" [emphasis added]. Wilson also sent a note to

Attorney General T. W. Gregory and cautioned him against making Hillquit a "martyr" by paying "any attention to his recent outrageous utterances about the Liberty Loan." Yet the president simultaneously encouraged Gregory to continue to investigate the Hillquit situation.[28]

Gregory wrote back to Wilson shortly before the election to inform him that Hillquit had "been very close to the line a number of times but, in my judgment, any proceedings against him would enable him to pose as a martyr and would be likely to increase his voting strength." But Gregory continued to monitor Hillquit in the hopes that he would say "something considerably more disloyal than the utterances so far reported to me."[29] As predicted, Hillquit failed to win the race, but he received nearly five times more votes than any previous Socialist candidate for the New York mayor's office. Hillquit was part of a national trend; Socialist candidates throughout the country dramatically increased their percentage of the vote in the 1917 fall elections.[30] Such voting behavior suggested that the Socialist Party's antiwar and anticonscription politics were clearly increasing its popularity, thereby provoking the Wilson administration's more sustained program of repression in 1918.

Perhaps of even greater concern to the Wilson administration than the political threat posed by the Socialists, however, was the ongoing labor unrest, for it threatened to paralyze economic mobilization for the war effort as well as derail Wilson's efforts to secure working-class support for his reformist agendas both at home and abroad.

THE ECONOMIC SPHERE

In the immediate aftermath of the U.S. declaration of war, as the Socialist Party met to frame its antiwar platform, AFL President Samuel Gompers convened a meeting of the Labor Committee of the Council of National Defense to develop a policy for promoting industrial peace during the war. The Labor Committee subsequently issued a statement asking that neither employees nor employers take advantage of the wartime situation to "change existing standards." Although the statement met with a mixed reception in labor circles, government officials at first widely praised the policy as visionary and cooperated with Gompers in developing adjustment commissions for individual industries that were designed to resolve disputes between management and workers with this principal in mind. Staffed by trade union, business, and government representatives, many praised the adjustment commissions for exemplifying industrial democracy in action.

As Joseph McCartin has persuasively argued, this system of adjustment commissions became the model for America's subsequent twentieth-century collective bargaining system.[31]

Initially, however, this system failed to stem the tide of industrial unrest; strike activity increased dramatically during the first five months of the war. Presidential advisor Franklin Lane, writing to Wilson in early November 1917, explained that a wide discrepancy existed between wartime labor policy and the reality of wartime labor relations. The Council of National Defense, Lane reminded the president, had called for maintaining existing standards. Yet the nation experienced 221 strikes affecting 179,103 workers between April 6, 1917, and October 19, 1917.[32] Felix Frankfurter, sent to investigate Western labor troubles, noted that the foreign-born dominated a number of the key industries critical to the war effort, but argued that Gompers had largely failed to win their trust. Among these were workers in the steel, meatpacking, mining, and clothing industries. Although he praised Gompers's "leadership" as "indispensable," he nonetheless warned that it would be "fatal to the handling of the labor situation to assume that Mr. Gompers controls all labor." Among those whom Frankfurter identified as responsible for inspiring labor unrest among the foreign-born were the Industrial Workers of the World as well as the Socialist-led unions—both outside and within the American Federation of Labor.[33]

Always opposed to U.S. involvement in the European war, the IWW leadership had nonetheless counseled its membership to avoid participating in antiwar and antipreparedness political activities after efforts to stage a general strike to end the war in Europe faltered. As the IWW paper *Solidarity* explained, it would be a mistake to "sacrifice working-class interests for the sake of a few noisy and impotent parades and antiwar demonstrations." Political actions like those proposed by the Socialists, they believed, would never empower workers. Instead they argued that IWW members should "get on the job of organizing the working class to take over the industries" and in that way "stop all future capitalist aggression that leads to war and other forms of barbarism."[34] But when the AFL pledged its loyalty to the government in the event of war in March of 1917, the IWW felt compelled to respond. Gompers, argued the editors at *Solidarity*, behaved like a "bell sheep" who had "placed himself at the head of 'his flock' to steer them into the shambles." The paper also published an antiwar statement from the IWW's 1916 convention alongside the AFL's declaration of labor loyalty. The IWW statement, in contrast to the AFL's, firmly condemned "all wars" and committed the IWW to "antimilitarist propaganda in times of peace" as well as to promoting "class solidarity among the workers of the entire world" during times of war. The editors then asked the rhetorical question, "Who will be to blame if the workers of America are betrayed and led into the bloodiest slaughter of history?"[35]

As tensions between the United States and Germany increased in late 1916 and early 1917, some Wobblie activists attempted to resurrect the idea of a general strike to prevent a U.S. declaration of war against Germany. But the general executive board, operating on the advice of William Haywood, tabled the resolution. Although details are sketchy, many apparently believed that labor had not reached a sufficient stage of industrial development to sustain such a strike; the unemployed would be recruited as replacement workers and used by militias to shoot down the strikers.[36] The IWW leadership steadfastly opposed a general strike even after the government enacted conscription. By contrast, many IWW locals actively resisted the draft. In Rockford, Illinois, for example, police arrested the entire membership of an IWW local after it staged a protest against conscription on Registration Day. In the West, IWW activist Frank Little became an outspoken critic of both the draft and the war and was lynched for his efforts. IWW as well as Socialist activists were also blamed, probably wrongly, for spontaneous armed rebellions against the draft such as the Green Corn rebellion in Oklahoma during the summer of 1917. Yet the leadership, while believing conscription to be the "rankest, rawest, crudest piece of work that was ever attempted to be 'put over' in the interests of Big Business under the lying mask of 'patriotism,'" nonetheless argued that it would be a strategic mistake to stage a general strike to prevent conscription. Such a strike would only land IWW members in jail where they would have no chance of continuing their industrial work.[37]

Instead the IWW leadership pursued what it perceived to be a cautious approach, focusing on organizing campaigns it initiated before the war among farm workers, miners, and lumbermen. Yet all of these industries, as Melvyn Dubofsky has noted, were critical to the war effort. Soldiers had to eat and lumber was necessary for the construction of ships. The coal excavated by miners fueled ships and factories; copper was an essential ingredient in instruments of wartime communication. According to Dubofsky, the IWW likely doubled its membership between 1916 and 1917, from about forty thousand to more than one hundred thousand, due in no small part to organizing campaigns in these war-related industries. Although AFL unionists also represented workers in these fields, when workers in all three industries struck in the spring and summer of 1917, the government blamed the IWW. Federal and state authorities raided IWW offices, shut down IWW publications, and arrested hundreds of IWW activists.[38]

In part, the government's campaign against the IWW might be understood as a logical, if highly undemocratic, response to the economic threat posed by IWW strikes to the war effort. In the Northwest lumber industry, for example, IWW strikes and slowdowns likely reduced output by around 40 percent. Yet statistics suggest that IWW strikes accounted for only one in six lost workdays during the war between April and October of 1917, its period of greatest strength. The demands made by IWW unions, moreover, were not substantively different than those of AFL or independent unions. In the lumber industry, both IWW and AFL unions struck primarily for an eight-hour day and an increase in wages sufficient to offset inflation. In the copper mines around Bisbee, Arizona, suggests Dubofsky, the membership of AFL and IWW unions proved so fluid, and their demands so similar, that it became "impossible without a scorecard to distinguish Wobblies, AFL men, and labor spies."[39]

Given that the AFL and independent unions were responsible for vastly more strikes and made demands quite similar to that of the IWW in industries where they competed for members, the repressive policies pursued by the government toward the IWW cannot be explained by economics alone. Instead, as Francis Shor has convincingly argued, the government feared the oppositional culture and discourse that grew in tandem with IWW unions. In this sense, the IWW's words mattered more than their actions, despite its often stated preference for the latter.[40]

Particularly important in wartime was the IWW's irreverent humor and talent for ridiculing patriotic appeals made to workers in order to encourage support for military enlistment, military conscription, or industrial peace. Declaring patriotism to be "gorgeous bunk," the *Industrial Worker* argued that "[a]ll wars have their roots in the economic field, notwithstanding fine-sounding palaver about 'small nationalities,' scraps of paper, 'Kultur,' etc." The paper declared that "real war insanity" reigned when workers who "own no ships and no homes, social outcasts, modern slaves, talk of 'our country.'" Workers, the editors insisted, had no vested interested in fighting for a country that was not theirs and never would be. Big business would reap the profits of war while the "damphool worker" paid with his life.[41] The editors of *Solidarity* used the cartoon figure "Mr. Block" to ridicule the unenlightened worker who was deluded by nationalist propaganda into becoming a soldier and murdering workers from other countries, or even killing American strikers, for the sake of the "International Plunderbund (Figure 4.2)."[42] The anticonscription

CLEVELAND, OHIO SATURDAY, OCTOBER 10, 1914.

THE THINKER!

MR. BLOCK: "It takes some hard thinking to understand how the European war is responsible for the high prices of food and other necessities in this country. Let me see—there's more produced this year than ever, and there's less demand for it, on account of Germany and other countries being cut off from the market. Wouldn't it be better for the respectable papers to put the blame for the high prices on the I. W. W.? Let's hope it will be done. In the meantime, let's be cheerful and patriotic."

Figure 4.2. *Solidarity*, October 10, 1914, 1. IWW publications used the iconic "Mr. Block" to represent the U.S. worker who was deluded by patriotic "bunk" and to highlight what they believed to be workers' real interests.

sentiments of the IWW were neatly summed up in a popular stickerette it produced declaring "Don't Be a Soldier! Be a Man!" Also effective in conveying this sentiment was one of its more memorable verses:

I love my flag, I do, I do,
Which floats upon the breeze,
I also love my arms and legs,
And neck and nose and knees.
One little shell might spoil them all
Or give them such a twist,
They would be of no use to me;
I guess I won't enlist.[43]

In addition to attacking patriotism itself, the IWW also ridiculed Wilson's war aims. On the one hand, they insisted, Wilson had clearly not made the world safe for democracy; rather, "the war with Germany [had] already been used by the masters of industry to destroy the small measure of democracy which existed in the United States." In Wilson's America, it declared, "Free speech is against democracy!" "Free assembly is against democracy!" "Working Class Organization is against Democracy!"[44] Wilson's plans for a League of Nations, moreover, could not be used to justify the war; this proposed body, far from revolutionizing International affairs, would primarily ensure more efficient international "exchanges of wealth . . . in the interests of the [master class]." Only when both capitalism and nationalism were destroyed, and international labor solidarity took their place, could permanent peace be achieved through a "League of Commonwealths" in which wealth was produced and exchanged "for the use and benefit of the entire human race." As the *Shilka* incident demonstrated, the IWW increasingly embraced Russia as the best hope for inspiring a worldwide workers revolution that would transform international relations.[45]

Although the IWW did not directly oppose the war, its culture and rhetoric, in combination with its strike activity, thus proved as threatening to the Wilson administration as the more overt antiwar activities of the Socialist Party. At times, concerns about the IWW seemed to approach near hysteria as authorities imagined its appeal to be potentially so great among unskilled immigrant workers that it might breed total anarchy.

Yet astute observers like Frankfurter continued to caution that the IWW was but a small part of the problem. The AFL, already far larger than the IWW at the onset of the war, doubled its membership between 1915 and 1920. Much of the new growth occurred in mass industries such as meatpacking in which new immigrants dominated. Although Gompers often failed to win their trust, many local AFL organizers proved more successful; in Chicago, for example, John Fitzpatrick launched a highly successful organizing campaign among Eastern European and African American stockyard workers. The New York–based International Ladies' Garment Workers' Union, meanwhile, employed a talented cadre of female organizers that included Rose Schneiderman to recruit women clothing workers from an extraordinarily diverse range of immigrant backgrounds in cities across the country.[46]

AFL unionists, suggests David Montgomery, accounted for at least 75 percent of all strikers in three war-related industries: the metal trades, shipbuilding, and coal mining.[47] In part, this strike activity was inspired by the desire of workers to improve wages and benefits during a time of labor shortages. Joseph McCartin has suggested that the new wartime adjustment commissions also functioned as "Trojan horses" in increasing the expectations of industrial workers. Yet equally important, although far more neglected by historians, was the international context. As David Montgomery has argued, many of the same immigrant neighborhoods that supported strikes teemed with antiwar politics. Many immigrant organizers and workers, moreover, were strongly influenced by the rumblings of revolution abroad. This included not only the Russian Revolution but also the Irish anticolonial struggle against Britain that commenced with the Easter Rebellion. John Fitzpatrick, as previously discussed, became heavily immersed in Irish nationalist politics after the Easter rebellion. Although these revolutions would later disappoint many American labor activists, for a short period they inspired far grander visions of industrial democracy and international transformation than those promoted by Gompers.[48]

That Gompers recognized politics as well as economics fueled AFL strikes became apparent when he created the American Alliance for Labor and Democracy in the summer of 1917. The immediate impetus for the formation of the AALD came from Gompers's concerns about labor unrest in the Jewish-dominated garment districts of New York City. Gompers blamed the People's Council, which he correctly assumed was quite popular among Jewish Socialists in the city. In June, Gompers traveled to New York to meet with Ernest Bohm, the secretary of the New York Central Federated Union. The two agreed on the need to "Americanize the labor movement in greater New York" and developed plans for a new organization designed to inspire patriotism and educate workers about the duties of citizenship. Leading prowar Socialists such as John Spargo and Chester Wright soon took an interest in the proposed organization and joined AFL representatives at a foundational meeting on

July 28. The meeting attacked the "so-called Peoples council" for attempting to "prostitute the labor movement to serve the brutal power responsible for the infamous rape of Belgium" and declared that the goal of the AALD would be to encourage workers to accept responsibility for "carrying the present war for justice, freedom and democracy to a triumphant conclusion." In the aftermath of the meeting, President Wilson supplied Gompers with a statement emphasizing the importance of opposing "dangerous elements" who promoted disloyalty during wartime in an effort to help promote the new organization.[49]

Shortly after this meeting, George Creel of the Committee on Public Information offered to fund the AALD, thereby providing it with enough finances to become a national organization.[50] When the People's Council tentatively planned its conference for Minneapolis in September, the AALD also chose to arrange a national conference there, hoping to engage in a direct challenge to the Socialist-led organization. Representatives from the People's Council, however, found that all the major halls and auditoriums were closed to them, perhaps because of unfavorable publicity they received from the Minneapolis State Federation of Labor. The People's Council therefore chose to hold a shortened meeting in Chicago, while the AALD met in Minneapolis. AALD leaders used their conference to launch a new national organization and officially adopted an expanded set of principles. Their new declaration of principles emphasized "unswerving adherence to the cause of Democracy" and declared that "until autocracy is defeated there can be no hope of an honorable peace." It also strongly denounced the "words and actions of those enemies of the Republic" who assumed to "speak in the name of labor and democracy." In a comparison designed to win the heart of trade unionists, the AALD statement argued that "the betrayal of one's fellow-workers during a strike finds its exact counterpart in the betrayal of one's fellow citizens in time of war." Both were "offenses which deserve the detestation of mankind." Finally, the document insisted that labor standards had not been undermined by the commitment of the labor movement to the war; they had been significantly improved.[51]

In the aftermath of the convention, the AALD launched a major organizing initiative, with Alliance rallies occurring in every major city in the country. Gompers used such occasions, in combination with press releases, as a forum to attack key arguments made by antiwar Socialists, promote the president's war agenda, and defend the AFL's collaboration with the government during the war. At several meetings, Gompers disputed the notion that the decision for war was made undemocratically, arguing that only Congress had the power to declare war. A referendum vote, such as that promoted by the Socialists, was entirely impractical. If a band of men threatened your home and family, he inquired, would you call a vote to meet the threat? On other occasions he accused the American Socialist Party of having more loyalty to its German counterpart than to the United States. He also attacked the notion of a labor-negotiated peace as a German conspiracy. On a more positive note, Gompers spoke of Wilson's commitment to small nationalities, and especially expressed hope to Jewish audiences that this commitment would culminate in a Jewish homeland in Palestine. Finally, he emphasized that AFL loyalty and participation in government agencies during the war was helping to democratize both industry and politics.[52]

Yet the AALD quickly created a firestorm within the AFL. At the AFL convention in November, President Wilson spoke to commend the AFL on its wartime loyalty. Yet a recommendation by the Committee on Resolutions to fully endorse the "patriotic work" of the Alliance aroused significant debate that lasted for several hours. Some wanted to know exactly what patriotism meant; others doubted that it was the "proper purpose" of the convention to discuss patriotism. J. Mahlon Barnes, a Socialist and former vice president, ridiculed the notion that American workers needed to be Americanized. Others complained that the AFL had not emphasized its support for free speech enough. Delegate Fred Voight, a representative of the Electrical Workers of San Francisco, linked the AALD to the broader system of collective bargaining that had developed during the war and complained that workers in his union were "tired of our international officers signing agreements for us without our consent and making scabs of us." Florence Etheridge of the Federal Employee's Union seconded Voight's statement, suggesting that "we must all admit that the workers have been exploited in the name of patriotism."[53]

Perhaps the most critical statements came from the representatives of the Seattle Central Labor Council and the International Ladies' Garment Workers' Union. James Duncan of Seattle suggested that his central labor council still believed the war was a "family quarrel between royalists," and for that reason "could not enthuse the people about it." He also argued that there was no need for any other labor organization "through which to express ourselves." Sarah Shapiro of the International Ladies' Garment Workers' Union argued that the Alliance seemed designed to "take away the rights of the workers and to give them into the hands of the few who claim to be patriots." No one could be blamed, she argued, for failing to support this type of democracy. Gompers responded indignantly, arguing that anyone who would not sign the Alliance pledge was guilty of treason and disloyalty to the AFL.[54]

Unsurprisingly, given that the voting power within the convention rested overwhelmingly in the hands of a few international union leaders, the resolution in support of the AALD passed overwhelmingly. Yet, that dissidents succeeded in launching such a sustained frontal attack on one of Gompers's pet projects on the floor of the AFL convention was in itself a victory. More often, criticisms of Gompers's policies failed to even make it out of committee. In the aftermath of the convention, opposition to the AALD continued, albeit in different forms. John Fitzpatrick, for example, practiced passive resistance by deliberately ignoring written requests from Robert Maisel to form a branch in Chicago. When pressed for an answer, Fitzpatrick finally expressed concerns about the some of the tactics of the organization. Fitzpatrick continued to stall on requests to create a Chicago branch of the AALD throughout the war. Pennsylvania State Federation of Labor President James Maurer, by contrast, expressed his concerns about the AALD directly to Gompers. In response, the AFL sent men to Pennsylvania to try to prevent his reelection. They paved the way for federal agents who were instructed to arrest Maurer if he was not reelected. Maurer, however, managed to win his reelection bid by a margin of three to one in 1918. The Hebrew Trades Council in New York also became involved in a bitter public imbroglio with the AALD in 1917–1918.[55] The debate over the AALD proved symbolic of the broader debate within labor about the costs and benefits of collaborating with the government during wartime and the meaning of working-class citizenship.

CONCLUSION

In a letter written to the Petrograd embassy in May 1917 to convince Russia to stay in the war, Samuel Gompers argued that in the United States the war effort enjoyed the support of 99 percent of the American people, including workers.[56] Clearly he was wrong. The upsurge in Socialist political strength, tepid response to conscription, and pervasive labor unrest all suggested that significant numbers of workers remained unconvinced that the U.S. war effort was a holy crusade that deserved their unstinting allegiance. This lack of enthusiasm among workers for the war effort in turn helps explain Wilson's repressive policies toward the Socialists and Wobblies, as well as his willingness to underwrite the activities of the American Alliance for Labor and Democracy. Yet if Gompers and the prowar Socialists did not clearly triumph in their battle for the loyalties of American workers in 1917, they had scored one victory in their continuing war with dissidents; they had won the collective ear of the Wilson administration. In 1918 they would continue to use their influence with the administration to undermine their domestic opponents. The growing relationship between AFL leaders, prowar Socialists, and the administration also culminated in their appointment to several new diplomatic missions designed to win European labor and Socialist support for Wilson's peace initiatives. American labor and Socialist opponents of the Wilson administration, however, would continue to use their independent transnational contacts to undermine the credibility of AFL and prowar Socialists engaged in diplomatic activity in Europe even as they devoted primary attention to staying out of jail.

5 The AFL, International Labor Politics, and Labor Dissent in 1918

DURING FEBRUARY OF 1918, Samuel Gompers and William English Walling sent a long memo to President Wilson warning of a significant new threat to the Allied war effort: the spreading contagion of Bolshevism and German minority socialism. They argued that, although the American policy of encouraging Socialist and progressive forces in Germany to overthrow the government was understandable, a revolution there would likely prove "abortive" due to the control that the military autocracy exercised over the flow of information and the population. By contrast, Bolshevist and Socialist revolutionary tendencies were fanning the flames of pacifism and labor unrest in the freer political environments of Western Europe and Britain and had the potential to spread even to "Chicago, New York, San Francisco and our other foreign industrial centers in this country." Growing labor and pacifist unrest, they feared, would give momentum to the Stockholm movement, that is, the renewed effort by European labor leaders to stage a conference of labor leaders from all the belligerent countries in order to negotiate an immediate end to the war. If those favoring the Stockholm solution succeeded, suggested Walling and Gompers, it would be a disaster for the United States; Germany would dictate the terms and continue its domination of Eastern and Central Europe after the war.[1]

Upon receiving the report, President Wilson sent it to Secretary of State Lansing, suggesting that it seemed to "speak an unusual amount of truth" and should inform their policies. Lansing responded that the report provided a "remarkable analysis of the dangerous elements which are coming to the surface and which are in many ways more to be dreaded than autocracy; the latter is despotism but an intelligent despotism, while the former is a despotism of ignorance." Autocracy, he suggested, at least had the "virtue of order." By contrast, revolutionary socialism was productive only of "disorder and anarchy." Yet if Walling and Gompers's memo was insightful in identifying a new threat to Wilsonian foreign policy and war strategy on the left, in other ways it proved highly misleading. In particular, by painting all European Socialists and pacifists with one broad brushstroke, the report glossed over the enormous differences between them in 1918. Among the most prominent promoters of the Stockholm conference, for example, were so-called "social patriots" like British Labour Party leader Arthur Henderson who abhorred Bolshevism, distrusted the German Social Democratic Party (SDP), and strongly admired President Wilson. He sought an interbelligerent labor conference in 1918 not because he believed it would achieve immediate peace but because he thought that Wilson's Fourteen Points could be used as the basis for a reconsideration of the war aims of the leading powers. A labor conference could in this sense serve as a spur to a future conference among governments that would negotiate a Wilsonian-inspired peace.[2]

Yet the Wilson administration, alienated from the main body of the U.S. Socialist Party, relied throughout 1918 on the advice and diplomacy of AFL leaders and prowar Socialists in dealing with the European Left. When liberal supporters questioned the policy and encouraged the president to renew ties with leading U.S. Socialists such as Eugene Debs, they were censored or repudiated for their efforts. Social patriots such as Arthur Henderson nonetheless remained strong admirers of the president for, as Alan Dawley has written, the Fourteen Points proved to be a "magic mirror" in which progressives of all kinds saw their own programs reflected.[3] But by following AFL advice and strongly opposing the Stockholm Conference, Wilson undercut the political strength of his strongest supporters in Europe while giving succor to the forces of the "old diplomacy" who would help to destroy his agenda for a just peace at Versailles. Meanwhile, his excessive reliance on the AFL leadership and prowar Socialists for diplomatic counsel and diplomatic service abroad encouraged continued derision and ridicule within the American Left, helping to set the stage for further polarization at war's end.

BRITISH AND AMERICAN LABOR DIPLOMACY IN 1918

Not surprisingly, the AFL leadership devoted the lion's share of its wartime diplomacy to trying to convert the British labor movement to its viewpoints. Yet British labor soon took the lead in trying to promote inter-Allied labor action on the war, placing the AFL on the defensive. Gompers's closest confidante within the British labor movement was William Appleton, conservative leader of the General Federation of Trade Unions (GFTU) who emphasized economic over political action and opposed a meeting with belligerent labor unions. But the General Federation of Trade Unions represented only about one-quarter of British trade unionists. The real centers of power within British labor were the

British Trade Unions Congress (BTUC), its Parliamentary Committee, and the British Labour Party. The British Labour Party was, in its turn, something of an umbrella organization that often worked in coordination with the Socialist and Independent Labour parties. When war broke out in Europe in 1914, Socialist and Independent Labour Party activist James Ramsey MacDonald was chairman of the Parliamentary Labour Party. He soon resigned his position due to his opposition to British involvement in the war and the more moderate Arthur Henderson replaced him.[4]

Under Henderson's direction, the joint committee representing the GFTU, the parliamentary committee of the BTUC, and the Labour Party chose to support the British war effort. Yet in contrast to Gompers, Henderson continued to collaborate with antiwar Socialists in framing labor policy during the war. During 1917–1918, Henderson even sought the input of MacDonald and others on Labour Party committees created to deal with international questions. In part, the difference between Henderson and Gompers on this issue can be explained by Henderson's more conciliatory personality. As Henderson's biographer has written, a more rigid or opportunistic politician might have used the war to drive MacDonald and his Socialist colleagues "into the political wilderness."[5] But equally important were the political exigencies: Labour Party leaders continued to covet Socialist and Independent Labour Party votes. In this sense, British Labour Party politics encouraged compromise and unity in a way that Gompers's pure and simple unionism did not.

As a strong supporter of the British war effort and critic of the German invasion of Belgium, Henderson initially opposed a meeting of labor leaders from belligerent countries. But in the spring of 1917, Henderson traveled to the Soviet Union at the request of the government. His trip roughly coincided in terms of timing with that of James Duncan, but he arrived at startlingly different conclusions than the AFL vice president. In contrast to Duncan's upbeat report emphasizing that pragmatic Russian workers and peasants repudiated Bolshevism, embraced democracy, and remained loyal to the war effort, Henderson wrote to colleagues that the situation in Russia was "chaotic" and could "prove a disaster to Russia [and] to the Allied cause." He feared that an "exclusively" Socialist government might soon take the place of the Kerensky coalition and lead the country into commercial and financial collapse. Interviews with workers made Henderson even more skeptical about the industrial situation; freed from the oppression that had been visited upon them for generations, workers suffered from "intoxication" and sought "complete control of industry." No "steadying influence akin to our trade union movement," suggested Henderson, existed to temper the "outrageous" demands of the workers. Anti-Allied and pacifist sentiment flourished in this chaotic atmosphere, undercutting what little support still existed for the war effort.[6]

Henderson's visit to Russia convinced him of the necessity of an Inter-Allied Socialist and Labor Conference to revise war aims and to plan an interbelligerent labor conference. In a somewhat paradoxical fashion, he argued that these two gestures were necessary both to revive enthusiasm for the war effort in Russia and other Allied countries and to speed up the peace process. In contrast to many in Russia, Henderson did not seek to make the results of an interbelligerent labor conference binding; instead he hoped that such a meeting would encourage more dialogue between belligerent labor movements in ways that would facilitate a future peace conference among governments. In the short term, an endorsement by the Allies of plans for an interbelligerent labor conference would convince the Russians of the sincerity of the Allies in seeking peace and help keep them in the war. Although Henderson doubted that Russia would be able to contribute much militarily under any circumstances, he assumed that "a crippled partner ruled by men sympathetic to the Allied cause and Western democracy was far preferable to a Bolshevik Russia" that tilted toward Germany. But Henderson failed to gain the support of the British government, which accused him of "treachery" for his efforts to promote an interbelligerent conference without their prior approval, and he resigned from the War Cabinet.[7]

Ironically, Henderson's resignation increased his popularity within the rank and file of the Labour Party and British trade union movement, who had grown increasingly disillusioned with the collaborationist foreign policies of British labor leaders over the course of the war. This support in turn afforded Henderson the latitude necessary to launch an initiative to hammer out an independent statement of Labour Party War aims.[8] Even as various party committees worked on the war aims, two momentous new international events gave urgency to their task: the Bolshevik Revolution in the autumn of 1917, and the subsequent publication by the Bolsheviks of "secret treaties" signed between the Allies. The publication of the secret treaties, suggests Alan Dawley, exposed the "sordid deals that defined Allied war aims."[9] Among these were the famous Sykes-Picot agreement that proposed British and French control of many Middle Eastern areas at war's end despite previous pledges to Arab nationalists to support independent Arab states in the area. In return for these pledges, Arab military forces had agreed to reverse their allegiance to the Central Powers and instead fought on the side of the Allies in the expectation of political freedom after 1916. Other "secret" agreements established British, French, or Russian claims to former German colonies. The treaties clearly belied the notion that the Allies were fighting a disinterested war for democracy and undermined support for the war effort among the war-weary Allied populations, helping to catalyze the popular, if diffuse, movement for a "people's peace," or for a labor-negotiated settlement to the war that would put the needs of working people first.[10]

Against this backdrop, the *Statement of War Aims of the Labour Party* passed by a "joint conference of the societies affiliated with the British Trade Union Congress and the British Labour Party" at Westminster on December 28, 1917, had a distinctly reformist, if not radical, cast to it that drew liberally on the rhetoric of President Wilson. The statement announced that whatever the original causes of the war "the fundamental purpose of the British Labour movement in supporting the continuance of the struggle is that henceforth the world be made safe for democracy." To this end, it announced its support for the "democratisation of all countries," and for the elimination of secret diplomacy and imperialism. It also called for the placement of foreign policy powers under the control of popularly elected political bodies within nations, disarmament, and the promotion of a League of Nations that would include an International Legislature comprised of elected representatives. Territorial adjustments were to be based on the principal of "allowing all people to settle their own destinies." Most of these adjustments dealt with areas occupied by the Germans. But the party also took aim at the secret treaties signed by the Allies and "disclaim[ed] all sympathy with the imperialist aims of governments and capitalists who would make of . . . territories now dominated by the Turkish hordes merely instruments either of exploitation or militarism." Anticipating the mandate system that would be created at Versailles, the party emphasized that these areas should be placed under the administrative supervision of the League of Nations. Similarly they suggested that the territories of Tropical Africa should be put under the League's trusteeship. The party also declared itself against protectionism and economic imperialism and advocated for the principle that all countries should support government policies designed to develop natural resources for the benefit of people throughout the world. Finally, it suggested the need for international labor legislation and for an international administrative agency that would allocate available world resources and commodities according to need.[11]

Viewed in retrospect, the party's war aims seem striking both for the extent to which they illuminated the racial paternalism that continued to undergird British Labour Party thinking about the international order and for their radical repudiation of the old diplomacy. Arab nationalists had clearly not asked for British protection from "Turkish hordes" or for political supervision under an administrative body of the League of Nations but for full independence, a point well understood by the Bolshevists who embraced self-determination for former colonies without qualification. Similarly, British Labour Party activists never consulted with representatives from Africa about whether they needed international supervision. Other British colonies were ignored altogether, although these issues would be taken up by the party in 1918 and 1919. Yet the *Statement of War Aims* also clearly demonstrated that, under the press of international events, the party had traveled light years from the War Cabinet in developing a war agenda based on the perceived needs of the world's working classes rather than its ruling elites.

Less than two weeks later, on January 8, 1918, President Wilson announced his own Fourteen Points program. In the aftermath of the president's speech, British Labour Party leaders not only commended him on his vision but announced that his peace program was "in essential respects" quite similar to their own.[12] Yet while the British Labour Party's *Statement of War Aims* often bogged down in specifics, the Fourteen Points expounded general principles, thereby allowing those seeking change throughout the world to read into them what they wished. For example, the first of Wilson's points called for "Open Covenants of Peace, Openly Arrived at," but avoided making any commitments to the democratization of foreign policy decision making highlighted in the British Labour Party statement, or in previous platforms of the American Socialist Party. The Fourteen Points proved similarly vague on territorial adjustments and questions of granting national independence, especially when it came to areas that would likely be claimed by Britain and France under the terms of the secret treaties. Issues of tropical Africa were avoided altogether as were questions of international labor legislation and redistributing the world's natural resources and wealth in a more equitable fashion.[13] Finally, although the president clearly championed the idea of a League of Nations, he failed to outline a possible organizational structure for it. Long hailed as the hallmark of a "new diplomacy" for the world, the Fourteen Points proved remarkably short on details.[14]

Yet the Fourteen Points came at an opportune time for the British Labour Party, helping to rationalize its plans for an Inter-Allied Labor Conference in February of 1918 to clarify war aims and to consider the question of whether to promote and organize an interbelligerent labor meeting. Arthur Henderson personally wrote Gompers informing him that they had chosen to send an invitation only to the AFL despite a request from the American Socialists that they also be represented at the conference. But Gompers claimed that he did not receive the telegram and subsequent letter, sent January 10 and January 16, respectively, until February 9. Since the conference was scheduled to begin February 20, the AFL did not have time to send a representative. In a return letter to Henderson declining the invitation, Gompers emphasized not only the impossibility of sending a representative on such short notice but also that the AFL did not support an interbelligerent labor conference with "those who are aligned against us in this world war for freedom." Gompers, however, informed Henderson that the AFL would be sending its own mission to Britain shortly.[15]

The Inter-Allied meeting proceeded as planned and adopted a statement of war aims that resembled that of the British Labour Party yet incorporated even more Wilsonian language. According to historian Arno Mayer, the new language illuminated the "expanding bonds between European non-Bolshevik Socialism and Wilsonian Liberalism." In particular, suggests Mayer, the new statement placed an emphasis on the League of Nations as a mechanism for resolving sticky territorial and colonial problems that might otherwise inhibit peace negotiations. Yet despite its Wilsonian leanings, the Inter-Allied meeting also declared in favor of an interbelligerent labor conference against the wishes of both the AFL and President Wilson, provided that the labor movements of the Central Powers agreed to support the basic principles of no annexations, no punitive indemnities, and the right of all peoples to self-determination as a precondition for beginning negotiations. To ascertain the support of the labor movements of the Central Powers for these principles, the representatives of the Allied labor meeting sent their statement of war aims to them and waited for a response. In the interim, they sought to travel to the United States in an effort to convince U.S. labor and the Wilson administration to support the proposed conference.[16]

Wilson, however, wrote to Edward House asking him to strongly discourage Henderson from coming to the United States because he believed that the "whole plan" for an International Socialist Labor conference "is outrageous and fraught with the greatest mischief." Secretary of State Lansing concurred with the president, suggesting that "[t]he meeting of this element of society, imbued with the idea of an international revolution, might become a very real menace to all existing forms of government, democratic as well as monarchical." For his part, Secretary of Labor William B. Wilson expressed fear that if Henderson came to the United States and started "preaching Socialism," it "might divide [American] labor." Also influencing Wilson were his increasing concerns about German aggression and his fear that Germany would use a labor meeting to rationalize continued occupation of portions of Russia and

Eastern Europe. In addition he believed German Socialists would capitalize on labor sentiment to justify avoiding indemnities for reconstructing nations like Belgium that had suffered as a result of German invasion.[17]

President Wilson soon communicated with Allied governments that he was opposed to the Henderson mission. Allied Socialist leaders, whether due to the opposition of their governments or other factors, canceled their plans to visit the United States. Meanwhile, Allied leaders Georges Clemenceau, Lloyd George, and Vittorio Orlando met in conference in March and determined that they were collectively opposed to an interbelligerent labor conference on the grounds that peace negotiations should be an affair of governments and that premature negotiations by labor leaders might favor the Germans. Reinforcing such feelings were the harsh terms imposed by Germany on Russia in the Brest Litovsk treaty.[18]

Interestingly, Wilson also vetoed efforts by a number of liberals to encourage a reconciliation between himself and Eugene Debs during the winter and spring of 1918. Like many other U.S. Socialists, Debs had been impressed both by the president's Fourteen Points speech and by the effort of the British Labour Party to align the international labor movement behind a peace based on Wilsonian principles. By contrast, Debs expressed harsh criticism of Germany for its treatment of Russia. On these grounds, Debs temporarily supported an effort to encourage the U.S. Socialist Party to revise its war platform. Among those suggesting that the president invite Debs to the White House for a meeting were James Hamilton Lewis and Allen Ricker. As Ricker explained in a letter to Colonel House, "There are three men in this nation who have a bigger personal following than any of our other citizens." The first was the president, the second was Roosevelt, and the third was Debs, whom "radicals will follow . . . as they will no other man." But Wilson declined to meet with Debs because it might cause the administration "serious embarrassment."[19]

The president's hostile actions toward Henderson and Debs raise questions about the communion that Allied Socialists and labor leaders believed existed between Wilson's international goals and their own. For all that the president spoke the language of a new diplomacy, he had long opposed U.S. Socialist efforts to democratize American diplomacy and displayed no more desire to see the international labor and Socialist movements usurp the diplomatic functions of governments than European leaders. The president denied passports to American Socialists seeking to travel to a Stockholm meeting on roughly the same grounds as European leaders; the issue of peace was an affair of governments and not of parties or social movements. By contrast, many European Socialists and labor activists had grown so disillusioned with their governments following the publication of the secret treaties that they believed it was necessary to at least temporarily circumvent traditional diplomatic channels to bring peace to Europe. Over the long run, both European and American Socialists argued that diplomacy must also be systematically democratized, first by establishing more popular and parliamentary/congressional controls over foreign policy within states, and second, by ensuring that the League included a democratic parliamentary body within it. Wilson, on the other hand, was a believer in representative rather than more direct forms of democracy and defended executive supremacy in foreign affairs if government leaders had been legitimately elected to office. The president's Fourteen Points thus stressed the need for "Open Covenants, Openly Arrived at" rather than calling for a more democratic foreign policy on the part of nation-states. The president also failed to embrace plans for a parliamentary body within the League of Nations that would be democratically elected. Instead, he continued to envision the League of Nations very much as a league of governments rather than as the "league of peoples" that the British Labour Party and others promoted. The differences between the social patriots who rallied behind the Inter-Allied War Aims and the Wilson administration, however, would become fully discernible only with the publication of the peace treaty.

THE FIRST U.S. LABOR MISSION TO EUROPE

In the meantime, the British government, in cooperation with the American Committee on Public Information, sought to take advantage of the rift between British labor and the AFL by inviting the latter to participate in a private diplomatic mission to Britain that would also include leading American journalists, academics, and businessmen. The ostensible goal of the mission was to "give to the people of Great Britain an opportunity of learning first hand something of the spirit and determination with which the United States of America are prosecuting the war." Yet as AFL appointee John P. Frey, an executive of the International Molder's Union and editor of its journal later emphasized, the "camouflaged" goal of both the American and British governments in supporting a strong AFL presence on the mission was to undermine pacifism within the British labor movement and to thwart the effort to force a negotiated peace through a Stockholm meeting.[20] In addition to Frey, Gompers appointed eight other AFL members to the mission: James Wilson, president of the Patternmaker's League of North America; William H. Johnston, president of the International Association of Machinists; George Berry, president of the International Printing, Pressmen's and Assistant's Union; Martin Ryan, president of the Brotherhood of Railway Carmen of America; Melinda Scott, president of the Straw Hat, Trimmers and Operatives Union; Agnes Nestor, vice president of the International Glove Workers Union; William Short, president of the Washington State Federation of Labor; and Chester Wright, representative from the International Typographical Union and director of publicity for the American Alliance for Labor and Democracy. At a time when the government regularly denied passports to American Socialists, it issued passports for the AFL delegates, as Agnes Nestor would later write, in "record time."[21]

Of the nine AFL members, Nestor was perhaps the most surprising appointment to the commission because she was not a part of Gompers's inner circle. In addition to her roles within the Glove Workers Union, she served as president of the Chicago branch of the Women's Trade Union League, and had sometimes differed with Gompers over women's trade union issues. Of Irish heritage and feminist conviction, Nestor had also been active in the pacifist movement before the U.S. intervened in the war. Yet Nestor gained national prominence following the U.S. declaration of war due to her appointment to several federal committees dealing with women's labor issues. Indeed, national WTUL President Margaret Dreier Robins discouraged Nestor from taking the position on the labor mission on the grounds that her current work on women's issues in federal government circles, including the Advisory Council of National Defense and the Committee on Women in Industry, was a "thousand fold" more important. Robins even wondered whether the "invitation, coming as it does, might easily have been offered with the hope of getting you out of the way." She noted that Gompers had refused to consider Nestor's name for a position on the Advisory Commission just a few months before and she therefore questioned the "sincerity" of his motives. But Nestor joined others in believing that after the war, international strategies would prove critical in advancing the cause of women workers. The mission, she believed, would afford many opportunities to cultivate contacts with other women labor leaders that could be vital in the future. Nestor's letters and autobiographical accounts of the trip also convey a personal motivation; as a girl sitting at a glove-making machine back in Chicago, she had never imagined she would enjoy such travel opportunities.[22]

Before leaving, Gompers carefully briefed the mission on its duties and on issues that he believed might arise during the trip. In a letter to participants, Gompers explained that the goal of the mission was to carry a message of goodwill to fellow workers and to make sure that nothing caused different groups of workers to become "estranged from each other." In a thinly veiled reference to the Stockholm movement, Gompers suggested that efforts to "wean us from the prosecution of our aims [in the war] should be resisted and repudiated." Another goal of the mission was to investigate working conditions prevailing in England and France during the war. The mission was not given the authority to negotiate war aims but only to explain previously enunciated positions of the AFL and to "confer" with British and French labor representatives on these points.[23]

At a gathering held immediately before the mission set sail, Gompers gave a long speech highlighting elements of the AFL's international record that he clearly wished U.S. labor delegates to stress in their meetings with British and French labor representatives. The AFL, he emphasized, had been in the "advance guard" of efforts to "maintain international peace." Yet the German trade unionists had largely ignored AFL efforts to encourage negotiations. England, suggested Gompers, was the "mother of the modern trade union movement." Of late, however, the British trade unions had been "subordinated" to the British Labour Party and had therefore surrendered their right to strike. By contrast, the American trade union movement had "lost none of its virility." American workers still enjoyed the right to strike, but felt no need to do so because of the wartime agreements signed by the AFL. Gompers defended the AALD, which he likely knew would be criticized by British Socialists, on the grounds that it was necessary "to fight the . . . organized effort put forth by the Socialist Party, by the ultra pacifists, by the pro Germans, and by the German propagandists to divide the people of the United States into opposite camps, and to weaken the country's ability to maintain its position as against German aggression and German atrocity." Gompers then encouraged delegates to read copies of "Our Program," that, significantly, was drawn not from past statements of the AFL about the war or peace conference but was taken verbatim from President Wilson's Fourteen Point speech.[24]

During their stays in Britain and France, the delegates were entertained not only by labor delegations but also by government dignitaries, including Lloyd George, Georges Clemenceau, and Winston Churchill. King George, Queen Mary and Princess Mary even received them at Buckingham Palace. In France the mission visited the front and spoke directly with "clear-eyed and manly" American soldiers who demonstrated great enthusiasm about the war. By contrast, French and British soldiers seemed grimmer to the mission members but maintained a "firm resolve" to see the war through to a successful conclusion. At first, according to John Frey, a sense of unity pervaded the labor component of the mission. But internal divisions soon arose because James Wilson of the Patternmakers tried to dominate labor events as well as press coverage, while the trade union women went off in their own direction.[25]

In part, the women's independent role on the mission was preordained because the British and French governments arranged multiple meetings for them with women trade unionists and labor leaders. But Nestor also displayed a more sympathetic attitude toward the Stockholm plan promoted by British unionists than her male comrades, suggesting that if the Germans would accept the war aims laid down by the Inter-Allied Socialist and Labor Conference, then progress might be possible. Nestor also demonstrated her independence by traveling with a small group from the mission to Ireland despite the disapproval of the British government. While there, Nestor met with a diverse range of Irish nationalists, including some women leaders of Sinn Fein and Cumann na mBan (the women's auxiliary of the Irish national army) and reported extensively on it in her subsequent writings.[26]

Upon returning, the mission met briefly with President Wilson who was reportedly "anxious" to hear their observations. The president proved particularly pleased to learn that the Fourteen Points had been well received in labor circles in both Britain and Europe. His attitudes toward divisions within international labor, by contrast, were less clear. At subsequent press conferences, Nestor and Melinda Scott emphasized the contribution of women to the war and the growing spirit of internationalism among workers in all countries, including Britain, Scotland, France, and Ireland. As one Chicago newspaper aptly summarized her message, "Agnes Nestor, Home From Abroad, Tells What Her Sex Is Doing, Predicts Internationalism." A photo showed the diminutive Nestor keeping "Swell Company" with British dignitaries that likely included Lloyd George. But in other news accounts, male members of the mission highlighted the continuing division over Stockholm and claimed that British Labour Party leaders were misrepresenting rank-and-file union members in Britain, most of whom did not favor an "inconclusive peace." These members argued that even in France only a minority of extremists, influenced by German propaganda, favored "parleys with German workingmen."[27]

In the official report of the mission to the AFL convention, the delegation highlighted the "unanimity" with which all labor groups in Europe supported the war aims of President Wilson that were endorsed by the American Federation of Labor. Yet they also continued to emphasize the "marked divergence of opinion" that existed between the AFL and some labor groups in Britain and France over the issue of the Stockholm conference. British and French labor, they further argued, were divided among themselves over the wisdom of an interbelligerent conference, and even those who supported the meeting disagreed about whether its results should be "binding." The American mission reported that, when pressured on the issue, they responded that they had no authority to negotiate regarding war aims or Stockholm and instead reiterated the AFL position that it was opposed to an international conference of labor representatives from belligerent countries "until German armies were no longer a menace." The report concluded that, despite the war weariness among the people of France and Britain, "the will to win remains unshaken" except for "a pacifist minority that would yield to Prussianism upon any pretext or none." It recommended a permanent AFL representative in Europe to report on conditions there. The AFL International Committee in turn accepted this recommendation and also recommended that Gompers go to Europe.[28] The AFL convention subsequently endorsed the report overwhelmingly, although three delegates from the always independent International Ladies' Garment Workers' Union voted against it because of the way it portrayed European Socialists.[29]

Concurring with the mission's report of its successes was British GFTU leader William Appleton who wrote Gompers to congratulate him and the mission on the way it remained loyal to the U.S. war effort despite the enormous efforts made by the "Defeatists" to convert the American delegation to the Stockholm viewpoint. British Socialist leader James Ramsey McDonald, by contrast, wrote American Socialist Party secretary Adolph Germer complaining that the labor mission had demonstrated that the American Federation of Labor was "hopelessly out of date" and entirely "aloof" from the realities of British and French working-class opinion.[30] Germer sent the letter to Eugene Debs who, after receiving a cold shoulder from the Wilson administration, renewed his attacks not only against Wilson but against the AFL during the spring of 1918. In his famous speech in Canton, Ohio, on June 16, 1918, Debs spoke only circumspectly about the war, but he directly attacked the Wilson administration for failing to seek democratic approval of its war policies, for its suppression of free speech, and for its jailing of leading Socialists like Kate Richards O'Hare. He then sarcastically compared the courage of Socialists and IWW activists imprisoned for exercising their right to free speech with Gompers and other AFL leaders whom the "capitalist press" now spoke of with "praise and adulation" for their patriotism and their willingness to enjoy lavish banquets with "Elihu Root, Andrew Carnegie and the rest of the plutocratic civic federationists" while promoting the war effort. Debs would be sentenced to ten years in prison for his remarks at Canton.[31]

With leading Socialists and IWW activists effectively muzzled and their presses censored, the nonlabor members of the American mission to Britain and France and the liberal press emerged as the most vocal critics of AFL diplomacy. Several of the mission members who came from academic and journalistic backgrounds complained that AFL members of the mission had acted with "bad manners" and in a "harsh and arrogant spirit" during their travels that tended to provoke resentment rather than understanding among their French and British counterparts. Professor Lovejoy of John Hopkins University also criticized AFL leaders for faulty assumptions about the proposed Stockholm meeting. Due to the conditions attached to such a meeting by Allied labor leaders, suggested Lovejoy, it was extremely unlikely that the Germans could use such a conference to bolster their own position. Rather, the more likely scenario was that the German government would refuse to permit German labor or the German Socialists to participate in a conference in which the terms were dictated by the Allies. In this sense, suggested Lovejoy, the conference was a "chimera" not worth the antagonism it engendered.[32]

But the *New Republic* disagreed, suggesting that Henderson's approach was really an exercise in political psychology. They doubted that even Henderson and the other Allied labor leaders supporting the conference believed that the German government would agree to allow German delegates to attend an interbelligerent labor meeting given all the stipulations. However, in promoting the conference, the British Labour Party advanced the democratic and just aims of the Allied war effort in ways that helped to ensure the continued support of workers for the war. Additionally, they helped bring attention to a distinctly labor international agenda and assured it greater prominence at any future peace conference. By contrast, suggested the *New Republic*'s editors, American labor offered as their postwar agenda only the "naïve assumption" that the world would be "made safe for democracy merely as a consequence of German military defeat." If the AFL wanted a seat at the peace conference, they argued, it must show that labor had something distinctive to bring to the solution of international problems.[33]

The *New Republic* had a point because, apart from opposing the interbelligerent labor conference, the AFL devoted very little time to developing a peace program in early 1918. So unsatisfactory did several international officers find Gompers's vague proclamations about the war that they asked him to clarify the principles for which American workers were fighting. In responding, Gompers failed to identify who the international officers were, but they may have hailed from the old antiwar Indianapolis group that had coalesced around the United Mine Workers in 1915–1916. During 1918, these groups scored an electoral victory over Gompers within the AFL, electing five members affiliated with their coalition to the Executive Council despite Gompers's endorsement of other candidates. The election of these members reflected growing disenchantment with Gompers's war policies. Yet when pressed for more specifics on war aims, Gompers fell back on familiar platitudes: the U.S. was fighting a war for freedom against an undemocratic government that enslaved workers and mutilated women and children. It was also fighting for a free-trade union movement and the ideal of equal opportunity that the United States embodied. In other speeches, Gompers emphasized Wilson's Fourteen Points while failing to highlight a distinctly labor peace agenda.[34]

The problem lay not just with Gompers's relatively rigid understanding of international politics but with the lack of an infrastructure within the AFL for considering political issues. In contrast, the British Labour Party functioned as a veritable idea factory in 1918, forming committees and producing briefing papers on a broad array of international issues that it believed would be of vital concern to workers in the postwar era. The briefing papers were often written by such Left intellectual luminaries as Sidney Webb, Beatrice Webb, Leonard Woolf, and James Ramsey McDonald, and frequently they offered highly original perspectives on a diverse range of issues that included the international legislature proposed for the League of Nations, international labor legislation, freedom of the seas, the international control of vital resources, the democratization of the foreign service, Russia, and the disposition of colonies and occupied territories in the postwar world. The recommendations contained in these reports then made their way up the bureaucratic ladder to the Labour Party Executive Committee that used them to formulate an increasingly complex labor peace program in the summer and fall of 1918. As the Executive Committee admitted in its report to the annual Labour Party Conference in 1918, their work had been dominated that year by activities on "behalf of a democratic diplomacy."[35]

With the support of his impressive staff, Henderson increasingly became the spokesperson for a "new" diplomacy in 1918 that differed from that promoted by either Lenin or Wilson, Henderson's reliance on Wilsonian rhetoric notwithstanding. On the one hand, Henderson differed from Lenin in emphasizing evolutionary and democratic rather than revolutionary change. On the other hand, he differed from Wilson in increasingly recognizing the need to eliminate British as well as German imperialism, in seeking to address some of the underlying economic causes of warfare, and in promoting a far more democratic League of Nations than that imagined by Wilson. Aware that he would likely win few converts for the British Labour Party program among the leaders of the AFL, Henderson increasingly used the American press to appeal directly to American workers and the American people. In a "Letter to American Workers," published in the *Atlantic Monthly*, Henderson noted that Americans seemed to have some "misapprehension" about the war aims formulated at the last Inter-Allied Conference. But British labor, he insisted, was patriotic and fighting to make the world safe for democracy just like American workers. U.S. and British labor, he emphasized, disagreed primarily on a tactical issue: American labor was committed to an exclusively military approach in defeating the Germans, while British labor sought to use political and diplomatic tactics in addition to military strategies in encouraging the Germans to support a negotiated peace. He urged Americans to join in this effort.[36]

In other articles, Henderson moved beyond the proposed interbelligerent conference, emphasizing that the war marked the final stage in the "disintegration and collapse of the political and economic system that was founded upon the private ownership of property." It was particularly crucial during this period for working-class parties to unite behind "democratic peace policies." Labor in the United States, he predicted, would "be compelled by the logic of events to enter into a closer alliance with the international working-class movement in Europe and will have to assert itself more actively in national politics in the interests of the common ideal of democratic self-determination to which workers everywhere are consciously pledging themselves." In yet other articles he emphasized that the League of Nations would be the linchpin of the new international system. The League, however, must not be merely an alliance of governments but must contain a democratically elected international legislature that would speak "for the public opinion of the world as a whole" and help to "create a common mind in the world."[37]

In appealing to American workers directly through the American press, Henderson threw down the gauntlet to Gompers who, in the summer of 1918, announced that he would soon lead a second labor mission to Great Britain, France, and Italy at the request of Allied governments.[38]

THE SECOND LABOR MISSION TO EUROPE

Gompers's planned mission, while greeted with enthusiasm in government circles, was not welcomed by everyone. The liberal journal, the *Nation*, argued that U.S. labor missions sent abroad had so far proven "singularly unproductive of information." The problem, the journal suggested, was that American trade unionists went as "propagandists rather than reporters." Yet what was currently needed was someone who could report in an informed way on "the whole state of European labor." Such information was as necessary for the American people as it was for the president. Yet Gompers, they suggested, would not go to Europe as an interested observer but as a "partisan drummer" to sell his idea of "victory to the pacifist elements in Allied countries, especially England." The editors therefore proposed that in lieu of Gompers going to Europe, British and European labor and Socialist leaders representing a broad spectrum of opinion should come to the United States so that Americans could hear their perspectives firsthand. The last thing the country needed right now, suggested the magazine, was another "bitter and shameful experience" comparable to the Root mission. The Postmaster Department in turn responded to these criticisms and suggestions by temporarily banning the edition of the magazine in which this article appeared from the mails. When Oswald Garrison Villard, editor of the *Nation*, complained and asked for an explanation, William H. Lamar of the Washington Post Office Department explained that "Mr. Gompers has rendered inestimable services to this government during this war in holding union labor in line and while this war is on we are not going to allow any newspaper in this country to attack him." Wilson later rescinded Lamar's order, but the incident suggested how much the government had come to value Gompers's loyalty and service as well as its intolerance of criticism about the partnership that had developed between the AFL and the government.[39]

Prowar Socialists such as John Spargo, William English Walling, Algie Simons, and Charles Edward Russell also increasingly voiced their concerns about the AFL's diplomatic talents and sent their own mission to Europe in advance of the Gompers mission in an effort to court European Socialists and British Labour Party activists. But the U.S. prowar Socialists had their own public relations problem; many British and European Socialists corresponded frequently with antiwar U.S Socialists and refused to recognize the prowar Socialists as legitimate representatives of the American party. James Ramsey MacDonald, for example, again wrote Adolph Germer assuring him that the Socialist mission was not recognized as the legitimate voice of American socialism.[40] Italian and French Socialists, for their part, continued to insist that the majority wing of the American Socialist Party should be represented at Allied Socialist and labor gatherings alongside the AFL.[41]

Gompers, however, shunted such criticism aside, arguing that there was "no such thing as an American Socialist Party but a German adjunct in America of the German Socialist Party."[42] Gompers planned his trip to coincide with the British Trade Union Congress at Derby in late August to which the AFL had already committed to send delegates. But he also wrote Arthur

Henderson and Léon Jouhaux of France asking for a meeting of Allied labor movements during his stay in Britain. Henderson gladly complied, for he eagerly sought AFL cooperation despite Gompers's abrasive personality. The conference was also welcomed by conservative elements of the British labor movement who hoped that Gompers could help restrain the movement for a labor-negotiated peace.

To assure that he could better control this mission than he had the last one, Gompers appointed only five other members, all of whom were loyal supporters: John Frey, who had also been on the first mission; Charles L. Bain, secretary of the Boot and Shoe Workers Union; William J. Bowen, president of the Brick Layers and Plasterers International Union; Edgar Wallace, the new prowar editor of the *United Mine Workers Journal*; and Guy Oyster, Gompers's personal secretary. The mission left on August 16 and arrived eleven days later, giving Gompers some time to visit relatives in London before the Derby Conference. At the Derby meeting both Gompers and Henderson toned down their rhetoric, with Gompers offering a speech praised by American Ambassador Walter Hines Page on the grounds that it emphasized the "warlike ardor and the loyalty of working men" even while it "did not say a word which could offend "either the Appleton-Wilson or the Henderson-Bowerman factions in Britain. For his part, Gompers found Henderson and James Ramsey MacDonald "surprisingly cordial" at Derby.[43]

Renewed tensions surfaced at the subsequent Inter-Allied Conference, but participants were still able to find some common ground. One source of tension arose from the failure of the conference organizers to invite American Socialists or Russian Bolshevists; Italian Socialists boycotted the meeting due to these exclusions while the French Socialists attended but protested the decision and asked that the AFL not be given the full American vote. Gompers responded by denouncing the French Socialists as "intellectuals" and by emphasizing that the French Socialist Party represented only thirty thousand members of mixed backgrounds while the AFL represented three million wage earners. The French motion to deny full voting power to the AFL was denied. The other issue that divided the meeting was, unsurprisingly, the Stockholm question. By the time of the September conference, German Socialist and labor leaders had rejected Henderson's efforts to make acceptance of the February Allied War Aims statement a precondition for labor peace negotiations. Henderson, according to Ambassador Walter Hines Page, was "bitterly disappointed" with the German response and favored a resolution that declared the German attitude an "obstacle" to any future interbelligerent labor peace conference. By contrast, the French favored immediate peace negotiations despite the German attitude. Gompers, on the other hand, proposed an amendment stating that Allied labor would meet only with those "of the Central Powers who are in open revolt against their autocratic governments." The Gompers's amendment was overwhelmingly defeated and the meeting went on record as favoring an interbelligerent labor peace conference provided that the Germans accepted the Allied Labor War Aims as a basis for negotiation. In this sense, the American presence helped the Henderson faction, since Gompers's team on the right offset the French left-wing Socialists.[44]

On the important issue of a new statement of war aims, on the other hand, the Americans seemed to gain the upper hand. Although Henderson had hoped that the AFL would accept the February memo in relatively unaltered form, Gompers arranged for Frey to serve on the war aims committee and encouraged him to be aggressive and "start the fight at the drop of a hat." Frey pressed forward the American war aim program, that now included Wilson's Fourteen Points, a demand for labor representation in the peace delegations and for a labor congress at the same time and place as the peace conference, and an industrial charter proposed by the AFL outlining fundamental workers' rights and "aspirations" that ought to be recognized by the peace conference in some fashion. The latter included the following:

> (a) That in law and in practice the principle shall be recognized that the labour of a human being is not a commodity or article of commerce.
> (b) Involuntary servitude shall not exist except as a punishment for crime whereof the party shall have been duly convicted.
> (c) The right of free association, free assemblage, free speech and free press shall not be abridged.
> (d) That the seamen of the merchant marine shall be guaranteed the right of leaving their vessels when the same are in safe harbor.
> (e) No article or commodity shall be shipped or delivered in international commerce in the production of which children under the age of 16 years have been employed or permitted to work.
> (f) It shall be declared that the basic work day in industry and commerce shall not exceed eight hours per day.
> (g) Trial by jury should be established."[45]

Responding to the American proposals, the conference first agreed to endorse the Fourteen Points, suggesting that they were a "concise summary of the main principles which the [February] Memorandum of War Aims expounds in detail." It also approved the AFL proposal for labor representation in the peace delegations and for a world labor congress at the same time and place as the peace conference. It even appointed Gompers to the planning committee, along with Henderson, Albert Thomas of France, and Emile Vandervelde of Belgium. Finally it expressed sympathy with the industrial principles suggested by the AFL but emphasized that they might not be universally applicable and might need to be modified.[46]

In the aftermath of the Inter-Allied Conference, U.S. Ambassador Walter Hines Page heaped additional praise on Gompers and even the usually critical liberal press expressed some positive opinions regarding Gompers's diplomacy. *Survey*, for example, emphasized that while Gompers had not brought "Henderson's head back on a platter," as he had apparently wished, he had achieved most of the AFL's other goals—with the exception of preventing the labor peace conference. The Inter-Allied meeting, moreover, had brought "new world" and "old world" labor together in ways that were bound to have positive repercussions. The *Nation* also applauded the new spirit of labor unity, although it attributed it more to Henderson than to Gompers and wondered whether the AFL was ever going to make a "real contribution . . . to the problem of international reconstruction" that would be so vital after the war. William English Walling, on the other hand, worried about the lack of support for Gompers's resolution opposing an interbelligerent labor conference and feared it signaled that the "growth of Bolshevik pacifism is continuous and ceaseless," a claim that government advisor William Bullitt dismissed as "alarmist." Bullitt suggested that as long as the governments of France, England, and Italy followed the liberal policy of Wilson there would be "no upheaval" in these countries. However, if the Allies chose to indefinitely continue the "war for imperialistic purposes," then the fears of Walling might be borne out.[47]

After the Allied conference, Gompers traveled to France and Italy where, according to government reports, he was enthusiastically received by the crowds, government and military leaders, King Emmanuel, and many labor groups, but not by Socialists. In particular, Gompers quarreled with the editors of the antiwar Socialist paper *Avanti* in Italy. But U.S. diplomats also scored these visits a propaganda success, emphasizing that Gompers had demonstrated forcefully that U.S. labor supported the war, thereby undermining the positions of antiwar Socialists who claimed to support a Wilsonian peace. They also noted that the honors paid to the unofficial mission by government and military personnel in Britain, France, and Italy were "absolutely without precedent" and demonstrated the esteem in which they held both Gompers and Wilson, boding well for the peace conference as well as for the future of international labor relations. Some also seemed to hint at the possibility of using patriotic labor leaders as diplomatic representatives in the future, perhaps at the peace conference.[48]

Yet hubris would soon catch up with Gompers for, even as he basked in the glow of praise from his apparently successful diplomatic debut in Britain and Europe, he received some tragic personal news. After a banquet in Turin, Italy, John Frey approached Gompers and handed him a cablegram from Secretary of Labor William B. Wilson informing him that his beloved daughter Sadie had died of influenza after only a short illness. Gompers arranged to travel home immediately and on reaching Paris discovered multiple bright and cheerful letters from his daughter awaiting him at the embassy that had been written only a few weeks earlier. Upon returning to the United States, Gompers would be forced to confront not only his own personal grief but a growing rebellion within the ranks of the AFL: a Labor Party movement inspired at least in part by Gompers's nemesis, the British Labour Party.[49]

THE LABOR PARTY MOVEMENT AND POLARIZATION WITHIN U.S. LABOR AND SOCIALISM AT WAR'S END

To AFL leaders, the Labor Party virus in the United States during the winter of 1918–1919 may well have seemed a bit like the influenza virus; the origins were difficult to track and it attacked healthy AFL unionists and unions without warning. Among the first to exhibit signs of the disease was the Chicago Federation of Labor; at a meeting on November 3, 1918, it officially announced its intent to establish a labor party and secured passage at the meeting of a Declaration of Labor Party Principles that included demands not only for industrial democracy but also for democratic representation for workers in future "international tribunals" in proportion to "their numbers in the armies, navies and workshops of the world." Shortly afterward, the CFL created the Chicago Labor Party. The CFL's actions were likely a surprise to Gompers, for he had worked closely with Chicago Federation of Labor leader John Fitzpatrick to help ensure federal mediation of labor disputes in the Chicago stockyards during the war. But whereas Gompers believed this mediation had been a success, Fitzpatrick had become convinced by the end of 1918 that the Council of National Defense and other war labor boards were not composed predominantly of labor sympathizers but of "labor baiters and labor crushers." His experiences with government mediation in turn made him critical of the entire collaborative partnership that had developed between the AFL and the Wilson administration and led him to believe that more could be achieved politically for labor through an independent labor party similar to Britain's.[50]

Although an admirer of the British Labour Party, Fitzpatrick's Labor Party activity was also fueled by his opposition to British imperialism, which he viewed as perhaps the greatest single threat to the well-being of the world's workers. Before Wilson's declaration of war, the CFL had been a center of antiwar agitation (see chapter 3) and had criticized the Wilson administration for its pro-British leanings. Since 1917, the CFL had toed the AFL line and supported the war effort, but its leaders remained suspicious of Wilsonian foreign policy. The Chicago Labor Party, while drawing on British Labour Party precedents in endorsing a democratic league of peoples rather than governments, distinguished itself by embracing complete independence rather than home rule or mandate status for British colonies like Ireland and India in its early platforms. The Chicago Labor Party soon attacked even U.S. imperialism in Latin America. That a local labor party should place so much emphasis on international issues was in some respects surprising, but it clearly reflected the tenor of the times. The war had convinced both local and national AFL leaders that the domestic well-being of American workers was inextricably intertwined with the seismic changes occurring in international politics. Yet, in contrast to AFL leaders, the Chicago Labor Party proved skeptical that a partnership with the Wilson administration would by itself ensure that the needs of the world's workers were adequately served by the new institutions that were to be created to preserve peace. American labor, like British labor, needed its own independent labor party voice in international affairs.

The Labor Party movement quickly spread like a "prairie fire"—or like a virus, depending on one's analogy—to small and midsize towns throughout the American Midwest. Several large AFL municipal affiliates, including those in Seattle and New York, also announced their support for labor party politics at war's end and soon launched their own Labor parties. Alarmed by the new movement, Gompers took time from his grieving for Sadie in December of 1918 to warn of the dangers of labor party politics. In a long speech in New York, Gompers highlighted past failed efforts to form a labor party in the United States and also commented extensively on the ways he believed Labour and Socialist Party politics had weakened the British and European labor movements. The fruits of the new Labor Party movement within the AFL, he believed, would be to divide American labor at a critical time. Yet local labor leaders like Fitzpatrick, who had loyally supported AFL policy during the war crisis, were not inclined to do so following the signing of the armistice on November 11, 1918. Even as Gompers made plans to travel anew to Europe for the peace conference, the CFL joined others in launching the national Labor Party. Although the new party proposed to act like a "jack screw—slow but sure" in politically organizing American workers, it would gather momentum as Gompers labored at Versailles in 1919 and would emerge as one of the strongest critics of the AFL president's international handiwork. In 1920, the party would be reorganized as the Farmer-Labor Party.[51]

The Socialist Party and IWW, for their part, remained preoccupied with legal battles designed to keep their leaders out of jail at war's end, as well as with internal divisions. In the spring of 1918, Wilson's Fourteen Points, in conjunction with the harsh terms meted out to Russia by the Brest Litovsk Treaty, convinced some previously antiwar Socialists to reverse their positions and support the war effort. Among these were the editors of the popular Socialist paper *Appeal to Reason*, which changed its name to *New Appeal*. Even Eugene Debs, as discussed previously, proved disgruntled by German actions surrounding Brest Litovsk and considered encouraging the party to reformulate its war aims. But relentless government persecution, in combination with their strong antiwar ideals, ultimately prevented the center and left-wing leaders of the party from reversing course and throwing their weight behind the Wilson administration's war policies before the signing of the armistice.[52] Although the party would come apart at its seams in 1919, various fragments of the party would nonetheless play an important role in impeding Gompers's efforts to align U.S. labor behind the Versailles Peace Treaty, League, and International Labor Organization. The IWW would also prove to be a particularly dogged and insightful critic of the ILO. Adding to the political confusion following the armistice were African American and women workers, as well as immigrant Left groups, who also sought to assert themselves in international affairs in ways that posed a potential challenge to the Wilsonian foreign policy agenda. As Gompers set sail for Versailles in 1919, he thus left behind an increasingly polarized working class that proved to be fertile soil for oppositional labor and Left politics.

CONCLUSION

A comparison of U.S. and British labor diplomacy during the war suggests some significant differences. Although the main trade union organizations in both Britain and the United States supported their government's war policies and collaborated with them during the war, Labour Party politics ensured that British labor enjoyed more bargaining power within government circles than U.S. labor. Initially, British Labour Party votes helped to guarantee that

Henderson was included in the War Cabinet, a much more influential position than Gompers's purely advisory role on the Council of National Defense. When Henderson became critical of British war policy, he simply withdrew and supported an independent Labour Party agenda, a political threat from the outside that British politicians from other parties ignored at their peril. By contrast, Gompers's political power depended entirely upon the goodwill of Wilson. Assured Gompers's loyalty, Wilson felt free to repress other Left opposition, ranging from the Socialist Party to the IWW. Yet this approach had its costs for Wilson, as AFL leaders and prowar Socialists habitually gave questionable advice and offered flawed intelligence about the European Left, who might otherwise have been among Wilson's strongest supporters.

British Labour Party politics offered another advantage as well; it encouraged Henderson to promote unity rather than discord within the ranks of labor, if for no other reason than to garner working-class votes. No such imperative existed for Gompers, who continued to pursue a holy crusade against antiwar labor and Socialist activists in 1918. By 1919, Gompers's enemy list would grow to include the Labor Party movement within the ranks of the AFL. The fruits would be a polarized working class that proved remarkably difficult to rally behind a new international labor politics.

Figure P.4 *New Majority* (paper of the Chicago Federation of Labor), May 22, 1919, 16. This drawing was likely first used during a British Labour Party campaign but proved popular in the United States as well. It reflected the aspirations of a diverse array of labor groups to have a voice at the peace conference, in future international organizations, and in shaping a "new diplomacy" that would be more responsive to the needs of ordinary people.

PROLOGUE: VERSAILLES
AND ITS AFTERMATH

Two types of peace gatherings, suggests Alan Dawley, took place in Europe during the first half of 1919: the "official meeting of diplomats at the old Bourbon Palace of Versailles," and the "unofficial gatherings of people's representatives, most of whom were not welcome in Paris and had to find someplace else to meet." Among those groups that sent representatives to Paris but were denied entry to the peace conference were women's rights organizations, the NAACP and Pan African Congress, labor and Socialist organizations, and a host of anticolonial nationalists—ranging from Ho Chi Minh, to Emir Faisal and Colonel T. E. Lawrence (Lawrence of Arabia), to representatives of the Irish Sinn Féin movement. The peace conference quickly disappointed these people's representatives, for Wilson had promised far more than he could deliver.[1]

Almost immediately, Wilson compromised on the first of his Fourteen Points: the plenipotentiaries met in secret rather than practicing the "open diplomacy" that Wilson had promised. The notion of a nonpunitive peace was also quickly jettisoned at Versailles; the other Allied powers insisted upon saddling Germany with harsh reparations and a humiliating war guilt clause, as well as stripping it of its colonies. Many independent nation-states, such as Poland, emerged in areas of Eastern Europe formerly controlled by either the German or Austro-Hungarian empires. In the Middle East and Africa, however, former German and Austro-Hungarian colonies were "mandated" to the countries that conquered them, France and Britain in particular. Although mandate status was officially meant to be a halfway house between colonialism and full independence, it gave the supervisory nation extensive influence within the mandated area and "smacked of imperialism." Japan acquired China's Shandong province and Germany's islands in the Pacific even while unsuccessfully pressing for the inclusion of a racial equality clause in the treaty. Anticipating nationalist objections to his handiwork at Versailles in the United States, Wilson won special recognition of the Monroe Doctrine, and thus implicitly of a special sphere of influence for the United States in Latin America, in the treaty. Denied any hearing whatsoever by the plenipotentiaries were those British and French colonies that sought self-determination at war's end, ranging from Ireland to Egypt, India, and Vietnam.[2]

Although Wilson was unhappy with many of the compromises made at Versailles, he insisted that the League of Nations could iron out problems later. But reformers claimed that the League of Nations itself was problematic; the blueprint for the organization drawn up at Versailles included an influential executive council upon which the five big powers were to sit permanently as well as a general assembly composed of national delegations, with no provisions made for the democratic election or representative nature of these delegations as outlined by the British Labour Party. Critics complained that this structure would give the major imperial powers undue influence and would in no way ensure that the national delegations were representative of constituent groups within their respective countries.

Leading the charge in the attack upon the undemocratic structure of the League of Nations were labor and Socialist organizations throughout the world. Yet the plenipotentiaries made a concession to labor during the peace conference that they did not make to any other group of reformers. Although they failed to grant labor special status within the peace conference itself or to mandate the inclusion of labor representatives within the delegations of the plenipotentiaries, they established a special Commission on International Labor Legislation to meet during the peace conference. The commission marked a modest effort to stem the tide of industrial and class unrest that convulsed the world in 1919 and to halt the spread of Bolshevism. Yet European labor initially boycotted the meeting due to the refusal of the Allies to allow German labor leaders to attend. They instead held their international labor meeting in Bern, Switzerland. AFL President Samuel Gompers, however, chose an alternative path; he traveled to Paris and became chair of the Commission on International Labor Legislation. Under his direction, this commission created the League of Nations–affiliated International Labor Organization (ILO) and framed a bill of labor rights that was incorporated directly into the peace treaty.

Although European labor leaders were at first angry with Gompers for dividing the international labor movement at such a critical time, European members of the International Federation of Trade Unions reluctantly agreed to send representatives to the first meeting of the International Labor Organization planned for Washington, D.C., in October 1919. Gompers also won the tentative support of the Pan-American Federation of Labor for the ILO and League of Nations in 1919. In a strange reversal of fortunes, however, a formidable array of political forces in the United States emerged to oppose U.S. membership in both the League and the ILO. Although historians have traditionally blamed Republicans for the growing tide of opposition to the Versailles Peace Treaty in the United States in 1919, dissenting labor groups and left-leaning diaspora political coalitions purporting to speak on behalf of the world's workers also proved surprisingly important in turning U.S. public opinion against the League of Nations and ILO.

6 Making the World Safe for Workers?
The AFL, Wilson, and the Creation of the ILO at Versailles

IN EARLY DECEMBER 1918, the diplomat Raymond Fosdick related to President Wilson an interesting personal anecdote about working-class hopes and dreams on the eve of the Versailles Conference. Fosdick was taking a cab to the New York ferry at 6 A.M. when he noticed hundreds of working men and women, who were identified by his cab driver as sweatshop workers, getting off the ferry boat and "hurrying . . . away into the darkness" to find other transportation that would take them to their destinations. Fosdick subsequently spoke to one of the men as he bought a paper and asked how many hours a day he worked. According to Fosdick, the man replied "Fourteen hours. But do you see that boat (pointing across the river towards the *George Washington*), there's a man aboard her [Woodrow Wilson] that is going to Europe to change all that." Fosdick subsequently used the story to advise the president of the necessity of incorporating a "bill of human industrial rights" into the peace treaty that would include issues like maximum hours of labor, minimum wages, and unemployment insurance. But Wilson responded that it "frightened him to think how much the common people of the world expect of him." He voiced concerns that it would not be "possible to take up any such matter at the peace conference." Instead the president "hoped the international labor conference on which he looked with much favo[r] would press for these matters."[1]

Fosdick's story was likely accurate for the president refused, despite an intense lobbying effort by supporters of the AFL, to include a labor representative on the American peace commission and instead advised Gompers to use his energies to organize an international labor conference to consider questions of postwar reconstruction. By contrast, the British delegation sought to create a commission at the Versailles Peace Conference that would deal directly with international labor issues. The idea for the commission was the brainchild of former Labour Party M.P. and War Cabinet member George Barnes, who clearly hoped that the commission could develop a permanent body for promoting international labor legislation that would not only quell the spirit of labor and social unrest that threatened world peace at war's end but also provide a mechanism for the permanent uplifting of labor standards. Wilson, although initially cool to the idea of an industrial component to the peace conference, soon joined other plenipotentiaries in supporting the plan and appointed Gompers to represent the United States on the commission. Doubtless the looming specter of Bolshevism and social revolution helped convince the plenipotentiaries of the value of a modest nod in the direction of international labor reform.

But controversy marred the work of the commission from its very beginning; even moderate British and European labor and Socialist organizations largely refused to attend the Versailles Conference due to the unwillingness of French authorities to allow enemy labor leaders into the country. Both the reconstituted International Federation of Trade Unions and Socialist International instead met in Bern, Switzerland, and claimed for themselves the right to speak for international labor. With most European labor leaders in Bern, the Commission on International Labor Legislation created by the peace commissioners was staffed primarily by social policy experts from Allied Countries, with Gompers acting as chair. At thirty-five meetings during February and early March of 1919, the commission drew up the blueprints both for an industrial charter of labor rights to be incorporated directly into the Versailles Peace Treaty and for the International Labor Organization, a tripartite body designed to include business, state, and government representatives from member states and to work in cooperation with the League in solving international economic problems and promoting international labor legislation. Wilson, despite his initial reluctance to consider industrial issues at the conference, subsequently embraced both the labor provisions of the peace treaty and the ILO as a critical component of his international programs. For both Gompers and Wilson the labor component of the Versailles treaty came to seem a logical culmination and expansion of the wartime partnership that had developed between the AFL and the American government. But the Bern conference initially repudiated both the peace treaty and the labor charter, setting the stage for a showdown between European labor and Gompers, who also faced a growing challenge to his international programs at home.

PREPARING FOR THE PEACE CONFERENCE

In the heady days following the signing of the armistice on November 11, 1918, Gompers assumed as a "matter of course" that he would be appointed a peace commissioner. This assumption was not mere conceit on his part but grew from widespread speculation in the labor press that he was being considered for the position, as well as from his knowledge that several prominent Americans were agitating on his behalf. Among those who wrote letters urging that Gompers be appointed to the peace commission were Al Smith, governor of New York and future presidential candidate; leading businessman Bernard Baruch; Secretary of Labor William B. Wilson; labor lawyer and National War Labor Board chair Frank Walsh; and several leading AFL trade unionists. Indeed even the French ambassador and French government, while not specifically recommending a particular appointment for Gompers, suggested that it would be useful to have the AFL president in Paris during the peace conference so that he could serve as a "steadying influence."[2] Yet Wilson responded to all these suggestions in a similar way: the peace delegates, he insisted, should not represent particular classes or special interests but "the country as a whole." In an effort to counteract these arguments, William B. Wilson claimed that Gompers's attainments were sufficiently great, and his vision sufficiently broad, to "qualify him to represent the people of the United States." President Wilson, although commending Gompers's patriotism and accomplishments, insisted that appointing the AFL president to the peace commission would be taken as "indicating a desire to have the special field of labor represented" in a fashion distinct from other interest groups.[3]

To Gompers's critics within the AFL, especially those who had caught the Labor Party bug, Wilson's failure to appoint a labor representative on the peace commission signaled that the AFL had gained little from its collaboration with the government during the war and ought to consider an independent approach. The editors of the *Seattle Union Record*, for example, argued that "[t]he refusal or failure of President Wilson to include a labor representative in the delegation from the United States makes all the more apparent the futility of attempting to secure any recognition for labor through existing governmental machinery." The three lawyers appointed to the peace mission, they argued, were "honest" but envisioned an "America we knew before the war, an America of millionaires and middle class and working class rather than a future America of industrial democracy." They instead supported the Chicago Labor Party plan that called for a "summons for an international of all workers, to establish industrial democracy in place of commercial imperialism under a workers league of peoples," as well as for simultaneous agitation to create a Labor Party movement at local, state, and national levels.[4]

Gompers, unsurprisingly, failed to draw the same conclusions about the need for Labor Party politics or a workers' league of peoples. But he was also clearly annoyed with the president and informed contacts in the State Department he would not go to Paris as the French requested "unless he had a reason for being there." Doubtless the president's decision disappointed Gompers because it suggested that Wilson, although happy to use the AFL to promote its foreign policies both at home and abroad during the war, was apparently no more committed to incorporating labor into actual policymaking circles than he had been during the Pan American Financial Conferences in 1915. But President Wilson and his aides soon smoothed Gompers's ruffled feathers by convincing him that an AFL presence at any future international labor conference would be vital to its success. Yet when Gompers began trying to plan the postwar conference he faced new obstacles. Several Allied governments expressed concerns about a labor conference in Paris during the peace negotiations. Gompers, however, insisted that the conference must be held there, noting that the Allies should be embracing rather than undermining free speech. Privately, he also told Acting Secretary of State Frank Polk that if the plenipotentiaries refused to allow a labor conference in Paris the AFL would be "humiliated and made the laughing stock of the world."[5]

Whether due to pressure from Wilson or from their own constituencies, Allied leaders soon reconsidered and decided to allow Allied labor representatives to meet in Paris. But the French government refused to permit labor delegates from enemy countries into France. Arthur Henderson and Albert Thomas, who had been appointed to the organizing committee for a labor peace congress along with Gompers at the Inter-Allied labor meeting in September, then made the decision to transfer the congress to a neutral location, either Lausanne or Bern, Switzerland, so that delegates from the Central powers could attend. But Gompers objected strongly to these changes, suggesting that if the conference were held in a neutral country it would be "captured by the extremists and Bolsheviks." The president seemed inclined to agree with Gompers, but others argued that the AFL could play an important role at a conference in a neutral country in curbing the extremists.[6]

The issue remained unresolved when Gompers and a small AFL mission set sail for London on January 8 to meet with Inter-Allied labor leaders. Discussions there failed to yield a compromise and in late January the AFL mission and Belgian representatives, who also opposed meeting prematurely with German labor leaders, traveled to Paris in the hopes of influencing the peace commissioners. By contrast, the majority of European labor and Socialist organizations, with the exception of a few left-wing groups, chose to send representatives to Bern, Switzerland, for the International Labor and Socialist Conference. Among those left-wing groups boycotting the conference were the Swiss "Zimmerwaldians," who advocated direct action to achieve economic goals, and some groups sympathetic to Bolshevism.[7]

Despite defections from the right and left, the Bern conference planned an ambitious agenda that included advising the peace conference on a host of political issues as well as strictly labor and economic questions. Gompers and the AFL mission, on the other hand, apparently had no clear idea what their function in Paris might be if the international labor congress were not held there. Fortuitously for the AFL, the plenipotentiaries adopted a resolution creating a commission to consider international labor issues based on George Barnes's proposals only shortly before Gompers arrived in Paris. After a meeting with the AFL mission, Wilson appointed Gompers to serve, along with Edward Hurley of the U.S. Shipping Board, on the commission. At the suggestion of Wilson and Barnes, the committee then elected Gompers chair. Wilson, still concerned about upcoming events at Bern, sent American diplomats Pleasants Stovall and William Bullitt to observe events there while the Commission on International Labor Legislation met in Paris.[8]

THE BERN CONFERENCE AND THE COMMISSION ON INTERNATIONAL LABOR LEGISLATION

Despite the schism between the Bern and Paris labor meetings, they enjoyed some common intellectual ground. George Barnes, before submitting his plan for an international labor organization to the peace conference, consulted with Arthur Henderson and other British Labour Party leaders and apparently gained their approval for the plan. Although Barnes had been repudiated both by the Labour Party leadership and the party's electorate in the elections of 1918, he nonetheless remained in the War Cabinet and the Lloyd George administration appointed him to serve as its labor representative at the peace conference. More conservative than Henderson, Barnes had been critical of the Stockholm movement and unswervingly supported the British government's war policies. Despite their differences, both Barnes and Henderson supported the idea of an international labor organization to create international labor legislation. Yet where Barnes's vision was largely defensive, Henderson's was expansive. For Barnes, an international labor organization working in harness with the League of Nations was necessary both to damp the flames of social revolution spreading in Europe and to protect British workers from the growing economic threat posed by workers in colonial or other underdeveloped areas. "Industrialism," he argued, "had spread out so that [the] older nations had no longer the hold on the world markets which at one time they had enjoyed." Britain now faced competition even from its own dominions. He insisted that an international labor organization designed to work in cooperation with the League of Nations in promoting international labor legislation was needed because "to raise the bottom is to raise ourselves." He offered the example of factory operatives processing jute fiber in Calcutta and Dundee. "If Indian operatives," he suggested, were "left to work long hours of labour, then it was obvious that the standard of life of the Dundee operatives would be jeopardized. The only way, or at least the best way, to safeguard Dundee was to raise Calcutta."[9]

Barnes's plan, written in conjunction with several officials from the Ministry of Labour, called for an organization consisting of state, labor, and employing interests to help frame international labor legislation in cooperation with the League of Nations that could help raise industrial standards throughout the world. It drew for inspiration on the prewar International Association for Labour Legislation centered in Basel, Switzerland, that had sought to encourage more uniform labor standards within European countries. Yet Barnes's plans were distinctive in encouraging an affiliation between the proposed international labor organization and the League and in inviting nations and self-governing colonies outside of Europe to join.[10]

Henderson and other British Labour Party leaders agreed that an international body designed to create international labor legislation could be a valuable tool for safeguarding labor standards in the postwar era, but only if it were a part of a far broader package of international political reforms. The British Labour Party's foreign policy programs at war's end, it will be recalled, asked for a sweeping democratization of the process of foreign policy decision making at the nation-state and international levels, as well as for self-determination for British colonies. At Bern, the proposals for an international labor organization were considered as but one component of an expansive agenda that also included a consideration of war guilt, territorial questions, colonialism, Russia, and plans for a democratic League of Nations. Wilsonian precepts clearly influenced the work of labor leaders at Bern. But the conference also went significantly beyond Wilson's Fourteen Points in embracing a more comprehensive vision of democracy that included "people's representatives" in the halls of international power as well as a greater emphasis on global economic democracy and equality.[11]

In opening the conference, President Hjalmar Branting of Sweden emphasized that Wilson was "historically the champion of the international policy of the working class" and through his Fourteen Points sought to bring about "Intellectual Revolution." But in Paris, Wilson would represent only "one great power among many." The chosen representatives of the working class must therefore complete Wilson's "work on behalf of a League of Peoples."[12] That Branting placed emphasis in his opening remarks on the League was significant, for although the conference spent much time on other components of the agenda, the League was clearly viewed as the linchpin upon which all other reforms depended. The conference made extensive recommendations on territorial questions, but it followed the reasoning of the Inter-Allied Labor and Socialist Conference and President Wilson in assuming that continuing disagreements over these issues should not delay a peace settlement; border problems and other issues could instead be resolved by the future League. The conference embraced the notion of self-determination for all oppressed nationalities who sought it, but insisted that the League would need to oversee the process by which colonies or other subject groups became nation-states. The League would also oversee conditions in colonial dependencies and assure that injustices were not occurring there, as well as develop policies that would encourage disarmament throughout the world. In order to promote economic equality and prevent starvation in the aftermath of war, the League would additionally exercise control over world reserves of natural resources and food. Finally, the League would be entrusted with implementing, and ensuring compliance with, the protective labor legislation recommended by any international labor organization created at the Versailles Peace Conference.[13]

Yet British delegates in particular emphasized that such powers could be entrusted to the League of Nations only if it were democratically constituted. Speaking before the conference, J. W. Thomas and James Ramsay MacDonald argued that the League must not be a league of ministers and diplomats but rather one comprised of delegations from national parliaments in which all parties and factions would be [proportionally] represented. Such a system would ensure that people's representatives from Socialist and Labor parties finally had a voice in international affairs. If the League were not democratically constituted, MacDonald insisted, it might simply become another apparatus for reinforcing the status quo and would fail to eradicate imperialism, war, or oppressive working conditions. In this respect, the labor and Socialist leaders at Bern clearly departed from the Wilsonian vision, for the U.S. president never elucidated a plan for parliamentary elections of delegates and proportional representation of divergent political factions within national delegations attending League of Nations meetings.[14] Instead his emphasis remained on creating a league of governments, whose representatives would presumably be appointed by government leaders.

This disconnect between Wilson and European Socialist and labor leaders on the issue of a democratic League of Nations informed a set of telegrams about the conference sent to Secretary of State Lansing from Pleasants Stovall, one of the U.S. ambassadors at the conference. After recounting MacDonald's speech, Stovall offered his own editorial opinion of MacDonald's ideas about a League of Peoples as "either childishly naïve or based upon self imposed blindness." He emphasized that for "the people to get along with one another they must all have and develop strong governments," and he expressed confidence in militaries when they were "controlled by enlightened and vigilant democracies." Although Stovall left some of his ideas underdeveloped, he hinted that the strength of the League would ultimately rest upon the combined military power of strong, centrally run governments and that the national delegations to the League would be drawn from the executives of these governments.[15]

The extremely democratic vision of Bern labor leaders not only separated them from the Wilsonians but also from the Bolsheviks and others who failed to repudiate force as a mechanism for social change in 1919. Despite an extended debate on the subject, the conference failed to agree upon a single resolution about the Russian Revolution. The majority statement denounced the tendency of governments to treat Bolshevism as a "bogey," but nonetheless emphasized that democracy was an essential underpinning of socialism. Henderson, in speaking on behalf of the resolution, commented that he had witnessed the excesses of the Russian Revolution and was convinced that "Socialism without democracy was nonsense." The minority resolution, however, warned about prematurely judging the methods of Russian revolutionaries and noted that several European Socialist parties had boycotted the Bern conference due to its apparent hostility to Bolshevism. In a nod to the minority, the majority agreed to send a commission to Russia to investigate conditions there.[16]

In contrast to the Russian issue, the recommendations for international labor legislation aroused virtually no opposition. The recommendations, written by delegates from the former International Federation of Trade Unions who met in a room adjacent to the meeting place of the International Labor and Socialist Conference under the direction of French trade union leader Léon Jouhaux, included an extensive set of resolutions on child labor, women's labor and maternity benefits, social insurance, and unemployment as well as a demand that at least half of all representatives in any future international labor organization be comprised of labor representatives.[17] After endorsement of these recommendations by the Bern conference, Léon Jouhaux traveled to Paris to participate in the last several sessions of the Commission on International Labor Legislation. The Bern conference also sent another group of representatives to confer directly with the plenipotentiaries about their broader agenda. Yet the Bern group's efforts to influence either the peace conference or the evolving blueprints for the International Labor Organization and International Labor Charter would be largely frustrated.[18]

PARIS

To European labor leaders who played a role at Bern, the appointment of Gompers to chair the Commission on International Labor Legislation seemed like a "farce" because the AFL president enjoyed a reputation as an "apostle of voluntarism" who eschewed governmental intervention in labor affairs. Yet during the war Gompers's thinking about the relationship between labor and the state had undergone a subtle transformation. Although still opposed to legislative solutions to most labor problems, Gompers's work for the Council of National Defense convinced him of the value of business, state, and labor cooperation in solving both domestic and international problems. Indeed, only shortly before sailing for Britain in January, Gompers sent Wilson a long letter suggesting that he make the Council of National Defense a permanent body for promoting industrial cooperation. In a similar vein, he welcomed the possibility of creating a voluntary international body to encourage cooperation between national delegations comprised of business, labor, and state representatives in resolving international economic problems. Like Barnes, he particularly feared that the increasing competition from poorer nations and colonies would undermine labor standards in allegedly mature industrial societies such as the United States. Yet where Barnes was concerned primarily about competition from Asia, Gompers feared competition from Mexico and the Caribbean. In addition, Gompers hoped to encourage voluntary agreements on immigration, since he believed that heavy influxes of immigrants from low-wage countries also threatened U.S. industrial standards. Finally, Gompers sought to use his position to encourage the incorporation of the general principles proposed by the AFL and accepted by the Inter-Allied Labor and Socialist Conference directly into the treaty (Figure 6.1).[19]

But Gompers soon found that guiding the commission along a voluntarist path was more difficult than he had assumed, despite the absence of most of his adversaries from the British and European labor and Socialist movements. The commission included two-member delegations from Great Britain, France, Japan, Italy, Belgium, and the United States; Cuba, Poland, and Czechoslovakia were each represented by one delegate. Most European

Figure 6.1. Commission on International Labor Legislation, Paris, 1919 (© International Labour Organization). AFL President Samuel Gompers is center front. Used with the permission of the International Labour Organization, Geneva, Switzerland.

countries sent social policy experts, many with extensive experiences in the International Association of Labor Legislation (IALL), created in 1900 in Basel, Switzerland by reformist intellectuals. In the prewar period, the IALL made a name for itself by successfully encouraging several European states to ratify two conventions on the prohibition of night work for women and the elimination of the dangerous chemical white phosphorous in the production of matches. Those with social policy backgrounds within the labor commission at Versailles, suggests Jasmien Van Daele, comprised an "epistemic community" that shared a "progressive" reform mentality and a belief in the value of ameliorative labor legislation in preventing "social breakdown."[20]

Particularly important to the functioning of the Commission on International Labor Legislation were Emile Vandervelde, a Socialist politician who had been a member of the Belgian Worker's Party since 1894 and served as a minister for the Belgian government during World War I; Ernest Mahaim, a Belgian professor at the University of Liege and an "international expert on social law"; and the two British delegates on the commission, George Barnes and social policy expert Sir Malcolm Delevigne. The only other trade union official within the commission was Léon Jouhaux, General Secretary of France's Confédération Générale du Travail (CGT) and a bitter critic of Gompers, who arrived at the conference after the Berne meeting. To many of these delegates, Gompers doubtless seemed an unschooled and provincial outsider and they were therefore surprised when President Wilson and George Barnes exerted influence to have him appointed chair; they had assumed that either Barnes or one of the other delegates with extensive experience with social legislation would direct the commission's work. But according to Van Daele, they accepted Gompers's appointment as a "diplomatic compromise" in order to build U.S. Senate support for passage of the Versailles Treaty.[21]

Assisting Gompers in Paris were several loyal and trusted labor colleagues whose voluntarist views about government-state relations were roughly comparable to his own: James Duncan, president of the Granite Workers; John Alpine, president of the United Association of Plumbers; Frank Duffy, secretary of the United Brotherhood of Carpenters and Joiners; and William Green, secretary-treasurer of the United Mine Workers and future president of the AFL. Although sometimes contentious, these colleagues were more a source of support than of problems for Gompers. Also of great assistance to Gompers was historian James Shotwell, who attended the meetings primarily as an observer but was asked by President Wilson's advisors to intervene on several occasions to help craft compromises between the U.S. and European delegations. By contrast, Andrew Furuseth of the Seamen's Union proved a constant irritant to Gompers. He attended the meetings on a daily basis in order to make sure that none of the international agreements signed by the American delegation undermined the U.S. Seamen's Act of 1915. Furuseth also served as a conduit of information about the conference for the U.S. Labor Party movement, that, in turn, regularly publicized his hostile impressions and critiques of the commission's work.[22]

One other prominent U.S. labor activist who was present for part of the Paris Peace Conference deserves brief mention here. Frank Walsh, former chair of the National War Labor Board, traveled to Paris in 1919 to agitate on behalf of Irish independence. When Wilson finally granted Walsh a meeting, President Wilson scolded him for undermining U.S. relations with Britain through his work investigating British atrocities in Ireland. Walsh's ill treatment by Wilson provoked a backlash among Irish-American labor activists and led to the creation of the Labor Bureau of the American Commission on Irish Independence, chaired by none other than Walsh's longtime friend, Chicago Federation of Labor President John Fitzpatrick. Irish-American and Labor Party politics became increasingly intertwined, helping to drive Labor

Party activists toward an anti-imperialist condemnation of both the League and the ILO that would prove important in undermining working-class support of the Versailles Treaty.[23]

In future attacks on the ILO, Irish-American and U.S. Labor Party activists would highlight the role allegedly played by British representatives in shaping discussions within the Commission on International Labor Legislation in ways that served British imperial interests. Since Barnes, in conjunction with the British Ministry of Labour and British Labour Party, prepared the blueprint for a possible international labor organization before the peace conference, this was the draft that was used as a basis for subsequent discussions within the commission—much to Gompers's chagrin. Only toward the end of the conference were the AFL's much-prized set of labor principles discussed or considered for inclusion in the treaty. Yet the commission extensively revised the British proposals, and the AFL's Labor Charter was but one of many submitted to the group. In this sense, the final product of the commission's work was a group effort that involved significant compromise by all parties concerned.

In debates over the proposed structure of the future International Labor Organization, the delegates within the Commission on International Labor Legislation feuded over at least three separate but interrelated issues. Perhaps most important was the question of representation within the new organization. The British plan proposed that each member state send national delegations to the conventions of the future organization that would consist of three members—one state representative with two votes and one employer and one labor delegate with one vote each. Gompers opposed this plan, arguing that government delegates would more often side with employer than labor interests. But significantly, Gompers did not oppose a tripartite structure altogether; instead he favored national delegations modeled loosely on the American war boards in that they would consist of one business, one state, and one government representative, each enjoying one vote. Belgian delegate Emile Vandervelde then proposed an alternative scheme for national delegations of two government representatives, one labor and one business, each with one vote. The primary difference between Vandervelde's proposal and that of the British delegation's was that there would be two government representatives with one vote each rather than one government representative with two votes, presumably because it would increase the diversity of governmental perspectives.[24]

Gompers and Léon Jouhaux, however, opposed this plan as well. Gompers insisted vehemently that if "workpeople" were relegated to a "minority of one in four" within the national delegations, as called for by both the British and Vandervelde plan, the working classes of these nations would not support the new organization. Jouhaux also argued that the French working class would "hesitate to take part in the proposed scheme." By contrast, Barnes expressed surprise that some believed "Governments were always hostile to the workers," since governments had appointed the delegates to the current commission. Both Barnes and Vandervelde seemed to anticipate that in the future Socialist and Labor parties would wield even greater influence within governments in Europe. Vandervelde wondered whether the American and French delegations were "opposed to the British proposals because for different reasons the working classes in these two countries did not exert on their respective Governments so effective an influence as the working class organizations in Great Britain, Belgium, and Italy?"[25]

In making such arguments Vandervelde and Barnes cast the Americans and French as the backward countries within the convention. But on this issue, Gompers and Jouhaux may have been more in touch with the currents then rippling through the international labor movement than Vandervelde and Barnes. Working-class proponents of a people's peace and democratic diplomacy were unlikely to be satisfied with a structure for the ILO that they perceived as undemocratic. As Jouhaux explained, the expectations of the workers had been greatly magnified as a result of the war. What they now sought was "nothing less than the creation of a new world." At the very least, this goal required that workers—as the majority class—be given majority representation within the new organization. But the commission nonetheless adopted the Vandervelde voting formula of four representatives: two government, one labor, and one business, each enjoying one vote. Subsequent efforts by Gompers to introduce amendments whereby this decision could be overturned were unsuccessful.[26]

Gompers and the other American delegate Henry Robinson, who replaced Edward Hurley when he resigned due to other commitments, also raised questions about British and Belgian schemes for representation of self-governing colonies within the future ILO, as well as for the colonies of other European states. The British proposal called for giving self-governing colonies the same rights and representation within the ILO as other countries. The Belgian delegation tried to modify the British proposal by suggesting that self-governing colonies would be granted representation only if the mother country agreed to it. In the case of colonies not represented in the ILO, mother countries would apply conventions on a case-by-case basis, depending on their suitability. Gompers and Robinson then intervened to demand that individual states within the United States be treated as self-governing colonies and granted the same rights to representation as British Dominions. They argued that in the United States, the states were self-governing in most respects and that it was inequitable to give the United States, with a population of over one hundred million, the same number of votes as a single self-governing colony or a small country. But Barnes argued that if this applied to the United States, then Canada and Australia should also have more votes. Gompers and Robinson responded with a new demand: if the American states did not qualify for self-governing status, then countries should be given proportional representation in the ILO based on population.[27]

Gompers and Robinson unsuccessfully pressed their case and the commission instead agreed that the British Dominions and India would automatically be accorded the same rights as the signatories to the peace treaty. Colonies of other nations could also apply for representation in the ILO if they were fully self-governing. The commission mandated that member states should apply conventions they had ratified to colonies that were not fully self-governing "[e]xcept where owing to the local conditions the convention is inapplicable" or "subject to such modifications as may be necessary to adapt the convention to local conditions." These proposals were subsequently modified somewhat to conform to the policies toward colonies already adopted by the high contracting parties as part of the peace treaty, but the principle of representation for self-governing colonies and the application of conventions by the mother country to other colonies on the basis of how appropriate they were to local conditions was maintained. These articles proved fateful for they gave rise within the United States to claims that the ILO would give unfair representation to the British Empire and would also be used by imperial states to perpetuate substandard conditions in their colonies.[28]

Some of these same issues surfaced in debates about the structure of the governing office of the ILO, which was to include twelve government members, six worker delegates, and six business delegates. Under the provisions drafted by the commission, eight government members were to be from states of chief industrial importance, and four were to be selected by the other governmental delegates. But a protocol supported by the AFL was subsequently added that mandated that "no high contracting party, together with its Dominions and Colonies, was entitled to more than one member among the government delegates." This provision was particularly aimed at the British Empire, since the AFL and some others within the commission feared that Britain would exercise undue influence over delegates from its self-governing colonies who might be elected to the governing board. Significantly the AFL did not criticize the provision that eight states of major industrial importance would receive regular representation within the governing body, something about which delegates from non-European countries would later complain. Doubtless, the AFL delegates believed that industrial creditor nations should be disproportionately represented in the governing office.[29]

The next issue over which substantial controversy arose was the matter of how binding ILO conventions should be on member states. French and Italian delegates proposed resolutions that would have empowered the ILO with the authority to create international labor legislation that had to be implemented within one year by member states. Vandervelde, however, pointed out that these proposals amounted to "the creation of a super-parliament." Although this system might be desirable in the future, it was not currently practical due to the differing economic situations within individual countries. He argued that Belgium was currently in an "impoverished state" due to invasion and "could not bear restrictions which would be quite acceptable to prosperous countries." The American delegation emphasized that numerous constitutional obstacles existed to such a scheme in the United States. Vandervelde and Barnes therefore modified the proposals of the Italians and French by suggesting that legislation passed by the ILO should instead be referred to national legislatures as draft conventions—comparable to a treaty—so that national governments could in turn decide whether to ratify them or not. If national legislatures failed to ratify a draft convention they needed only to notify ILO authorities. But if they approved it, those countries could then be subject to sanctions if they failed to implement the convention.[30] Gompers and Robinson, however, objected even to this modified proposal, arguing that labor legislation in the United States was the preserve of the forty-eight states and that the federal government had no authority to impose it on them. They cited the example of the child labor law that had recently been declared unconstitutional by the Supreme Court. Gompers also warned that American plenipotentiaries at the conference were unlikely to accept a provision that might be deemed unconstitutional.[31]

The issue threatened to derail the work of the commission, much to the consternation of President Wilson's advisors Felix Frankfurter and Colonel Edward House. They recruited James Shotwell to work on the issue, fearing that it "would be nothing short of an international scandal if, after having promised labor legislation with such a magnificent gesture at the first meeting of the Peace Conference, there should be a complete breakdown on a technical question." Shotwell subsequently directed a subcommittee that crafted a compromise article whereby ILO legislation might take the form of either nonbinding recommendations or draft conventions. Federal states, however, could treat draft conventions as recommendations. The committee's revised article was accepted despite complaints that federal states would now be under a lesser obligation than others. A special protocol was also later inserted into the article in response to pressure from Andrew Furuseth and Samuel Gompers mandating that no high contracting party be "asked or required, as a result of the adoption of any recommendation or draft convention by the Conference, to lessen the protection afforded by its existing legislation to the workers concerned."[32] The compromise appeared to be a victory for the AFL, for it made compliance with ILO mandates largely voluntary. The article, however, would later be bitterly criticized by U.S. opponents of the ILO, including Andrew Furuseth.

With most of the constitutional and procedural issues resolved, a final showdown within the commission developed over the question of the labor charter to be inserted into the treaty. According to James Shotwell, Gompers had a "deep personal interest" in the charter because "it was the statement of those general principles for which he and the American Federation of Labor had fought."[33] The AFL submitted the first set of labor principles early in the deliberations but this draft soon competed with several others. The Bern labor conference, upset at being upstaged by Gompers, sent a "Manifesto" of demands only shortly after the commission's deliberations commenced in February. In subsequent weeks, the British, Italian and Belgian delegations also submitted draft statements of principles for inclusion in the treaty. Some of the principles, such as demands for an eight-hour day and the abolition of child labor, overlapped. But in other respects the drafts reflected divergent priorities. The Bern Manifesto championed by Jouhaux included far more specifics in its program than the other proposals and, in addition to demanding that one-half of the delegates to the proposed ILO be workers, insisted that any labor conventions adopted by the organization have the force of international law. The Italian delegation's proposals also anticipated the adoption of a body of specific international regulations governing work life that would be internationally enforced. Perhaps the most radical demands of the Italian delegation were that workers should claim the legal right to be consulted on questions of management in industry and agriculture, and a proposal for freedom of migration for workers between countries with international guarantees on the protection of their rights wherever they traveled.[34]

By contrast, the British delegation's original proposals seemed designed, as Irish-American labor activists later charged, to preserve imperial prerogatives in colonial areas and suggested a kind of racialized thinking about international labor standards; they supported the eight-hour day and forty-eight-hour week in principle, but emphasized the need for exceptions in areas such as "Asia and Africa, where owing to climate conditions, the general physique of the industrial population . . . or other special circumstances, the industrial efficiency of the workers is substantially inferior to the efficiency of the workers in other countries." The American proposals also proved unique; they emphasized safeguarding the rights of workers to free speech and free assembly, drew on language from the Clayton Antitrust Act in declaring that labor was not a commodity or article of commerce, and included a clause on the rights of seamen to leave their ships while in port—no doubt inspired by Andrew Furuseth's constant lobbying on the issue.[35]

In deliberations on the proposals, the British favored a relatively short list of flexible clauses for insertion in the treaty, while the Americans and French favored a longer charter that established clear universal principles. For example, when Barnes expressed doubts about including an eight-hour clause in the charter and suggested instead that a "careful" convention be framed at a future conference, Jouhaux responded that "an eight hours' day was unanimously demanded by the working classes in all countries" and that they would be unable to "comprehend the action of the commission" if it were not inserted directly into the treaty. Gompers also favored inserting a clause on the eight-hour day directly into the treaty.[36] Eventually, the commission appointed a subcommittee that whittled the list of demands from the four separate drafts of proposals down to nineteen. The commission then voted on these clauses and reduced the number of principles recommended for insertion into the treaty to nine. The adopted clauses enunciated the principle that labor was not a commodity and prohibited child labor. They also asserted the right of workers to free association, an eight-hour day and forty-eight-hour week, a weekly rest of twenty-four hours, and "a wage adequate to maintain a reasonable standard of life as this is understood in their time and country." Other clauses declared that workers were entitled to equitable economic treatment, and provided that each state create a system of inspection in which women should take part to ensure the enforcement of labor laws.[37]

Omitted from the final proposals of the labor commission were several American clauses, including one that delineated the rights of seamen. Not surprisingly, the elimination of this clause from the treaty outraged Andrew Furuseth, who wrote Wilson personally to complain and soon became a bitter critic of the labor provisions of the treaty.[38] Other controversies arose when the commission sent the labor clauses to the plenipotentiaries at the peace conference and they in turn made further changes in the wording.

Most members of the labor commission disliked the changes but they differed about whether the new language substantively undermined the labor provisions. Emile Vandervelde argued that the peace commissioners had only "slightly scumbled" the meaning of the original proposals. Others, however, were far more critical, charging that the changes "materially emasculated" the Labor Charter.[39]

Gompers proved particularly upset by the alterations because he had already left Paris by the time the plenipotentiaries met to discuss the Labor Charter; the AFL delegation apparently presumed that peace delegates would have power only to accept or reject the work of the Commission on International Labor Legislation. Instead Sir Robert Borden of Canada proposed amendments that, from Gompers's perspective, "practically nullifie[d] [the] whole program." One important change involved the elimination of the clause strongly supported by the American delegation regarding the composition of the ILO Executive Office. This clause decreed that "no member, together with its Dominions and Colonies, whether self-governing or not, shall be entitled to nominate more than one member [to the governing body of the ILO]." From the American perspective, the chief virtue of this clause was to prevent excessive influence within the ILO by representatives of the British Empire. Borden, on the other hand, insisted that labor conditions in the British Dominions were entirely different than in the mother country and that they should be treated as independent members, a point to which President Wilson acceded, even while noting that he had more concerns about India in this respect than Canada. By contrast, Gompers and Robinson argued that the exclusion of this safeguard from the ILO constitution would prove "disastrous" in terms of rallying U.S. public opinion behind the treaty, since many Americans already believed that the British would wield too much power in the League of Nations and ILO. In contrast to Borden, Gompers and Robinson assumed that representatives of British Dominions would be subservient to Britain in international governing bodies.[40]

Even more significant to the AFL delegation were changes in the much prized Labor Charter that was to be incorporated directly into treaty. Most important to the AFL delegation was the inclusion of the word "merely" in the proposed clause that "labor should not be regarded *merely* as a commodity or article of commerce." As Furuseth pointed out, the addition changed "an absolute negative into an equally absolute positive." He compared it to saying that "Andrew Furuseth is not a scab" and then amending it to say that "Andrew Furuseth is not *merely* a scab." President Wilson was so concerned that the changes might lead the AFL to repudiate the Labor Charter that he

cabled Gompers, who was back in the United States by the time the plenipotentiaries met, and explained that he did not think the changes "introduced
any weakness or threat of weakness into the labor provisions."[41]

Furuseth later claimed that Gompers privately called the proposed ILO a
"Frankenstein." Wilson aide Joseph Tumulty also informed the White House
of rumors circulating in Washington, D.C., that Gompers believed he had
been "sold out" with respect to the international labor program and felt "very
bitter." But publicly Gompers insisted that, although the Labor Charter and
proposed ILO were not "perfect" due to the necessity of compromising with
other nations, they nonetheless marked a "glorious advance for labor." The
American press widely praised Gompers for his leadership in constructing
the ILO and Wilson administration officials warmly congratulated him.[42]
Wilson, for his part, became convinced that the labor provisions would be
one of the few noncontroversial elements of the peace treaty and could well
be a political selling point. During the summer and fall of 1919, Wilson extensively used the labor provisions in promoting the peace treaty, insisting
that they were a "Magna Charta" for labor and pointed the way toward international industrial peace and conciliation, as well as industrial democracy.
That the president liked the labor provisions was not surprising, because they
embodied the progressive ideals for which he had long fought. Their goals
were class collaboration rather than class conflict and the uplifting of labor
standards without resort to the socialization of production or a dictatorship
of the proletariat as envisioned by the Bolsheviks.[43]

EARLY OPPOSITION TO THE LABOR PROVISIONS

But trouble soon brewed both in Europe and the United States. Representatives from the Bern trade union group insisted that the manifesto they had
drawn up represented the real demands of international labor and ought to be
used in lieu of the charter agreed upon by the Commission on International
Labor Legislation. They also demanded fundamental structural changes in the
proposed International Labor Organization, including the requirement that
half of all delegates be worker delegates, that Germany and Austria immediately be invited to join the organization, and that a mechanism be developed
to make all legislation passed by the new organization binding.[44]

The leaders of the Socialist and political side of the labor conference at Bern
doubted that the international regulation of labor could be effective without
a fundamental revision of the entire Paris Peace Treaty, whose preliminary
terms they viewed as reactionary. The group complained not only about

the harsh peace meted out to the Germans but also about the rewarding of German colonies to other imperial powers as spoils of war. Until colonial imperialism ended, they suggested, the "exploitation of native races" would undermine the effort of all workers to improve their economic well-being. Colonies of both the Allied and Central powers must be afforded the right to self-determination. Perhaps most disappointing and problematic from the perspective of the Bern Socialist and labor leaders were the structural blueprints drawn up for the League of Nations at Versailles. Much as they had feared, the leading powers constructed a "League of Governments and Executives and not of peoples and parliaments." As such, the League seemed designed "to be an instrument of a victorious coalition dominated by five great powers rather than an organ of international justice upon which all nations ought to find a place." Bern leaders argued that, given its proposed composition, the League was unlikely to undertake the tasks of ending imperialism, redistributing world resources and food in a more equitable fashion, and establishing ways to control the "vast capitalist organizations" that now determined the conditions under which the world's workers labored. In the absence of a democratic league committed to these kinds of fundamental reforms, the proposed International Labor Organization would likely be of limited value.[45]

The British Labour Party summed up the sense of betrayal felt by many Bern Leaders, suggesting that in "essential particulars" the Peace Treaty was "opposed to the declarations of President Wilson, the Inter-Allied conferences and the Bern conference and in its general spirit does not conform to the working classes' conception of a peace of justice and right." In essence, the British Labour Party believed that the treaty negotiated painstakingly by President Wilson over several months was not Wilsonian enough! Beginning in the spring of 1919, both the British Labour Party and Bern group committed themselves to forcing a fundamental revision of the treaty, including its labor provisions.[46]

Also flashing early warning signals about the ILO was Andrew Furuseth of the Seamen's Union. In a press release widely published in Labor Party, Socialist and liberal newspapers and magazines across the United States, Furuseth indicted the proposed ILO on several counts. First, he questioned the composition of the Commission on International Labor Legislation itself, arguing that only a "very small minority of the delegates were even representatives of organized labor." Next, he charged that the proposed national delegations to the ILO would be "stacked against workers," since they would be comprised of only one labor delegate but would include two government representatives and one employee representative. Third, Furuseth complained that the article concerning recommendations and draft conventions would tend to undermine the authority of national governments over labor legislation despite the safeguards. Fourth, he highlighted the disproportionate vote of the British, arguing that they would control the votes of their self-governing colonies in the ILO. Finally, he argued that the U.S. Seamen's Act would be imperiled because Britain had long disliked it and would use its influence in the ILO to undermine it.[47]

Foreshadowing its opposition to the ILO and labor provisions, the Chicago Labor Party newspaper, the *New Majority*, published Furuseth's criticism under the banner headline "Furuseth Reports Inside Peace Dope—May God Save the Working People." Chicago labor reporters also did some of their own independent investigating and detailed the way "conservative British labor delegate" George Barnes allegedly "nullified the standard wage principle" by including in the Labor Charter a conditional clause excluding those colonies or countries in which "climactic conditions, the imperfect development of industrial organization, or other special circumstances make industrial conditions substantially different." This coverage of the ILO meshed harmoniously with the paper's increasingly harsh indictments of British imperialism and with its growing disillusionment with the negotiations in Versailles.[48]

Also offering early criticism of the proposed labor provisions was the IWW press, which remained committed to worker empowerment rather than government intervention on behalf of workers. The editors of the IWW paper *Solidarity* argued that the labor charter was full of "glittering generalities that mean nothing other than a determination to exploit the workers of the world to the fullest extent." It particularly criticized one of the treaty's clauses on child labor, arguing that in tone it was comparable to a "stock grower's convention discussing the age at which colts should be broken to harness, or in a horticultural magazine in writing of the right time to market fruit." The issue of child labor, they suggested, should not be reduced to "a matter of putting the commodity on the market at the right time to make the most of it." In other articles, the editors expressed "disgust" at a clause stating that "Every worker has the right to a wage adequate to maintain a reasonable standard of life, having regard to the civilization of his time and country." The editors pointed out that it was workers themselves who should determine what constituted a "reasonable standard of life." Instead, "[t]he Paris conferees have decided that they themselves are the ones to select who shall decide for all the world just how much sugar and clothing and social life would be 'reasonable' for workers. They have arrogated to themselves the positions of

Great I Am's to tell hundred [*sic*] of millions of workers of the world just how much these workers shall and shall not have to live on." *Solidarity*'s editors concluded that the labor provisions must be rejected because they had the power to "forthwith stop all progress of the human race."[49]

With criticism mounting both in Europe and the United States, Gompers chose to launch a vigorous campaign in defense of the entire Versailles "package"—including the treaty, League, Labor Charter, and ILO. Whatever his personal misgivings about some of the changes made to the labor provisions, Gompers apparently believed that the League and ILO would both prove critical in protecting the future well-being of the world's workers. On the one hand, the League would help prevent a future war in which working men and women might again lose their lives. On the other hand, the ILO would help to guarantee certain fundamental human rights to workers across the globe and slowly uplift labor standards. In the frenzied summer of 1919, Gompers sought and won the endorsement of three major labor conventions for the Versailles package: those of the American Federation of Labor, the newly created Pan American Federation of Labor (PAFL) and the reconstituted International Federation of Trade Unions (IFTU). He also garnered the cooperation of these conventions in planning for the first meeting of the International Labor Organization, which the plenipotentiaries had agreed should be held in Washington, D.C., in October 1919.

THREE CONVENTIONS

First on Gompers's agenda was the AFL convention scheduled for Atlantic City in late June 1919. Although the AFL convention usually rubber-stamped Gompers's foreign policy decisions, fireworks exploded when Gompers locked horns with Furuseth in a four-hour debate over the labor provisions at the 1919 meeting. According to Furuseth, the ILO sought nothing less than to take "jurisdiction over the daily lives of the working people throughout the world." But it was problematic, he emphasized, to entrust the new organization with such powers due to its undemocratic structure. Building on arguments he first made in the press, Furuseth emphasized that national delegations would be stacked against workers by a ratio of three to one. The British Empire, moreover, would control twenty-four votes in the new organization in contrast to the U.S.' four due to the representation that was to be given to self-governing colonies. They would use this influence to pursue policies advantageous to the British Empire but often discriminatory toward U.S. workers. Furuseth also continued to warn that the conventions passed by the ILO would tend over time to have the force of international law, the protective protocols inserted by the American delegation notwithstanding. He insisted that even the Labor Charter had now been eviscerated: it sanctified the treatment of labor as a commodity and failed to protect the right to free speech, the right of seamen to leave their ship, and even the right of workers not to be held in slavery. Furuseth aptly summarized his objections by suggesting that to trust such a structure and charter one would have to assume that "men all of a sudden [had] become saints" and would work against their own self-interest. Demonstrating the strong connections that existed between ideas about manliness and voluntarism in American working-class culture, Furuseth also questioned why "full-grown men" should need protective legislation like the minimum wage rather than "having it set by themselves," presumably through collective bargaining and strike activity.[50]

Gompers responded to Furuseth by admitting that as chair of the Commission on International Labor Legislation he had been in an "awkward and uncomfortable position" for "nine-tenths" of the time. He emphasized that he had fought hard for greater democratization of the ILO but had been opposed as much by Socialists as by capitalists. The AFL president nonetheless defended the ILO and Labor Charter by suggesting that although they were not "perfect," they laid the basis for improving the lives of workers—particularly in the "most backward countries." He insisted vehemently that the ILO would not "by any stretch of the imagination" undermine U.S. labor standards due to the safeguards that the American delegation had succeeded in including in the final draft of the treaty. He noted that Furuseth himself had at first accepted that these safeguards would be sufficient to ensure the safety of seamen. Gompers lamented that "some people are so constituted that if you gave them paradise, they would find fault with it." He then emphasized that U.S. workers wanted peace and goodwill as well as to raise the standards of others. For this reason they recognized the political importance of supporting the Versailles package. "What was there left to stand as a barrier against war," suggested Gompers, "if the proposed covenant were defeated?"[51]

Joining Gompers in singing the praises of both the ILO and League were a host of his supporters, with only a few voicing support for Furuseth in the debate on the floor of the convention. Among those endorsing Gompers's handiwork at Versailles were new leaders from the United Mine Workers such as William Green and John Walker; former president John White who had previously opposed U.S. intervention in the war no longer occupied a position in the union's hierarchy. Indeed, the entire Indianapolis group that had previously been so important in opposing Gompers's war policies seemed largely absent from the debate on the League and ILO. Also missing from the debate were leaders of the new Labor Party movement. Both the *New York Times* and *Nation* noted that John Fitzpatrick was not a delegate to the convention, thereby preventing a revolt among the central federated bodies supporting the Labor Party. But they also argued that Fitzpatrick's decision not to make the Labor Party movement an issue at the convention symbolized that it was a "secession movement" and would proceed independently anyway. Among the few defenders of Furuseth's position on the floor of the convention were delegates from the International Ladies' Garment Workers' Union (ILGWU). Although doubting that the ILO would ever turn into the super-parliament that Furuseth imagined, they nonetheless asserted that government delegates were overrepresented within the proposed national delegations and could not be trusted; such delegations would typically serve the interests of the capitalist class rather than workers. On the other hand, the ILGWU delegates announced their support for the League of Nations idea and eventually voted for the Versailles package resolution.[52]

If Furuseth's objections had little support, however, the concerns of Irish-American labor delegates did. They succeeded in inserting into the Versailles package resolution an amendment stating that "nothing in the indorsement [sic] should be construed as to deny the right of self-determination to the people of Ireland." The proposal acknowledged concerns that both the League of Nations and ILO might be used by major powers—especially Britain—to reinforce the imperial status quo and serve the economic interests of their empires. The Versailles package resolution passed, with the Irish amendment attached, by a vote of 29,750 for and 420 against.[53] In the aftermath of the convention the Socialist *New York Call* woefully complained that "[n]o surrender was ever more willingly made than that of the A.F. of L. convention to the international imperialists when it endorsed the Peace of Paris." The paper argued that the AFL was the "only labor body in the world" that had endorsed the treaty "without reservation" and insisted that the "surrender was made because of the 'labor charter' that served as a rider for the general peace pact."[54]

Second on Gompers's agenda was the newly created Pan American Federation of Labor convention that followed quickly on the heels of the AFL convention in New York City from July 7–10. The new federation, created during November of 1918, grew from the contacts Gompers had developed with Mexican labor leaders during the Mexican revolution. Also aiding in its organization was Gompers's longtime friend Santiago Iglesias, who greatly appreciated Gompers's efforts on behalf of Puerto Rican labor. Seventy-six delegates attended the first meeting, forty-six from the AFL, twenty-one from various Mexican unions, and one delegate each from Puerto Rico, Guatemala, El Salvador, Costa Rica, and Columbia. The organization would expand to include representatives from other Latin-American countries in the future. The official goal of the new federation was to encourage cooperation and solidarity among labor organizations in the Americas. But Gompers also clearly hoped to use PAFL both to fight radical labor influences in Latin America and to counteract the predominance of European Socialist and Labor Party movements in international labor affairs.[55]

Gompers commenced the conference with a plea to pass a package resolution on the Versailles Treaty, League, Labor Charter, and ILO comparable to that passed by the AFL. Some delegates seemed inspired by the work of the Commission on International Labor Legislation, noting that Central American countries also sought the "English Industrial Week" of an eight-hour day with salary increases and were interested in being a part of the universal movement advocating these goals. But they noted the disagreements that arose between Gompers and British labor leaders and wondered whether the economic interests of European workers and of workers in the Americas might in some respects be different. The Mexican delegation inquired whether the AFL's statement of labor principles, endorsed by the first PAFL convention in 1918, had been fully implemented at the conference. Gompers admitted successes and failures in this regard. The Mexican delegation also expressed concern that some of the countries of the Americas, including Mexico, had not yet even been invited to join the League of Nations or ILO. They implied that they could hardly be expected to support an organization that they were not allowed to join.[56]

The Mexicans, in fact, had reason to worry because Mexico was considered one of the outlaw nations—along with Russia and Ireland—in 1919. This was due not only to continuing instability in the country but also to provisions of the 1917 constitution that vested the subsoil rights of Mexico in the Mexican nation, thereby allowing for the expropriation of foreign business owners. The *New York Times* commented in 1919 that Great Britain, France, and the United States were unlikely to welcome Mexico into the League because they had all allegedly been victims of Mexico's "confiscatory legislation." The unwillingness of the peace commissioners to consider Mexico for membership in the League or ILO reflected how much their thinking about peace and stability was intertwined with capitalist notions of respect for property. The peace commissioners' attitudes in this regard made labor movements in many underdeveloped nations trying to free themselves from economic domination suspicious of the goals of the proposed League and ILO. But ultimately, the Mexican labor delegation chose to compromise with the AFL by using a tactic similar to that of Irish-Americans within the AFL convention: they developed an amendment to Gompers's resolution in support of the Versailles Treaty asking that all countries be admitted to the League of Nations. With this amendment included, PAFL then voted unanimously to support the resolution endorsing the League of Nations, ILO, Labor Charter, and Versailles Peace Treaty. Gompers, for his part, expressed hope that when the ILO finally went into operation "every country in the two Americas" would be represented in both the conference and the governing body. Gompers was no doubt sincere, for this would have afforded him an effective way to counteract what he viewed as the potentially deleterious influence of European labor movements within the ILO. As a final gesture, PAFL gave the AFL authority to represent it at the upcoming session of the IFTU, thereby affording him additional voting power and clout at the European meeting.[57]

An exhausted Gompers sailed for Europe only one day after the PAFL conference ended in order to attend the IFTU Conference that commenced in Amsterdam on July 25. Not surprisingly, Gompers received a hostile reception, for many were still angry with the AFL president for dividing international labor during the peace conference. The Dutch labor leader Jan Oudegeest claimed that European labor leaders invited America to the IFTU meeting "only because we want to have a go at that man Gompers. It is about time that farce was ended." Edo Fimmen, another Dutch labor delegate, argued that Gompers "deserved the disapproval" of European labor and was "very much to blame for his attitude towards his comrades of the old International."[58] Despite Gompers's opposition, the newly reconstituted IFTU endorsed the more radical Bern program rather than the Labor Charter and passed a number of resolutions calling for socialization of the means of production. But significantly, European labor representatives, despite their annoyance with Gompers and their more socialistic orientation, agreed to participate in a founding conference for the ILO in Washington, D.C., in October if two conditions were met: German trade unions needed to be invited and worker delegates could be represented only by IFTU member organizations. When Gompers and the Wilson administration agreed to these conditions, the IFTU in turn gave its tentative approval to the Washington ILO conference.[59] Apparently European labor leaders, although disappointed by the blueprint outlined for the ILO in Paris, believed that a glass half-full was better than no glass at all and decided to work from within the organization to achieve change.

By the end of the summer it seemed as though Gompers had successfully aligned much of international labor behind the Versailles Peace Treaty. Armed with endorsements from the AFL, PAFL, and the IFTU, both Wilson and Gompers enthusiastically prepared for the first meeting of the ILO in Washington in October. So eager was Gompers to see the conference succeed that he overcame his anti-German animus and insisted to a skeptical State Department that the Germans and Austrians be invited to the conference. Wilson, for his part, told aides that he was "anxious for the conference to take place" because there has been "practically no criticism of the labor sections of the treaty." He instructed aides to reassure worried European leaders that the conference would go forward regardless of whether the Senate had ratified the treaty and that he would find a way to ensure that U.S. representatives participated.[60] In his whistle stop tour of the United States in September, Wilson included sections praising the ILO and Labor Charter during speeches in places as diverse as Columbus, Ohio; Des Moines, Iowa; St. Paul, Minnesota; Seattle, Oregon; San Diego, California; and Reno, Nevada.[61]

The speeches suggested that the president had come full circle in his attitude about incorporating labor into international governance. Before the peace conference, Wilson had supported an international labor conference but believed its activities should be conducted separately from that of governments. But the blueprints developed by the Commission on International Labor Legislation convinced him that labor could play a valuable role in resolving economic problems that created tensions between nation-states. Equally important, by incorporating respectable labor into international governance, world leaders could help tame the labor unrest and damp the fires of social revolution spreading throughout the world, as well as win political support for the peace treaty. But both Wilson and Gompers would soon discover that labor opposition to the ILO and to the peace treaty in the United States was a multiheaded hydra. Rather than a political asset, the labor provisions would prove a political liability.

7 U.S. Labor Irreconcilables and Reservationists and the Founding ILO Conference in Washington, D.C., November 1919

INCLUDED IN THE BRITISH DELEGATION THAT traveled to the founding convention of the ILO in Washington, D.C., in the fall of 1919 was George Barnes, the British architect of the initial plan for the ILO. In his memoirs, Barnes would write of his experiences that "we were received very coldly in Washington." In part, Barnes blamed the frosty reception on President Wilson's stroke, for it was Wilson who first extended the invitation for the international conference to meet in the United States. Barnes also noted the irony that the United States could not officially participate in the conference because the Senate had yet to ratify the treaty, although American labor and business delegates were invited to send informal observers. In addition, Barnes suggested that two bitter nationwide strikes among miners and transport workers distracted attention from the conference. American newspapers, he and other labor delegates argued, exacerbated the situation by providing incomplete and often biased coverage of their meeting. Barnes particularly complained about one editorial that associated the labor unrest in the United States with the ILO conference and suggested that the labor delegates to the conference should "all be deported as undesirable aliens." With an air of British understatement, Barnes described the experiences of foreign delegates in the United States for the conference as being of a "most inauspicious character."[1]

Yet if Barnes emphasized circumstantial factors distracting attention and support from the conference, the roots of the problem lay deeper. Not only the Senate but public opinion was deeply divided on the question of U.S. membership in the League and the ILO by the time of the conference. Although progressive, labor, and Left groups throughout the world were disappointed by the Versailles Peace Treaty, much of the non-Bolshevik Left in Europe, as we have seen, nonetheless chose to support the ILO in the hopes that it could be changed from within. By contrast, a unique confluence of class, diaspora, race, and isolationist politics in the United States drove many centrist labor and moderate Left groups purporting to speak on behalf of U.S. workers in

1919 toward "irreconcilable" or harshly reservationist positions on the question of U.S. participation in the League and ILO. Significant opposition to the ILO among American labor and Left groups in turn created an opening for Republican Senator Robert LaFollette, a strong supporter of labor causes, to launch a devastating attack on the ILO in Congress at the same time as the ILO conference met in Washington, D.C. In a case of politics making for strange bedfellows, LaFollette's proposals soon won support from some of labor's most bitter enemies in the Senate and became a critical component of ongoing discussions over the treaty. Largely neglected by historians, the debate over the ILO illuminated the critical role of economic considerations and ideas about the racialized division of labor in shaping Congressional responses to Wilson's foreign policy programs in 1919.

Also meeting in Washington at the same time as the ILO Conference and debate in the Senate over the ILO was the International Congress of Working Women (ICWW), staged by the Women's Trade Union League (WTUL) with the cooperation of British women trade unionists. For the women of the WTUL who organized the women's congress, the ILO held promise if it could be restructured to more fully incorporate women's representatives and women's concerns. In this sense, the WTUL proved a rarity in the polarized U.S. politics of 1919; few other groups stepped forward to offer sympathetic reservations designed to improve the ILO rather than to undercut its chances for ratification by the Senate. Initially modest in its goals, the meeting of the ICWW drew women's labor representatives from nineteen countries and soon outgrew its own narrowly defined parameters, producing revolutionary ideas about the very meaning of work for women and the kinds of international programs necessary to ensure the well-being of families throughout the world. Despite the ICWW's generally sympathetic posture toward the ILO, the Wilson administration adopted a hostile attitude toward the conference, thereby alienating potentially valuable allies in the fight on behalf of the treaty. The simultaneous meetings of the ILO, the International Congress of Working Women, and the U.S. Senate in Washington in the late autumn of 1919 thus afford unique lenses through which to reevaluate Wilsonian internationalism and the debate over the Versailles Treaty.

PUBLIC OPINION AND EARLY PRESS COVERAGE OF THE ILO

During his whistle-stop tour across the country in September 1919, President Wilson lamented that the labor provisions of the Versailles Peace Treaty had not been given enough attention by the press. Subsequent articles in liberal journals such as the *New Republic* also emphasized the lack of attention devoted to either the ILO issue or the upcoming Washington ILO conference in the press. Historians, apparently taking a cue from the president and these journals, have largely neglected the ILO in their studies of the treaty debate.[2] Yet computer indexes of historical newspapers now make it possible to better assess newspaper coverage of particular events. These indexes suggest that the ILO issue received significant attention in both the mainstream presses of major U.S. cities and the Main Street newspapers of small-town America.[3] Two factors help explain this attention. First, many newspapers covered Wilson's speeches during his tour, which often included significant segments extolling the virtues of the ILO. Second, and more ominously, Wilson's Republican opponents quickly responded to his efforts to promote the International Labor Organization by raising questions about its constitutionality and structure, as well as its possible impact on workers of different races. Southern senators voiced concerns about whether the ILO would be allowed to regulate "negro" labor; Western commentators speculated that Japan could use the ILO as an instrument to force equal treatment of Japanese workers in the United States. Senator Thomas of Colorado insisted that the ILO, rather than raising the standards of workers in poorer countries as European trade union leaders claimed, would more likely reduce labor standards for (white) American workers to those of laborers in China and India. Thomas also questioned the constitutionality of American membership in the ILO. Many Wisconsin newspapers explored Senator Robert LaFollette's concerns about the undemocratic structure of the ILO.[4]

The problem, then, was not so much one of the quantity of press coverage as its generally negative overtones. With the exception of Wilson himself, the only other positive voice that the major urban newspapers as well as presses of small and midsize towns regularly included in its articles on the ILO was that of Gompers. And Gompers's detractors too easily found ways to turn his words against him. For example, when Gompers declared that the labor provisions were "written by labor men for labor," critics used it to claim that the ILO would serve a special class interest at the expense of other economic groups in ways that would undermine social peace.[5] If Gompers's allies in the AFL stepped up to defend him or the ILO, it went largely unrecorded in the popular press. Even more troubling for Wilson's supporters, many labor and Left groups joined the chorus of those complaining about or denouncing the ILO and League, albeit for very different reasons than most Republican senators.

THE ILO AND THE INTERSECTION OF CLASS, DIASPORA, AND ISOLATIONIST POLITICS IN 1919

Throughout the world, the publication of the Versailles Peace Treaty gave impetus to the far Left at the expense of centrist labor forces. Disgusted by Wilson's failure to deliver on his promises of self-determination for oppressed nations such as Ireland, India, Egypt, and Vietnam, as well as by his decision to bow to British and French imperial designs for control over the Middle East and Africa, many workers' groups embraced the seemingly stronger anti-imperialist agenda of Vladimir Lenin and Comintern. New communist parties and Soviet workers' organizations sprouted across the globe, even as communists also tried to infiltrate long-standing trade unions and labor political organizations. The United States was no exception to this trend; in 1919 two Communist parties emerged from the left-wing section of the U.S. Socialist Party.

Leading the secessionist movement were foreign-language federations from Eastern European countries who sought to spread the Russian Revolution to their homelands as well as to inspire class upheaval in the United States. Among these were the Slavic, Hungarian, Lithuanian, Lettish, Russian, and Polish Language Federations. The two Communist parties spawned by these foreign-language federations quickly moved to align with the Comintern and became bitter enemies of the International Federation of Trade Unions and the International Labor Organization.[6] By the early 1920s, U.S. Communists would develop a color code to explain their attitudes toward the competing labor internationals of the era. They dubbed the European-based International Federation of Trade Unions the "yellow" international due to its cowardice in promoting working-class interests throughout the globe and coded the ILO the "black" international due to its betrayal of the international working class. By contrast, the Comintern was nicknamed the "red international" due to its brave support for revolutionary upheaval throughout the world.[7]

The embattled centrist core of the U.S. Socialist Party, by contrast, remained more ambivalent in its attitudes toward competing internationals in the postwar era. As historian David Shannon argued, one might have expected the center core of the party to shift to the right after the expulsions and defections on the left. Instead, the party continued for a time to swing to the left. From his jail cell, an embittered Eugene Debs recommended affiliating with the Third International (Comintern) rather than the Bern group that had voted to exclude Communists. The 1919 Socialist Party convention also repudiated the Bern conference, and the party membership, by a referendum, voted to affiliate with the Third International. Yet by the spring of 1920, the party convention expressed concern about the dictatorial methods of the Soviets and voted to recommend affiliation with the Third International only if it "should relax its attitude toward dictatorship of the proletariat" and move toward "an international embracing all 'true Socialist forces.'" Morris Hillquit and Victor Berger also persuaded Debs to withdraw his support for affiliation with the Communist International on the grounds that the U.S. Socialist Party had always been faithful to democratic ideals and methods.[8]

But even as the party distanced itself from the Third International, it remained a strong critic both of the Bern group and of those forces on the Left conditionally supporting the League and the ILO as flawed organizations that should nonetheless be embraced as stepping-stones to a better future. The influential Socialist paper the *New York Call* perhaps best explained why many U.S. Socialists adopted an irreconcilable attitude toward Wilsonian institutions. On the one hand, the paper continued to dismiss the ILO as an insignificant "rider" to a flawed peace treaty. On the other hand, it emphasized that the League would create a new "Holy Alliance" among the imperial powers, which gave them a powerful mechanism to "put down revolutions." They pointed in particular to Article 10 of the League Covenant, which pledged member states to protect each other's territorial integrity, as a reactionary clause that would be used as a pretext by the powers that lay behind the League to suppress nationalist rebellions. Similar arguments were widespread within the Irish-American community at war's end. But Socialists expanded on these critiques by emphasizing that the mandate system established for the Middle East represented a new era in the history of imperialism. By pooling their resources through the League of Nations, suggested the editors, the major powers could now avoid costly wars and annexations and instead agree to collectively make little nations "satellites" that served the needs of the international capitalist class. The editors warned that "as the earlier Alliance [of 1815] outlawed democratic republics, so this one outlaws industrial republics."[9]

Significantly, even Socialist papers like *Appeal to Reason* that had tentatively thrown their support to the war effort and toward President Wilson after his Fourteen Points Speech in 1918 also adopted an uncompromising attitude toward the "imperialist deals" contained in the peace treaty. Preoccupied with the amnesty campaigns on behalf of Eugene Debs and Kate Richards O'Hare, the paper nonetheless documented the disillusionment of many prowar Socialists such as Upton Sinclair with the peace treaty and League. By contrast, other pro-war Socialists such as William English Walling and

Charles Edward Russell remained loyal to the president. In the spring of 1919, the paper officially called for nominating Debs for president from his jail cell and in 1920 it published the uncompromising Socialist Party platform, that called for the dissolution of the "mischievous organization called the 'League of Nations'" and instead demanded the creation of "an international parliament composed of democratically elected representatives of all the nations of the world." No mention was made of the ILO, but presumably as an affiliate of the League it would have been dissolved as well.[10]

If in some respects the party's ideas for an international parliament drew on the intellectual legacies of the British Labour Party, it differed in seeking to dissolve the League rather than merely reform it and in failing to support the creation of the ILO. American Socialists also demanded direct democratic elections for members of its proposed international parliament rather than proportional representation of parties based on the composition of nationally elected bodies.[11] Even the beleaguered centrist component of the Socialist Party thus proved more uncompromising than its European counterparts in opposing the League of Nations and its affiliated institutions in the immediate postwar period. In part, the brutal repression visited upon leading Socialists during the war may have played a role in the party's irreconcilable attitude. But even more important was the U.S. Socialist Party's long-standing commitment to an arguably more pacifist, democratic, and anti-imperialist agenda than many European Socialist parties.

The IWW also remained staunchly opposed to the ILO and League of Nations. Like the Socialist Party, the IWW suffered heavily under the weight of government repression during the war. Over one hundred members of the IWW were found guilty in one trial alone in 1918, including infamous Big Bill Haywood. With so much of its leadership in and out of jail in 1919, the organization often pursued seemingly inconsistent policies or divided on key questions.[12] Yet on the issue of the League and ILO, the IWW hewed a relatively straightforward path that seemed very much in tune with its long-standing distrust of centralized political power. Despite its diverse immigrant and racial membership, diaspora politics seemed to play little role in its policies. The IWW press condemned the League because it would serve as the world's greatest "strike breaking agency," and help to keep the "smaller nations in a lootable condition," even while it enabled larger nations to increase their "own fighting capacity." In a typically sarcastic tone, the IWW press also highlighted Wilson's hypocrisy, announcing that "The League of Nations guarantees the right of peoples to self determination, except in the case of China, India, Ireland, Mexico, Porto Rico, the Philippines,

South Africa, Egypt, Russia, and a few score others."[13] More than most other groups, the IWW also continued to hammer away at the ILO, denouncing the "vague platitudes" that were to guide the organization as well as the class collaboration upon which the organization was based. Standards for workers, the organization continued to insist, must be determined by the workers themselves and not by some distant bureaucrats.[14] For the IWW in 1919, as before the war, industrial democracy could be achieved only though direct worker control of the means of production.

Ironically, the IWW's distrust of centralized power and vision of industrial democracy also ultimately led it to reject overtures from Comintern and Profintern (Comintern's trade union affiliate). Inspired by the success of the Communist revolution, IWW activists at first divided on the question of affiliating with the Communist Internationals. Further muddying the waters was the decision of Big Bill Haywood to jump bail and flee to the Soviet Union. Yet as Melvyn Dubofsky has written, Haywood was never at home among Russia's emerging political and industrial bureaucrats and died a lonely alcoholic. Although the IWW sent a delegate to the Profintern Convention in 1921, it criticized the domineering attitude of Soviet Communists at the meeting. In 1922, the IWW decided against further affiliation with the Communist Internationals, arguing that "[w]e believe the character of the state will not permit that institution to aid the proletariat in its class struggle."[15] In a strange fashion, the IWW thus gave momentum to traditional isolationist impulses in American culture, urging U.S. workers to eschew entangling alliances with either the European Socialist and labor forces promoting the ILO or the Communist forces seeking IWW participation in the Comintern. Instead American workers were urged to trust only their own capacities for building industrial democracy at the point of production. Although IWW activists ultimately envisioned one big union spreading throughout the world, their vision of industrial democracy mandated against centralized coordination to achieve this end.

Also encouraging unique alignments on international issues was the blossoming U.S. Labor Party movement, that perhaps more than any other coalition of labor groups embodied the intersection of working-class and diaspora politics in 1919. In part, the Chicago leaders of the movement grew suspicious of the ILO because their wartime experiences, in combination with the business offensive against labor at war's end, led them to distrust class collaboration. Fitzpatrick argued that, although the wartime defense boards included some labor representatives, they had mostly been filled with "labor baiters and labor crushers" who had used their positions to advance the interests of business and finance at the expense of workers. Chicago Labor Party leaders insisted that labor, as the majority class, should exercise majority control within national governing institutions as well as within international bodies. Yet, drawing on Furuseth's critiques, they noted that labor representatives within the ILO would be outnumbered by approximately three to one. Given this fact, the new organization would tilt toward business in most of its decisions. Chicago labor leaders instead continued to promote a "League of Peoples" with workers represented "in proportion to their numbers in the armies, navies and workshops of the world."[16]

The influential Seattle Labor Party press concurred in the conclusions of the Chicago movement about the ILO, arguing that its proposed structure was "artificial." Editors at the *Seattle Union Record* noted that because national delegations were to consist of two governmental representatives, one capitalist, and one labor man—all hand-picked by the government—the prospects for "anything acceptable to the rank and file" coming from the ILO were "not very good."[17] As Belgian Socialist Emile Vandervelde had anticipated during deliberations in Paris, American labor activists calculated the possibilities of class collaboration differently than their European counterparts because the United States lacked a strong national Socialist or Labor Party. Although American Labor Party activists sought to remedy this situation, they were convinced that for the near future the two government representatives on national delegations would usually vote against labor interests. As a result, they assumed that the ILO might initially harm rather than help American workers.[18]

Perhaps even more important than the mathematical calculations made about the ILO by the Chicago and Seattle Labor parties were their broader indictments of the League and its affiliated institutions as products of British and European imperialism that would serve to reinforce the imperial status quo. These critiques grew logically from the immersion of CFL leaders, and to a lesser extent Seattle Labor Party leaders, in Irish nationalist politics. During the period from 1919–1921, CFL leaders John Fitzpatrick, Edward Nockels, and Robert Buck participated actively in no less than three Irish-American groups: the Friends of Irish Freedom, the American Association for the Recognition of the Irish Republic, and the American Commission on Irish Independence. In 1920, Fitzpatrick's close friend Frank Walsh, the former War Labor Board Chairman and a part of the American mission sent to Ireland to investigate British atrocities there during the peace conference, also appointed Fitzpatrick to chair the Labor Bureau of the American Commission on Irish Independence; subsequently the CFL served as headquarters for the organization. With so much Irish activity emanating from the Chicago labor council, the causes of Irish independence and Labor Party politics inevitably became intertwined; the Labor Party regularly voiced support for Irish independence and Irish voluntarist organizations regularly served as conduits for Labor Party appeals. When Frank Walsh asked Fitzpatrick to launch a labor boycott of British goods, Fitzpatrick used over two hundred and fifty cooperating city labor councils to launch the initiative. Among these was the Seattle Central Labor Council, a Labor Party stronghold.[19]

The linkages between Irish nationalist politics and the CFL in turn proved important in shaping the Labor Party movement's position on the League and, indirectly, the ILO. President Wilson insisted that those oppressed nationalities who had not obtained their independence by virtue of the peace treaty would be given a chance to have their case heard before the League of Nations. But the Irish-American press denounced Wilson's claims as "ridiculous tommyrot." They pointed out that the League Covenant required a member state to demand a hearing for a colony requesting its freedom. Yet League members would inevitably refuse to champion the rights of subject nationalities because if one colonial power were to work for the "destruction of another's colonies, then that power would vote for the destruction of the other's colonies." Even worse, Article 10 of the League Covenant required member states to protect each other's territorial integrity. This clause might force the United States to help Britain militarily or economically suppress the Irish rebellion, since the British officially claimed Ireland as a part of its territory. Highlighting the counterrevolutionary tendencies of the League, one Irish newspaper argued that "Were a League of Nations in existence in the days when George Washington fought and won, we would be still an English colony."[20]

For their part, Labor Party newspapers dubbed Britain the "Pirate Empire," emphasizing that it had successfully swindled other nations, including the United States, at Versailles. "[N]ever before in history," argued one editor, "has there been such a steal and all accomplished under the cry of 'saving the world for democracy,' and the 'protection of small nations.'" During the spring of 1919, many local and state parties included demands both for Irish and Indian independence in their platforms and used them as rallying cries in street rallies. When the national Labor Party Convention met in December of 1919, it joined Irish-American newspapers in highlighting the ways in which the League would reinforce an imperial status quo that favored Britain and a few other imperial powers, but added an economic dimension to the critique. American workers, it proclaimed, would "not be satisfied with a League of imperialist governments, dominated by an international League of money bosses, to cement an international control of industry by a small group of men who manipulate the bulk of the world's wealth." Such indictments seemed to preclude support for the ILO, an organization that Chicago labor leaders had earlier implied was designed to do the dirty work of the British Empire by maintaining substandard conditions in colonial areas (see chapter 6).[21]

Yet if Labor Party activists disliked the League and its affiliates, they were also not attracted to its alternatives: the Bern program or that of Comintern. Instead, Labor Party leaders pursued a foreign policy that seemed to draw on the intellectual legacies of both the Irish Sinn Féin movement supported by CFL leaders and American isolationist traditions. Although the phrase Sinn Féin literally translates into English as "ourselves" or "we ourselves," Irish revolutionaries of the period widely translated it to mean "ourselves alone." This phrase aptly summarized the separatist approach of the Sinn Féin group in Ireland in 1919. In theory, they sought to encourage a peaceful separation of Ireland from Britain by withdrawing from British political institutions and creating alternative, exclusively Irish, ones. Violence, they argued, became necessary only because of British efforts to suppress Irish independence.[22]

Inspired by the Sinn Féin movement, the Irish-American leaders of the Labor Party called for a policy of nonintervention in other countries, even those undergoing revolutions, on the grounds that the people of those countries were the ones best suited to determine their own political fates and fight for their own freedom. At its 1919 national convention, Labor Party activists thus not only called for a policy of Ireland for the Irish but of "America for the Americans . . . Russia for the Russians . . . Mexico for the Mexicans and freedom for all peoples." In its 1920 platform, the renamed Farmer-Labor Party demanded that the United States recognize the legitimate governments of Mexico, Ireland, and Russia and refrain from further intervention in these countries. It additionally asked the United States to withdraw from "imperialistic enterprises upon which we have already embarked in the Phillipines [sic], Hawaii, Cuba, Samoa and Guam."[23]

The emphasis in the Labor Party platforms of 1919–1920, in sum, was on nonintervention in the affairs of other countries rather than on participation in international institutions. In this way the party repudiated Wilson, whose idealistic rhetoric had emphasized the missionary role of the United States in making the world safe for democracy. By contrast, the Labor Party emphasized that the form of governments that people adopted in their own countries should be of no concern to others. If this noninterventionist ideology drew in part on the Sinn Féin thinking of Irish revolutionaries, it also had roots in pre-Wilsonian American isolationist traditions dating back to George Washington that counseled against involvement in the political affairs of European countries. Yet it is important to emphasize that while Washington and other early American leaders in no way precluded the possibility that the United States would develop its own empire, the foreign policy vision of Labor Party leaders was distinctly anti-imperialist in intent.

The anti-imperial message of the Labor Party movement proved attractive to a host of immigrant aid and nationalist organizations that used city labor councils with strong Labor parties as a hub for many of their activities. Among those groups at least occasionally using city labor councils and affiliated Labor parties as a base for their activities were the Friends of Irish Freedom, American Association for the Recognition of the Irish Republic, Labor Bureau of Irish Independence, Irish Women's Purchasing League, the Friends of Freedom for India, the Friends of Soviet Russia, the Alliance for Trade Relations with Russia, and the Bazaar for Relief of Jewish War Sufferers. These organizations in turn often served as a conduit for Labor Party critiques of the League and ILO and helped further to swell the growing tide of opposition to American participation in these organizations.[24]

Although the Labor Party movement successfully brought the progressive and left-wings of some diaspora communities under its umbrella, the support of others proved more problematic. Eastern Europeans, as we have seen, tended to flock to the Communist parties or remain allied with the Socialist Party. Some African Americans in Chicago drifted toward Labor Party candidates, but nationally the party failed to attract significant numbers from this community. Despite Fitzpatrick's efforts to unionize African Americans in the city, neither the domestic or international agenda of the Labor Party specifically addressed African American concerns. Instead, African American workers and left-leaning groups moved in at least three other directions in 1919. Some, like W. E. B. Du Bois and the NAACP, chose to support the Wilsonian international agenda despite its perceived flaws. A second, more disillusioned, set of groups proved increasingly attracted to the black nationalist thinking of Marcus Garvey and became bitter critics of the treaty. A third tier of groups devoted more fully to working-class interests became increasingly disaffected with the Socialist Party and white-led labor movement and drifted toward Communism.[25] This latter tier of groups also proved to be strong critics of the treaty, League of Nations, and ILO, particularly emphasizing the way they would serve the interests of white capitalists from the major imperial nations at the expense of workers of color throughout the world. Although much of the debate within the African American community occurred outside the parameters of the white-led labor and Socialist movements, it nonetheless forms a critical piece in any imagined jigsaw puzzle representing working-class foreign policy opinion in 1919.

THE AFRICAN AMERICAN DIASPORA, PAN-AFRICANISM, AND THE DEBATE OVER THE TREATY

When Woodrow Wilson was elected to office in 1912, few African Americans likely cheered for he was widely regarded as a segregationist and a "representative of the southern negro-hating oligarchy."[26] Wilson's policies during his first few years in office did little to change the minds of his critics within the African American community. Yet after the United States declared war against Germany, many leading African American organizations urged people of color to support the war effort. Among these was the influential National Association for the Advancement of Colored People (NAACP), led by prominent African Americans such as W. E. B. Du Bois and James Weldon Johnson, as well as by sympathetic white progressives such as Oswald Garrison Villard. At its annual conference in 1917, the organization passed resolutions emphasizing that although England, Belgium, and the United States all had poor records in "dealing with colored peoples," the history of German colonialism in Africa was even more "wretched." Therefore it encouraged African Americans to support the Allied war effort. In a famous editorial in 1918 in the NAACP magazine *The Crisis*, W. E. B. Du Bois appealed to African Americans to "forget our special grievances and close our ranks shoulder to shoulder with our own white fellow citizens and the allied nations that are fighting for democracy."[27]

Yet Du Bois and the NAACP by no means necessarily reflected the opinions of all African Americans. Indeed, recent historical studies suggest that the African American community was quite divided on the war. Poor African Americans, like poor whites, often evaded the draft and responded apathetically to war campaigns. Those within the African American community seeking to avoid the draft, suggests Jeannette Keith, often employed the "weapons of the weak"; they simply disappeared down the back roads of the rural South or the back alleys of Northern cities. During a time when federal record keeping was primitive by today's standards, draft-dodging could prove remarkably easy.[28] In Harlem, African American Socialists such as A. Philip Randolph and Chandler Owen, and recent Caribbean immigrants, such as Marcus Garvey, Cyril Briggs, and former Socialist Hubert Harrison, criticized

Du Bois for not using the wartime situation to demand greater democratic rights for African Americans. These radicals, under the direction of Harrison, launched the Liberty League in the summer of 1917 and championed the idea of a "New Negro" who would be more assertive in demanding that the South be made "Safe for Democracy" and that the lynching and disenfranchisement of African Americans be ended.[29]

Although proclaiming their loyalty to the United States during wartime, some of these radicals also voiced early concerns about Wilson's foreign policies. Historian Minkah Makalani, for example, suggests that Caribbean immigrants such as Cyril Briggs "saw an irony in President Woodrow Wilson standing at the helm of an ever-expanding American empire while asserting that the United States should enter the war to help make the world safe for democracy." They questioned "Wilson's commitment to self-government" as a rationale for war and raised concerns about whether self-government would be applied to those areas in the Caribbean and Africa under British or American imperial control. The *Messenger*, an African American Socialist paper edited by A. Philip Randolph, raised similar concerns.[30]

Although the African American community did not entirely unify behind the war effort as Du Bois hoped, he nonetheless sought to use the gallant record of African and African American soldiers who fought on behalf of the Allies to make a bid both for greater racial equality within the United States and for a hearing for the claims of Africa to at least partial self-determination before the peace conference. Du Bois first laid out his plans for Africa in a memo to President Wilson in late November 1918. Noting that the fate of German colonies in Africa would be determined at the peace conference, Du Bois argued that "to take German Africa from one imperial master, even though a bad one, and hand it over to another, even though a better one," would "arouse a suspicion of selfish aims on the part of the Allies." Instead Du Bois recommended internationalizing a large section of Africa that might include German, Portuguese, and Belgian colonies under the "guidance of organized civilization." Among those who would play a role in administering this new area of Africa would be experts (presumably of all races) from the fields of science, commerce, social reform, religious philanthropy and government representing "modern culture." In addition, Du Bois's plans called for including a variety of "Negro" voices in decision making about Africa, including African Chiefs, the educated classes and "intelligent Negroes" of Africa, independent "Negro governments," and the "civilized Negroes of the United States." Although Du Bois emphasized the role of educated men of color as well as whites in initially supervising the new African state, he asserted that "[t]axation and industry could follow the newer ideals of industrial democracy, avoiding private land mon[o]poly and poverty, promoting cooperation in production and the socialization of income."[31]

Du Bois, who had at one time been a Socialist, may have been somewhat influenced by the schemes of the British Labour Party, whose international activities and proposals for internationalizing Africa *The Crisis* reported upon with interest during the war.[32] But he also clearly drew on his ideas about the role of the "Talented Tenth" in uplifting the colored races. Such ideas invited derision from Marcus Garvey, who charged that Du Bois's plans for the "internationalization of Africa" would ensure that the "capitalistic class of white men" remained in control there.[33] He appointed Socialist A. Philip Randolph, antilynching crusader Ida Wells Barnett, and Haitian activist and mechanic Eliézer Cadet to represent his newly created organization, the United Negro Improvement Association (UNIA), independently at the peace conference. At a mass meeting in New York in November 1918, UNIA developed a petition articulating nine peace aims for the delegates to bring with them to Paris, among them the principle that full self-determination be applied to Africa and to "all European controlled colonies in which people of African descent predominate"; that former German colonies in Africa be "turned over to the natives with educated Western and Eastern Negroes as their leaders"; that racial discrimination and segregation be eliminated throughout the world; that native land in Africa be restored to its original owners; that "Europeans who interfere with, or violate African tribal customs be deported and denied re-entry to the continent"; and that "Negroes be given proportional representation in any scheme of world government."[34]

Demonstrating no favoritism, the Wilson administration failed to grant a hearing before the peace conference both to the Du Bois and Garvey factions and even denied them passports to travel to Paris. Du Bois, however, was able to use his contacts with influential whites to secretly secure passage to Paris, where he worked in cooperation with Blaise Diagne, a Senegalese delegate to the French Chamber of Deputies, to stage the Pan-African Congress that met in Paris from February 19–21, 1919. Fifty-seven delegates attended the Congress—sixteen from the United States, thirteen from the French West Indies, seven from Haiti, seven from France and three from Liberia, with the remainder representing various colonies in Africa. Since most African Americans, including the representatives from UNIA, failed to secure passports to attend the conference, the U.S. delegates included white prowar Socialists like William English Walling and Charles Edward Russell. In many respects the conference followed the blueprints outlined by Du Bois in his letter to Wilson. But the conference proved even more cautious in its demands for independence for African states than Du Bois, perhaps because it wished to avoid alienating French Premier George Clemenceau as well as the white administrators of colonial areas upon whose goodwill the conference depended. Plans for formerly German-held areas of Africa emphasized "colonial administration under international supervision," ostensibly by the League of Nations.[35]

Other resolutions passed by the Congress highlighted the need to protect and to develop the Negro race, especially in Africa. For example, the conference asked that African lands be held in trust for natives and that investment capital be directed in ways that would prevent exploitation. The conference demanded that slavery be outlawed and that the right of children to learn to read and write in their own language as well as the language of the "trustee nation" be recognized. Natives were to be guaranteed the right to participate in political life "as fast as their development permits," with the long term goal of Africa being ruled by the "consent of the Africans." Significantly, the Congress also seemed influenced by the concurrent meeting of the Commission on International Labor Legislation in Paris. As one of its first principles, it called on the Allied Powers to establish a code of laws for the international protection of the Natives of Africa similar to the proposed international code of labor prepared by the Commission on International Labor Legislation and also recommended the establishment of a bureau to oversee these laws. In addition, it demanded that all international labor legislation passed by the ILO and League be extended to Native workers.[36]

The program clearly fell far short of the demands made by UNIA and outraged Marcus Garvey, who viewed Du Bois as an "imperial stooge."[37] Yet the peace conference ignored even the very modest demands of the Pan-African Congress. When the terms of the Versailles Peace Treaty were published, nearly all segments of the African American community expressed disappointment, if not outrage, because it left Africa largely in the hands of white colonial administrators. Under the complicated terms of the tripartite mandate system established for Africa under the supervision of the League of Nations, some areas were granted partial autonomy under the supervision of a mandatory power (Class A mandates); others were to be ruled directly by mandatory powers as separate entities (Class B mandates); still others were to be governed by the mandatory country as "integral parts of its own territories" (Class C mandates). The system accorded most Middle Eastern countries Class A status and placed them under the supervision of Britain and France; Britain gained direct control of the former German colonies of

Tanganyika in East Africa as well as parts of Togoland and the Cameroon, mostly as Class B mandates; the remainder of Germany's former colonies in Africa were divided up for control either by the white-ruled state of South Africa or Belgium as Class B or Class C mandates; colonies held by Allied Nations at the time of the peace conference were left untouched. The League of Nations in theory supervised the mandatory powers, but the requirements were minimal; the mandatory powers were required only to submit a yearly report to a League of Nations commission on the territories they controlled or supervised.[38]

Although Du Bois and the NAACP were disappointed by the treaty, they nonetheless urged African Americans to support the League of Nations despite its flaws. "In its current form," an editorial in *The Crisis* asserted in November 1919, the League of Nations is "oligarchic, reactionary, restricted and conservative, and it gives Imperial England unwarranted preponderance." Yet the editorial insisted that the League should be embraced because "it has a democratic assembly, it recognizes no color line, and it can enforce peace." No other group, the paper argued, had offered anything that stood a chance of being adopted. Sounding a great deal like the moderate Socialists of Europe, the editors counseled, "Let us have the League with all its autocracy and then in the League let us work for Democracy of all races and men." In 1921, DuBois would visit ILO headquarters to ask that a separate section of the ILO central office be established to deal specifically with questions of "Negro labor."[39]

Marcus Garvey, by contrast, sent an impassioned petition to Congress on behalf of UNIA urging senators to reject U.S. participation in the League. Emphasizing that there was nothing in the League constitution that suggested a "spirit of good will toward a struggling race," Garvey extensively quoted from the section of the League constitution specifically dealing with the establishment of mandates for the Middle East and Africa. He then queried of senators, "Can you not read between the lines and see that it is the intention of the European powers to shackle the millions of black people on the continent of Africa and to further exploit them for the development of their respective nations[?] " He then asked the senators to refuse their consent to U.S. membership in the League of Nations on the grounds that it would be the "'hangman' of all future aspirants to that liberty which you fought and won for yourselves not many centuries ago."[40] At mass UNIA meetings that attracted between three thousand and ten thousand people in the spring and fall of 1919, Garvey sought to mobilize the entire African American community to work against U.S. participation in the new international body, arguing that "the League of Nations must be defeated by every Negro in America, or it will mean that Africa will have to fight the combined nations of the world" in order to obtain its independence. At such meetings, Garvey also often emphasized his plans to encourage African American emigration to Africa through his newly created *Black Star Line* and highlighted the UNIA goal of creating an independent "Negro empire" in Africa. "We have a whole continent to redeem," exhorted Garvey to his massive audiences in 1919.[41]

Equally critical of the League of Nations were those Socialists and ex-Socialists who had coalesced around the Liberty League in 1917. Hubert Harrison, for example, argued that behind the League of Nations lay the "capitalist international" whose goal was "to unify and standardize the exploitation of black, brown and yellow peoples in such a way that the danger to the exploiting groups of cutting each other's throats over the spoils may be reduced to a minimum." Like Garvey, Harrison particularly denounced the mandate system, suggesting that "darker peoples" did not want to be "'wards of the nations' of Europe any longer." Harrison instead called for an "international of the darker races."[42] In the *Messenger*, Chandler Owen joined the chorus, attacking the League of Nations as a reactionary body designed to perpetuate the imperial and racial status quo, and the mandate system as a monstrosity created by the "white capitalist nations" in order to "use Africa as a beast of burden to feed the belly of Europe." The paper also explicitly dismissed the ILO, charging that Gompers had been "chloroformed with a bit of capitalist deception which is about as valuable to labor as the belief of a hungry man that a brick is a sausage."[43]

Although the Garvey and Socialist critiques of the League and ILO initially seemed to share much in common, tensions increasingly developed between the two factions. Ultimately, the Garveyites would veer in a different direction from the Socialist/labor contingent, with Garvey using his *Black Star Line* in an effort to encourage African Americans to return to Africa to develop a black-led empire in their ancestral homeland. From the perspective of African American Socialists and ex-Socialists, this approach was shortsighted because a black-led empire in the absence of proletarian revolution would prove as exploitative of working people as the British or European empires. Socialist Cyril Brig established the African Blood Brotherhood (ABB) in 1919 to "infuse class into black nationalist thought." Although a smaller group than either Garvey's UNIA or Du Bois's NAACP, the ABB boasted a disproportionately working-class membership that included both skilled and migrant laborers. Eventually many of the leaders of this organization would ally with Comintern, reflecting the disillusionment felt by African American Socialists and workers with the U.S. Socialist Party, as well as their belief that Comintern was the one group unequivocally committed to proletarian revolution in Africa and Asia.[44]

Despite their differences after 1920, both Garveyites and African American Socialists and Communists initially proved important in rallying African American workers against the peace treaty, League, and ILO. African American mobilization on foreign policy issues, in concert with the plague of race riots that gripped the country in 1919, in turn helped fuel the fears of racist white politicians and businessmen. As the arguments of southern senators suggested, these latter groups ironically opposed the League and ILO for reasons diametrically opposed to those of African Americans: they feared that these organizations would undermine their ability to control restive African American workers and would threaten the racial status quo.

By the time that ILO delegates began to arrive in Washington, D.C., in late October of 1919, important segments of public opinion had thus shifted decisively against the League and its affiliated organizations, making the delegates' reception cold indeed. Had any of the disaffected within the American public and within Congress chosen to listen to the proceedings in Washington, they might have discovered that the delegates at least partially resolved some of the problems and weaknesses with which they were concerned. But Congress would seize upon the fears voiced by varied sectors of the American population while ignoring many of the actual programs and structures created in Washington.

THE ILO CONFERENCE

Doubtless, ILO delegates felt confused by the cold reception they received in part because the State Department devoted such extraordinary effort to making arrangements for the conference on quite short notice. The sheer logistical problems of finding steerage for so many delegates on the limited number of passenger ships crossing the Atlantic in 1919 proved a daunting task, as did finding hotel rooms for them in crowded Washington, D.C. The ILO organizing committee and U.S. government also faced complex decisions about who should be invited to the conference, since some nations were in the process of applying for League membership but had not yet been accepted. An even thornier set of questions revolved around Germany and Austria; Gompers had officially told the IFTU that he would seek to assure that any bars to the membership of these nations in the ILO were removed. Wilson and the plenipotentiaries agreed but argued that the ILO conference itself must consent to seat them. Faced with this dilemma the State Department finally invited the Germans and Austrians to attend the conference and informed them they would be accorded representation pending the approval of their membership by the conference. But the invitations arrived too late for travel arrangements to be made. And then there was the question of the United States itself, which had not yet signed the treaty and was therefore ineligible to participate in the conference that it was organizing. These considerations led George Barnes to suggest that the conference be postponed.[45]

Some State Department officials also voiced reservations about holding the conference in the autumn of 1919. Their concerns, however, were different than those of Barnes; they worried not so much about the logistical difficulties but about the possible dominance of the British in the conference. Although the ILO organizing committee emphasized that it would be possible for U.S. labor and employer delegates to participate unofficially in the conference, State Department personnel expressed concerns that if the United States lacked voting power, the British would inevitably dominate the conference. In a telegram to Raymond Fosdick, a U.S. diplomatic functionary in London who identified himself only as "Sweetser" emphasized that "two English-men" might be chosen for the positions of secretary-general of the League of Nations and secretary of the Labor Conference. This development would prove "disastrous [for] American public opinion" because "[a]nti-British feeling" was already "very strong" due to the belief that Britain was unfairly represented in both organizations. Another State Department memorandum emphasized that the recommendations of the organizing committee of the ILO were "essentially English" in character, as well as "exceedingly conservative and almost reactionary." The memo insisted on the need for a strong American delegation in the conference that would counteract the influence of the British. By contrast, Wilson remained upbeat about the upcoming ILO meeting and continued to assume that the ILO would prove a public relations asset in the battle for the League.[46]

After a number of delays caused by the difficulty of making arrangements, the ILO conference finally opened on October 29, 1919, in the Pan Am building in Washington, D.C. Thirty-nine countries participated, among them the newly minted states of Poland and Czechoslovakia. Also represented for the first time as what British organizing committee member Harold Butler called "independent international entities" were Canada, India, and the Union of South Africa. Gompers, of course, had strongly contested the inclusion of Canada and India since they were still a part of the British Empire. Asia was strongly represented with delegations from China, India, Japan, Persia, and

Siam; many South American countries also sent delegates. Not invited to the conference were the U.S.S.R, Mexico, or Ireland, due to their unstable political conditions. Also missing from the conference were the four Central Powers of Germany, Austria, Hungary, and Bulgaria, who received their invitations too late to attend.[47]

At its first meeting on October 29, the conference invited the United States to send unofficial delegates from the American Federation of Labor and U.S. Chamber of Commerce, designated by Secretary of Labor Wilson as the most representative organizations of U.S. labor and U.S. business, respectively. After a significant delay, the Chamber of Commerce declined to send any representatives due to a lack of consensus within that organization over whether to support the ILO. The AFL appointed Samuel Gompers as their representative. But after attending one session and giving one speech during which he talked about the miner's strike, Gompers chose not to attend any other sessions. According to British representative Harold Butler this was because Gompers's "unofficial position without the right to vote placed him in a somewhat difficult position." Likely, Gompers found the experience not simply difficult but excruciating; the European leaders with whom he had long sparred were now able to dominate the organization that he had played such a critical role in creating.[48]

Apart from Gompers, the only other American participating in the meeting in an official capacity was Secretary of Labor William B. Wilson, who presided over the conference. According to ILO historian Antony Alcock, Secretary Wilson at first refused this role because Congress had not authorized U.S. participation in the conference. Secretary of State Robert Lansing then dodged the decision regarding who should preside over the conference because he feared it would be used in arguments against ratification of the treaty in the Senate. At this point, suggests Alcock, Edith Bolling Galt Wilson stepped in and insisted that Secretary Wilson preside. The incident suggested that many within the Wilson administration, with the exception of Wilson himself, now recognized the ILO as a political hot potato.[49]

Among the surprises at the meeting was the assertiveness of the representatives from what the British delegates termed the "over-sea countries," including their own independently represented colonies. In particular, the non-European delegates objected to the dominance of European representatives in the governing body of the ILO. India challenged the designations of the eight states of chief industrial importance within the governing group, arguing that six of the eight were from Europe. The Indian delegates insisted that they belonged on the list before smaller European countries. Even more importantly, South African Delegate William Gemmill sponsored a resolution expressing "disapproval of the composition of the Governing Body of the International Labor Office inasmuch as no less than 20 of the 24 members of that body are representatives of European countries." The resolution asked that a maximum limit be placed on the number of delegates within the governing body that could be from Europe. Arthur Fontaine of France countered that, for practical reasons, Europeans should be disproportionately represented on the governing body; the ILO permanent office would be in Europe. Since the governing body was primarily administrative, its disproportionately European composition would not adversely impact "over-sea countries." Finally, Fontaine emphasized that representation within the governing body should not be determined by geographical distribution but by "industrial development and experience, and by the importance of their industrial interests."[50]

But Gemmill's motion was overwhelmingly supported by the "over-sea countries" and passed by a vote of forty-four to thirty-nine. Among those voting for the resolution were Guatemala, India, Japan, Peru, and South Africa. British delegate Harold Butler, writing about the conference in the 1930s, would comment on this development, "[t]hus began a movement towards readjusting the balance between the old industrial world and the new, which has continued without interruption until the present day." Particularly important, the International Labor Office would expand its governing board from twenty-four to thirty-two in 1922. Of the sixteen government members of the board, six were to be from non-European states. Of the eight employer and eight worker delegates on the governing board, two from each group were to be from non-European countries. Actual implementation of this plan, however, was delayed by the League of Nations and did not come into effect until the late 1930s.[51]

If actual change to the ILO's structure came slowly, the assertiveness of the "over-sea countries" nonetheless suggested that at least one American concern about the new organization was partially unfounded. British colonies represented independently within the ILO did not vote as a block with Britain on all issues. Indeed, the international organization sometimes provided a format for colonies and economically underdeveloped countries to challenge imperial prerogatives.

One other unforeseen structural development also occurred at Washington. The labor and employer delegates formed their own blocs at the conference and began meeting regularly. The separate labor and employer groups within the ILO in turn tended to undercut nationalist loyalties and to encourage alignments along lines of class in ways that brought fresh perspectives to international economic and labor issues. On the other hand, labor delegates were unsuccessful in their quest to change representation within the ILO so that labor delegates would represent one-half of all representatives. Similarly, they failed in efforts to reduce the number of government representatives within the national delegations from two to one. As a consequence, the aggregate breakdown of delegates within the conference remained 50 percent for government, 25 percent for labor and 25 percent for employers. On many committees, however, it was agreed that there would be equal representation of government, labor, and employer delegates. Previous proposals to require the democratic election of all delegates were also not taken up by the convention, although procedures were established for reviewing the credentials of labor representatives to assure that they came from the most "representative" labor organizations in their respective countries. These procedures were developed in response to protests regarding labor delegates from Argentina, Cuba, France, Japan, and South Africa.[52]

Finally, the conference adopted six conventions that began the process of building an international code of labor legislation. These included one establishing an eight-hour day and forty-eight-hour week. Two others dealt with child labor: one prohibited children under the age of fourteen from employment in industry; another outlawed night work for those under eighteen, with certain exceptions. Japan, however, successfully lobbied for lower standards for itself in some cases, as did India. A fourth convention dealt with the question of unemployment. Two others provided protection for women workers. One prohibited night work for women while another allowed women six weeks leave before childbirth and six weeks afterward, with provisions made either by the state or by private insurance groups within particular nations for some kind of monetary allowance during these periods. Those seeking a convention or resolution asking the League to work toward a better redistribution of the world's raw materials were defeated.[53]

Far from revolutionary, the conventions nonetheless signaled a paradigm shift in international governing circles. Before the Versailles conference, even Wilson had expressed doubt that new institutions of international governance should take up the burden of international labor legislation. Yet at the Washington Conference large numbers of nations, even while disagreeing about specifics, seemed to accept the assumption that peace between nations was inextricably linked to industrial peace between classes and to the realization of higher labor standards throughout the world. Without such standards, imperial exploitation of underdeveloped areas would increase, fomenting revolutions like those occurring in Russia, Ireland, and Mexico. Unequal labor standards throughout the world would also increase economic competition and the race for empire among industrially developed countries in ways that might foment another world war. As the preamble to the ILO constitution explained with admirable succinctness, "peace can be established only if it is based upon social justice."[54] The conference would thus close on a triumphant note, with delegates proud of the role they had played in inaugurating a new era in the history of international politics. Representatives would soon discover, however, that the most difficult component of their task lay ahead; the process by which individual states ratified conventions created by the ILO conference proved painfully slow. More immediately, the conference would face opposition from the two other groups meeting in Washington at the same time: the International Congress of Working Women and the U.S. Congress. The ICWW offered reservations that would arguably have strengthened the ILO; by contrast, the debate in the U.S. Senate demonstrated that significant elements within both the American political Left and Right lay outside the growing global consensus in support of international labor legislation.

THE INTERNATIONAL CONGRESS OF WORKING WOMEN

If the State Department and diplomatic service scored a major organizational triumph in organizing the ILO conference on short notice, the efforts of Margaret Dreier Robins in arranging the International Congress of Working Women despite government hostility and with only private resources proved truly superhuman. Robins had first become interested in the ILO when she heard of the deliberations of the Commission on International Labor Legislation in the spring of 1919. Seeking to ensure that women were represented within the commission and in any future organization, Robins quickly appointed Rose Schneiderman and Mary Anderson to represent the WTUL in Paris. The two sailed for Europe in March, but the Commission on International Labor Legislation had adjourned by the time they arrived. Schneiderman and Anderson subsequently arranged a meeting with President Wilson and asked that women's representatives be included in any future meeting. The president engaged them in cordial conversation and even inquired of them why AFL President Samuel Gompers was so hostile to the Germans but apparently Wilson proved noncommittal about questions of female representation.[55]

Following their meeting with the president, Schneiderman and Anderson traveled to London where they met with the British women's trade union leader Margaret Bondfield. The three of them discussed the possibility of staging a women's international conference at the same time as the ILO conference scheduled for Washington, D.C., in the autumn. Margaret Dreier Robins also liked the idea and soon fully devoted herself to planning the conference. Yet Robins faced formidable problems in organizing the women's meeting. She enlisted historian James Shotwell in an effort to win State Department sanction and support for the conference. In particular, she hoped to use the State Department's cables to announce the conference to women's groups throughout the world. But both the Departments of Labor and of State remained largely hostile to the conference and refused to give any material support to it. Labor Secretary William B. Wilson wrote President Wilson warning that three separate groups dominated the WTUL: the "radicals" led by Mrs. Raymond Robins, the "extra-radicals" led by Rose Schneiderman, and a more conservative group dominated by Mary Anderson. Robins, he suggested, was an opponent of the Versailles Treaty who might be turned around if the president strongly supported the labor clauses and a women's meeting. But he warned that the president needed to be careful because the manufacturers were opposed to it.[56]

Shortly after his letter to the president, Secretary Wilson told the WTUL that he could not sanction their meeting without Congressional mandate. He gave his approval for their announcements to be sent out on State Department cables, but the State Department in turn claimed that it needed Congressional authorization to send out their invitations and refused their request. Denied the cooperation of the State Department, Robins was forced to use private cables at great personal expense to send the announcements. Robins preferred to keep quiet about the issue, but both the New York Socialist press and Rose Schneiderman publicized the government's hostility to the conference. Schneiderman detailed the problems that the WTUL was encountering in organizing the conference at a meeting for an actresses union and was scolded severely by Robins for her indiscretion. Making light of the issue, Schneiderman responded that "I was scared stiff by your letter. I thought I had murdered my mother or something." Schneiderman claimed that it was already a "public secret" in New York that the government opposed the women's conference.[57]

Despite the lack of government support, Robins secured the necessary ship berths for those women wishing to attend the conference and used her connections to wealthy, mostly female, patrons to secure luxurious accommodations for many in private homes. In addition, she solicited the cooperation of "the wives of official Washington" to help entertain the war-weary visitors. As Rose Schneiderman admiringly wrote, Robin's "heart went out to all the women who had gone through four years of war and she saw that they had every comfort within her power." Unsurprisingly, none of the women delegates complained about being coldly treated in Washington. Indeed, the conference nurtured friendships that lasted a lifetime.[58]

The conference opened on the same day as the ILO conference, October 29, 1919, with women from nineteen countries attending. Robins was elected president and Maud Schwartz of the United States was appointed secretary-treasurer. Delegates were also chosen to represent each of the major "races" on an executive committee. Mary Macarthur of England, represented the "Anglo-Saxons"; Betty Kjelsberg of Norway the Scandinavians; Mme Landova Stychova of Czechoslovakia the Slavs, and Jeane Bouvier of France, the "Latin Races"; with a fifth position to be filled by a representative from the Central Powers. Elizabeth C. Carter, Honorary President of the National Association of Colored Women's Clubs, spoke on behalf of "Negro women laborers" (Figure 7.1)[59]

The American delegation consisted of ten women, with some chosen by the Women's Trade Union League and others by the American Federation of Labor. Among the most prominent of these were Robins herself, Mary Anderson, Rose Schneiderman, Agnes Nestor, and Leonora O'Reilly. True to the WTUL's mission, each of these women had been active in the struggles for industrial democracy, women's suffrage, and world peace for many years and saw strong interconnections between them. Leonora O'Reilly, who represented the Women's Trade Union League at the International Women's Peace Congress at the Hague in 1915, perhaps best articulated this interconnected vision. From her perspective, industrial democracy was the bedrock upon which a permanent peace must be built. Only workers, she argued, could create a "Society based on production and eliminate a Society based on War." Yet "woman" was essential to this task "first, because she is the mother of all industries and second, because to earn a living today she has followed the industries into the factory, mill, office and market." Over eight million women in the United States, O'Reilly emphasized, now worked in industry. Working men needed the votes of working women to help ensure a revolution at the ballot box that would make industrial democracy possible without resorting to "bullets" or violence. Working together, men and women could then build an "Industrial Democracy" that eliminated war. This kind of integrated vision in turn informed the actions of the American delegation at the International Congress of Working Women, where they would play a prominent role in many debates, especially those pertaining directly to women's labor.[60]

Perhaps the single-most important issue with which the ICWW concerned itself was the question of how to ensure that women were better represented

Figure 7.1. Panoramic of the International Congress of Working Women, October 1919, Courtesy of the Library of Congress.

in the national delegations to the ILO. Although several nations included women as technical advisors to their delegations, no nation appointed a woman as one of its voting representatives. Robins, in her opening address, argued that the problem with this arrangement was that "the power of the woman technical advisor . . . is entirely dependent upon the good will of the man delegate whom she is appointed to assist." To remedy this situation the International Congress of Working Women unanimously demanded a fundamental restructuring of the national delegations to include six rather than four representatives, distributed as follows: two delegates "representing the Government, one of whom shall be a woman"; two delegates "representing Labor, one of whom shall be a woman"; and two delegates "representing the Employers," with no special mandate that a woman be included in this final category.[61]

Resolutions on several other issues such as hours limitations, child labor, and unemployment overlapped those of the ILO but were slightly more radical in their demands. For example, the child labor resolution set the minimum age for employment at sixteen rather than fourteen. This may have been due as much to the all-labor composition of the congress as to its female representation, since many labor groups throughout the world favored this more mature age for entering the work force. On the question of hours, women were particularly adamant about the need for slightly shorter hours than those recommended by the ILO (a forty-four rather than a forty-eight-hour week) and an "uninterrupted one day and a half rest" due to the additional need for women to do housework before the Sunday holiday. In addition, the women succeeded in passing a resolution calling for the equal redistribution of raw materials throughout the world as essential to uplifting international labor standards, as well as one calling on the governments of the world to end the blockade of Russia.[62]

But perhaps unsurprisingly, the conference most diverged from that of the ILO in its discussions and resolutions on matters pertaining specifically to women. On the one hand, debate evolved within the congress over the prohibition of night work for women, a measure strongly supported by the ILO convention. The Scandinavian delegates within the women's congress strongly opposed this measure on the grounds that it would prevent women from working in certain lucrative fields; what was instead needed was the prohibition of night work for everyone. But while the WTUL agreed that the goal of the labor movement should eventually be to ensure the protection of all workers, women were particularly vulnerable in industry. Therefore, they urged that protective legislation for women should be embraced as a first step in the fight for protective legislation for all. The congress endorsed the prohibition of night work for women but added a proviso urging that night work for men also be prohibited except when absolutely necessary.[63]

The debate on maternity leave and insurance proved far more expansive. The ILO's maternity convention was designed to ensure that women in industry and commercial fields would be allowed to take a six-week leave before and after childbirth. It also suggested that some kind of monetary allowance should be given to these women during their maternity leaves. But this proposal, generous by today's standards, was deemed insufficient by the delegates attending the International Congress of Working Women. Some of the delegates, for example, wondered about the wives of working men; should they not also be eligible to receive monetary compensation? Many also believed that it was essential to guarantee women and their babies health care during the period of "confinement." The American delegation insisted that all women, regardless of class, should be eligible for health and maternal benefits; by contrast, some of the European delegates argued that only working women and the wives of working men should be granted these benefits. Others suggested that a maximum wage level be used to determine whether women were eligible for benefits. Disagreements also arose as to whether the state or private insurance companies should pay the maternity award. In the end, the delegates agreed to disagree, with Robins emphasizing that the lack of consensus was to be expected given the divergent work traditions from which the delegates hailed. The resolutions of the congress on maternity insurance therefore included a majority report that proposed giving maternal benefits to all women, and two minority reports that established different criteria for giving benefits only to wage-earning women and the wives of wage-earning men.[64]

The debate was significant for it suggested that many women within the ICWW defined work differently than the men of the ILO. The American delegation implied that all women deserved benefits because mothering was in itself work, whether or not their husbands fit into a class defined as "wage-earners." Equally important, society as a whole stood to benefit from giving all women health care and support during childbirth. This approach in turn suggested the integrative world view of many WTUL representatives. By contrast, some European women understandably thought the benefit should be tied to the financial need of working-class families.

In the end, the ILO paid very little attention to either group, targeting only women who worked in industry and commerce in its resolution. Similarly, it largely ignored the other recommendations of the ICWW on the prohibition of night work for women, although women technical advisors from France, Great Britain, and Sweden did play a role in this ILO discussion.[65] Most importantly, the ILO failed to take seriously the ICWW's demand for equal representation for women in the ILO. Yet despite the ILO's failure to address many of its demands, the ICWW, and its subsequent organization the International Federation of Working Women, remained sympathetic to the goals of the ILO and continued to cooperate with it until 1923. At this point, the Europeans voted to merge with the International Federation of Trade Unions over the objections of the Americans, and the International Federation of Working Women ceased to exist as an independent entity.[66]

Yet if the International Federation of Working Women proved short-lived, the Wilson administration clearly missed an opportunity to curry support for its international agenda among a new constituency in U.S. politics: working women. In the meantime, the administration had also lost the support of many predominantly male labor organizations. As the Senate took aim at the ILO during its meetings in November of 1919, progressives from both parties could thus join hands with conservative Republicans in opposing U.S. membership in the new organization without apparent fear of political consequences.

THE DEBATE IN CONGRESS

By the time the ILO conference convened in Washington, the Senate had been debating the treaty for many months. Yet whether by coincidence or design it postponed the major discussion of the ILO until late October and early November of 1919, exactly the time that the ILO and ICWW conferences were meeting in Washington. Significantly, the first sustained attack on the labor provisions of the Versailles Treaty and ILO came not from a conservative but from Senator Robert LaFollette of Wisconsin. So strong was LaFollette on most labor issues that he was courted by the Labor Party to be its presidential candidate in 1920. LaFollette had also worked closely with Andrew Furuseth in securing Congressional passage of the Seamen's Act of 1915 that guaranteed essential rights to sailors and merchantmen. Many labor activists further admired LaFollette for his unwavering opposition to U.S. involvement in World War I. LaFollette's record on labor and antiwar measures ensured him the overwhelming support of his Irish and German working-class constituencies in elections.

So convinced was LaFollette that the ILO could do irrevocable harm to American workers that he moved to strike the labor provisions from the

Versailles Peace Treaty entirely rather than try to amend them or qualify them through reservations. LaFollette's arguments, unsurprisingly, drew on those of labor opponents like Andrew Furuseth and the Labor Party rather than those of southern or western senators who had expressed concern about the ILO in September. In his opening address before the Senate, LaFollette argued that the labor clauses "set up an international legislative body, undemocratic in character, which has broad power to reach out into the internal affairs of our country." He argued that the ILO was undemocratic because no provisions were made for the election of delegates and that governments would be overrepresented in the national delegations. Like other labor opponents, he doubted that government representatives would usually side with labor, noting that in recent industrial conferences in the United States quite the opposite had been the case.[67]

LaFollette also questioned whether the safeguards included by Shotwell and Gompers in the treaty were sufficient to prevent the ILO from subverting democratic procedures for the passage of labor legislation in the United States. He had no problems with ILO recommendations, but he argued that if the ILO submitted a draft convention to the United States, the Senate might decide to use its treaty-making powers to pass the draft convention into law without consulting the far more democratic House of Representatives or state governments. For LaFollette this kind of scenario was problematic not only because it was undemocratic but also because he assumed that the ILO might, due to the preponderance of government and business delegates within it, pass legislation that was actually hostile to labor. "Think of the possibility, he suggested, "of putting through in the form of a 'draft convention' a law against collective bargaining, against strikes and combinations of labor without any opportunity for labor to be heard and resist such legislation." He insisted that the protocol inserted into the covenant stating that "no nation could be asked or required by the ILO to diminish the protections afforded for workers by 'existing' national legislation" was a "deadly joker" because it offered protection only for legislation existing at the time the treaty was passed by Congress. The door would therefore be open for the Senate to pass draft conventions that undermined U.S. labor legislation adopted after the treaty was ratified. Missing from LaFollette's analysis was any sense of the concurrent debates within the ILO conference over conventions that were overwhelmingly prolabor, if not terribly radical, in intent.[68]

LaFollette further argued that Great Britain and its empire would allegedly enjoy at least a twenty-four to four voting advantage over the United States within the ILO and would use it to "habitually assail the advanced position of American labor." LaFollette and Senator Medill McCormick used as an example the case of seamen. Britain and Indian governmental delegates, they argued, would try to undermine the U.S. Seamen's Act in order to protect Indian seamen in the employ of the British navy who were paid an "oriental wage." It was telling, they suggested, that Gompers was "beaten on every important point" by the British within the Commission on International Labor Legislation. Senator McCormick also raised concerns that European nations with imperial empires would form a "bond" against the United States in trying to diminish immigration restrictions and tariff barriers that had traditionally protected U.S. workers.[69]

In a case of politics making for strange bedfellows, LaFollette's proposal to strike the labor provisions also drew support from those southern senators who feared the proposed ILO would undermine rather than reinforce the imperial status quo and would subvert the existing racial division of labor within the global system. Senator James Reed of Missouri argued that the ILO would empower small nations with predominantly black populations by giving them representation on tribunals created to enforce ILO conventions. He was clearly horrified by the prospect and asked fellow senators to imagine a scenario in which "Uncle Sam" might be brought before a Commission of Enquiry because Southern plantation owners had allowed Negroes to pick cotton past dark in violation of an ILO-imposed eight-hour day. Sitting in judgment over Uncle Sam on the commission would be "colored gentlemen" from Liberia, the Arab World, and Haiti who had only recently undertaken to "garb themselves in the accouterments of civilization." Reed assumed that such a prospect was so outrageous that it needed no further explanation. The Senator from Missouri also waxed splenetic against the idea that the American laborer should "sacrifice himself for the benefit of the Chinaman, or the group of men of India, or the man of Siam, or the inhabitants of other even less favored parts of the world." He urged his fellow senators to play the part of a "manly nation" and strike the labor provisions.[70]

Still others objected that the ILO would subvert the international division of labor by giving undue influence to organized labor at the expense of other economic groups. Senator Charles Thomas of Colorado expressed fear that the ILO would establish a "wage-earning oligarchy" that would become despotic in its power and subvert class relations within the world system; he complained that neither farmers nor intellectual workers had been accorded similar privileges. He also expressed concerns about the influence of Social-ist leaders from Bern in a future conference. Other senators worried about possible Bolshevik subversion within the ILO. The labor provisions of the treaty, argued Thomas, "were not a Magna Charta of labor," but a "sentence of death to free institutions."[71]

LaFollette's resolution to strike the labor provisions from the treaty failed by a narrow margin of thirty-four to forty-one.[72] But two additional amendments on the labor provisions were proposed almost immediately. Senator Porter McCumber of North Dakota proposed a resolution that called on the United States to withhold its assent to the labor provisions unless Congress, by a joint resolution, decreed that it wanted representation in the ILO. The idea here was to include the House of Representatives in the vote because labor issues more clearly fell within the purview of the House. In addition, it would allow Congress time to more fully consider the details of U.S. inclusion in the ILO and to join at some future date if it so chose. But Senator King of Utah proposed a substitute resolution that eliminated the language about a joint Congressional Resolution and called on the United States to withhold its assent from the labor provisions without qualification and to decline "to participate in any way" in the ILO. McCumber declared the difference between the two resolutions to be comparable to the difference between "the use of an ax and an anesthetic in [a] . . . surgical operation." He noted that his resolution would leave the door open to future participation.[73]

In subsequent debate, supporters of the ILO finally had the chance to defend it on the grounds that it was a moderate solution to the class unrest currently raging throughout the world and would strengthen the "responsible elements" of labor at the expense of the Bolshevist elements. They also argued that the ILO was not based on the idea of "compulsion" but on the ideas of cooperation and free discussion. In other words, suggested Senator Henderson from Nevada, "It is an application in the industrial sphere of the free representative institutions for which the United States and Great Britain have long stood in the political sphere."[74] By contrast, opponents argued that the new organization would be used by "official meddlers" of the radical faith to keep industry in a "state of perpetual stew." Others continued to sound racial themes, arguing that the idea that U.S. labor standards should be determined by an organization that included representatives from Hejaz, Siam, Liberia, India, and Japan was "preposterous." American workers, they insisted, could only be hurt by participating in an organization in which most member nations had lower labor standards than in the United States. The historic U.S. policy of protectionism afforded the best means of protecting America.[75]

When the resolutions were finally put to a vote, King's substitute "ax" resolution calling for a definitive vote against the labor provisions and U.S. participation in the ILO failed by a vote of forty-three to forty-eight.

But McCumber's original resolution withholding U.S. assent to the labor provisions unless Congress approved them by a joint resolution passed by a vote of fifty-four to thirty-five. McCumber's resolution subsequently became one of the fourteen reservations to the treaty.[76] As is well known, the Senate subsequently failed to ratify the treaty both with and without reservations, due primarily to President Wilson's insistence that Democrats not compromise the integrity of the Versailles Treaty by supporting the reservations. The United States would therefore not join the ILO until 1934, when the Roosevelt administration used its influence to secure U.S. membership despite the continuing absence of the United States from the League of Nations.

CONCLUSION

The debate over the ILO in Congress suggested that many had made up their minds about the organization even before the ILO conference met in October and November of 1919 in Washington, D.C. The American Left opposed the ILO because they believed its structure to be undemocratic, distrusted the class collaboration it encouraged, and assumed it would become a powerful tool used by imperial powers to reinforce an imperial status quo and undermine labor standards throughout the world. Those on the right, by contrast, argued that the ILO would be used to subvert the racialized division of labor both within the United States and abroad. In so doing, it would undermine U.S. economic supremacy and subvert the authority of white elites. Despite the role of Gompers and Wilson in creating the ILO, the United States thus remained outside the growing consensus in favor of international labor standards as an essential underpinning for guaranteeing peace between nations.

Conclusion

THE SENATE'S FINAL REJECTION OF THE Treaty of Versailles brought to an end the eight-year war of position waged among U.S. labor and Socialist groups in an effort to influence the Wilsonian international agenda. No clear winners emerged from the war; it ended in stalemate. Although the AFL clearly enjoyed more direct influence within the Wilson administration, labor and Left opponents of Wilson's foreign policies retained their own residuals of power that, when combined with those of the political Right, successfully defeated the administration's foreign policy programs as they were embodied in the Versailles Treaty. Yet no single labor or Left group enjoyed sufficient power to implement their own international vision in 1919. The treaty's defeat thus served the political ends of the Republicans more than the Left, perhaps explaining the historical amnesia that has developed surrounding labor and Left critiques of the Wilsonian international agenda. Both the Democratic Party and the U.S. Left would remain weak throughout the 1920s. The Socialist Party and IWW would never recover from the wounds inflicted on them by government persecution and internal fragmentation during World War I.

Yet as students and scholars of President Wilson have often emphasized, the Republican victory over Wilsonian principles proved temporary; Wilsonian ideas about American exceptionalism, democracy, international law and governance, and international capitalism would cast a long shadow over the twentieth, and even the twenty-first, century.[1] For this reason, understanding the full range of objections that emerged to Wilson's efforts to reform the world between 1912 and 1920 also seems important. Although historians have often assumed widespread Left political support for Wilson, opposition to his foreign policies emerged among Socialist, labor, and diaspora Left groups from the earliest days of his administration. In the case of Wilson's Mexican policies, labor dissidents throughout the Americas criticized Wilson for camouflaging his real goals behind lofty rhetoric. Wilson claimed that he sought to end U.S. imperialism in Latin America, but groups that ranged from the Partido Liberal Mexicano, to the U.S. Socialist Party, to the United Mine

Workers, argued that instead his real goal was to create a more efficient and less costly form of U.S. capitalist domination over the Western hemisphere. Greater capital mobility and freer economic flows within the Western hemisphere, argued labor dissidents, would come at the expense of workers. Only the AFL leadership accepted Wilson's political rhetoric surrounding a new Monroe Doctrine for the Western hemisphere at face value and attempted to forge a stronger relationship with the administration.

The AFL leadership's initiatives yielded few tangible benefits until World War I, when the Wilson administration systematically incorporated AFL leaders into policymaking circles. But antiwar sentiment remained strong within the American labor and Socialist movements. In contrast to the president and AFL leaders, antiwar fragments within U.S. labor did not include protecting U.S. economic interests abroad, or the international laws that Wilson invoked to defend these interests, in their definitions of vital U.S. national security interests. Although dissenters recognized that the economic well-being of workers was linked to the well-being of American business, they insisted that exports and foreign investments were not the only way to achieve prosperity. Instead they emphasized that industrial democracy could end the quest for easy foreign profits and lead to domestic reinvestment as well as a redistribution of wealth that would stimulate the economy. Although many working-class contributors to the debate over national security expressed a willingness to fight to defend their homes, they invoked religious ideas dictating against murder in opposing a war beyond American borders. With these sentiments in mind, Socialists and some AFL unions pursued efforts to make foreign policy subject to greater democratic checks and balances.

When Wilson led the country into war anyway, U.S. dissidents continued to oppose the war in surprisingly large numbers and faced brutal repression for their efforts. That many rank-and-file workers remained either opposed or indifferent to the war was evident in the unprecedented strike levels, high Socialist vote tallies, and large numbers of American men who sought to avoid the draft—either through legal or illegal means. In the meantime, AFL leaders enjoyed unprecedented input over U.S. foreign policy and served on multiple diplomatic missions. Yet AFL leaders did not acquit themselves well in the diplomatic arena. They often sowed the seeds of discord with European labor and Socialist movements in ways that undercut support for the president's agenda and inhibited British Labour Party efforts to forge a third way in international politics that differed from that of both President Wilson and the Bolsheviks.

On the other hand, Gompers's actions at Versailles helped to ensure the creation of the International Labor Organization as an affiliate to the

League of Nations. Although far from perfect, moderate European labor and Socialist leaders, as well as labor delegates from a surprisingly diverse range of other countries and commonwealths throughout the world, chose to participate in the ILO's founding convention in the hopes that they could change it from within. Subsequently, the constituent national labor movements represented in the International Federation of Trade Unions became a mainstay of the ILO. By contrast, a unique combination of labor, Left, and racial politics inhibited support for the ILO and League in the United States and contributed to the defeat of the peace treaty. The United States would not become a member of the ILO that Gompers played such an important role in creating until 1934.

The U.S and transnational labor and Left debate over the Versailles Treaty, League, and ILO exposed fundamental contradictions in Wilsonian internationalism too often ignored by Wilson scholars, who tend to emphasize the opposition to Wilsonianism that emerged on the political Right within the United States and among the leaders of the imperial powers at the peace conference. Particularly neglected by historians have been the disagreements that developed between some Left groups and the Wilson administration over the League of Nations. Although most labor and Socialist groups supported the idea of a League of Nations, their blueprints for the proposed organization were significantly different than those of the Wilson administration. Energized by the popular demand for a "people's peace" and a "people's diplomacy," at the end of the war, a diverse array of groups that included the British Labour Party, Bern International Labor and Socialist Conference, U.S. Socialist Party, and U.S. Labor Party, among many others, sought to establish firm rules guaranteeing that national delegations to the League were either democratically elected or included representatives from political groups within parliamentary systems proportionate to their numbers in national assemblies. Wilson, however, proved uninterested in these designs and instead preferred to allow nations to develop their own systems for designating delegates. Yet from the perspective of Left activists, a League comprised of the same government elites who had caused World War I was unlikely to fundamentally alter the imperial status quo in ways that would advance the interests of the world's workers or ensure future peace and prosperity. Further undermining the potential of the League of Nations to promote genuine change was the power vested in its executive council; this governing body was to be comprised primarily of permanent representatives of the major imperial powers with only a few elected representatives. As the U.S. Socialist Party complained, this kind of structure would lend itself to the emergence of another "Holy Alliance" that would find ever more creative ways to repress the rights of workers throughout the globe.[2]

Labor and Socialist groups also found Wilson's rhetoric about national self-determination misleading. As workers in the Americas had long recognized, Wilson's racial paternalism precluded his support for independence for some groups. The president instead believed that these groups needed to be tutored in the ways of democracy before they would be ready for independence. In other cases, Wilson assumed that nations had proved themselves unready for independence by virtue of the social revolutions that erupted within their borders. Yet, as Robert Lansing warned, the term self-determination was "loaded with dynamite" and raised "hopes that can never be realized."[3] This proved as true in labor and Socialist circles as it did in those countries that failed to gain a hearing at the peace conference because many Left activists participated extensively in the diaspora politics of oppressed nationalities. Particularly important in the United States were the diaspora campaigns of the Irish, Mexicans, Russians, Poles, Slavs, and Pan-African groups. Left activists defended the rights of these groups to include the attainment of industrial democracy in their definitions of national self-determination.

Closely related to labor and Socialist concerns about Wilson's inconsistent and incomplete use of the term *self-determination* was his sense of American exceptionalism. Although some groups purporting to speak for workers, both in the United States and Europe, welcomed the president's efforts to "make the world safe for democracy," others doubted the wisdom, as well as desirability, of one nation trying to impose democracy on another. In this sense, they objected to Wilson's efforts to make spreading democracy a unique national mission of the United States. This proved particularly true of the U.S. Socialist and Labor parties. In contrast to the president, they interpreted self-determination to mean nonintervention in the internal affairs of other nations, or would-be nations, by outside powers and advanced the common sense idea of allowing other people to determine their own form of governments. This especially applied to countries in states of revolutionary upheaval, such as Ireland, Mexico, and Russia, that clearly had their own ambitious agendas for self-governance and industrial democracy. Socialist and labor activists unmasked the Wilson administration's tendencies toward what William Appleman Williams would later call the "imperialism of idealism" or the belief that other nations could be immeasurably improved by reshaping them in an American mold. In contrast to Wilson, labor and Left activists suggested that American political and economic institutions were not necessarily the best models for all other countries, or even for the United

States.[4] In this sense, the most constructive role that the United States could play in international affairs was a primarily negative one; it should seek, as the Chicago Labor Party argued, to withdraw from the "imperialistic enterprises upon which we have already embarked" in areas that ranged from the Philippines to the Dominican Republic, and to avoid neoimperialistic interventions in countries such as Mexico. U.S. policymakers should also use their influence to encourage the major European powers to dismantle their empires. Yet Labor Party activists remained skeptical that the United States would move in this direction until industrial democracy was achieved in the United States because the U.S. business class had a vested interest in economic expansion abroad.[5]

The one area in which Wilson's quest to "make the world safe for democracy" seemed at first to converge with the efforts of labor and Socialist groups to make the world safe for workers was in the ILO. Although the ILO was clearly no panacea, Wilson, Gompers, and many European Socialist and labor leaders assumed that it would, in modest ways, advance the cause of industrial democracy. But a broad range of U.S. labor, Socialist, and diaspora Left dissidents joined Republicans in rejecting the ILO. They argued that the undemocratic structures and compositions of the ILO and League of Nations would assure that these institutions worked in tandem in ways that reinforced the existing imperial and racial division of labor and undermined rather than promoted the struggle for industrial democracy.

The worst fears of American labor dissidents about the ILO would not be borne out in the twentieth century. Instead, the ILO has functioned as a moderate voice for reform for much of its nearly one-hundred-year history.[6] Yet the larger questions raised by the debate over the ILO in 1919 still seem relevant. In promoting the ILO, British Labour Party leader George Barnes highlighted one of the central dilemmas that would face twentieth- and twenty-first-century labor movements: the standards of workers in "Dundee" (wealthier countries) could be safeguarded only by raising labor standards in "Calcutta" (poorer nations).[7] In some cases, the ILO has, through its conventions and recommendations, realized its goal of incrementally improving global labor standards. Yet more often, it has proved relatively ineffective in countering the ever-expanding global power and mobility of multinational corporations committed to lowering production costs and slashing wages. Continuing global economic inequities, some of them originating in the more shortsighted components of the Versailles Peace Treaty, would contribute mightily to the political tensions that produced the twentieth century's ongoing pattern of hot and Cold wars, as well as the more recent wars in Afghanistan and Iraq.[8] In this sense the ILO has not proven an adequate mechanism for resolving some of the problems created by the relatively unfettered form of international capitalism championed by Wilson in his Fourteen Points and later implemented, at least in part, by some of his successors. The time thus seems ripe for a reconsideration of some of the alternative strategies for achieving industrial democracy, national security, and collective international security promoted by World War I–era labor dissidents and Socialists, both in the United States and abroad.

Notes

Introduction

1. Erez Manela, *The Wilsonian Moment: Self-Determination and the International Origins of Anticolonial Nationalism* (Oxford: Oxford University Press, 2007).

2. The literature on Wilson's foreign policy is vast. For sympathetic accounts of Wilson's foreign policy, see especially Arthur Link, *Woodrow Wilson: Revolution, War, and Peace* (Arlington Heights, Ill.: Harlan Davidson, 1979) and his many other books on Wilson; John Milton Cooper, *Breaking the Heart of the World: Woodrow Wilson and the Fight for the League of Nations* (Cambridge: Cambridge University Press, 2001); Thomas Knock, *To End All Wars: Woodrow Wilson and the Quest for a New World Order* (Oxford: Oxford University Press, 1992). For revisionist accounts of Wilson's diplomacy, see especially William Appleman Williams, *The Tragedy of American Diplomacy*, 2d ed. (New York: Delta Publishing, 1982), 52–159; Lloyd Gardner, *Safe for Democracy: The Anglo-American Response to Revolution, 1913–1923* (New York: Oxford University Press, 1984); N. Gordon Levin, *Woodrow Wilson and World Politics: America's Response to War and Revolution* (New York: Oxford University Press, 1968); Carl Parrini, *Heir to Empire: United States Economic Diplomacy, 1916–1923* (Pittsburgh: University of Pittsburgh Press, 1969); Thomas McCormick, *America's Half Century: United States Foreign Policy in the Cold War and After*, 2d ed. (Baltimore: John Hopkins University Press, 1995), 1–42.

3. See especially Lloyd Ambrosius, *Woodrow Wilson and the American Diplomatic Tradition: the Treaty Fight in Perspective* (Cambridge: Cambridge University Press, 1987); Ambrosius, *Wilsonian Statecraft: Theory and Practice of Liberal Internationalism during World War I* (Wilmington, Del.: Scholarly Resources, 1991) and his many other writings on Wilson; John Coogan, *The End of Neutrality: The United States, Britain, and Maritime Rights, 1899–1915* (Ithaca: Cornell University Press, 1981); Ross Kennedy, *The Will to Believe: Woodrow Wilson, World War I, and America's Strategy for Peace and Security* (Kent, Ohio: Kent State University Press, 2009); Mary A. Renda, *Taking Haiti: Military Occupation and the Culture of U.S. Imperialism, 1915–1940* (Chapel Hill: University of North Carolina Press, 2001); Alan Dawley, *Changing the World: American Progressives in War and Revolution* (Princeton: Princeton University Press, 2003); Robert Tucker, *Woodrow Wilson and the Great War: Reconsidering America's Neutrality: 1914–1917* (Charlottesville: University Press of Virginia, 2007).

4. *New Majority*, September 6, 1919, 1, 3, and July 26, 1919, 5; Elizabeth McKillen, *Chicago Labor and the Quest for a Democratic Diplomacy: 1914–1924* (Ithaca: Cornell

University Press, 1995), 141–142; Geert Van Goethem, *The Amsterdam International: The World of the International Federation of Trade Unions (IFTU), 1913–1945* (Aldershot, England: Ashgate Publishing, 2006), 175; "Preliminary Peace Proposals, Manifesto of the Committee of Action of the Berne International Labour and Socialist Conference," in Labour Party, *Report of the Nineteenth Annual Conference,* 1919, Appendix, XI, 212–213.

5. Knock, *To End All Wars,* viii–x; Dawley, *Changing the World,* 1–140.

6. The best synthetic account of the AFL during these years is David Montgomery, *The Fall of the House of Labor: The Workplace, the State, and American Labor Activism, 1865–1925* (Cambridge: Cambridge University Press, 1987). See also Paul Buhle, *Taking Care of Business: Samuel Gompers, George Meany, Lane Kirkland and the Tragedy of American Labor* (New York: Monthly Review Press, 1999), 73–90. On the AFL's approach to politics, see Julie Greene, *Pure and Simple Politics: The American Federation of Labor and Political Activism, 1881–1917* (Cambridge: Cambridge University Press, 1998). For Socialist activism within the AFL, see Nick Salvatore, *Eugene V. Debs: Citizen and Socialist* (Urbana: University of Illinois Press, 1982), 267. On labor party sentiment, and the antiwar and anti-imperialist sentiment of local unions, see McKillen, *Chicago Labor,* and Andrew Strouthous, *U.S. Labor and Political Action, 1918–1924: A Comparison of Independent Political Action in New York, Chicago, and Seattle* (New York: St. Martin's Press, 2000).

7. On the conservatism of AFL leaders, see Buhle, *Taking Care of Business,* 17–90.

8. Delber Lee McKee, "The American Federation of Labor and American Foreign Policy" (PhD diss., Stanford University, 1952), 134; David Montgomery, "Workers' Movements in the United States Confront Imperialism: The Progressive Era Experience," *Journal of the Gilded Age and Progressive Era* 7:1 (January 2008), 7–42; Rhodri Jeffreys Jones, "Organized Labor and the Social Foundations of American Diplomacy, 1898–1920," in *The U.S. Public and American Foreign Policy,* Helen Laville and Andrew Johnson, eds. (New York: Routledge, 2010); Elizabeth McKillen, "Organized Labor," in *Encyclopedia of American Foreign Policy,* 2d ed., Alexander DeConde et al., eds. (New York: Simon and Schuster, 2002), 47–48; Julie Greene, *The Canal Builders: Making America's Empire at the Panama Canal* (New York: The Penguin Press, 2009).

9. Philip Yale Nicholson, *Labor's Story in the United States* (Philadelphia: Temple University Press, 2004), 174.

10. "Minutes, Conference in Executive Council Room," March 6, 1917, Conference Collection-Gompers Microfilm Collection (CC-GMC), State Historical Society of Wisconsin (SHSW); "Excerpts from the Minutes of a Meeting of the Executive Council of the AFL," March 9, 1917, in *The Samuel Gompers Papers,* v 10, Grace Palladino and Peter Albert, eds. (Urbana: University of Illinois Press, 2007), 23–29 (hereafter *SGP*).

11. Joseph A. McCartin, *Labor's Great War: The Struggle for Industrial Democracy and the Origins of Modern American Labor Relations, 1912–1921* (Chapel Hill: University of North Carolina Press, 1997); James Weinstein, *The Corporate Ideal and the Liberal State, 1900–1918* (Boston: Beacon Press, 1968); Michael Hogan,

"Corporatism," in *Explaining the History of American Foreign Relations*, 2d ed., Michael Hogan and Thomas Paterson, eds. (Cambridge: Cambridge University Press, 2004), 137–148; John Horne, *Labour at War: France and Britain, 1914–1918* (Oxford: Oxford University Press, 1991); Jasmien Van Daele, "Engineering Social Peace: Networks, Ideas, and the Founding of the International Labour Organization," *International Review of Social History* 50 (2005), 435–466.

12. On diplomatic historians and the corporatist model, see particularly Michael Hogan, "Corporatism," 137–148; Thomas McCormick, "Drift or Mastery? A Corporatist Synthesis for American Diplomatic History," *Reviews in American History*, 10 (December 1982), 318–330. For the AFL's corporatist approach during this era, see Ronald Radosh, *American Labor and United States Foreign Policy: The Cold War in the Unions from Gompers to Lovestone* (New York: Random House, 1969) and Gregg Andrews, *Shoulder to Shoulder? The American Federation of Labor, the United States, and the Mexican Revolution, 1910–1924* (Berkeley: University of California Press, 1991). Three case studies have explored the opposition of particular AFL unions or municipal labor councils to World War I, but none has offered a synthetic view of the role of Socialist and labor dissent in shaping Wilson's and the AFL's foreign policies and the partnership between the two. See McKillen, *Chicago Labor*; Simeon Larson, *Labor and Foreign Policy: Gompers, the AFL, and the First World War, 1914–1918* (London: Associated University Presses, 1975); Frank Grubbs, *The Struggle for Labor Loyalty: Gompers, the A.F. of L and the Pacifists, 1917–1920* (Durham: Duke University Press, 1968). On the IWW's antiwar activities, see Francis Shor, "The IWW and Oppositional Politics in World War I: Pushing the System beyond Its Limits," *Radical History Review* 64 (Winter 1996), 74–94. On the current state of literature on the history of the international labor movement during this period, see Dana Frank, "Where Is the History of U.S. Labor and International Solidarity: Part 1: A Moveable Feast," *Labor: Studies in Working-Class History of the Americas* 1 (Summer 2004), 95–119.

13. The best synthetic accounts of U.S. socialism are still James Weinstein, *The Decline of Socialism in America: 1912–1925* (New York: Monthly Review Press, 1967) and David Shannon, *The Socialist Party of America: A History* (New York: Macmillan, 1955). More recent studies have illuminated significant regional variations within the U.S. Socialist Party and the importance of women. See especially James R. Green, *Grass-Roots Socialism: Radical Movements in the Southwest, 1895–1943* (Baton Rouge: Louisiana State University Press, 1978); Mari Jo Buhle, *Women and American Socialism, 1870–1920* (Urbana: University of Illinois Press, 1983); David Chang, *The Color of the Land: Race, Nation and the Politics of Land Ownership in Oklahoma, 1832–1929* (Chapel Hill: University of North Carolina Press, 2010).

14. For the 1915 Socialist Party Peace Program, see William English Walling, *The Socialists and the War* (New York: Holt and Co., 1915), 466–468.

15. Knock, *To End All Wars*, viii–x.

16. *Solidarity*, February 17, 1917, 2. Melvyn Dubofsky, *We Shall Be All: A History of the Industrial Workers of the World* (New York: Quadrangle Books, 1969), 349–468.

17. See especially chapter 7 and Jeffrey B. Perry, *Hubert Harrison: The Voice of Harlem Radicalism, 1883–1918* (New York: Columbia University Press, 2009); *Garvey: Africa, Europe, the Americas*, Rupert Lewis and Maureen Warner Lewis, eds. (Trenton: Africa World Press, 1994); Minkah Makalani, *In the Cause of Freedom: Radical Black Internationalism from Harlem to London, 1917–1939* (North Carolina: University of North Carolina Press, 2011).

18. For European perspectives on these issues, see especially Reiner Tosstorff, "The International Trade Union Movement and the Founding of the International Labour Organization," *International Review of Social History* 50 (2005), 399–433, and Markku Ruotsila, "'The Great Charter for the Liberty of the Workingman': Labour, Liberals and the Creation of the ILO," *Labour History Review* 67 (2002), 29–47.

19. See, for example, *Workers across the Americas: The Transnational Turn in Labor History*, Leon Fink, ed. (Oxford: Oxford University Press, 2011). Fink, in his essay, notes that transnational historians "emphasize the supranational or subnational aspect of their subjects" and he argues that historians have too often assigned "nation-states outsized influence as both historical agents and sources of identity" (xi–xiii). In her essay, Julie Greene argues that nation-states and their policies are still important to transnational historians, but that they seek to move "beyond approaches that see any nation-state as discrete and distinct or that study it unproblematically as a self-contained unit, essentialized or ahistorical" (13). None of the essays in this large volume focuses primarily on questions of labor and national foreign policies or deals extensively with the large literature in diplomatic history or international politics. See also Marcel van der Linden, "Transnationalizing American Labor History," *Journal of American History* 86 (December 1999), 1078–1092.

Inspired by the new Cold War history as well as the recent blossoming of an antiwar movement within the ranks of U.S. labor associated with the group U.S. Labor Against the War, a number of studies of U.S. labor and Cold War foreign policy have emerged in the last two decades. See especially "Workers, Labor, and War: New Directions in the History of U.S. Foreign Relations," Elizabeth McKillen, ed., *Diplomatic History* 34 (September 2010), 641–736, and Victor Silverman's groundbreaking work, *Imagining Internationalism in American and British Labor, 1939–1949* (Urbana: University of Illinois Press, 2000). See also John Bennett Sears, *Generation of Resistance: The Electrical Unions and the Cold* War (Conshohocken, Pa: Infinity Publishing, 2008); Brandon Williams, "Labor's Cold War Missionaries: The IFPCW's Transnational Mission for the Third World's Petroleum and Chemical Workers, 1954–1975," *Labor: Studies in the Working-Class History of the Americas* 7:4 (2010), 45–69; Edmund Wehrle, *Between a River and a Mountain: The AFL-CIO and the Vietnam War* (Ann Arbor: University of Michigan Press, 2005). By contrast, the question of U.S. and international labor responses to Wilson's foreign policies remains an understudied subject, except for the few case studies and older works mentioned in note 12.

Antonio Gramsci used the idea of a "war of position" primarily to explain a cultural war between counter-hegemonic and hegemonic forces in society. In recent years it has been at the heart of many debates in cultural studies. My purpose here is not to engage this theoretical debate. Rather, I use the term *war of position* in a historically specific way, grounded in common usage, to refer to the simultaneous economic, political, and intellectual battles waged between different labor/Left groups in an effort to influence U.S. foreign policy. On the Gramscian notion of a war of position and the debates about it, see especially Antonio Gramsci, *Selections from the Prison Notebooks of Antonio Gramsci*, Quintin Hoare and Jeoffry Nowell Smith, eds. (New York: International Publishers, 1971), 210–276; Michael Denning, *The Cultural Front: The Laboring of American Culture in the Twentieth Century* (New York: Verso, 1998), 22–25; Nathan Godfried, "Labor," *The Handbook of Communication History*, Peter Simonson, Janice Peck, Robert T. Craig, and John P. Jackson Jr., eds. (New York: Routledge, 2013).

20. Older corporatist literature, in particular, tended to assume that the AFL enjoyed a lopsided victory over its opponents, at least in terms of shaping U.S. foreign policy. See note 12.

21. Arno Mayer, *Political Origins of the New Diplomacy* (New Haven: Yale University Press, 1959); Mayer, *Politics and Diplomacy of Peace-Making, 1918–1919* (New York: Alfred Knopf, 1967). See also Radosh, *American Labor and United States Foreign Policy* .

22. For an introduction to the debate over the new cultural and multiarchival approaches to the field, see Hogan and Paterson, eds., *Explaining the History of American Foreign Relations*. On the successes of World War I propaganda, see Steven Vaughn, *Holding Fast the Inner Lines: Democracy, Nationalism and the Committee on Public Information* (Chapel Hill: University of North Carolina Press, 1980). For a skeptical review regarding World War I propaganda utilizing gender themes, see Elizabeth McKillen, "Pacifist Brawn and Silk Stocking Militarism: Labor, Gender and Antiwar Politics, 1914–1918," *Peace and Change* 33 (July 2008), 388–425.

23. Although an extensive literature exists on African American responses to World War I, as well as the appeal of international communism to African American radicals in its aftermath, alignments within this community surrounding the League of Nations and ILO have been surprisingly neglected. See chapter 7.

24. See, for example, Robert Ford, editor of the *Irish World and American Industrial Liberator* to Garvey, n.d., *Marcus Garvey and Universal Negro Improvement Association Papers (UNIA)*, v 1, Robert Hill, ed. (Berkeley: University of California Press, 1983), 287.

25. David R. Roediger, *Working toward Whiteness: How America's Immigrants Became White: The Strange Journey from Ellis Island to the Suburbs* (New York: Basic Books, 2005), 3–130; James Barrett and David Roediger, "The Irish and the 'Americanization' of the 'New Immigrants' in the Streets and in the Churches of the Urban United States, 1900–1930," *Journal of American Ethnic History*, 24 (Summer 2005), 4–33; David Brundage, "Recent Directions in the History of Irish American Nationalism," *Journal of American Ethnic History* 28 (Summer 2009), 82–89. As Roediger perceptively points out, "ethnic" was not used as a noun in

the early twentieth century. Instead, immigrants tended to conflate race and nationality in often confusing ways in explaining their ancestral backgrounds and in defining themselves relative to Anglo-Saxon–Protestant elites in American society (*Working toward Whiteness*, 19–22).

26. To date, three articles have been written on the International Congress of Working Women (ICWW). None of these articles places the activities of the ICWW in the context of the broader debate in the United States over the League and Versailles Peace Treaty. See Ulla Wikander, "Demands on the ILO by Internationally Organized Women in 1919," in *ILO Histories: Essays on the International Labour Organization and Its Impact on the World during the Twentieth Century*, Jasmien Van Daele, Magaly Rodríguez García, Geert Van Goethem, Marcel van der Linden, eds. (Bern: Peter Lang, 2010), 67–89; Dorothy Sue Cobble, "U.S. Labor Women's Internationalism in the World War I Era," *Revue Française D'Etudes Américaines* 122 (4 Trimestre, 2009), 44–58; Geert Van Goethem, "The International Federation of Working Women, 1919–1924," www.globallabour.info, 1–24 (accessed December 12, 2012). See also Robin Miller Jacoby, *The British and American Women's Trade Union Leagues, 1890–1925* (New York: Carlson Publishing, 1994).

27. See, for example, Alan Dawley, *Struggles for Justice: Social Responsibility and the Liberal State* (Cambridge: Belknap Press, 1991), vii–13.

Part I. Mexico and the Western Hemisphere

1. Knock, *To End All Wars*, 39, 42–43, 71; Mark Gilderhus, *Pan American Visions: Woodrow Wilson and the Western Hemisphere, 1913–1921* (Tucson: University of Arizona Press, 1986), 1–80.

2. Thomas G. Paterson et al., *American Foreign Relations: A History to 1920*, v 1, 6th ed. (Boston: Houghton Mifflin, 2005), 240–244; Renda, *Taking Haiti*, 39–181; Bruce Calder, *The Impact of Intervention: The Dominican Republic during the Occupations, 1916–1924* (Austin: University of Texas Press, 1984); Emily S. Rosenberg, *Financial Missionaries to the World: The Politics and Culture of Dollar Diplomacy, 1900–1930* (Durham: Duke University Press, 2003), 79–93.

3. Trygve Throntveit, "The Fable of the Fourteen Points: Woodrow Wilson and National Self-Determination," *Diplomatic History* 35 (June 2011), 445–481; Knock, *To End All Wars*, 4–7; Link, *Woodrow Wilson: Revolution, War, and Peace*, 4–7; Rosenberg, *Financial Missionaries to the World*.

4. Paterson et al., *American Foreign Relations*, v 1, 244.

5. John Mason Hart, *Empire and Revolution: The Americans in Mexico since the Civil War* (Berkeley: University of California Press, 2002); Mark T. Gilderhus, *Diplomacy and Revolution: U.S.-Mexican Relations under Wilson and Carranza* (Tucson: University of Arizona Press, 1977), 1–70; Freidrich Katz, *The Secret War in Mexico: Europe, the United States, and the Mexican Revolution* (Chicago: University of Chicago Press, 1981); Gardner, *Safe for Democracy*, 45–70.

6. Manela, *Wilsonian Moment*.

Chapter 1. The Mexican Revolution as Catalyst

1. *Appeal to Reason (AR)*, April 25, 1914, May 2, 1914, April 24, 1915, 1, May 27, 1915, 1; *Solidarity*, April 25, 1914, 1, May 16, 1914, 1, May 23, 1914, 1, May 20, 1911, 1; "Situation in Mexico," in "Report of the Executive Council in the Philadelphia Convention," in AFL, *Labor and the War: The American Federation of Labor and the Labor Movements of Europe and Latin America* (Washington, D.C.: AFL, 1918), 7–10; *American Federationist*, August 1916, 633–646; Alan Dawley, *Changing the World*, 27–33; Dubofsky, *We Shall Be All*, 350–351; Thomas G. Paterson et al., *American Foreign Relations: A History, since 1895*, v 2, 5th ed. (Boston: Houghton Mifflin, 2000), 50–51.

2. Ibid. *United Mine Workers Journal (UMWJ)*, April 30, 1914, 1, 4; *Milwaukee Leader (ML)*, April 23, 1914, 1, 8, April 25, 1914, 1, 10; Diana K. Christopulos, "American Radicals and the Mexican Revolution, 1900–1925" (PhD diss., State University of New York at Binghamton, 1980), 236–238 (quote); *New York Call (NYC)*, June 17, 1915, 6, August 15, 1915, 1; Andrews, *Shoulder to Shoulder?* 33.

3. "Manifesto to Fellow Workers from the Organizing Junta of the Mexican Liberal Party," May 1911, per R. Flores Magón in U.S. Congress, Senate Committee on Foreign Relations, *Investigation of Mexican Affairs, 66th Cong., 2d sess., 1920, S. Doc. 285*, v 2, 2501; "Manifesto of the Organizing Junta of the Mexican Liberal Party to the Workers of the United States," *Regeneración*, March 6, 1915, 4. See also John Kenneth Turner, *Barbarous Mexico*, with an introduction by Sinclair Snow (Austin: University of Texas Press, 1969 [1910]); Elizabeth McKillen, "Hybrid Visions: Working-Class Internationalism in the Mexican Borderlands, Seattle and Chicago," *Labor: Studies in the Working-Class History of the Americas* 2 (Spring 2005), 77–107.

4. On the PLM, see especially Colin MacLachlan, *Anarchism and the Mexican Revolution: The Political Trials of Ricardo Flores Magón in the United States* (Berkeley: University of California Press, 1991); James Sandos, *Rebellion in the Borderlands: Anarchism and the Plan of San Diego, 1914–1923* (Norman: University of Oklahoma Press, 1992); W. Dirk Raat, *Revoltosos: Mexico's Rebels in the United States, 1903–1923* (College Station: Texas A&M University Press, 1981); Juan Gómez-Quiñones, *Sembradores: Ricardo Flores Magón y el Partido Liberal Mexicano: A Eulogy and Critique* (Los Angeles: Aztlán Publications, University of California at Los Angeles, 1973); James D. Cockcroft, *Intellectual Precursors to the Mexican Revolution: 1900–1913* (Austin: University of Texas Press, 1968).

On the importance of immigrant and refugee communities in fostering anti-imperialist movements, see especially "Good Neighbors: Popular Internationalists and United States' Relations with Mexico and the Caribbean Region (1918–1929)" (PhD diss., University of Minnesota, 2001); Erin Murphy, "Anti-Imperialism during the Philippine-American War: Protesting 'Criminal Aggression' and Benevolent Assimilation'" (PhD diss., University of Illinois, 2009); Sandos, *Rebellion in the Borderlands*; Elizabeth McKillen, "Ethnicity, Class and Wilsonian Internationalism Reconsidered: The Mexican-American and Irish-American Immigrant Left and U.S. Foreign Relations, 1914–1922," *Diplomatic History* 25 (Fall 2001), 553–588.

5. Juan Gómez Quiñones, *Mexican American Labor, 1790–1990* (Albuquerque: University of New Mexico Press, 1994), 39.

6. Ibid.

7. Benjamin Heber Johnson, *Revolution in Texas: How a Forgotten Rebellion and Its Bloody Suppression Turned Mexicans into Americans* (New Haven: Yale University Press, 2003), 9; David Montejano, *Anglos and Mexicans in the Making of Texas: 1836–1986* (Austin: University of Texas Press, 1987), 3–6; Ramón Eduardo Ruiz, *The People of Sonora and Yankee Capitalists* (Tucson: University of Arizona Press, 1988); Samuel Truett, *Fugitive Landscapes: The Forgotten History of the U.S.-Mexico Borderlands* (New Haven: Yale University Press, 2006). Truett suggests that state-centered history has obscured the history of the Borderlands and that "Arizonans viewed their neighbors to the south as siblings in an interlocking family history." They expected "economic development to knit Mexico and the United States together and carry them as progressive partners into a modern future" (5–6). Yet while this may have been true of some business groups, my own studies suggest that workers overwhelmingly feared such integration. As they well understood, U.S. imperial power reinforced a racialized division of labor in the Southwest as well as Mexico. With this in mind, they politically mobilized to oppose U.S. intervention in Mexico. The state and national identity therefore remain vital to an understanding of the Borderlands.

8. Montejano, *Anglos and Mexicans in the Making of Texas*, 316–318; Gómez-Quiñones, *Mexican-American Labor*, 45–52; Heber Johnson, *Revolution in Texas*, 110.

9. Montejano, *Anglos and Mexicans in the Making of Texas*, 5–10, 113; Gómez Quiñones, *Mexican American Labor*, 45. Emilio Zamora, *The World of the Mexican Worker in Texas* (College Station: University of Texas Press, 1993), 14–15.

10. Ibid.

11. Zamora, *World of the Mexican Worker*, 49–73; Raat, *Revoltosos,* 13–62; Sandos, *Rebellion in the Borderlands*, xv–xviii.

12. On dependent economic development, see Louis Pérez, "Dependency," in Hogan and Thomas Paterson, eds., *Explaining the History of American Foreign Relations*, 162–175.

13. Hart, *Empire and Revolution*, 17, 169, 236; Sandos, *Rebellion in the Borderlands*, 5; MacLachlan, *Anarchism and the Mexican Revolution*, 88.

14. Turner, *Barbarous Mexico*, 128; Hart, *Empire and Revolution*, 136.

15. Hart, *Empire and Revolution*, 236.

16. MacLachlan, *Anarchism and the Mexican Revolution*, 3; John Mason Hart, *Anarchism and the Mexican Working Class, 1860–1931 (Austin: University of Texas Press, 1978)*, 88; Cockcroft, *Intellectual Precursors*, 5, 51, 86–87.

17. Sandos, *Rebellion in the Borderlands*, 3–23; Cockcroft, *Intellectual Precursors*, 5, 51, 86–87.

18. Sandos, *Rebellion in the Borderlands*, 3–23; Raat, *Revoltosos*, 3–62.

19. Raat, *Revoltosos*, 65–91; Sandos, *Rebellion in the Borderlands*, 10–11, 15–22, 58–62; McKillen, "Wilsonian Internationalism Reconsidered," 558–559; Mike Casillas,

"The Cananea Strike of 1906," *Southwest Economy and Society* 3 (Winter 1977/1978), 15–32.

20. See especially Zamora, *World of the Mexican Worker*, 133–134, and, in general, Sandos, *Rebellion in the Borderlands*, 10–23, 129, 205–209.

21. Andrews, *Shoulder to Shoulder?* 15–18, 24, 37; Gómez-Quiñones, *Mexican-American Labor*, 78–85; Gómez-Quiñones, "The First Steps: Chicano Labor Conflict and Organizing, 1900–1920," *Aztlan* (Summer 1973), 31–34; Philip J. Mellinger, *Race and Labor in Western Copper: The Fight for Equality, 1896–1918* (Tucson: University of Arizona Press, 1995), 197, 201–202; AFL Resolutions, in AFL, *Labor and the War*, 136–137; AFL, *Proceedings*, 1916, 57; *American Federationist*, August 1916, 637. Samuel Gompers, *Seventy Years of Life and Labor* (New York: E. P. Dutton, 1925), v 2, 303–323.

22. "Manifesto of the Mexican Liberal Party," signed September 23, 1911, in *Regeneración*, June 13, 1914, 8.

23. Ibid. Lowell Blaisdell, *The Desert Revolution: Baja California, 1911* (Madison: University of Wisconsin Press, 1962). On the contradictions of the PLM's attitudes toward women, see Emma Pérez, *The Decolonial Imaginary: Writing Chicanas into History* (Bloomington: Indiana University Press, 1999).

24. *Solidarity*, June 24, 1911, 1, March 22, 1911, 1–2; "Manifesto of the Mexican Liberal Party," 1911, in *Regeneración*, June 13, 1914, 8; *Douglas Munroy*, "Fence Cutters, Sediciosos, and First-Class Citizens: Mexican Radicalism in America," in *The Immigrant Left in the United States*, Paul Buhle and Dan Georgakas, eds. (Albany: State University of New York Press, 1996), 11–44.

25. Eugene Debs, "The Crisis in Mexico," in *Writings and Speeches of Eugene V. Debs*, Arthur M. Schlesinger Jr., ed. (New York: Hermitage Press, 1948), 337–339; AR, June 17, 1911, July 8, 1911; Christopulos, "American Radicals," 145–149.

26. Mother Jones to Manuel Calero, October 25, 1911, in *The Correspondence of Mother Jones*, Edward M. Steel, ed. (Pittsburgh: University of Pittsburgh Press, 1985), 97–100; Christopulos, "American Radicals," 145–146; Andrews, *Shoulder to Shoulder?* 23, 104.

27. *Regeneración*, June 13, 1914, 7–8, August 22, 1914, 4.

28. *Regeneración*, May 9, 1914, 8; McKillen, "Hybrid Visions," 82.

29. *Regeneración*, May 24, 1913, 4; McKillen, "Wilsonian Internationalism Reconsidered," 561–562.

30. McKillen, "Wilsonian Internationalism Reconsidered," 561–562; *Regeneración*, June 13, 1914, 2.

31. McKillen, "Hybrid Visions," 85–86; Hart, *Anarchism and the Mexican Working Class*, 129; Sandos, *Rebellion in the Borderlands*, 154; Ramón Eduardo Ruiz, *Labor and the Ambivalent Revolutionaries: Mexico, 1911–1923* (Baltimore: John Hopkins University Press, 1976), 39–72.

32. *Solidarity*, August 21, 1915, 2, March 11, 1916, 3; *El Rebelde*, March 18, 1916, 4; Andrews, *Shoulder to Shoulder?* 33; Raat, *Revoltosos*, 285–290; Sandos, *Rebellion in the Borderlands*, 135–140; Gómez-Quiñones, *Mexican American Labor*, 5.

33. *Solidarity*, August 21, 1915, 2, March 11, 1916, 3; *El Rebelde*, March 18, 1916, 4, May 26, 1916, 2, July 8, 1916, 3, June 6, 1916, 1; Andrews, *Shoulder to Shoulder?* 33; Raat, *Revoltosos*, 285–290; *Sandos, Rebellion in the Borderlands*, 135–140; Gómez-Quiñones, *Mexican American Labor*, 5.

34. See especially *Mother Earth*, August 1910, 185, December 1911, 301–302, April 1915, 85, August 1916, 570–577; Raat, *Revoltosos*, 285–290; Sandos, *Rebellion in the Borderlands*, 135–140.

35. AFL, *Proceedings*, 1913, 364; Andrews, *Shoulder to Shoulder?* 24–31; Christopulos, "American Radicals," 281.

36. Gompers to Wilson, September 22, 1915, and Wilson to Gompers, September 24, 1915, in a letter to Carranza, March 9, 1916, 812.0017847, RG59-R 162, National Archives and Record Administration (NARA); Report of the AFL Executive Council, 1915, in AFL, *Labor and the War*, 21–25; Gompers, *Seventy Years*, 311–313; *American Federationist*, August 1916, 640–641; AFL, *Proceedings*, 1916, 57; McKillen, *Chicago Labor*, 121–122.

37. Report of the AFL Executive Council, 1915, 21; "Minutes, Conference in the Executive Council Room, March 6, 1917," in CC-GMC, and Gompers Letter to the Advisory Commission, April 12, 1917, and April 5, 1917, in the Letterbooks, Gompers Microflim Collection (Lb-GMC) at the SHSW; *New Republic*, June 10, 1916, 137–138.

38. Report of the AFL Executive Council, 1915, 22–25; Andrews, *Shoulder to Shoulder?* 36–37; Sinclair Snow, *The Pan American Federation of Labor* (Durham: Duke University Press, 1964), 3–73; Santiago Iglesias, "American Organized Labor Crusaders for Liberty," in AFL, *Labor and the War*, 163–165. See also Gompers to Wilson, enclosing a letter from Santiago Iglesias, December 4, 1916, *PWW*, v 40, 146–148.

39. Andrews, *Shoulder to Shoulder?* 49; Ruiz, *Labor and the Ambivalent Revolutionaries*, 39–72; Hart, *Anarchism and the Mexican Working Class*, 126–129; Sandos, *Rebellion in the Borderlands*, 156; McKillen, "Wilsonian Internationalism Reconsidered," 563–564; U.S. Senate, Investigation of Mexican Affairs, 1920, 2820–2822; *Regeneración*, May 3, 1916, 1, 4; November 25, 1916, 2, 4; September 30, 1916, 4.

40. *American Federationist*, August 1916, 645–646; Gompers, *Seventy Years*, 314–315; AFL, *Labor and the War*, 130–137; Christopulos, "American Radicals," 320–326; Gompers to Carranza, March 9, 1916, 812.0017847, RG59-R162, NARA.

41. Ibid. Andrews, *Shoulder to Shoulder?* 50–62.

42. *UMWJ*, April 30, 1914, 1; *Seattle Union Record (SUR)*, April 25, 1914, 1.

43. *UMWJ*, May 28, 1914, 4, June 10, 1915, 4.

44. *UMWJ*, July 13, 1916, 12; see also chapter 3.

45. *Regeneración*, May 2, 1914, 4, July 4, 1914, 4, July 18, 1914, 4.

46. Christopulos, "American Radicals," 195; Knock, *To End All Wars*, 29–30, 101. Victor Berger and the *Milwaukee Leader*, meanwhile, were inconsistent on Mexico, sometimes seeming to advocate an even more aggressive policy than Wilson toward Mexico and at other times siding with the antiwar majority in the Socialist Party. See *ML*, April 20, 1914, 4, April 21, 1914, 8, April 23, 1914, 1, 8, April 25, 1914, 4, 10, April 27, 1914, 8.

47. See the Socialist Party statement on the war, *ML*, April 25, 1914, 4; (Hallettsville) *Rebel*, July 24, 1915, 3, January 5, 1916, 1, January 29, 1916, 1; Turner, *Barbarous Mexico*, xi–xxix.

48. *AR*, May 27, 1915, 1.

49. Christopulos, "American Radicals," 101–128, 252–257; *AR*, April 24, 1915, 1, 4, May 1, 1915, 1, May 27, 1915, 1–2, October 28, 1916, 4; *NYC*, August 15, 1915, 1.

50. *AR*, July 22, 1916, 1, September 23, 1916, 1, October 14, 1916, 1–2, October 28, 1916, 4.

51. *AR*, October 28, 1916, 1.

52. *AR*, July 22, 1916, 1.

53. *AR*, July 15, 1916, 1, October 28, 1916, 4; Christopulos, "American Radicals," 252–257.

54. *AR*, November 25, 1916, 2.

55. Monroy, "Fence Cutters, Sedicioso, and First-Class Citizens," 22; Montejano, *Anglos and Mexicans in the Making of Texas*, 117–128; Sandos, *Rebellion in the Borderlands*; McKillen, "Hybrid Visions," 88–89; McKillen, "Wilsonian Internationalism Reconsidered," 568–570.

56. Heber Johnson, *Rebellion in Texas*, 136–137; McKillen, "Hybrid Visions," 88–89; Zamora, *World of the Mexican Worker*, 81–82; MacLachlan, *Anarchism and the Mexican Revolution*, 57–58, 63, 71, 80; Sandos, *Rebellion in the Borderlands*, 88, 208–209; Sandos, "The Plan of San Diego: War and Diplomacy on the Texas Border, 1915–1916," *Arizona and the West* 14 (1972), 22; U.S. Senate, *Investigation of Mexican Affairs*, 1920, 1222–1226, 1233–1236.

57. *Mother Earth*, April 1916; "Address of Enrique Flores Magón," in MacLachlan, *Anarchism and the Mexican Revolution*, 130–131.

58. MacLachlan, *Anarchism and the Mexican Revolution*, 60–112; Sandos, *Rebellion in the Borderlands*, 133–140, 167–69; Raat, *Revoltosos*, 285–290; McKillen, "Hybrid Visions," 89. In *Regeneración*, see especially February 26, 1914, 4, March 18, 196, 4, July 8, 1916, 4.

59. *Regeneración*, April 21, 1917, 4, July 28, 1917, 4, November 11, 1916, 4, January 29, 1916, 1; McKillen, "Wilsonian Internationalism Reconsidered," 566–567.

60. Ibid. Heber Johnson, *Rebellion in Texas*, 151–152.

61. See especially Sandos, *Rebellion in the Borderlands*, 167–68; MacLachlan, *Anarchism and the Mexican Revolution*, 60–112.

62. *Rebel*, December 26, 1914, 1–4, July 24, 1915, 3, May 20, 1916, 1, August 19, 1916, 1; Christopulos, "American Radicals," 185–186; Green, *Grass-Roots Socialism*, 330–335; Zamora, *World of the Mexican Worker*, 15–16, 133–145.

63. MacLachlan, *Anarchism and the Mexican Revolution*, 79; Zamora, *World of the Mexican Worker*, 15–16, 133–145; Mellinger, *Race and Labor in Western Copper*, 201–202; Gómez-Quiñones, "First Steps," 33–34.

64. Pan-American Federation of Labor (PAFL), *Report of the Proceedings of the Second Congress of the Pan-American Federation of Labor*, July 7–10, 1919, 4–40; Andrews, *Shoulder to Shoulder?* 82–86; Raat, *Revoltosos*, 285–290.

Part II. World War I and the U.S. Labor Debate over Neutrality and Preparedness

1. Paterson et al., *American Foreign Relations*, v 1, 6th ed., 269–270. For an account that emphasizes the mobilization of African and Indian soldiers, see John Morrow Jr., *The Great War: An Imperial History* (New York: Routledge, 2004).

2. The literature on Wilson's neutrality policies is extensive. For contrasting interpretations of these policies, see especially Ross Gregory, *The Origins of American Intervention in the First World War* (New York: Norton, 1971); Tucker, *Woodrow Wilson and the Great War*; Coogan, *End of Neutrality*; Paterson et al., *American Foreign Relations*, v 1, 263–301.

3. *Seattle Union Record (SUR)*, May 22, 1915, 2.

4. See especially Knock, *To End All Wars*; Link, *Woodrow Wilson: Revolution, War and Peace*; Ambrosius, *Wilsonian Statecraft*; Ross Kennedy, "Woodrow Wilson, World War I, and American National Security," *Diplomatic History* 25 (Winter 2001), 1–31.

5. See especially Knock, *To End All Wars*, 34, and, in general, Tucker, *Woodrow Wilson and the Great War*, 24, and Kennedy, *Will to Believe*, 25, 38.

6. Kennedy, *Will to Believe*, 25, 38; Dawley, *Changing the World*, 1–179. Social historians have, of course, long emphasized the peace activities of these groups, but their scholarship has only rarely made its way into the debates over American foreign policy in books about diplomatic history. For an examination of these issues as they pertain to issues of class, see McKillen, ed., "Workers, Labor, and War." See also the many forums on recent literature on Wilson in the innovative online series *H-Diplo*.

Chapter 2. The Outbreak of World War I and the Socialist "War on War"

1. *NYC*, August 9, 1914, 1–2.

2. Ibid. For more on Anne Maley, see Buhle, *Women and American Socialism*, 152–154.

3. Dawley, *Changing the World*, 109. For examples of other events like the one in New York, see *ML*, August 8, 1914, 11; August 14, 1914, 10; *American Socialist (AS)*, August 8, 1914, 1.

4. Interestingly, the Socialists actually encouraged foreign-born workers to hold their own meetings for the purpose of emphasizing the "fraternity and solidarity of all working people." *AS*, August 8, 1914, 1. This was a quite different strategy from that of President Wilson who attacked "hyphenated Americans" for their allegedly narrow obsessions with their former homelands. See McKillen, *Chicago Labor*, 8–9.

5. For a good introduction to the diverse cultural makeup of the Socialist Party, see Paul Buhle, "Socialist Party," in *Encyclopedia of the American Left* (Oxford: Oxford University Press, 1998), 767–774. Green, *Grass-Roots Socialism*; Richard Judd, *Socialist Cities: Municipal Politics and the Grass Roots of American Socialism* (Albany: State University of New York Press, 1989); and Mary Jo Buhle, *Women and American Socialism*, were among the early pioneers in the study of regional Socialist subcultures. *The Immigrant Left in the United States*, Paul Buhle and Dan

Georgakas, eds. (Albany: State University of New York Press, 1996) contains much useful information on socialism in immigrant communities. See also Paul Buhle, *Marxism in the United States: Remapping the History of the American Left* (London: Verso Press, 1991), and Nick Salvatore, *Eugene V. Debs: Citizen and Socialist* (Urbana: University of Illinois Press, 1982).

More recently, scholars have begun to focus on questions of race and religion in Socialist subcultures. See especially Chang, *The Color of the Land*; Jim Bissett, *Agrarian Socialism in America: Marx, Jefferson, and Jesus in the Oklahoma Countryside, 1904–1920* (Norman: University of Oklahoma Press, 1999); Makalani, *In the Cause of Freedom*; Perry, *Hubert Harrison*.

6. Although earlier literature on the Socialist Party duly noted the importance of its foreign policy activities, it largely neglected analyses of these groups' foreign policy ideas and the ways in which they shaped the national debate over foreign policy during the war. See, for example, Weinstein, *Decline of Socialism in America*; Shannon, *Socialist Party*; and Philip Foner, *History of the Labor Movement of the United States* (New York: International Publishers, 1987), v 7, 1–39.

7. Morris Hillquit to Mr. Walter Lanfersiek, September 21, 1914, Hillquit papers (HP) Box (B) 2, File (F) 4 at the State Historical Society of Wisconsin (SHSW); William English Walling, *The Socialists and the War* (New York: Henry Holt and Co., 1915), 406–407.

8. Morris Hillquit, *Loose Leaves from a Busy Life* (New York: Macmillan Co., 1934), 160. See also Letter from Dr. Albert Sudekun to Hillquit, September 24, 1914, HP, B2-F4; *ML*, September 21, 1914, 8.

9. Victor Berger to President Wilson, December 1, 1914, and Berger to Hon. William Redfield, December 1, 1914, Berger papers (BP), Microfilm Edition at SHSW, R15; Hillquit to Walter Lanfersiek, November 21, 1914, HP B2-F4.

10. Hillquit to NEC, December 28, 1914, HP B2-F4; Lanfersiek to Hillquit, January 23, 1915, HP B2-F5; Hillquit to Mr. Theodore Stainig (Denmark), December 28, 1914, and Hillquit to H.M. Hyndman (London), December 31, 1914, HP B2-F4. The letter to Hyndman suggests that some British Socialists believed the conference of neutrals would actually be pro-German. See also letter from Henry Ford to Hillquit, November 27, 1915, HP B2-F5, urging him to join a peace pilgrimage. Berger to Hillquit, June 3, 1916, HP B2-F5; Walling, *Socialists and the War*, 424.

11. Hillquit, *Loose Leaves*, 153–157; Froelker at the Hague to Hillquit, June 29, 1917, HP B2-F5. On Eugene Debs and his support for the Zimmerwald Conference, see Eugene Debs, "The Prospect for Peace," in *Eugene V. Debs Speaks*, Jean Y. Tussey, ed. (New York: Pathfinder, 1970), 232–233; Algie Simmons to Eugene V. Debs (EVD), October 1915, in *Letters of Eugene V. Debs (Letters of EVD)*, J. Robert Constantine, ed. (Urbana: University of Illinois Press, 1990), v 2, 194–195, and explanatory note.

12. Lanfersiek to EVD, December 23, 1915, and EVD to Walter Lanfersiek, December 24, 1915, in *Letters of EVD*, v 2, 212–214.

13. Hillquit, *Loose Leaves*, 161–162.

14. Kate Richards O'Hare, *Montana Socialist*, March 20, 1915, R1, microfilm collection at SHSW.

15. *AR*, September 22, 1914, 4; *NYC*, April 5, 1915, 4; *AS*, September 15, 1914, 4, September 12, 1914, 2, September 19, 1914, 1, September 26, 1914, 1.

16. Foner, *History of the Labor Movement*, v 7, 6–7, 26–27; *AS*, September 12, 1914, 2. On the AFL and the embargo movement, see AFL, *Labor and the War*, 12.

17. *International Socialist Review*, March 1914, 534–544, September 1914, 144–145, October 1914, 198–199, November 1914, 292–300, March 1915, 528–529, 561, November 1916, 291, 305, December 1916, 367. On the IWW, see chapter 4, 186–188, and accompanying notes.

18. Hillquit, *Loose Leaves*, 160.

19. On the emergence of the radio industry and its importance for working-class struggles, see Nathan Godfried, *WCFL: Chicago's Voice of Labor, 1926–1978* (Urbana: University of Illinois Press, 1997).

20. On the circulation of the *Appeal to Reason*, see Knock, *To End All Wars*, 17.

21. Walling, *Socialists and the War*.

22. On charges that the Socialist newspapers were pro-German, see especially George Herron to Hillquit, April 5, 1915, B2-F5, HP. On the cutting of the transatlantic cables, see Frederick C. Leubke, *Bonds of Loyalty: German Americans and World War I* (Dekalb: Northern Illinois University Press, 1974), 89–90; *ML*, August 13, 1914, 2.

23. See especially *NYC*, March 14, 1915, 3, September 3, 1914, 7 (mag.), August 30, 1914, 4, August 31, 1915, 16; *AR*, August 15, 1914, 4.

24. See especially William English Walling in *NYC*, August 29, 1915, 3.

25. *AR*, August 15, 1914, 1; *NYC*, August 31, 1915, 6.

26. *NYC*, March 7, 1915, section s 2, 1, August 29, 1915, s 2, 3, March 21, 1915, s 2, 9; Hillquit in Walling, *Socialists and the War*, 22–23.

27. Victor Berger in Walling, *Socialists and the War*, 384–387; Sally Miller, *Victor Berger and the Promise of Constructive Socialism, 1910–1920* (Westport, Conn.: Greenwood Press, 1973), 127–128. See also Berger's evolving positions in the *Milwaukee Leader*, as well as the paper's coverage of the Socialist antiwar movement in Germany, especially August 3, 1914, 8, August 8, 1914, 10, August 10, 1914, 8, September 22, 1914, 9, September 28, 1914, 9, December 4, 1914, 2.

28. *NYC*, March 14, 1915, s 2, 3, March 21, 1915, 1, 9; *Rebel*, May 15, 1915, 1–4.

29. Hillquit and Berger in Walling, *Socialists and the War*, 381, 384–387.

30. *International Socialist Review*, March 1915, 523–527; *Solidarity*, May 27, 1916, 2; *Rebel*, May 20, 1916, 1; *NYC*, September 3, 1914, 7.

31. George Herron to Hillquit, April 5, 1915, HP B2-F5, and *AR* and *NYC*, 1916.

32. Debs, "The Prospect for Peace," 233.

33. For an earlier version of some of the research in this section, see Elizabeth McKillen, "Pacifist Brawn and Silk-Stocking Militarism: Labor, Gender and Antiwar Politics, 1914–1918," *Peace and Change* (July 2008), 388–425.

34. John Gary Clifford, *The Citizen Soldier: The Plattsburg Training Camp Movement, 1913–1920* (Lexington: University of Kentucky Press, 1972), 3–6, 19, 37.

35. See especially Leonard Wood to Samuel Gompers, September 20, 1915, in Robert Cuff, "Samuel Gompers, Leonard Wood and Military Preparedness," *Labor History* (Spring 1971), 285.

36. Clifford, *Citizen Soldier*, 85.

37. Ibid., 187, 200. *AR*, November 27, 1915, 1.

38. Michael Kimmel, *Manhood in America*, 1st and 2d eds. (New York: Free Press, 1996, and New York: Oxford University Press, 2006), 187, 124; *AR*, November 27, 1915, 1; *NYC*, July 25, 1915, s 2, 10, August 1, 1915, s 2, 5.

39. John Whiteclay Chambers, *To Raise an Army: The Draft Comes to Modern America* (New York: Free Press, 1987), 81–83; Gail Bederman, *Manliness and Civilization: A Cultural History of Gender and Race in the United States: 1880–1917* (Chicago: University of Chicago Press, 1995), 7–17.

40. Chambers, *To Raise an Army*, 95–96; *AR*, June 13, 1915, 1.

41. Kathleen Kennedy, *Disloyal Mothers and Scurrilous Citizens* (Bloomington: Indiana University Press, 1999), xix.

42. *AR*, September 31, 1915, 1.

43. Kennedy, *Disloyal Mothers*, 9–10; Susan Zeiger, "She Didn't Raise Her Boy to Be a Slacker: Motherhood, Conscription and the Culture of the First World War," *Feminist Studies* 2 (Spring 1996), 7–39.

44. *NYC*, June 20, 1915, 1; *AR*, August 14, 1915, 1, September 13, 1915, 1.

45. *AR*, September 31, 1915, 1, August 14, 1915, 1.

46. *AR*, March 17, 1917, 4; *NYC*, June 19, 1915, 1, August 29, 1915, 1. For further analysis of the use of gender in antiwar campaigns, see McKillen, "Pacifist Brawn and Silk-Stocking Militarism," and Kathleen Kennedy, "Declaring War on War: Gender and the American Socialist Attack on Militarism, 1914–1918," *Journal of Women's History* (Summer 1995), 27–51.

47. *NYC*, March 7, 1915, s 2, 1, April 11, 1915, 1, 5. See also Eugene Debs, "Letter of Acceptance," in *Writings and Speeches of Eugene Debs*, Arthur Schlesinger, ed. (New York: Hermitage Press,1948), 395–397.

48. Eugene Debs to Upton Sinclair, January 12, 1916, *Letters of EVD*, v 2, 227.

49. *AR*, August 22, 1914, 2.

50. Ibid. *AR*, February 15, 1916, 1; *AS*, September 26, 1914, 1.

51. *AR*, August 22/24, 1914, 2, November 27, 1915, 2. *NYC* (Debs), August 31, 1915, 6. Victor Berger was unique among Socialists in believing from an early date in the value of a limited form of preparedness and military service based on the Swiss army model. See *ML*, December 10, 1914, 12.

52. *AR*, November 27, 1915, 1.

53. Ibid. *AR*, March 31, 1917, 8; *NYC*, June 5, 1915, 1.

54. *AR*, May 19, 1917, 1, June 13, 1915, 1, August 14, 1915, 1, November 27, 1915, 3, January 6, 1916, 1.

55. *AR*, May 1914, 1.

56. *NYC*, April 11, 1915, s 2, 5.

57. *AR*, December 4, 1915, 1, June 9, 1917, 3.

58. Mary E. Marcy, "The Real Fatherland," and "Better Any Kind of Action than Inert Theory," in *You Have No Country*, Franklin Rosemont, ed. (Chicago: Charles H. Kerr Publishing, 1984), 17–19, 25–29; Marcy, "Where We Stand on War," *ISR*, March 1915, 561; Marcy, "The Value of Immorality, *ISR*, March 1915, 528–529.

59. On Debs's masculinity, see particularly Kathleen Kennedy "Manhood and Subversion during World War I: The Cases of Eugene Debs and Alexander Berkman," *North Carolina Law Review* 82 (2004), 1661–1703.

60. *NYC*, August 30, 1914, Women's Sphere Section (WSS), 15, June 18, 1915, Special Suffrage Edition, 3; *National Rip-Saw*, May 1915, 7, August 1915, 5–7.

61. *NYC*, June 2, 1915, 4, October18, 1914, WSS, 3; *AS*, September 26, 1914, 1.

62. *NYC*, July 29, 1915, 5, August 8, 1915, s 2, 1; *AR*, November 27, 1915, 1.

63. *NYC*, October 68, 1914, WSS, 13, April 18, 1915, 13.

64. Kate Richards O'Hare, "World Peace," in *Kate Richards O'Hare*, Philip Foner and Sally Miller, eds. (Baton Rouge: Louisiana State University Press, 1982), 160, 151–163.

65. For an analysis of O'Hare and the politics of motherhood during World War I, see especially Kennedy, *Disloyal Mothers and Scurrilous Citizens*, 18–38; Kennedy, "Declaring War on War: Gender and the American Socialist Attack on Militarism, 1914–1918," *Journal of Women's History* (Summer 1995), 27–51.

66. Mary Marcy, "Morals and War Babies," *ISR* June 1915, 719–723; Marcy, "When We Go to War," and "Better Any Kind of Action than Inert Theory," *You Have No Country*, Rosemont ed., 34–37, 25–29.

67. Mary Field, "Babes Bred for War," *ISR*, January 1915, 394–397.

68. *AR*, April 24, 1915, 2, September 19, 1914, February 20, 1915, 1; *Rebel*, October 20, 1916, 1.

69. Allan Benson to EVD, February 21, 1915, 130–131, and editorial notes; Allan Benson to EVD, March 19, 1915, 138–139; EVD to Allan Benson, March 22, 1915, 141–143; Allan Benson to EVD, March 24, 1915, 144; Allan Benson to EVD, April 1, 1915, 146–147: all in *Letters of EVD*, v 2. *AR*, September 19, 1914, 1, February 20, 1915, 1, 5, May 22, 1915, 1, July 15, 1916, 1, February 3, 1917, 1; Ernest C. Bolt, *Ballots before Bullets: The War Referendum Approach to Peace in America: 1914–1941* (Charlottsville: University Press of Virginia, 1977); Clifford, *Citizen Soldier*, 147–148.

70. *AR*, September 19, 1914, 1, February 20, 1915, 1.

71. Weinstein, *Decline of Socialism in America*, 125.

72. See especially Paterson et al., *American Foreign Relations*, 6th ed., v 1, 272, 269–275, v 2, 68–85.

73. Paterson et al., *American Foreign Relations*, v 1, 264–275; Kennedy, *Will to Believe*, 83–93.

74. *Irish World and American Industrial Liberator*, May 15, 1915, 4, February 10, 1917, 4; *Gaelic American*, May 15, 1915, 1; *Chicago Citizen*, February 9, 1917; 5 McKillen, *Chicago Labor*, 28; Leubke, *Bonds of Loyalty*, 133–134.

75. Hillquit, *Loose Leaves*, 163–165; *NYC*, May 24, 1915, 2, July 25, 1915, s 2, 1; *AR*, August 4, 1915, 1, May 22, 1915, 1; *Rebel*, May 15, 1915, 1–4.

76. *NYC*, May 11, 1915, 6, May 30, 1915, s 2, 7, June 13, 1915, s 2, 7; *Rebel*, May 15, 1915, 1–4, February 12, 1916, 1.

77. *NYC*, June 16, 1915, 2.

78. Walling, *Socialists and the War*, 466–468; *AS*, May 15, 1915, 1; Hillquit, *Loose Leaves*, 160; Miller, *Victor Berger*, 125; Weinstein, *Decline of Socialism in America*, 119–124.

79. Kennedy, *Will to Believe*, 94–96. See also Tucker, *Woodrow Wilson*, for a critical analysis of Wilson's ideas about security.

80. EVD to *New York Sun*, November 29, 1915, 204–205, and EVD to Upton Sinclair, January 12, 1916, 227, both in *Letters of EVD*, v 2.

81. *AR*, October 9, 1915, 1, July 15, 1916, 1.

82. *AR*, October 9, 1915, 1, July 15, 1916, 1, May 27, 1916, 4, June 7, 1916, 4.

83. Paterson et al., *American Foreign Relations*, 6th ed., v 2, 82–85; Kennedy, *Will to Believe*, 104–127.

84. *AR*, October 28, 1916, 4.

85. *AR*, July 15, 1916, 1.

86. Ibid. *AS*, October 21, 1916, 4.

87. *AR*, February 3, 1917, 1; Miller, *Victor Berger*, 136–137; Weinstein, *Decline of Socialism in America*, 114–125; Salvatore, *Eugene V. Debs: Citizen and Socialist*, 280; Knock, *To End All Wars*, 18–19, 101–102.

88. Knock, *To End All Wars*, 15–69, 101.

Chapter 3. Antiwar Cultures of the AFL, the Debate over Preparedness, and the Gompers Turnabout

1. *SUR*, September 25, 1915, 6.

2. Ibid. *SUR*, November 18, 1915, 3.

3. *SUR*, September 4, 1915, 1–3, "Minutes, Central Labor Council of Seattle and Vicinity," August 25, 1915, 34, in King County Central Labor Council Records at the University of Washington, Seattle, Washington (hereafter, "Minutes," CLCS).

4. "Minutes," CLCS, May 10, 1916, 107; *SUR*, January 13, 1917, 7, February 24, 1917, 7.

5. See especially "Minutes," CLCS, June 16, 1915, 18, July 28, 1915, 27.

6. On working-class Americanism, see Gary Gerstle, *Working-Class Americanism: The Politics of Labor in a Textile City, 1914–1960* (Cambridge: Cambridge University Press, 1989).

7. "Report of the Executive Council at the Philadelphia Convention," AFL, *Labor and the War*, 3–10.

8. Foner, *History of the Labor Movement*, v 7, 44; Gompers, *Seventy Years*, v 2, 322–326, 339, 359; Montgomery, "Workers' Movements in the United States Confront Imperialism," 28–36.

9. Woods to Gompers, September 20, 1915, and Gompers to Wood, October 6, 1915, in Robert Cuff, "Samuel Gompers, Leonard Wood and Military Preparedness," *Labor History* (Spring 1971), 280–288; Larson, *Labor and Foreign Policy*, 69; Clifford, *Citizen Soldier*, 157.

10. *American Federationist*, January 1916, 48, and March 1916, 174–180; Chambers, *To Raise an Army*, 128; McKillen, *Chicago Labor*, 65.

11. "Minutes of Executive Council Meeting," March 9, 1917, in *SGP*, v 10, 23–28.

12. McKillen, *Chicago Labor*, 11–12.

13. *SUR*, March 31, 1917, 1; Dana Frank, *Purchasing Power: Consumer Organizing, Gender and the Seattle Labor Movement, 1919–1929* (Cambridge: Cambridge University Press, 1994), 15–25.

14. Strouthous, *U.S. Labor and Political Action*, 78; Frank, *Purchasing Power*, 15–18; Janice Reiff, "Urbanization and the Social Structure: Seattle, Washington, 1852–1910" (PhD diss., University of Washington, 1981); Frank Miyamoto, *Social Solidarity among the Japanese in Seattle*, 1st ed., 1931, repr., Seattle: University of Washington Press, 1981); Yuji Ichioka, *The Issei: The World of the First Generation Japanese Immigrants, 1885–1924* (New York: Free Press, 1988).

15. David Roediger, *Wages of Whiteness: Race and the Making of the American Working Class* (New York: Verso, 1991), 65–92.

16. *SUR*, February 26, 1916, 7, January 30, 1915, 4, November 30, 1915, 4; "Minutes," CLCS, February 28, 1917, March 4, 1917, March 28, 1917, 191–198.

17. *SUR*, May 26, 1917, 1.

18. *SUR*, August 8, 1914, 1.

19. *SUR*, November 28, 1914, 4, 1, November 21, 1914, 1.

20. *SUR*, June 12, 1915, 4, May 22, 1915, 1.

21. On "paytriots" see *SUR*, October 20, 1917, 4. For the response to Wilson, see *SUR*, January 1, 1916, 1, May 20, 1916, 1; "Minutes," CLCS, May 24, 1916, 110–111, February 7, 1917, 184, February 21, 1917, 188, March 28, 1917, 198.

22. On Mexico, see *SUR*, July 1, 1916, 4, July 5, 1916, 1, July 15, 1916, 1, September 9, 1916, 1.

23. *SUR*, November 18, 1915, 3.

24. *SUR*, May 22, 1915, 2.

25. "Minutes," CLCS, March 28, 1917, 198.

26. *SUR*, March 31, 1917, 1.

27. McKillen, *Chicago Labor*, 4, and chap. 1; John M. Allswang, *A House for All Peoples: Ethnic Politics in Chicago, 1890–1936* (Lexington: University of Kentucky Press, 1971), 21; David Montgomery, "Immigrants, Industrial Unions, and Social Reconstruction in the United States, 1916–1923," *Labour/Le travail* 13 (1984), 101–113. See also James Barrett, *Work and Community in the Jungle: Chicago's Packinghouse Workers, 1894–1922* (Urbana: University of Illinois Press, 1987).

28. McKillen, *Chicago Labor*, 14, 44–55; Barrett, *Work and Community in the Jungle*, 191. See also Chicago Federation of Labor, "Chicago Federation of Labor Minutes" (m. ed.) (CFL, "Minutes") and the John Fitzpatrick papers (FP) at the Chicago Historical Society.

29. John Fitzpatrick, Speech to the First Convention of the American Association for the Recognition of the Irish Republic, n.d., B11-F78, FP.

30. CFL, "Minutes," May 21, 1916, 18–19; McKillen, *Chicago Labor*, 51; *Regeneración*, May 16, 1914, 4.

31. AFL, *Labor and the War*, 12; McKillen, *Chicago Labor*, 52.

32. *Gaelic American*, February 20, 1915, 4; *Irish World and American Industrial Liberator*, May 15, 1915, 4.

33. CFL, "Minutes," May 16, 1915, June 20, 1915, 18–19.

34. *SUR*, January 8, 1916, 1.

35. CFL, "Minutes," February 6, 1916, 12–17, April 16, 1916, 10–11, May 16, 1916, 10–11, May 21, 1916, 4; *SUR*, February 19, 1916, 3.

36. CFL, "Minutes," February 6, 1916, 17, April 16, 1916, 10–11.

37. CFL, "Minutes," April 16, 1916, 20–11, May 21, 1916, 10–11, 14–16, January 7, 1917, 10–17.

38. CFL, "Minutes," May 21, 1916, 18–19.

39. See especially Friends of Irish Freedom to Fitzpatrick, 1916, B5, FP; Resolutions Passed at the Mass Meeting of the Friends of Irish Freedom, General John Stark Branch at St. Annes, B9-F56, FP.

40. Telegram, Fitzpatrick and Ed Nockels to Gompers, February 4, 1917, CC-GMC; CFL, "Minutes," February 8, 1917.

41. Foner, *History of the Labor Movement in The United States*, v 7, 40–77; "Minutes," SCLC, June 6, 1915, 18.

42. Richard Jensen, "United Mine Workers of America," in *Encyclopedia of U.S. Labor and Working-Class History*, v 3 (London: Routledge Press, 2007), 1430–1434; *United Mine Workers Journal (UMWJ)*, November 26, 1914, 4–5, December 13, 1914, 2; Montgomery, *Fall of the House of Labor*, 356–365.

43. On the militia and Boy Scouts issue, see especially *UMWJ*, March 19, 1914, 4, December 3, 1914, 30, May 24, 1917, 4; John W. Hevener, "John P. White," in *Biographical Dictionary of American Labor*, Gary Fink, ed. (Westport, Conn.: Greenwood Press, 1974), 582–583. On the other antiwar positions of the UMWA, see especially *UMWJ*, August 13, 1914, 8, August 27, 1914, September 3, 1914, 1, November 26, 1914, 4, June 13, 1915, 15, March 9, 1916, 4. On the coal wars, see Montgomery, *Fall of the House of Labor*, 333–347.

44. *UMWJ*, May 28, 1914, 4, June 8, 1916, 9.

45. *UMWJ*, June 8, 1916, 9.

46. Ibid.

47. *UMWJ*, July 19, 1915, 1, October 28, 1915, 1.

48. *UMWJ*, January 27, 1916, 19, October 5, 1916, 19, January 4, 1917, 19. Thanks to Alex Grab for translations from Italian to English.

49. *NYT*, May 15, 1915; *UMWJ*, June 13, 1915, 15.

50. *Indianapolis Star*, May 28, 1915; *New York Times*, May 15, 1915; *UMWJ*, June 3, 1915, 10, June 13, 1915, 10; Montgomery, *Fall of the House of Labor*, 359; Larson, *Labor and Foreign Policy*, 52–53.

51. *UMWJ*, November 23, 1915, 4, December 21, 1916, 7, June 6, 1915, 4 (Mexico), February 1, 1917, 4.

52. *Ladies Garment Worker*, August 1914, 22, October 1915, 25; Nancy MacLean, "Juliet Stuart Poyntz," *Encyclopedia of the American Left*, 631–632.

53. For general background on the International Ladies' Garment Workers' Union, see Paul Buhle, "International Ladies Garment Workers Union," *Encyclopedia of the American Left*, 370–373; Kenneth C. Wolensky, "International Ladies' Garment Workers' Union," *Encyclopedia of U.S. Labor and Working-Class History*, v 2, 679–682; Gus Tyler, *Look for the Union Label: A History of the International Ladies' Garment Workers'*

Union (Armonk, N.Y.: M. E. Sharpe, 1995); Ruth Waldinger, *Through the Eye of the Needle* (New York: New York University Press, 1986); Kenneth C. Wolensky, Nicole H. Wolensky, and Robert P. Wolensky, *Fighting for the Union Label* (University Park: Pennsylvania State University Press, 2002).

54. Robin Miller Jacoby, *The British and American Women's Trade Union Leagues, 1890–1925* (New York: Carlson Publishing, 1994), xxiii. See also Elizabeth Anne Payne, *Reform, Labor, and Feminism: Margaret Dreier Robins and the Women's Trade Union League* (Urbana: University of Illinois Press, 1988).

55. See, for example, *NYT*, November 26, 1912, 3. O'Reilly emphasized that college women should not try to correct the grammar of working girls or "boss us."

56. Leonora O'Reilly, "Report on the International Congress of Women at the Hague," in *Proceedings of the Fifth Biennial Convention of the National Women's Trade Union League of America*, 6; O'Reilly, "Industrial Democracy," in *The Woman Voter*, June 1915, both in Leonora O'Reilly papers at Schlesinger Library, Radcliffe College, Boston (hereafter, OP), R9. *Life and Labor* (*LL*), paper of the Women's Trade Union League), April 15, 1915, 65, June 1915, 112–113, July 1915, 116–117; *NYT*, April 11, 1915, C 3.

57. *LL*, October 1914, 315; Jane Addams, *Peace and Bread in Time of War* (New York: King's Crown Press, 1945), 7. Harriet Hyman Alonso, *Peace as a Women's Issue: A History of the U.S. Movement for World Peace and Women's Rights* (Syracuse: Syracuse University Press, 1993), 66–69; Leila Rupp, *Worlds of Women: The Making of an International Women's Movement* (Princeton: Princeton University Press, 1997), 45–52.

58. *Ladies Garment Worker*, November 1914, 1, 4–5.

59. *Ladies Garment Worker*, November 1915, 6–8, December 1915, 5.

60. *Ladies Garment Worker*, December 1914, 12; John Holmes, "American Jewish Communism and Garment Unionism in the 1920s," *American Communist History* 6 (2007), 177; Tony Michels, *A Fire in Their Hearts: Yiddish Socialists in New York* (Cambridge: Harvard University Press, 2005).

61. *Ladies Garment Worker*, December 1916, 4–7.

62. AFL, *Proceedings*, 1916, 232, 303–311; *SUR*, November 25, 1916, 1.

63. Gompers, "Address before Fifty Fourth Annual Convention of the New York State Federation of Labor, August 31, 1917," in Gompers, *American Labor and the War* (New York: George H. Doran and Co., 1919), 93.

64. *American Federationist*, May 1917, 357; Montgomery, *Fall of the House of Labor*, 360; AFL, Executive Council Report, in AFL, *Labor and the War*, 12.

65. Statement of Samuel Gompers, in "Excerpts from the Minutes of a Meeting of the Executive Council of the AFL, March 9, 1917," *SGP*, v 10, 33; Gompers to Newton Baker, January 9, 1917, 1–2; CC-GMC, Gompers to Executive Council, September 15, 1916, CC-GMC; Gompers to Newton Baker, June 12, 1917, in *American Federationist*, July 1917, 543–544; AFL, *Proceedings*, 1916, 109; Gompers, "Anti-Disloyalty Mass Meeting in Carnegie Hall," November 2, 1917, in Gompers, American *Labor and the War*,135.

66. John White to Gompers, March 3, 1917, CC-GMC; Gompers to Executive Council, February 28, 1917, CC-GMC; "Minutes Conference in Executive Council Room,"

March 6, 1917, Conf. Collection-GMC; William Z. Foster, *History of the Communist Party of the United States* (New York: International Publishers, 1952), 132.

67. "Excerpts from the Minutes of a Meeting of the Executive Council of the AFL," March 9, 1917, in *SGP*, v 10, 23–29.

68. "Excerpts," *SGP*, v 10, 29–33.

69. "Excerpts," *SGP*, v 10, 32–39.

70. "Labor's Position in Peace or in War," *SGP*, v 10, 39–45.

71. *American Federationist*, April 1917, 269; James Duncan to Gompers, March 17, 1917, CC-GMC; *Chicago American*, March 13, 1917, 1; March 14, 1917, 1; Foner, *Labor and the War*, v 7, 102–103. See also Larson, *Labor and Foreign Policy*, 77–89; Radosh, *American Labor and United States Foreign Policy*, 54–71.

72. Tobin to Gompers, March 30, 1917, CC-GMC.

73. See, for example, E. J. Bicket, IAM Lodge 379, to Gompers, March 24, 1917, CC-GMC; Jim Rothberg, Wage Earner, to Gompers, March 14, 1917, CC-GMC; "Minutes," CLCS, April 4, 1917, 200; *SUR*, April 14, 1917, 1.

74. CFL, "Minutes," April 1, 1917, 23–44, April 15, 1917, 4–5, May 20, 1917, 14–15; McKillen, *Chicago Labor*, 77–79.

75. Gerald Horne, "Who Lost the Cold War? Africans and African Americans," *Diplomatic History* 20 (Fall 1996), 619, 613–626.

Part III. U.S. Belligerency

1. For a summary of these issues see especially Link, *Woodrow Wilson: Revolution, War and Peace*, 47–71; Paterson et al., *American Foreign Relations*, 6th ed., v 1, 264–301; Kennedy, *Will to Believe*, 128–162.

2. Wilson's war speech, in AFL, *Labor and the War*, 56–63. The AFL included the speech in its entirety in their book on the war because they wanted "to aid in immortalizing it." See also *Congressional Record*, LV (April 2, 1917), Part 1, 102–104.

3. Theodore Roosevelt, quoted in Mayer, *Political Origins of the New Diplomacy*, 344–345. On the Socialist Party, see their manifesto on the war, published in *AS*, April 21, 1917, 1.

4. "Wilson Proclaims U.S. War Aims: The Fourteen Points, 1918," in Dennis Merrill and Thomas G. Paterson, *Major Problems in American Foreign Relations, V1: To 1920*, 7th ed. (Boston: Cengage Learning, 2010), 433–435; Throntveit, "Fable of the Fourteen Points," 445–481; Manela, *Wilsonian Moment*, 37–42; Lloyd Ambrosius, *Wilsonianism: Woodrow Wilson and His Legacy for American Foreign Relations* (New York: Palgrave Macmillan, 2002), 51–64, 125–134.

5. Ibid. Williams, *Tragedy of American Diplomacy*, 58–107. Williams and other revisionists argued that American policymakers first began to promote an "Open Door" approach to international politics in the late nineteenth century when they sought access to markets and investments in China. By World War I, they sought to internationalize their ideas about the virtues of freer trade among nations. Yet free trade, as this school of diplomatic historians pointed out, tends to benefit the

strongest economic power at the expense of those less able to compete. For this reason, the United States maintained high tariff barriers for much of the nineteenth century when it was developing its industrial infrastructure.

6. Kennedy, *Will to Believe*, 128–159; Mayer, *Political Origins of the New Diplomacy*, 36, 220, 388–389.

7. Dawley, *Changing the World*, 237.

Chapter 4. Dialectical Relationships

1. Report of Special Diplomatic Mission to Russia to Secretary of State, *FRUS*, 1918, Russia, v 1, 131–146; *NYT*, May 16, 1917, 2, May 12, 1917, 9, June 19, 1917, 3. Gompers Memo, January 11, 1918, *SGP*, v 10, 310–311. On the decision to appoint Duncan, see Gompers to Wilson, May 4, 1917, 763.72/4391-1/2, v 351, RG59, NARA.

2. James Duncan, "Report on the Diplomatic Mission to Russia," AFL, *Proceedings*, 1917, 326, 334, 323–346.

3. Ibid., 327.

4. "Report of the Committee on International Relations," 1917, in AFL, *Labor and War*, 72–73.

5. *AS*, May 12, 1917, 1, May 26, 1917, 4; *AR*, May 5, 1917, 1; Letter to Charles Edward Russell from Victor Berger, May 15, 1917, BP.

6. *Solidarity*, August 14, 1917, 2; *Industrial Worker* (*IW*), October 13, 1917, 8, January 5, 1918, 2, September 22, 1917, 2; *Seattle Daily Call* (*SDC*), December 2, 1917, 1.

7. Mother Jones to John H. Walker, n.d. circa 1917, *Correspondence of Mother Jones*, Edward Steel, ed. (Pittsburgh: University of Pittsburgh Press, 1985), 178–180; "Minutes," CLCS, December 11, 1918, 357.

8. Walter Lippmann to Edward Mandell House, October 17, 1917, *PWW*, v 44, 393–394; Knock, *To End All Wars*, viii–x, 135–137.

9. *AS*, April 14, 1917, 1.

10. *AS*, April 21, 1917, 1. See also "Wilson's War Message to Congress," World War I Document Archive, http://wwi.lib.byu.edu (accessed August 26, 2011).

11. Ibid. *AR*, June 23, 1917, 4.

12. Ibid. Shannon, *Socialist Party*, 97. For a discussion of the divisions within the convention by an insider, see Hillquit to Ni and La, April 10, 1917, HP.

13. For Baker's views of Hillquit as well as Lansing's meeting with Hillquit, see Robert Lansing to the President, May 19, 1917, *PWW*, v 42, 350. On the concerns of President Wilson and others about how Gompers or other close AFL associates might be received by Russian Socialists, see Woodrow Wilson to Mr. Secretary, April 19, 1917, and E. M. House to Governor [President Wilson], April 20, 1917, *PWW*, v 42, 95, 110–111.

14. William English Walling to William B. Wilson, May 2, 1917, enclosed in a letter to President Wilson from Robert Lansing, May 3, 1917, 763.724390-1/2, v 351, RG59, NARA.

15. President Wilson to Robert Lansing, May 3, 1917, 763.724390-1/2, v 351, RG 59, NARA. William English Walling to William Bauchop Wilson, May 2, 1917, *PWW*,

v 42, 197–199; Lansing to President Wilson, May 7, 1917, with enclosure from Frank Lyon Polk to Lansing, May 7, 1917, *PWW*, v 42, 239–240; President Wilson to Walling, May 14, 1917, *PWW*, v 42, 291; Wilson to Lansing, May 14, 1917, *PWW*, v 42, 289.

16. Radosh, *American Labor and United States Foreign Policy*, 85.

17. Consul at Petrograd (Winship) to Secretary of State, May 15, 1917, *FRUS*, Russia, 1918, v 1, 55. AFL Executive Council to "all who have aided in establishing liberty in Russia," in letter from Samuel Gompers to Robert Lansing to be conveyed to Mr. Nstcheidze, April 23, 1917, 861.328, v 1276, RG 59, NARA. For Pravda editorial, see Radosh, *American Labor and United States Foreign Policy*, 93.

18. Gompers to James Duncan, relayed via telegram from the Secretary of State to the Ambassador in Russia (Francis), June 28, 1917, *FRUS*, 1917, supplement (s) 2, v 1, 745.

19. Gompers Address to 54th Annual Convention of the New York State Federation of Labor, August 29, 1917, in *SGP*, v 10, 196; Gompers to Appleton, January 9, 1918, *SGP*, v 10, 309; AFL, Committee on International Relations Report, 1917, AFL, *Labor and the War*, 74; Gompers, *Seventy Years*, v 2, 401.

20. Russell to Lansing, May 15, 1917, *PWW*, 42, 350–351; Lansing to President, with enclosure from Walling, May 17, 1917, *PWW*, 42, 318–319; Walling to William B. Wilson, May 3, 1917, 763.724390-1/2, RG 59, NARA (quote).

21. Hillquit to Lansing, May 10, 1917, *PWW*, 42, 268; Lansing to the Ambassador in Great Britain Page, August 7, 1917, *FRUS*, 1917, S2, v 1, 752; "Report of the Executive Council on International Relations, 1917," AFL, *Labor and the War*, 52; William Kerry, State Department to Berger, May 23, 1917, BP; Hillquit, *Loose Leaves*, 155–157; *AS*, June 2, 1917, 1.

22. *AS*, April 21, 1917, 1, 3, May 26, 1917, 1. Gilbert Fite and H. C. Peterson, *Opponents of War: 1917–1918* (Seattle: University of Washington Press, 1957), 23.

23. *AS*, May 26, 1917, 1, June 16, 1917, 1; *AR*, June 9, 1917, 1; *New York Times (NYT)*, June 8, 19, 1917, 1; Gerald Edwin Shenk, *Race, Gender and the Draft in World War I* (New York: Palgrave Macmillan, 2005), 155; Jeanette Keith, *Rich Man's War, Poor Man's Fight: Race, Class and Power in the Rural South during the First World War* (Chapel Hill: University of North Carolina Press, 2004); Christopher Capozzola, *Uncle Sam Wants You: World War I and the Making of the Modern American Citizen* (Oxford: Oxford University Press), 30; Chang, *Color of the Land*, 185–186.

24. Steven Vaughn, *Holding Fast the Inner Lines: Democracy, Nationalism and the Committee on Public Information* (Chapel Hill: University of North Carolina Press, 1980), xi; Leslie Midkiff Debauche, *Reel Patriotism: The Movies and World War I* (Madison: University of Wisconsin Press, 1997); Zeiger, "She Didn't Raise Her Boy to Be a Slacker," 7–39; Robert Zieger, *America's Great War: World War I and the American Experience* (Lanham, Md.: Rowman and Littlefield, 2000), 83.

25. *AR*, March 17, 1917, 4; June 9, 1917, 3; McKillen, "Pacifist Brawn and Silk Stocking Militarism," 413; Kathleen Kennedy, "Declaring War on War," 27–51; Keith, *Rich Man's War, Poor Man's Fight*, 85–86.

26. *AS*, July 30, 1917, 1 (quote); Grubbs, *Struggle for Labor Loyalty*, 22–34, Dawley; *Changing the World*, 167–169; *NYT*, June 1, 1917, 1, June 15, 1917, 8; June 16, 1917, 1,

June 21, 1917, 1; *AR*, June 16, 1917, 2; David Kennedy, *Over Here: The First World War and American Society* (Oxford: Oxford University Press, 1980), 26.

27. (David) Kennedy, *Over Here*, 26; (Kathleen) Kennedy, *Disloyal Mothers and Scurrilous Citizens*, 18–19; Reports of Commanding Officer, Neutrality Squad to Corps of Intelligence Police, February 21, 1918, R 6-Frame 138; P. E. Merrinan, Report from Boise Idaho, July 15 and July 30, 1917, R 6-Frames 135–136, and Gordon Johnson to Assistant Chief of Staff, Intelligence, Sixth Corps Area, October 21, 1920, R6-Frames 124–125: all in *U.S. Military Intelligence Reports: Surveillance of Radicals in the United States, 1917–1941*; Adam Hodges, "'Enemy Aliens and Silk Stocking Girls': The Politics of Class Internment in the Drive for Urban Order during World War I," *Journal of the Gilded Age and Progressive Era*, 6 (2007), 431–458.

28. Lippman to the President, October 8, 1917, 333–334; Lippman to House, October 17, 1917, 393–394; Herbert Croly to the President, October 19, 1917, 408–410; Wilson to Burleson, October 23, 1917, 428; Wilson to Attorney General (Thomas Gregory), October 29, 1917, 463, all in *PWW*, v 44.

29. T. W. Gregory to Wilson, November 3, 1917, *PWW*, v 44, 504.

30. Chambers, *To Raise an Army*, 208; Weinstein, *Decline of Socialism in America*, 145–149; Nathan Fine, *Labor and Farmer Parties in the United States, 1828–1928* (New York: Russell and Russell, 1961 [1928]), 225–226.

31. Gompers to Advisory Commission, April 5, 1917, in GLB-GMC; "Resolution Adopted at Meeting of Executive Committee, Labor Committee—Conservation of Health and Welfare of Workers," April 5, 1917, B 331, RG 62, NARA. For an example of a favorable response, see "Newark Labor Council in Ohio to Gompers," March 29, 1917, B 331. For the far more numerous unfavorable responses, see especially letter from Wm. Green to Gompers, April 23, 1917, B 331, RG 62, NARA. See also Montgomery, *Fall of the House of Labor*, 375; McCartin, *Labor's Great War*; Zieger, *America's Great War*, 118.

32. Franklin Lane to President, November 3, 1917, *PWW*, v 44, 498–501. See Montgomery, *Fall of the House of Labor*, 370, for a historical analysis of increased strike activity.

33. Newton Baker to the President, September 7, 1917, enclosing a memo from Felix Frankfurter, September 4, 1917, *PWW*, v 44, 161–162.

34. *Solidarity*, February 17, 1917, 2. See also *Solidarity*, December 18, 1915, 2.

35. *Solidarity*, March 24, 1917, 1–2; *IW*, August 25, 1917, 2.

36. Dubofsky, *We Shall Be All*, 353–355; Shor, "The IWW and Oppositional Politics," 81–83; Bill Haywood, *The Autobiography of Big Bill Haywood* (New York: International Publishers, 1929), 295–299; *Solidarity*, April 7, 1917, 2, May 12, 1917, 2.

37. Ibid. *Solidarity*, May 12, 1917, 2 (quote), June 6, 1917, 2; Green, *Grass-Roots Socialism*, 360–366.

38. Dubofsky, *We Shall Be All*, 349–359. See also Elizabeth Gurley Flynn, *The Rebel Girl: An Autobiography* (New York: International Publishers, 1955), 217–276.

39. Dubofsky, *We Shall Be All*, 365–371; Montgomery, *Fall of the House of Labor*, 370.

40. Shor, "The IWW and Oppositional Politics," 75–94; Shor, "'Virile Syndicalism' in Comparative Perspective: A Gender Analysis of the IWW in the United States and Australia," *International Labor and Working-Class History* 56 (Fall 1999), 65–77.

41. *IW*, April 1, 1916, 1–2; February 24, 1917, 2.

42. See, for example, *Solidarity*, October 31, 1914, 3, November 21, 1914, 2.

43. Haywood, *Autobiography*, 294–295; Dubofsky, *We Shall Be All*, 355; Shor, "The IWW and Oppositional Politics," 82.

44. *IW*, June 23, 1917, 2.

45. *Solidarity*, January 27, 1917, 2; *IW*, July 7, 1917, 4; see also note 6.

46. Newton Baker to the President, September 7, 1917, enclosing a memo from Felix Frankfurter, September 4, 1917, *PWW*, v 44, 161–162. James R. Barrett, *Work and Community in the Jungle: Chicago's Packinghouse Workers, 1894–1922* (Urbana: University of Illinois Press, 1987), 188–239; McKillen, *Chicago Labor*.

47. Montgomery, *Fall of the House of Labor*, 370–371.

48. Ibid. McCartin, *Labor's Great War*, 100; McKillen, *Chicago Labor*.

49. Grubbs, *Struggle for Labor Loyalty*, 35–45 (quote 45); Wilson to Gompers, August 31, 1917, *PWW*, v 44, 95–102; Gompers, *Seventy Years of Life and Labor*, v 2, 378; Creel to Gompers, July 26, 1917, *SGP*, v 10, 156–157; *American Federationist*, October 1917, 837–838.

50. Chairman, AALD, to Robert Maisel, August 2, 1917, and Maisel to Gompers, October 6, 1917, CC-GMC.

51. "The Declaration of Principles Adopted by the American Alliance for Labor and Democracy Convention in Minneapolis," September 7, 1917, in *SGP*, v 10, 210–213; Gompers, *Seventy Years*, v 2, 380–384; AFL, *Proceedings*, 1917, 95–97.

52. See especially Gompers address, "Americans Fight for the Preservation of Democracy," speech before the AALD meeting in Minneapolis, September 7, 1917; "Antidisloyalty Meeting in Carnegie Hall," November 2, 1917, and "In Canada for Victory," Canadian Victory Loan Meeting, November 28, 1917; Gompers, *American Labor and the War*, 110, 135, 146–154; AALD Resolution on Small Nationalities, September 7, 1917, GMC.

53. AFL, *Proceedings*, 1917, 283–314.

54. Ibid., 289–296.

55. Ibid., 284–314. McKillen, *Chicago Labor*, 84–85; Maurer to Gompers, October 12, 1917, *SGP*, v 10, 240; Shannon, *Socialist Party of America*, 118; Grubbs, *Struggle for Labor Loyalty*, 93–100.

56. Lansing to Petrograd Embassy, transmitting cable of Samuel Gompers, May 7, 1917, 861.00/328, v 1276, RG 59, NARA.

Chapter 5. The AFL, International Labor Politics, and Labor Dissent in 1918

1. Gompers to Wilson, February 9, 1918, *PWW*, v 46, 310–313.

2. Wilson to Mr. Secretary, February 13, 1918, *PWW*, v 46, 334; Lansing to My

Dear Mr. President, February 15, 1918, *PWW*, 46, 349–350. Mayer, *Political Origins of the New Diplomacy*, 192–249.

3. Dawley, *Changing the World*, 186.

4. Henry Pelling, *A History of British Trade Unions*, 2d ed. (Middlesex, Britain: Pelican Books, 1971), 149; F. M. Leventhal, *Arthur Henderson* (Manchester: Manchester University Press, 1989), 49–78; Peter Stansky, *The Left and War: The British Labour Party and World War I* (Oxford: Oxford University Press, 1969). On Gompers's and the AFL's close relationship with the GFTU, see especially Gompers to Appleton, January 9,1918, *SGP*, v 10, 309; and "Report of the American Federation of Labor Delegates to the Inter-Allied Conference League held in England, September 10, 1917, to the Buffalo Convention, November 1917," in AFL, *Labor and the War*, 77.

5. Leventhal, *Arthur Henderson*, 53.

6. Henderson to "Jack" [J. Gilbert Dale], June 19, 1917; Henderson to "Ralph," [R. W. Raine Esq., J. P.], June 19, 1917, Reel (R) 16, 1, 28–30, Henderson Papers (Hen. P), Series (S) 3-Part (P) 9A Archives of the British Labour Party (ABLP), microfilm edition (m. ed.).

7. Henderson to G. H. Roberts, June 21, 1917, R 16, 1/31, Hen. P; British Labour Party, "Report of the Executive Committee," 1918, in *Report of the Seventeenth Annual Conference of the Labour Party*, 1918, 3–11 (m. ed.); Address of the Right Hon. Arthur Henderson at a Special Party Conference, August 10, 1917, in Labour Party, *Report of the Annual Conference*, 1918 (m. ed.), 49–51; Leventhal, *Arthur Henderson*, 66 (quote); Mayer, *Political Origins of the New Diplomacy*, 44.

8. Pelling, *A History of Trade Unionism*, 149–159; Leventhal, *Arthur Henderson*, 64–78. See also James Hinton, *The First Shop Stewards' Movement* (London: George Allen and Unwin, 1973).

9. Dawley, *Changing the World*, 174.

10. Ibid., 155–156, 237–243.

11. "Statement of War Aims of the British Labour Party," December 28, 1917, in Stansky, *The Left and War: The British Labour Party and World War I*, 318–326; Mayer, *Political Origins of the New Diplomacy*, 315–321.

12. Mayer, *Political Origins of the New Diplomacy*, 387–388.

13. "The Fourteen Points, 1918," in Dennis Merrill and Thomas G. Paterson, eds., *Major Problems in American Foreign Relations*, 5th ed., v 2 (Boston: Houghton Mifflin, 2000), 41; Kennedy, *Will to Believe*, 132.

14. Mayer, *Political Origins of the New Diplomacy*, 353–354.

15. Telegram from British Trades and Labour Party and Arthur Henderson to Gompers, January 1, 1918, R5, JSM1-16; J. S. Middleton Papers (MP), in S3-P9A, ABLP (m. ed.); Henderson to Gompers, January 16, 1918; Gompers to Henderson, February 18, 1918, in AFL, *Labor and the War*, 91.

16. Mayer, *Political Origins of the New Diplomacy*, 388–389; "Inter-Allied Labour War Aims," in Arthur Henderson, *The Aims of Labour* (New York: B. W. Heuebsch, 1918), 99–110; Ambassador Page to Secretary of State, March 1, 1918, enclosing a

report from F. M. Gunther, "Memorandum on War Aims," adopted by the Inter-Allied Labor and Socialist Conference at London, February 23, 1918, *FRUS, Supplement 1: The World War*, 1918, 154–167; Ambassador Page to Colonel House, March 1, 1918, 763.72119 S076, B 7054, RG 59, NARA; British Labour Party, *The Labour Party Memoranda on the International Meeting*, R8, LPIAC, Memos and Docs, 1–80, S3-P8, ABLP (m. ed.).

17. Wilson to House, March 22, 1918, *PWW*, v 47, 105–106; Lansing to Wilson, February 15, 1918, *PWW*, v 46, 349–350; Diary of Josephus Daniels, March 18, 1918, *PWW*, v 46, 581–582; Ambassador Sharp to the President and Secretary of State, March 19, 1918, *PWW*, v 47, 73–77; Mayer, *Political Origins of the New Diplomacy*, 388–389.

18. Ibid.

19. Eugene Debs to Adolph Germer, April 8, 1918, in *Letters of EVD*, v 2, 397; Allen Ricker to House, April 31, 1918, *PWW*, v 47, 471; President to Joseph Tumulty, December 18, 1917, enclosing a letter from James Hamilton Lewis to the President, December 13, 1917, *PWW*, v 45, 318–319; Salvatore, *Eugene V. Debs*, 289–290.

20. Geoffrey Butler, British Pictorial Services, to Agnes Nestor, February 21, 1918, R 2, in Agnes Nestor Papers (ANP), original collection at the Chicago Historical Society (m. ed.), in the Women's Trade Union League Papers at Schlesinger Library, Radcliffe Institute for Advanced Studies; John P. Frey, "The Reminiscences of John P. Frey," 1957, v 2, 326–327, in the Columbia University Oral History Collection, Butler Library, Columbia University, New York.

21. AFL, *Proceedings*, 1918, 52, AFL to Fellow Workers, announcing the members of the mission, March 25, 1918, R2, ANP; Agnes Nestor, *Woman's Labor Leader: An Autobiography of Agnes Nestor* (Rockford: Bellevue Books, 1954), 185.

22. M. D. Robins to Agnes Nestor, February 4, 1918, R2-ANP; Olive Sullivan to Agnes Nestor, February 2, 1918, R2-ANP. On Nestor's personal excitement about the trip, see especially her letters sent from Britain and France, April 1918, R2, ANP, and Nestor, *Woman's Labor Leader*, 184–221.

23. Gompers to Nestor, March 18, 1918, ANP, R2; "Report of the Labor Mission to Great Britain and France," adopted at the St. Paul Convention of the AFL in 1918, in AFL, *Labor and the War*, 107, and in AFL, *Proceedings*, 1918, 138–141.

24. Report of the Conference at AFL Headquarters, including typescript of Gompers's speech, March 28, 1918, 5–19, R2, ANP, 5–19.

25. "Report of the Labor Mission to Great Britain and France, 1918," AFL, *Labor and the War*, 112–115; Frey, "Reminiscences," 326–355.

26. Agnes Nestor to Mary [Nestor?] April 13, April 15, April 30, and May 10, May 17, May 19, 1918; Nestor to Olive [Sullivan?], April 18, 1918, and May 10, 1918; United Irish League to Nestor, April 25, 1918, Cumann na mBan Executive to Nestor, May 19, 1918, all in R2-ANP; Nestor, *Woman's Labor Leader*, 184–221; Frey, "Reminiscences," v 2, 326–355.

27. *Chicago Daily News* clipping, June 5, 1918, and poster for American Labor Mission Presentation in Chicago, in R 2, ANP; photo in Nestor, *Woman's Labor Leader*, 190, 190–221; anonymous clippings, May 1918, R 2, ANP.

28. "Report of the Labor Mission to Great Britain and France," 104–122.

29. AFL, *Proceedings*, 1918, 151. See press reports of the AFL convention in *SGP*, v 10, 469–471.

30. Appleton to Gompers, May 15, 1918, *SGP*, v10, 445–446; Adolph Germer to Eugene Debs, enclosing a letter from J. Ramsey MacDonald, June 5, 1918, in *Letters of EVD*, v 2, 428–429.

31. For the Debs speech, see Tussey, *Eugene V. Debs Speaks*, 243–279.

32. *New Republic*, June 15, 1918, 190–193, 206–207.

33. Ibid.

34. Gompers to the Toilers of America, April 8, 1918, *SGP*, v 10, 413–414; *SUR*, July 6, 1918, 1; Montgomery, *Fall of the House of Labor*, 386.

35. British Labour Party, "Report of the Executive Committee," 1918, 3. See, for example, British Labour Party, Minutes of the Meetings of the Advisory Committee on International Relations, June 14, 1918, 1, 5, July 5, 1918, 1, 8, September 27, 1918, October 22, 1918, R7, S3-P8, ABLB (m. ed.). See also British Labour party, "Memos and Documents of the Labour Party International Affairs Committee," 2, 1918–1919, 1–160, R 8, S3-P8, ABLP (m. ed.).

36. Arthur Henderson, "A Letter to American Workers," *Atlantic Monthly*, 122 (September 1918), 301–302; Alfred Gardiner, "Mr. Henderson and the Labor Movement," *Atlantic Monthly* 122 (August 1918), 221–230.

37. Ibid. Arthur Henderson, "A New International Order," *Yale Review* NS7 (July 1918), 676–687; Henderson, *League of Nations and Labor* (Oxford: Oxford University Press, 1918), 4–13; *NYT*, February 21, 1918, 3, May 26, 1918, July 14, 1918, 7.

38. Gompers, *Seventy Years*, v 2, 407–408.

39. "The One Thing Needful," *Nation*, September 14, 1918, 283. The President to Joseph Patrick Tumulty, with Enclosures, September 18, 1918, in *PWW*, v 51, 55, and accompanying note.

40. Report of American Socialist Mission to Robert Lansing, from A. M. Simons et al., September 25, 1918, 763.72119 S072, B7054, RG 59, NARA. Germer to Morris Hillquit, October 11, 1918, HP. Radosh, *American Labor and United States Foreign Policy*, 218–219, 185–221.

41. See, for example, Gompers's recounting of the Allied Socialist and Labor Conference in September, in Gompers, *Seventy Years*, v 2, 419–429.

42. Ibid., 420–421.

43. Frey, "Reminiscences," 356; Gompers, *Seventy Years*, v 2, 409; Page to Lansing, August 20, 1918, RG 59-B7019, 763.72/11051, NARA; Page to Secretary of State, September 12, 1918, 032.G58, B309, RG59 NARA; Gompers to John Alpine (Acting President of AFL), September 4[3], 1918, *SGP*, v 10, 520–522.

44. Page to Secretary of State, September 3, 1918, 032.G58, B309, RG59, NARA; Gompers, *Seventy Years*, v 2, 434–435; Frey, "Reminiscences," v 2, 362–364; Labour Party, "Confidential Labour Party Memoranda on the International Meeting, German Response," June 28, 1918, IAC 1918–1919, Memos and Documents, R8, S3-P8, ABLP; Radosh, *American Labor and United States Foreign Policy*, 162–165.

45. Frey, "Reminiscences," v 2, 362–364; Frey, "An Excerpt from an Account of the Inter-Allied Labour and Socialist Conference in London," September 20, 1918, in *SGP*, v 10, 529–532; British Labour Party, "Report of the Executive Committee," June 1918–June 1919, in *Report of the Nineteenth Annual Conference of the British Labour Party, 1919*, 3–7.

46. Frey, "An Excerpt from an Account of the Inter-Allied Labour and Socialist Conference in London," *SGP*, v 10, 529–532.

47. Page, Memo to Secretary of State, September 20, 1918, 032.G58, B309, RG59, NARA; *Survey*, v 41, November 2, 1918, 125–126; *Nation*, October 12, 1918, 414–415; Walling to Lansing, September 24, 1918, and William Bullitt to Joe Grew, October 7, 1918, RG59-B7054, 763.72119 S081, Box 7054, RG59, NARA; Radosh, *American Labor and United States Foreign Policy*, 161.

48. The Gompers mission in Europe was reported on extensively by American diplomats. See especially Irwin Lauchlin to Secretary of State, November 1, 1918 (quote); William Buckler to the Secretary of State, November 1, 1918; North Winship to American Consulate, October 17, 1918, enclosed in North Winship to Secretary of State, September 15, 1921; Thomas Nelson Page to Secretary of State, October 31, 1918, all in 032.G58, B309, RG 59, NARA. See also Daniella Rossini, Anthony Shugaar (trans.), *Woodrow Wilson and the American Myth in Italy: Culture, Diplomacy, and War Propaganda* (Cambridge: Harvard University Press, 2008), 124.

49. Gompers, *Seventy Years*, v 2, 468–469.

50. McKillen, *Chicago Labor*, 86–88, 128–129; Barrett, *Work and Community in the Jungle*, 224–231.

51. Samuel Gompers, "'Should a Political Labor Party Be Formed?' An Address by Samuel Gompers, President of the American Federation of Labor, to a Labor Conference Held at New York City, December 9, 1918," *SGP*, 11, 8–17. Strouthous, *U.S. Labor and Political Action, 1918–1924*; McKillen, *Chicago Labor*, 131.

52. See especially *AR*, December 15, 1917, 1; *New Appeal (NA)*, January 12 and January 18, 1918, 1; Carl D. Thompson to EVD, April 12, 1918, *Letters of EVD*, v 2, 397–398; Salvatore, *Eugene V. Debs*, 289–290.

Part IV. Versailles and Its Aftermath

1. Dawley, *Changing the World*, 237. For contrasting views see especially Cooper, *Breaking the Heart of the World*; Margaret MacMillan, *Paris 1919: Six Months that Changed the World* (New York: Random House, 2003); Kennedy, *Will to Believe*; Ambrosius, *Woodrow Wilson and the American Diplomatic Tradition*; Arno Mayer, *Politics and Diplomacy of Peace-Making: Containment and Counterrevolution at Versailles* (New York: Knopf, 1967); Levin, *Woodrow Wilson and World Politics*.

International social movements and their agendas in 1919 have been far less studied. For an introduction to this subject and to the emerging literature, see Dawley, *Changing the World*. On anticolonial activists in 1919, see Manela, *Wilsonian Moment*. Perhaps the most neglected historical subject matter of all, suggests

Dawley, are studies that place "social reform and foreign policy" in the "same frame of analysis"(*Changing the World*, 5–6).

2. Paterson et al., *American Foreign Relations*, sixth ed., v 1, 285–286; Dawley, *Changing the World*, 219–256; Kennedy, *Will to Believe*, 182–227; Manela, *Wilsonian Moment*.

Chapter 6. Making the World Safe for Workers?

1. Diary of William Bullitt, December 11, 1918, in *PWW*, v 53, 366–367.

2. Gompers, *Seventy Years*, v 2, 477; *UMWJ*, January 15, 1919, 6; *SUR*, November 30, 1918, 2, December 14, 1918, 2; Wilson to Alfred Emmanuel Smith, November 26, 1918, *PWW*, v 53, 206; Wilson to Frank Morrison, November 27, 1918, *PWW*, v 53, 216; W. B. Wilson to Wilson, November 21, 1918, *PWW*, v 53, 154–156; Bernard Baruch to Wilson, January 20, 1919, *PWW*, v 54, 172; William B. Wilson to Wilson enclosing a recommendation from Frank Walsh, November 28, 1918, *FRUS*, 1919, v 1, 173. Lansing to Wilson, November 29, 1918, 763.72119So/42a, B7054, RG 59, NARA (quote).

3. W. B. Wilson to President Wilson, November 21, 1918, *PWW*, v 53, 154–156; Wilson to Secretary of the AFL Morrison, November 22, 1918, *FRUS*, 1919 (Paris Peace Conference) v 1, 168; Wilson to Frank Morrison, November 27, 1918, *PWW*, v 53, 206; Wilson to W. B. Wilson, November 28, 1918, *FRUS*, 1919 (Paris Peace Conference), v 1, 173.

4. *SUR*, December 7, 1918, 2; December 14, 1918, 2, November 30, 1918, 2.

5. [Frank] Polk, Acting Secretary of State, to Commission to Negotiate Peace, December 16, 1918, and Polk to Commission to Negotiate the Peace, December 21, 1918, *FRUS*, 1919 (Paris Peace Conference), v 1, 539–541, and Gompers to President Wilson, December 21, 1918, 551B2, B5499, RG59, NARA.

6. Ibid. Wilson to Mr. Secretary, December 24, 1918, in *FRUS*, 1919, v 1 (Peace Conference), 541; Mayer, *Politics and Diplomacy of Peace-Making*, 378–386; Lansing to Wilson with Enclosure from Bullitt, November 9, 1918, *PWW*, 53, 6–9.

7. John W. Davis to Secretary of State, January 31, 1919, 032.G58, B309, RG59, NARA; Gompers, "Memoranda No 1, January 30, 1919," *SGP*, v 11, 37–40; *American Federationist*, March 1919, 227–229; McKillen, *Chicago Labor*, 101; Mayer, *Politics and Diplomacy of the Peace-Making*, 386–387.

8. Ibid. Telegram from Pleasants Stovall, enclosed in a letter from "Your Obedient Servant" to the Secretary of State, February 4, 1919, 763.72119 So46, B7054, RG59, NARA.

9. George Barnes, *History of the International Labour Office* (London: William and Norgate Limited, 1926), 35–37; Barnes, *From Workshop to War Cabinet* (New York: Appleton, 1924), 162–273.

10. Ibid. "Memorandum . . . Prepared in the British Delegation, January 15–20, 1919," Document 25, *ILO*, v 2, 117–124; Edward Phelan, "British Preparations," *ILO*, v 1, 105–126.

11. To a surprising extent, the existing European literature on the Bern conference and Wilson has emphasized the overlap in their programs while ignoring the differences, especially with respect to the League of Nations. See, for example, Mayer, *Politics and Diplomacy of Peace-Making*, 169–170. More recent studies have added an important dimension by exploring the social and labor roots of the ILO. But these studies have largely avoided the larger political context and the connections made by World War I–era labor activists between the League and the ILO. See Ruotsila, "The Great Charter for the Liberty of the Workingman"; Van Daele, "Engineering Social Peace"; Tosstorff, "International Trade-Union Movement."

12. Telegram from Stovall, February 4, 1919, enclosed in a letter from "Your Obedient Servant" to Secretary of State, 763.72119 S046, B 7054, RG59, NARA.

13. Report and Text of Resolutions, "International Labour and Socialist Conference, Berne, January 26–February 10, 1919," in British Labour Party, *Report of the Nineteenth Annual Conference*, 1919, Appendix 8, 196–204; British Labour Party, "Report of the Executive Committee," June, 1918–June 1919, in *Report of the Nineteenth Annual Conference*, 9–23. For the origin of ideas about a parliament of the League of Nations, see "Parliament of the League of Nations," in "Memos and Documents, January 1919," R8-P8, ABLB; Mayer, *Politics and Diplomacy of Peace-Making*, 392–406.

14. Mayer, *Politics and Diplomacy of Peace-Making*, 392–403; telegram from Stovall, February 6, 1919, in enclosure from "Your Obedient Servant" to Secretary of State, 763.72119 S046, RG 59, NARA; British Labour Party, "Report of the Executive Committee," June 1918–June 1919, 12–23; Reports of Texts of "International Labour and Socialist Conference, Berne," 196–197.

15. Telegram from Stovall, February 8, 1919, in enclosure from "Your Obedient Servant" to Secretary of State, 763.72119 S046.

16. Report and Text of Resolutions, "International Labour and Socialist Conference, Berne," 196–204; Mayer, *Politics and Diplomacy of Peace-Making*, 403.

17. Ibid.

18. Ibid. Mayer, *Politics and Diplomacy of Peace-Making*, 398–399, 405–406.

19. W. M. Gunther to Secretary of State, July 25, 1919, with enclosure from *Het Volk* on the Meeting of the International Trade Union Congress, 555 1/35, RG59, NARA; Van Goethem, *Amsterdam International*, 27; Samuel McCune Lindsay, "The Problem of American Cooperation," *ILO*, v 1, 338–339; Gompers to Wilson, November 27, 1918, *PWW*, v 53, 217–220; Van Goethem, *Amsterdam International*, 27.

20. Van Daele, "Engineering Social Peace," 436–438, 449–450; Phelan, "British Preparations," *ILO*, v 1, 129–130; Tosstorff, "The International Trade Union Movement," 402; *NYT*, June 1, 1919, 79; Van Goethem, "Conflicting Interests: The International Federation of Trade Unions (1919–1945)," in *The International Confederation of Trade Unions*, Anthony Carew et al., eds. (Bern: Peter Lang, 2000), 80–81; Leifer Magnussun, "American Preparations," *ILO*, v 1, 57.

21. Van Daele, "Engineering Social Peace," 449–450.

22. Van Goethem, "Conflicting Interests," 80; *New Majority*, May 17, 1919, 14–15.

23. Frank Walsh, Diary of Frank P. Walsh at the Paris Peace Conference, 1919, April 2–June 12, 1919, 32–33, B29, Walsh Papers (WP) at the New York Public Library; American Commission on Irish Independence to Fitzpatrick, August 13, 1920, and Labor Bureau of American Commission on Irish Independence, unsigned, undated letter, B9-F67, FP; Julie Manning, *Frank P. Walsh and the Irish Question* (Georgetown: Georgetown University Press), 54–58; McKillen, "Ethnicity, Class and Wilsonian Internationalism Reconsidered," 576.

24. "Drafts of the Convention," *ILO*, v 1, 378; "Minutes of the Meetings of the Commission on International Labor Legislation," in *ILO*, v 2, 157–178.

25. "Minutes of the Meetings of the Commission on International Labor Legislation," 159–174.

26. McKillen, *Chicago Labor*, 88; "Manifesto of the International Trade Union Conference at Berne, February 10, 1919," *ILO*, v 2, 336–340; "Minutes of the Commission on International Labor Legislation," 159–237, 290–291; "Memorandum of the British Delegation on the Question of Voting Power at the Conference," *ILO*, v 2, 330–335; James Shotwell, *At the Paris Peace Conference* (New York: Macmillan, 1937), 209–224.

27. "Minutes of the Commission on International Labor Legislation," 178, 194–198, 209, 290–91.

28. "Drafts of the Labor Convention" and "Final Texts of the Labor Section," in *ILO*, v 1, 411–413, 444.

29. *NYT*, June 21, 1919, 3; "Drafts of the Labor Convention," 418–419.

30. "Minutes of the Commission on International Labor Legislation," 179–186, 209–237.

31. *Ibid*, 179–182, 209–237. See also Elizabeth McKillen, "Beyond Gompers: The American Federation of Labor, the Creation of the ILO and U.S. Labor Dissent," in Jasmien Van Daele et al., *ILO Histories: Essays on the International Labour Organization and Its Impact on the World during the Twentieth Century* (Brussels: Peter Lang, 2010), 41–66.

32. Shotwell, *At the Paris Peace Conference*, 199; "Minutes of the Commission on International Labor Legislation," 255–289, 315; "Report of the Subcommittee on Article 19 of the Labor Convention, March 19, 1919," *ILO*, v 2, 361; "Report of the Commission on International Labor Legislation, March 24, 1919," *ILO*, v 2, 373–375; "Final Texts of the Labor Sections," *ILO*, v 2, 436.

33. Shotwell, *At the Paris Peace Conference*, 211.

34. "Proposals Submitted by the Delegates of the United States of America, February 5, 1919," "Manifesto of the International Trade Union Conference on Berne, February 10, 1919, on International Labor Legislation," "Clauses Suggested for Insertion in the Treaty of Peace, March 13–15, 1919": all in *ILO*, v 2, 328–329, 336–340, 349–356.

35. Ibid.

36. "Minutes of the Commission on International Labor Legislation," 242–247.

37. "Final Texts of the Labor Sections," 448–449.

38. "Minutes of the Commission on International Labor Legislation," 312–317; Furuseth to Wilson, March 26, 1919, *ILO*, v 2, 433. For more on seamen and the ILO, see Leon Fink, *Sweatshops at Sea: Merchant Seamen in the World's First Globalized Industry from 1812 to the Present* (Chapel Hill: University of North Carolina Press, 2011), 145–160.

39. "Extract of the Minutes of the Plenary Peace Conference," *ILO*, v 2, 414–416; "Speech by Mr. Andrew Furuseth . . . at the Annual Convention of the American Federation of Labor," *ILO*, v 2, 423; "Speech by Mr. Samuel Gompers Defending the League of Nations and the International Labor Organization," *ILO*, v 2, 434–440; Gompers, *Seventy Years*, v 2, 499; *American Federationist*, August 1919, 718–721; Van Goethem, *Amsterdam International*, 175.

40. Guy Oyster, Secretary to Gompers, to Henry Robinson, n.d., 763.72119, B7054, RG 59, NARA; Gompers to President, April 12, 1919, and Gompers to Harry Robinson, April 12, 1919, 032.G58, B309, RG 59, NARA. Sir Robert Borden to Sir Thomas White, with Enclosure, May 3, 1919, *PWW*, v 58, 415–418; telegram from Acting Department of State to American Mission, September 10, 1919, 555E1, RG 59, Council of Four, Minutes of Meetings, April 28, 1919, *FRUS*, v 5, 1919 (Paris Peace Conference), 308–309.

41. "Extract of the Minutes of the Plenary Peace Conference, "*ILO*, v 2, 414–416, and "Speech by Mr. Samuel Gompers Defending the League of Nations and the International Labor Organization," *ILO*, v 2, 434–440; AFL, *Proceedings*, 1919, 401. Wilson Cable to Gompers, June 20, 1919, *ILO*, v 2, 441–443; Edward Phelan, "The Labor Proposals," *ILO*, v 1, 217.

42. "Speech by Mr. Andrew Furuseth . . . at the Annual Convention of the American Federation of Labor," *ILO*, v 2, 423; Joseph Tumulty, [The White House] no 127, May 16, 1919, *PWW*, v 59, 203; "Speech by Mr. Samuel Gompers Defending the League of Nations and the International Labor Organization," *ILO*, v 2, 434–440; Gompers, *Seventy Years*, v 2, 499; *American Federationist*, August 1919, 718–721; Van Goethem, *Amsterdam International*, 175; Lansing to Gompers, April 11, 1919, and Shotwell to Gompers, April 11, 1919, O32-G58, B309, RG59, NARA.

43. William Philips to the American Mission, September 22, 1919, 555E174B, B5499, RG 59, NARA; Wilson Presidential Address, 1919, *FRUS*, 1919, v 1, xvi; Markku Ruotsila, "Great Charter for the Liberty of the Workingman," 42; Wilson's speeches while on his "whistle-stop tour" in September 1919, *PWW*, v 63, 14–15, 78, 99, 147, 261–262, 357, 375, 535.

44. Van Goethem, *Amsterdam International*, 174–175; "Manifesto of the International Trade Union Conference at Berne," February 10, 1919, *ILO*, v 2, 336–340.

45. "Preliminary Peace Proposals, Manifesto of the Committee of Action of the Berne International Labour and Socialist Conference" and "Preliminary Peace Proposals, Manifesto of the National Executive of the Labour Party," in British Labour Party, *Report of the Nineteenth Annual Conference*, 1919, 212–217; "Peace Terms, Norman Angell," and "The International and the Treaties," May 1919, R8-S8, ABLP; Van Goethem, *Amsterdam International*, 174–175.

46. "Peace Terms, Norman Angell," and "The International and the Treaties," May 1919, R8-S8, ABLP; "Manifesto of the National Executive of the Labour Party," 212–217; Van Goethem, *Amsterdam International*, 174–175.

47. See, for example, *NM*, May 17, 1919, 1, 14–15; *NYC*, June 25, 1919, 8; *UMWJ*, May 1, 1919, 6, July 7, 1919, 1–2; *Nation*, June 28, 1919, 1002–1003; *NYT*, July 13, 1919, 3.

48. *NM*, May 17, 1919, 1, 14–15, April 26, 1919, 10; McKillen, *Chicago Labor*, 136–165.

49. *Solidarity*, June 14, 1919, 2, June 21, 1919, 2.

50. *NYT*, June 21, 1919, 3; AFL, *Proceedings*, 1919, 399–402, 24–31; "Speech of Mr. Andrew Furuseth," *ILO*, v 2, 421–426.

51. "Speech by Mr. Samuel Gompers Defending the League of Nations," 440; *NYT*, June 21, 1919, 3; AFL, *Proceedings*, 1919, 399–402. On Gompers's communication with the White House during the conference, see Gompers to Wilson, June 17, 1919, Tumulty Memo, June 13, 1919, Wilson to Tumulty, June 15, 1919, *PWW*, v 60, 645, 113, 197.

52. AFL, *Proceedings*, 1919, 398–416; McKillen, *Chicago Labor*, 118–119; Charles Patrick Sweeney, "Gompers Triumphant," *Nation*, June 28, 1919, 1002–1003; *NYT*, July 13, 1919.

53. AFL, *Proceedings*, 1919, 398–416; *NYT*, June 21, 1919, 3.

54. *NYC*, June 25, 1919, 8.

55. Sinclair Snow, *The Pan-American Federation of Labor* (Durham: Duke University Press, 1964), 51–73; Report of the American Labor Mission to Mexico to the AFL Convention, St. Paul, June 1918, AFL, *Labor and the War*, 123–144.

56. Pan American Federation of Labor, *Proceedings*, 1919, 4–31.

57. Ibid.; *NYT*, July 10, 1919, 19, July 11, 1919, 26, February 15, 1919, 3, March 30, 1919, 45; Snow, *Pan American Federation of Labor*, 51–73.

58. W. M. Gunther to Secretary of State, July 25, 1919, with enclosure from Het Volk on the meeting of the International Trade Union Congress, 555E1/35, RG 59, NARA; Van Goethem, *Amsterdam International*, 27, 176 (quotes); "Resolution on the International Federation of Trade Unions," *ILO*, v 2, 447; AFL, *Proceedings*, 1920, 148–150; *American Federationist*, October 1919, 940.

59. Van Goethem, *Amsterdam International*, 175–178; Tosstorff, "International Trade Union Movement," 425–433; AFL, *Proceedings*, 1920, 148–150.

60. On Gompers's support for inviting the Germans and Austrians, see especially Gompers to Hon. Alvey A. Adec, 2d Assistant Secretary of State, September 3, 1919, and Cable from Acting Secretary of State to President Wilson, September 4, 1919, 555E1/44 and 45, B5499, RG 59, NARA. On Wilson, see William Philips to the President, September 22, 1919, and William Philip to the American Mission, September 22, 1919 (quote), 555E174A and B, B5499, RG 59, NARA. See also telegram to William Philips, September 23, 1919, *PWW*, v 63, 463–464, and Davis to Secretary of State, August 30, 1919, 555E1/39, B5499, RG59, NARA, for early concerns of the British.

61. For discussions of the ILO during Wilson's speeches while on tour, see *PWW*, v 63, 14–15, 78, 144, 147, 261–262, 357, 375, 435.

Chapter 7. U.S. Labor Irreconcilables and Reservationists and the Founding ILO Conference in Washington, D.C., November 1919

1. George Barnes, *From Workshop to War Cabinet*, 269–270; Barnes, *History of the International Labour Office*, 57–58; *NYT*, November 7, 1919, 10.

2. See, for example, Wilson's address in Columbus, Ohio, September 4, 1919, *PWW*, v 63, 14–15, and "The International Labor Conference," in the *New Republic*, December 24, 1919, 110–112. For brief discussions of the treaty debate and the ILO, see Cooper, *Breaking the Heart of the World*, 219–220, 235, 301; Edward C. Lorenz, *Defining Global Justice: A History of U.S. International Labor Standards Policy* (South Bend: University of Notre Dame, 2001), 73–74; Ambrosius, *Woodrow Wilson and the American Diplomatic Tradition*, 203; McKillen, "Beyond Gompers," and Elizabeth McKillen, "Integrating Labor into the Narrative of Wilsonian Internationalism: A Literature Review," *Diplomatic History* 34 (September 2010), 643–662.

3. A survey of *Newspaper Archive* for the term *International Labor Organization* in 1919 and 1920 yielded 157 results, most from small-town U.S. newspapers. The *New York Times* also devoted extensive coverage to the issue.

4. For coverage of Wilson's speeches, see, for example, *Syracuse Herald*, September 9, 1919, 1; *Daily News* (Frederick Maryland), September 18, 1919, 2; *Pinnacle News* (Middlesboro, Kentucky), 1; *Reno Evening Gazette*, September 8, 1919, 3; *Waterloo Evening Courier* (Waterloo, Iowa), October 24, 1919, 1. On the concerns of southern senators, see "Southerners against Labor Section," *Boston Globe*, October 12, 1919, 6. For treatment of the Japanese labor issue, see *Ogden Examiner*, September 3, 1919, 6, and for concerns about U.S. labor standards declining to those of China and India, see *Sandusky Register* (Sandusky, Ohio), October 31, 1919, 1. For other issues, see especially *Centralia Daily Chronicle* (Centralia, Washington), October 30, 1919, 1; *Janesville Daily Gazette* (Janesville, Wisconsin), October 29, 1919, 1; *Stevens Point Daily Journal* (Stevens Point, Wisconsin), June 6, 1919, 1; *Oxford Leader* (Oxford, Iowa), May 15, 1919; Steubenville Herald (Steubenville, Ohio), August 28, 1919, 1; *Sun Herald* (Lime Spring, Iowa), August 28, 1919, 1, 3; *Reno Evening Gazette*, September 3, 1919, 1; *Atlanta Constitution*, August 30, 1919, 1; *Fort Wayne News*, January 16, 1919, 1; *Washington Post*, September 2, 1919, 1; *Racine Journal* (Racine, Wisconsin), October 11, 1919; *Helena Daily Independent* (Helena, Montana), August 25, 1919, 2.

5. *Billings Gazette*, October 31, 1919, 9.

6. Manela, *Wilsonian Moment*; Shannon, *Socialist Party*, 126–149.

7. *Voice of Labor*, July 8, 1921, 10, October 18, 1921, 7. For background on early-twentieth-century communism, see especially Randi Storch, *Red Chicago: American Communism at Its Grassroots: 1928–1935* (Urbana: University of Illinois Press, 2009); James Barrett, *William Z. Foster and the Tragedy of American Radicalism* (Urbana: University of Illinois Press, 1999); Theodore Draper, *American Communism and Soviet Russia: The Formative Years* (New York: Viking Press, 1960); Draper, *Roots of American Communism* (New York: Viking Press, 1957).

8. Shannon, *Socialist Party*, 150–153; Salvatore, *Eugene V. Debs*, 322–323.

9. *NYC*, June 3, 1919, 8, June 10, 1919, 1, 8, June 19, 1919, 3, June 25, 1919, 8, July 12, 1919, 8, July 20, 1919, 8; Shannon, *Socialist Party*, 150–153.

10. *AR*, May 23, 1919, 11, June 7, 1919, 1–4, July 19, 1919, 4, August 30, 1919, 4, May 24, 1919, 1 (nomination of Debs), June 5, 1920, 4 (platform). Significantly, the *Appeal to Reason* changed its name to *New Appeal* after it reversed course and chose to support the war in 1918. But in the midspring of 1919, it changed its name back to *Appeal to Reason*.

11. For an examination of the generally more conciliatory attitude of British labor representatives toward the League and ILO, despite their disappointments with it, see chapter 6 and Leventhal, *Arthur Henderson*, 85–114.

12. Dubofsky, *We Shall Be All*, 423–468; Shannon, *Socialist Party*, 113–114.

13. *Solidarity*, March 5, 1919, 7, June 7, 1919, 2, June 14, 1919, 2, June 21, 1919, 2, September 3, 1919, 2.

14. *Solidarity*, September 3, 1919, 2.

15. Dubofsky, *We Shall Be All*, 460–464; *Solidarity*, July 14, 1920, 3, August 14, 1920, 1, 3.

16. McKillen, *Chicago Labor*, 86; *Independent Labor Party Platform*, B7-F51, FP; *NM*, May 17, 1919, 1, 14–15, December 19, 1919, 8.

17. *SUR*, October 4, 1919, 2; McKillen, "Hybrid Visions," 103.

18. See chapter 6.

19. See especially McKillen, *Chicago Labor*, 50–55, 166–192.

20. *Chicago Citizen*, October 10, 1919, 4, September 19, 1919, 1, October 2, 1919, 1, October 17, 1919, 1; McKillen, *Chicago Labor*, 172–173; Joseph Cuddy, *Irish America and National Isolationism* (New York: Arno Press, 1976), 194–195, 200.

21. *SUR*, September 20, 1919, 1; McKillen, *Chicago Labor*, 145; McKillen, "Hybrid Visions," 103.

22. Michael Laffan, *The Resurrection of Ireland: Sinn Féin, 1916–1923* (Cambridge: Cambridge University Press, 1999); F. S. Lyons, *Ireland since the Famine* (Great Britain: Collins-Fontana, 1971), 247–260. See Wikipedia, http://en.wikipedia.org/wiki/Sinn_F%C3%A9in_(slogan) (accessed February 20, 2012) for a good introduction to the evolving meaning of the term *Sinn Féin*.

23. *New Majority*, December 19, 1919, 1–2, July 4, 1920, 5; *Proceedings of the First National Convention of the Labor Party, 1919*, 7–15, 26–27.

24. McKillen, *Chicago Labor*, 146–192; Foner, *History of the Labor Movement*, 60–62.

25. See especially Perry, *Hubert Harrison*.

26. *The Crisis*, December 1916, 59.

27. *The Crisis*, June 1917, 59, July 1918, 111; William G. Jordan, *Black Newspapers and America's War for Democracy, 1914–1920* (Chapel Hill: University of North Carolina Press, 2001), 5–6, 114–115.

28. Keith, *Rich Man's War, Poor Man's Fight*, 3, 9, 118–119, 171, and, in general, Theodore Kornweibel, *"Investigate Everything": Federal Efforts to Compel Black Loyalty during World War I* (Bloomington: Indiana University Press, 2002), 76–117; Gerald Shenk, *"Work or Fight!" Race, Gender and the Draft in World War One* (New York: Palgrave Macmillan, 2005).

29. Perry, *Hubert Harrison*, 282, 281–327. Theodore Vincent, "The Evolution of the Split between the Garvey Movement and the Organized Left in the United States, 1917–1933," in *Garvey, Africa, Europe, the Americas*, Rupert Lewis and Maureen Warner-Lewis, eds. (Trenton: Africa World Press, 1994), 147–175.

30. Makalani, *In the Cause of Freedom*, 38; Winston James, *Holding Aloft the Banner of Ethiopia: Caribbean Radicals in Early Twentieth Century America* (London: Verso, 1999); *Messenger*, January 1918, 6.

31. William Edward Burghardt DuBois to Joseph Patrick Tumulty, with enclosure, November 27, 1918, *PWW*, v 53, 236–238.

32. See, for example, *The Crisis*, July 1917, 72, which discussed the Inter-Allied Labor Conference held in Britain and its proposals for international control of Africa under the League of Nations.

33. "Addresses Denouncing W. E. B. Du Bois (reprint from the *Negro World*, April 5, 1919), in *Marcus Garvey and Universal Negro Improvement Association Papers* (hereafter *UNIA*) (Berkeley: University of California Press, 1983), v 1, 396.

34. FBI Report of D. Davidson to Special Agent Finch, *UNIA*, v 1, 288–289; Brenda Gayle Plummer, *Rising Wind: Black Americans and U.S. Foreign Affairs, 1935–1960* (Chapel Hill: University of North Carolina Press, 1996), 17–18; *The Crisis*, March 1919, 224–225.

35. Plummer, *Rising Wind*, 17–18; *The Crisis*, March 1919, 224–225, April 1919, 271–274.

36. *The Crisis*, April 1919, 271–274, May 1919, 7–8.

37. Plummer, *Rising Wind*, 18.

38. For a brief explanation of the complicated tripartite mandate system created by the League for Africa, see *UNIA*, v 1, 290, footnote 12. See also "Petition by Marcus Garvey," *UNIA*, v 1, 366–369.

39. *The Crisis*, November 1919, 336–337; George Huggins, "Marcus Garvey and the League of Nations, 1921–1931: An Episode in the International Relations of the U.N.I.A.," in Lewis and Warner-Lewis, eds., *Garvey: Africa, Europe, The Americas*, 136–137.

40. "Petition by Marcus Garvey," February 21, 1919, *UNIA*, v 1, 366–369.

41. "Addresses Denouncing W. E. B. Du Bois (reprint of article from *Negro World*, April 5, 1919), *UNIA*, v 1, 397; Report of UNIA meeting, August 25, 1919, *UNIA*, v 1, 498–516; British Military Intelligence Report on Garvey, September 27, 1919, *UNIA*, v 2, 30–31.

42. Hubert Harrison, *When Africa Awakes* (New York: Black African Press, 1997 [1920]), 111–113. http://wwww.jeffreybperry.net (accessed February 4, 2013).

43. *Messenger*, June 1919, 14–17, October 1919, 9.

44. For details on the splits among African American radicals in 1919, see especially Minkah Makalani's excellent book, *In the Cause of Freedom*, 45–46 (quote), 63, and, in general.

45. On Barnes, see Davis to Secretary of State, August 30, 1919, 555E1/39, B5499, RG59, NARA. The other themes were discussed in voluminous correspondence throughout the late summer and autumn of 1919; see 555.E1–555.E1/153, B5499, RG59, at NARA.

46. Sweetser to Raymond Fosdick, September 10, 1919, 555.E1/55A, B5499, RG 59, NARA; John Davis to the Secretary of State for the Secretary of Labor from Ethelbert Stewart, August 9, 1919, 555.E1/12, B5499, RG 59, NARA; William Phillip to the American Mission, September 22, 1919, 555.E1/74B, B5499, RG59, NARA.

47. Numerical totals for delegations differ slightly depending on who was included. See League of Nations, *International Labor Conference: First Annual Meeting, October 29, 1919–November 29, 1919* (stenographic proceedings) (Washington, D.C.: Government Printing Office, 1920), 1–31, 176; Harold Butler, "The Washington Conference," in *ILO*, v 1, 306–313; *NYT*, November 11, 1919, 1; Antony Alcock, *Origins of the International Labor Organization* (New York: Macmillan, 1971), 37–38.

48. Butler, "The Washington Conference," 306–313; League of Nations, *International Labor Conference* (1919), 31–54; *NYT*, November 11, 1919, 1.

49. Ibid. Alcock, *Origins of the International Labor Organization*, 38, 317; League of Nations, *International Labor Conference* (1919), 11.

50. Butler, "The Washington Conference," 323–324; League of Nations, *International Labor Conference* (1919), 152–153, and in general.

51. Butler, "The Washington Conference," 320–324; Alcock, *Origins of the ILO*, 41.

52. Butler, "The Washington Conference," 312–319.

53. "The International Labor Conference," *New Republic*, December 24, 1919, 110–112; League of Nations, *International Labor Conference* (1919), 256–300.

54. "Final Texts of the Labor Section," *ILO*, v 1, 424.

55. Stenographers Report, International Congress of Working Women, October 30, 1919, 50, B12-F3, P3, International Federation of Working Women Records at Schlesinger Library, Radcliffe Institute for Advanced Studies (hereafter IFWWR); Rose Schneiderman with Lucy Goldwaite, *All for One* (New York: P. S. Eriksson, 1967), 131–138; Schneiderman to Mrs. Raymond Robins, March 10, 1919; Frances Perkins to Schneiderman, March 7, 1919, Leonora O'Reilly to Schneiderman, March 11, 1919, in R1 Schneiderman Papers (SP), Microfilm Edition held by Schlesinger Library, Radcliffe Institute.

56. Schneiderman, *All for One*, 135–138; Robins to Shotwell, June 12, 1919, copy in R2-SP; Shotwell Memo to the President, *PWW*, v 62, July 16, 1919; W. B. Wilson to the President, August 4, 1919, *PWW*, v 62, 132. W. B. Wilson to the President, September 5, 1919, *PWW*, v 63, 56–57.

57. Ernestine Friedmann to Robins, September 2, 1919, and September 15, 1919, in Margaret Dreier Robins Papers (MDRP) at Schlesinger Library, Radcliffe. *NYC*, August 28, 1919, and Rose Schneiderman to Robins, September 16, 1919, MDRP.

58. Friedmann to Robins, September 2, 1919, September 15, 1919, and September 30, 1919, MDRP; Schneiderman, *All for One*, 137–139; Nestor, *Woman's Labor Leader*, 225–227.

59. International Federation of Working Women Pamphlet in B12-F1, "Welcoming Address of Mrs. Raymond Robins," and report in *Life and Labor*, 307–314, B12-F2, Stenographer's Report, International Congress of Working Women, 35, B12-F3, P8: all in IFWWR.

60. Leonora O'Reilly, "Industrial Democracy," *Woman Voter*, June 1915, and Leonora O'Reilly, Report on the International Congress of Women at the Hague, in *Proceedings of the Fifth Biennial Convention of the National Women's Trade Union League of America*, R9, OP.

61. Robins, "Welcoming Address," 311, B12-F2, IFWWR; *Resolutions Adopted by the First International Congress of Working Women*, Washington, D.C., U.S.A., October 28 to November 6, 1919, 2; online pamphlet accessed through Harvard Library.

62. *Resolutions Adopted by the First International Congress of Working Women*, 3–10, Stenographers Report, International Congress of Working Women, 3–51, B12-F3, P5, IFWWR.

63. Ibid. Stenographer's Report, International Congress of Working Women, 14–32, B12-F3, P8, IFWWR; Ulla Wikander, "Demands on the ILO by Internationally Organized Women in 1919," in Van Daele et al., eds., *ILO Histories*, 80–81.

64. Stenographers Report, International Congress of Working Women, B12-F3, P7, 4–48, P8, 1–9, P9,1–23, IFWWR, *Resolutions Adopted by the First International Congress of Working Women*, 4–5; Wikander, "Demands on the ILO," 81.

65. League of Nations, *International Labor Conference* (1919), 102–107, 171–179, 244–249, 260–261.

66. Wikander, "Demands on the ILO," 79; Dorothy Sue Cobble, "U.S. Labor Women's Internationalism in the World War I Era," *Revue Française D'Etudes Américaines*, No 122 (4 Trimestre, 2009), 44–58; Van Goethem, "The International Federation of Working Women, 1919–1924," 1–24.

67. *Congressional Record*, 66th Congress, 1st Session (October–November 1919), 7669–7677.

68. Ibid., 7670–7672; McKillen, "Beyond Gompers." 62–64.

69. Ibid., 5674, 7660–7675, 7939–7940; for details, see McKillen, "Beyond Gompers," 62–63.

70. Ibid., 7966–7968.

71. Ibid., 7805, 7800, 7805, 7673.

72. Ibid., 7969; Cooper, *Breaking the Heart of the World*, 219–220.

73. *Congressional Record*, 66th Congress, First Session (November 1919), 8640–8641, 6702.

74. Ibid., 8704–8705.

75. Ibid., 8702, 8713.

76. Ibid., 8729–8730, 8773.

Conclusion

1. See especially Lloyd Ambrosious, "Woodrow Wilson and George W. Bush: Historical Comparisons of Ends and Means in Their Foreign Policies," *Diplomatic History* 30 (June 2006), 509–543; Dawley, *Changing the World*, 341–358; Frank Ninkovich, *The Wilsonian Century: U.S. Foreign Policy since 1900* (Chicago: University of Chicago Press, 1999).

2. *NYC*, June 25, 1919, 8, and chapter 7.

3. Louis Gerson, *The Hyphenate in Recent American Politics and Diplomacy* (Lawrence: University of Kansas Press, 1964), 76.

4. Williams, *Tragedy of American Diplomacy*, 59–89.

5. McKillen, *Chicago Labor*, 154.

6. For differing interpretations of the ILO in the twentieth century, see especially Van Daele et al., eds., *ILO Histories*, Robert Cox, "Labor and Hegemony," *International Organization* 31 (1977), 385–424; Victor Silverman, "Green Unions in a Gray World: International Labor Environmentalism at the UN," *Organization and Environment* 19:2 (June 2006), 191–213.

7. Barnes, *History of the International Labour Office*, 35–37; Barnes, *From Workshop to War Cabinet*, 162–273, and chapter 6.

8. See especially McCormick, *America's Half Century*, and Nathan Godfried, *Bridging the Gap between Rich and Poor: American Economic Development Policy toward the Arab East, 1942–49* (Westport, Conn.: Greenwood Press, 1987), for insightful examinations of the linkages between the international division of labor, political tensions, and war in the twentieth century.

Abbreviations and Primary Sources

Abbreviations

AALD: American Alliance for Labor and Democracy (AFL)
AFL: American Federation of Labor
BTUC: British Trades Union Congress
CFL: Chicago Federation of Labor
FOIF: Friends of Irish Freedom
GFTU: General Federation of Trade Unions
ICWW: International Congress of Working Women
IFTU: International Federation of Trade Unions
IFWW: International Federation of Working Women
ILGWU: International Ladies' Garment Workers' Union
ILO: International Labor Organization
IWW: Industrial Workers of the World
NAACP: National Association for the Advancement of Colored People
PAFL: Pan American Federation of Labor
PLM: Partido Liberal Mexicano
SCLC: Seattle Central Labor Council and Vicinity (also sometimes called the Central Labor Council of Seattle and King County)
Socialist Party: U.S. Socialist Party (all others designated)
UMWA: United Mine Workers of America
UNIA: United Negro Improvement Association
WTUL: Women's Trade Union League

Manuscript Collections and Unpublished Memoirs

ANP: Agnes Nestor Papers in the Papers of the Women's Trade Union League and Its Principal Leaders(Papers of the WTUL), microfilm ed. (m. ed.), at Schlesinger Library, Radcliffe Institute for Advanced Studies, Boston, Massachusetts. Original collection at the Chicago Historical Society.

BP: Victor Berger Papers, State Historical Society of Wisconsin (SHSW), m. ed., Madison, Wisconsin.

FP: John Fitzpatrick Papers, Chicago Historical Society, Chicago, Illinois.

———. John Frey, "The Reminiscences of John P. Frey," 1957, unpublished memoir in Columbia University Oral History Collection at Butler Library, Columbia University, New York.

Ge P: Adolph Germer Papers, SHSW.

GMC: Samuel Gompers Papers, SHSW, m. ed. (GMC).

Correspondence Collection (CC-GMC).

Letterbooks (LB-GMC).

Conference Collection (Conf. C-GMC).

Speeches and Writing Collection (SWC-GMC).

———. Carl Haessler Papers, Walter P. Reuther Library, Wayne State University, Detroit, Michigan.

———. Max Hayes Papers, Ohio Historical Society, Columbus, Ohio.

Hen P: Arthur Henderson Papers (Hen P), in Archives of the British Labour Party (ABLP), m. ed., series 3, part 9, A, at Lamont Library, Harvard University.

Her P: Lillian Herstein Papers, Chicago Historical Society.

HP: Morris Hillquit Papers (HP), SHSW.

———. Kate Richards O'Hare Papers, m. ed., SHSW.

MDRP: Margaret Dreier Robins Papers, Papers of WTUL.

MP: J. S. Middleton Papers in ABLP, m. ed., series 3, part 9, A.

OP: Leonora O'Reilly Papers, in Papers of the WTUL.

SP: Rose Schneiderman Papers, in Papers of the WTUL.

WP: Frank Walsh Papers (WP), New York Public Library, New York. Also in this collection, "Diary of Frank P. Walsh at the Peace Conference, 1919, 2 April–12 June 1919."

Published Collections of Personal Papers

Letters of EVD: J. Robert Constantine, ed., *Letters of Eugene V. Debs, (1913–1926)*, v 2–3 (Urbana: University of Illinois Press, 1990).

PWW: Arthur Link, ed., *The Papers of Woodrow Wilson*, v 35–64 (Princeton: Princeton University Press, 1966–1987).

SGP: Peter Albert and Grace Palladino, eds., *The Samuel Gompers Papers*, v 10–11 (Urbana: University of Illinois Press, 2007, 2009).

UNIA: Robert A. Hill, ed., *The Marcus Garvey and Universal Negro Improvement Association Papers*, v 1–2 (Berkeley: University of California Press, 1983).

OTHER COLLECTIONS

Herbert Aptheker, *The Correspondence of W.E.B. Du Bois: Selections 1877–1934*, v 1 (Amherst: University of Massachusetts Press, 1973).

Edward M. Steel, ed., *The Correspondence of Mother Jones* (Pittsburgh: University of Pittsburgh Press, 1985).

PUBLISHED MEMOIRS: FOR THE ABUNDANT AND OFTEN INSIGHTFUL
PUBLISHED MEMOIRS AND OTHER CONTEMPORANEOUS WRITINGS OF LABOR
ACTIVISTS, SEE THE APPROPRIATE ENDNOTES.

U.S. Government Documents

NARA: National Archives and Record Administration, Washington, D.C.
Record Group 59, State Department Records.
Record Group 62, Advisory Commission, Committee on Labor, Records of the
Council of National Defense.

Published Records

FRUS: United States Department of State, *Papers Relating to the Foreign Relations
of the United States*, 1913–1920.
U.S. Senate, Committee on Foreign Relations, *Investigation of Mexican Affairs*, 66th
Congress, 2d Session, 190, S. Doc., 285.
Congressional Record, 66th Congress, 1st Session, 1919.

Minutes, Proceedings, and Document Collections of Labor Organizations

AMERICAN FEDERATION OF LABOR

AFL, *Labor and the War*
American Federation of Labor, *Labor and the War: The American Federation of
Labor and the Labor Movements of Europe and Latin America* (Washington, D.C.:
American Federation of Labor, 1918). Contains many important documents on
AFL foreign policy.
AFL, *Proceedings, 19—*
American Federation of Labor, *Report of the Proceedings of the . . . Annual Con-
vention of the American Federation of Labor*, 1913–1920 (Washington, D.C.: Law
Reporter Printing, Co., 1913–1920).

BRITISH LABOUR PARTY

Labour Party, *Report of the . . . Annual Conference, 1916–1919* (London: Labour Party,
1916–1919), m. ed. Contains British Labour Party Executive Council Reports,
as well as many documents from the Inter-Allied Labor Conference and Bern
International Labor and Socialist Conference.

Labour Party, Minutes and Papers of the International Affairs and Commonwealth Committees and Papers on Foreign Affairs, Part 8, Archives of the British Labour Party, m. ed., 1916–1920, Northwestern University, Evanston, Illinois.

CHICAGO FEDERATION OF LABOR

CFL, "Minutes"
Chicago Federation of Labor Minutes (of weekly meetings) at the Chicago Historical Society (1915–1920, m. ed.)

LABOR PARTY, PROCEEDINGS, 1919

National Labor Party of the United States, *Proceedings of the First National Convention of the Labor Party of the U.S.*, November 22–25, 1919, Chicago, Illinois.

INTERNATIONAL CONGRESS OF WORKING WOMEN

Stenographers Report, International Congress of Working Women, October–November of 1919, in International Federation of Working Women Records, Schlesinger Library, Radcliffe Institute for Advanced Studies, Box 12.

INTERNATIONAL LABOR ORGANIZATION

ILO, v 1 or 2
James Shotwell, ed., *The Origins of the International Labor Organization*, 2 vols. (New York: Columbia University Press, 1934). This book contains most of the documents produced by the Commission on International Labor Legislation that created the ILO, including the minutes of the commission's meetings, sub-committee reports, and drafts of the Labor Charter included in the Versailles Peace Treaty.
League of Nations, *International Labor Conference: First Annual Meeting, October 29, 1919–November 29, 1919* (stenographic proceedings) (Washington, D.C.: Government Printing Office, 1920), This provides the minutes of the Washington ILO meeting.

PAN AMERICAN FEDERATION OF LABOR

Pan American Federation of Labor, *Report of the Proceedings of the . . . Pan-American Federation of Labor*, 1919, 1920.

SEATTLE CENTRAL LABOR COUNCIL

"Minutes," *CLCS*
Central Labor Council of Seattle and Vicinity, "Minutes," at the University of Washington, Seattle, Washington, 1914–1920.

Newspapers, Journals, and Magazines

American Federationist (AFL)
AR: Appeal to Reason (Socialist)
AS: American Socialist (Socialist)
Chicago Citizen (Irish-American)
The Crisis (National Association for the Advancement of Colored People)
El Rebelde (IWW)
Gaelic American (*Irish-American*)
Irish World and American Industrial Liberator
ISR: International Socialist Review
IW: Industrial Worker (IWW)
Lady Garment Worker (International Ladies' Garment Workers' Union)
LL: Life and Labor (Women's Trade Union League)
Messenger (African American–Socialist)
ML: Milwaukee Leader (Socialist)
Mother Earth (Anarchist)
Nation
New Republic
NM: New Majority (Chicago Federation of Labor, Labor Party)
NYC: New York Call (Socialist)
NYT: New York Times
Rebel (Texas Socialist Party paper, based in Hallettsville, Texas)
Regeneración (Partido Liberal Mexicano)
Rip Saw (Socialist, St. Louis, Missouri)
SDC: Seattle Daily Call (Socialist)
Solidarity (IWW)
SUR: Seattle Union Record (Seattle Central Labor Council)
UMWJ: United Mine Workers Journal (official journal of the UMWA)
Voice of Labor (Communist)

Index

Furuseth, Andrew: at Versailles, 191, 196–197; opposed to Versailles Peace Treaty, 198–204, 213, 215, 237

Garvey, Marcus, 10, 218, 221–225. *See also* UNIA
George, Lloyd, 159, 162–163, 185
German Americans, 3, 82–83
Germer, Adolph, 164, 168
GFTU (General Federation of Trade Unions), 153–154, 164
Gompers, Samuel: and AALD, 148–150, 162; background, 5–7, 9–11, 13, 15; and Commission on International Labor Legislation, 179–180, 189–199; and Council of National Defense, 7, 13, 17, 95, 116–117, 139, 141–142, 161, 189; criticized by liberals and Socialists, 142–143, 164–168; early responses to World War I and military preparedness, 52, 55, 90, 93–96, 110–111, 116–121; and ILO meeting in Washington D.C., 225–227; and labor missions to Europe, 161–172; and Labor Party 172–175; legacy, 242; and Mexico/Mexican labor issues, 27, 33, 39, 49–50; praised by Wilson officials and diplomats, 168, 171–172; and revolution in Europe, 152–154; and Socialists, 90, 128, 134, 162, 168, 174; and Stockholm movement, 127, 135, 152, 160–164, 168–169; and the Versailles Peace Conference, 182–185, 189–199; and the Versailles Peace Treaty, 202–207; view of British labor, 162. *See also* specific topics

Haenisch, Conrad, 65, 67
Harrison, Hubert, 10, 219–220, 224
Haywood, William/Big Bill, 37, 63, 143, 213–214
Henderson, Arthur, 11, 14, 153–155, 157–159, 165–171, 175, 184–186, 188. *See also* Labour Party, British

Herron, George, 68
Hickey, Tom, 48. *See also* Irish Sinn Féin movement and Socialist Party (U.S.)
Hillquit, Morris: and Communist International, 212; early responses to World War I, 59–62, 64–68, 72, 74–75, 83; at Emergency Convention, 1917, 132; and ILGWU, 114; and New York mayoral campaign, 140–141; and People's Council, 139; and referendum on war, 79; and Stockholm movement, 136; and Wilson administration, 134, 140–141. *See also* Berger, Victor
House, Edward, 131, 158–159, 195
Huerta, Victoriano, 21–22, 37–38, 43, 45

ICWW (International Congress of Working Women), 10, 16–17, 209, 230–236, 252n26
IFTU (International Federation of Trade Unions), 182, 188, 202, 211, 236; and Amsterdam conference of July 1919, 206–207; and ILO, 225, 236, 243
IFWW (International Federation of Working Women), 236
ILGWU (International Ladies' Garment Workers' Union), 4, 10, 111–116, 149, 164, 204
ILO (International Labor Organization): and AFL, 11, 202–205; and African Americans, 222–224; background, 1, 3, 9, 11; and Bern conference, 3, 11, 185–186, 199–200, 206; and communists, 211; and Congress, 209–210, 236–240; creation of at Versailles, 179–180, 182, 186–189, 192–199; founding conference in Washington D.C., 180, 208–209, 225–230; and Furuseth, Andrew, 200–201, 202–203; and ICWW/WTUL, 209, 230–236;

ILO (International Labor Organization) (*continued*): and IFTU, 206, 236; and IWW, 201–202, 213–214; and Labor Party movement, 3, 201, 191–192, 214–219; legacies, 245–246; and PAFL, 204–206; and press coverage, 209–210; and Socialists, 211–213; and Wilson, 178, 182, 207, 209–210

industrial democracy, 3–4, 7–8, 25, 49–50, 244; and AFL, 7, 41, 141, 199; and Du Bois, W. E. B., 221; and international organizations, 13, 245–246; and IWW, 214; and Labor Party, 147, 172, 183, 245; and Socialists, 8, 68, 74, 85, 88, 136; and WTUL, 112, 232

Inter-Allied Labor and Socialist Conference of September 1918, 169–171, 184, 187, 189

Inter-Allied Labor Conference of February 1918, 157–158

International Association of Labor Legislation, 186, 190

Irish Americans, 3, 10, 15, 82–83, 102–105, 106, 196–197, 215–218. *See also* CFL; Fitzpatrick, John; Walsh, Frank; White, John

Irish Easter Rebellion, 67, 104

Irish Sinn Féin movement, 163, 178, 217

IWW (Industrial Workers of the World): background, 4, 9; and Labor Charter of Treaty of Versailles, 201–202; and Mexico 26–27, 29, 33, 36–37, 48; and postwar isolation from international labor groups, 213–214; and World War I, 63, 130, 142–146, 164

Jewish Americans, 16, 57, 59, 111–116, 147, 149

Jones, Mother, 33–34, 130

Jouhaux, Léon, 11, 188–189, 191, 192–193, 196–197

labor missions to Europe (AFL): first, 160–167; second, 167–172

Labor Party (U.S.), 172–174, 203–204, 214–219

Labour Party (British), 11, 153–157, 158–160, 174–175, 185–188; and a democratic diplomacy, 166–167, 187–188, 213. *See also* Arthur Henderson and individual topics

LaFollette, Robert, 209, 210, 236–239

Lansing, Robert, 134, 136, 152, 158, 227, 244

Larkin, Jim, 92

League of Nations: and AFL, 198–199, 203–204; and African-Americans, 222–225; background, 1–3; and Bern Conference, 185–188, 200; and British Labour Party, 156–157, 159–160, 167, 187–188; and Inter-Allied labor, 158–160, 187–188; and IWW, 213–214; and Labor Party, 215–218; and Socialists, 160, 212–213; and Wilson, 54, 126, 157, 160, 179

Liebnecht, Karl, 67

Lippmann, Walter, 131, 140

Little, Frank, 143

London, Jack, 65, 73

London, Meyer, 59, 61, 74, 76, 114

Lovejoy, Professor, 165

Lusitania, 53, 82–86, 94, 98–99

MacDonald, James Ramsey, 154, 168, 187–188

Madero, Franciso, 21, 26–27, 34

Maley, Anne, 57

Marcy, Mary, 59, 63, 65, 74–75, 77–78

Marsh, E. P., 91–92

Maurer, James, 62, 80, 150

messianic Americanism/U.S. exceptionalism, 54, 57–58, 86. 89, 241, 244

Mexican revolution, 8, 21–22

Minor, Robert, 65, 72, 75–76, 83–84

speech, 126, 157; and Hill quit mayoral campaign, 140–141; and labor at the Versailles Peace Conference, 181–185; and labor clauses of the Versailles Peace Treaty, 195, 199, 209–210; and League of Nations, 2, 126, 159–160, 166–167, 179; and Mexico, 16, 22–23, 35–37, 80–85; and neutrality, 6, 17, 52–53; and Pan-Americanism, 20; and Pan-Africanism, 221; and preparedness, 86; and Stockholm movement, 159–160; and U.S. Left, 4, 9, 14, 89–90, 131–132, 154, 157–159, 175, 241–246; and Versailles Peace Conference, 178–179

Winship, North, 135

WTUL/NWTUL (Women's Trade Union League/National Women's Trade Union League), 10, 112–113, 209, 230, 234–235

Zimmerwald Meeting, 61

ELIZABETH MCKILLEN is a professor of history at the University of Maine and the author of *Chicago Labor and the Quest for a Democratic Diplomacy: 1914–1924.*

The Working Class in American History

The University of Illinois Press
is a founding member of the
Association of American University Presses.

University of Illinois Press
1325 South Oak Street
Champaign, IL 61820-6903
www.press.uillinois.edu